THE CHARTER

OF THE

CITY OF DETROIT,

AS AMENDED; TOGETHER WITH

ACTS OF THE LEGISLATURE.

RELATING TO THE CITY.

COMPILED AND PRINTED BY ORDER OF THE COMMON COUNCIL.

DETROIT:
TRIBUNE COMPANY, PRINTERS TO THE CITY, 212 JEFFERSON AVE.
1867.

CONTENTS OF CHAPTERS.

PART FIRST.

CHARTER OF THE CITY.

		PAGE
CHAPTER I.	INCORPORATION: CITY AND WARD BOUNDARIES, . .	9
CHAPTER II.	OFFICERS: WHO ELECTED, WHO APPOINTED, QUALIFICATIONS, BONDS, OFFICIAL TERMS, REMOVAL, VACANCY,	11
CHAPTER III.	ELECTIONS: HOW CONDUCTED, ...	26
CHAPTER IV.	OFFICERS: THEIR RIGHTS, POWERS, AND DUTIES, . .	34
HAPTER V.	COMMON COUNCIL: POWERS AND DUTIES.	46
CHAPTER VI.	RECORDER'S COURT, ...	78
CHAPTER VII.	OPENING, ALTERING, AND CLOSING STREETS, . - .	95
CHAPTER VIII.	TAXATION AND FINANCE, ...	114
CHAPTER IX.	ASSESSMENT OF TAXES AND THEIR COLLECTION, . . .	133
CHAPTER X.	FIRE DEPARTMENT, ...	149
CHAPTER XI.	MISCELLANEOUS PROVISIONS, ...	156
CHAPTER XII.	ACTS CONTINUED AND REPEALED, , ...	161
CHAPTER XIII.	POLICE DEPARTMENT, ...	164

CONTENTS OF CHAPTERS.

PART SECOND.

ACTS OF LEGISLATURE.

			PAGE.
CHAPTER	I.	CORPORATE LIMITS OF THE CITY OF DETROIT, ...	175
CHAPTER	II.	BOARD OF WATER COMMISSIONERS, ...	179
CHAPTER	III.	POLICE DEPARTMENT, ...	193
CHAPTER	IV.	COURTS OF THE CITY, ...	224
CHAPTER	V.	HOUSE OF CORRECTION, ...	232
CHAPTER	VI.	FIRE DEPARTMENT, ...	247
CHAPTER	VII.	TAXES, ...	261
CHAPTER	VIII.	REGISTRATION AND ELECTIONS, ...	267
CHAPTER	IX.	PUBLIC SCHOOLS, ...	300
CHAPTER	X.	DRAINAGE, ...	317
CHAPTER	XI.	MISCELLANEOUS PROVISIONS, ...	321

ERRATA.

On foot of page 183, for "Section 345 *ante*," read Section 245 *ante*.
On page 289, at end of Section 498, for "1863" read 1864.

PART FIRST.

CHARTER

OF THE

CITY OF DETROIT.

An Act to Revise the Charter of the City of Detroit.

[*Approved February 5th*, 1857. *Laws of* 1857, *p.* 73.]

CHAPTER I.

INCORPORATION: CITY AND WARD BOUNDARIES.

SECTION
1. Incorporation; name and powers of the corporation; seal of.

SECTION
2. City boundaries established. Creation of Wards; their boundaries; how altered.

CHAPTER I.

(§ 1.) SECTION 1. *The People of the State of Michigan enact:* That the corporation heretofore created and now known as "The Mayor, Recorder, Aldermen, and Freemen of the City of Detroit," shall be and continue to be a corporation by the name of "The City of Detroit," and by that name may sue and be sued, implead and be impleaded, complain and defend, in any court of record, and in any other place whatsoever; may have a common seal and alter it at pleasure, and may take, hold, purchase, lease, convey and dispose of any real, personal, or mixed estate for the use of said corporation. Corporat'n. Name and powers of. Seal of.

(§ 2.) SEC. 2. The district of country in the county of Wayne, and State of Michigan, hereinafter particularly described, is hereby constituted and declared to be a city Boundaries.

by the name of Detroit, and subject to the municipal government of said corporation, said district of country being bounded as follows, viz: Beginning at a point on the national boundary line in the Detroit River, directly opposite and in a line with the dividing line between the Baker and Woodbridge farms, so called, and running thence north twenty-two degrees and forty-seven minutes west, to the margin of said river; thence north twenty-two degrees and forty-seven minutes west, along said dividing line to the rear or northerly line of the Baker farm aforesaid; thence northeasterly along the rear or northerly line of the Baker, Labrosse, and Forsyth farms, so called, to the northwesterly corner of the Jones farm, so called; thence north sixty degrees east, on a course parallel with Jefferson Avenue to a point opposite the dividing line between the Dequindre and Witherell farms, so called; thence south twenty-six degrees east to the northeasterly corner of the Dequindre farm aforesaid, being the northwestern corner of the Witherell farm aforesaid; thence south twenty-six degrees east along said line of said farms, to the margin of the Detroit River aforesaid; thence south twenty-six degrees east to the national boundary line in said river, and thence southwesterly along said national boundary line to the place of beginning.[a] The wards of said city shall be and remain as heretofore laid out and constituted, until altered by the Common Council of said city, as authorized by this act.[b]

Wards established; how altered

[a] See Section 302, enlarging city limits.

[b] See Sections 303, 506.

CHAPTER II.

OFFICERS: WHO ELECTED, WHO APPOINTED, QUALIFICATIONS, BONDS, OFFICIAL TERMS, REMOVAL, VACANCY.

SECTION

3. What officers of corporation elected on general ticket, and on ward ticket.
4. What officers appointed by Council. New offices; how created.
5. Board of officers of corporation: Water Commissioners; terms of office, and how determined. Board of Education. Board of Inspectors of Election. Board of Sewer Commissioners; how appointed, and powers. Engineer, how appointed, and duties of.
6. Justices of the Peace; their terms of office, jurisdiction, powers, and duties.
7. Officers to be resident electors of city.
8. Qualifications of Attorney.
9. Defaulters ineligible to office.
10. Ignorance a disqualification for office.
11. Aldermen to hold no other office.
12. Persons interested in contracts disqualified for office.
13. Officers becoming interested in contracts to be removed. Punishment.
14. Bribery of members of Council, and how punished.
15. Terms of office.
16. Commencement of terms of office.
17. Oath of office.

SECTION

18. Officers elected, when to enter upon duties. Officers appointed, when, etc.
19. Offices; how discontinued.
20. Recorder subject to impeachment.
21. Expulsion from office; in what cases charges to be made; mode of trial; what officers Mayor may suspend.
22. Removal of officers.
23. Temporary suspension from office; how made.
24. Vacancies.
25. Resignations; how made.
26. Filling vacancies in appointed offices.
27. Vacancies in the office of Mayor or Aldermen; how filled.
28. Vacancies in elective offices other than Mayor, Recorder, or Aldermen; how filled.
29. Official bonds.
30. Condition of official bonds.
31. Constables' bonds.
32. Renewal of official bonds.
33. Notice of election to office; how given; neglect to qualify.
34. Sureties on bonds may be required to justify.
35. Clerk to report those neglecting to qualify.
36. Aldermen may exercise powers of Policemen.

(§ 3.) SECTION 1. The following officers of the corporation shall be elected at the annual city election, on a general ticket, by the qualified electors of the whole city, viz: Mayor, Recorder, City Clerk, Attorney, Treasurer, City Surveyor, and Director of the Poor.

Officers elected on gen'l ticket.

On ward ticket.

The following officers of the corporation shall be elected at said election on a ward ticket, in each ward, by the qualified electors thereof, viz: Two Aldermen, two School Inspectors, a Collector, Overseer of highways, and Constable. [*As amended by Laws of* 1861, *p.* 180.

Officers appointed by Com. Council.

Stadler vs. City of Detroit, 13th Mich., 346.

(§ 4.) SEC. 2. The following officers shall be appointed by the Common Council, at a meeting to be held on the second Tuesday of January in each year, viz: Superintendent of Alms House, a Sealer of Weights and Measures,[a] a Clerk of the Recorder's Court, who shall be appointed on the recommendation of the Recorder, one or more Collectors, one or more Physicians, one or more Street Commissioners, a Marshal, one or more Assistant Marshals,[b] and one or more Clerks of the Markets, and such other officer, deputies, assistant officers and agents, as may be necessary, and whose appointment shall be authorized by prior resolution of the Common Council. A Controller shall be appointed on the second Tuesday of March preceding the expiration of his term of office, and on the nomination of the Mayor, a Receiver of Taxes, whose term of office, shall be two years; a Superintendent of the House of Correction, whose term of office shall be three years, and a Counselor, who shall be a practicing attorney, and whose term of office, duties and compensation shall be prescribed by the Common Council: *Provided,* That any appointment which shall not be made on the day named, may be made at any subsequent regular session of the Common Council: *And provided, further,* That any office created by ordinance or resolution

[a] See Section 345.

[b] See Section 373, abolishing office of Marshal and Assistant Marshals.

of the Common Council, may be filled at any time until the second Tuesday of January following, when, as in case of other officers, the regular term of service shall commence, and the office, if continued, be filled for the ensuing year, unless otherwise provided by the the ordinance or resolution creating such office. [*As amended by Laws of* 1861, *p.* 181.]

(§ 5.) SEC. 3. There shall also be the following board of officers of the corporation: A board of water commissioners, to be appointed and constituted as provided for in the act incorporating the Board of Water Commissioners of the City of Detroit, approved February 14, 1853;[c] a Board of Education, to be constituted as provided for in the act incorporating the Board of Education of the City of Detroit, approved February 17, 1842,[d] and all present and existing acts amendatory thereto; and a Board of Inspectors of Elections, to be appointed and constituted as hereinafter provided; and a board of three Sewer Commissioners, who shall be appointed by the Common Council, on the nomination of the Mayor, and who shall appoint a competent Engineer, and with his aid it shall be their duty to propose a plan for constructing sewers and drains for the whole city, having reference, however, to the sewers and drains already constructed or in process of construction; and said board shall have the control of all the public and private sewers within the city, and shall in the month of February, of each year, furnish to the Common Council a list of all the public sewers, together with the estimated cost of the

Water Commissioners.

Board of Education.

Board of Inspectors of Election.

Sewer Commissioners; duty of.

List of Sewers and cost.

[c] See Part II, Chapter II, Section 307, *et post.*

[d] See Part II, Chapter IX, Section 510, *et post.*

same, which they recommend to be constructed or built within said city, for the fiscal year ending January thereafter; and the Common Council shall decide which of the sewers, so recommended by the board they will have built or constructed under the supervision of said Sewer Commissioners; and the Common Council shall not have power to build, or contract to build, any sewer or sewers within said city that the Board of Sewer Commissioners has not recommended in their report in the month of February, as provided for in this act; and said board shall have such further powers and duties, in respect to the sewers and drains of said city, as said Common Council shall by ordinance prescribe; said Commissioners shall received no compensation for their services; shall hold their office for the term of five years, with the exception of the first board, who shall hold their office for the respective terms of three, four, and five years, and the respective terms of each shall be determined by lot, under the direction of the City Attorney and Controller, and when thus determined, such determination shall be certified by said Attorney and Controller to the Common Council, and entered upon their journal, and such certificate shall be evidence of the respective term for which the several members of said board have been elected; it shall be the duty of said Engineer, under the direction of said board, to superintend the construction and repairing of all the sewers. [*As amended by Laws of* 1867. *Vol. II., p.* 1110.]

Sewers that may not be built.

Compensa'n

Term of office.

Duty of Engineer.

(§ 6.) SEC. 4. There shall be six Justices of the Peace in and for said city, who shall be elected on the general ticket at the annual city election in the same manner, shall hold their offices for the same terms and by the

Justices of the Peace—their term of office, jurisdict'n, powers, and duties.

same tenure, possess the same jurisdiction and powers, subject to the act of the Legislature establishing a Police Court of the City of Detroit, and be subject to the same duties and liabilities, as provided by the general laws of this State in relation to the election, jurisdiction, powers, duties and liabilities of Justices of the Peace for townships; but the Justices of the Peace of said city, now in office, shall continue to hold their offices for the terms for which they have been elected, and in conformity to the general laws of this State: *Provided, however,* That at the election, to be held in April, 1857, a Justice of the Peace may be elected to fill the vacancy which will occur by the expiration of the term of such Justice, in July, 1857.

Justices now in office to continue.

Proviso.

(§ 7.) SEC. 5. No person shall be elected or appointed to, or shall hold any office under this act, who shall not be, at the time of his election, or appointment, and so long as he shall hold such office, a resident elector of said city; and no person shall be elected or appointed to, or shall hold office for any ward in said city, who at the time of his election or appointment, and so long as he shall hold such office, shall not be a resident elector of the ward from and for which he may be elected or appointed. If any person, elected or appointed to any office of the corporation, shall cease to be a resident of the city, or of the ward, for which he may have been elected or appointed, such office shall thereby be vacated: *Provided, however,* That a School Inspector shall not vacate his office by his removal from one ward to another ward in said city.[e]

Officers to be residents of Detroit.

Proviso.

---

[e] See Section 541.

Qualificat'n of Attorney. (§ 8.) SEC. 6. No person shall be elected to the office of Attorney, unless he be at the time of his election a Counselor of the Supreme Court of this State of two years' standing.

Defaulters ineligible. (§ 9.) SEC. 7. No person shall be elected or appointed to any office created by this act, who is now, or hereafter may be, a defaulter to said city, or to any board of officers thereof, or to the State of Michigan, or any county thereof; and any person shall be considered a defaulter who has refused, or neglected, or may hereafter refuse or neglect, for thirty days after demand made, to account for and pay over to the party authorized to receive the same, any public money which has come in his possession. If any person holding any such office shall become a defaulter, while in office, the same shall thereby be vacated.

Ignorance a disqualification for office. (§ 10.) SEC. 8. No person shall be elected or appointed to any office under this act, except the offices of Scavenger and Chimney Sweeper, unless he is able to read and write the English language intelligibly; and if any such person be elected or appointed, the Common Council shall declare such appointment or election void.

Inelligibil'y of members of the Council to hold certain offices. (§ 11.) SEC. 9. No member of the Common Council shall hold or be eligible to the office of Recorder of the city of Detroit, or hold or be eligible to any county office of the county of Wayne, except the office of Notary Public, and all votes cast for any such member for any such office shall be null and void, nor shall any member, after his election, and during the time for which he was elected, or within one year thereafter, be appointed to any office under this act, which shall have been created, or the emoluments of which shall have been increased, during such time: *Provided*, That this section shall not be construed to affect the members of the present Common Council, nor their right to hold county offices to which they have heretofore been elected. [*As amended by Laws of* 1867, *Vol.* II, *Page* 1114.] Proviso.

(§ 12.) SEC. 10. No person interested, directly or indirectly, either as principal or surety, in any contract or agreement, written or verbal, to which the corporation shall be a party in interest, or to which any officer or board under this act shall officially be a party, for the construction of any sewer, pavement, building, or performance of any pnblic work whatever, or for involving the expenditure, receipt or disposition of money or property of the corporation, Common Council, or by any officer or board under this act, shall be eligible or appointed to any office under this act; and if any person thus interested shall be elected or appointed to office, his election or appointment shall be void, and his office shall be deemed vacant. Persons interested disqualified for office.

(§ 13.) SEC. 11. If any member of the Common Council, or other officer of the corporation, after his election or appointment, or while in office, shall become, or cause himself to become interested, directly or indirectly, in any contract or agreement, written or verbal, to which the corporation shall be a party in interest, or to which any officer or board under this act shall officially be a party, or in any question, subject or proceeding, pending before the Common Council, with intent to gain, directly or indirectly, any benefit, profit, or pecuniary advantage, he shall be removed from his office, and his office declared vacant by the Common Council, and he shall be deemed guilty of willful and corrupt malfeasance in office, Officers becoming interested to be removed.

Punishme't. and may be prosecuted therefor, and on conviction, shall be punished by a fine not exceeding one thousand dollars, or imprisonment in the State Prison not exceeding one year, or both, at the discretion of the court.

Bribery. (§ 14.) SEC. 12. If any person shall offer, directly or indirectly, to a member of the Common Council, or if any member of the Common Council shall directly or indirectly accept, or agree to accept, or receive any money, goods or chattels, or any bank note, bank bill, bond, promissory note, due bill, bill of exchange, draft, order or certificate, or any security for the payment of money or goods and chattels, or any deed or writing containing a conveyance of land, or containing a transfer of any interest in real estate, any valuable contract, in force, or any other property or reward whatsoever, in consideration that such member of the Common Council will vote affirmatively or negatively, or that he will not vote, or that he will use his interest or influence on any question, ordinance, resolution, or other matter or proceeding pending before the Common Council, he shall be removed from office, and his office declared vacant by the Common Council, and both he and the person making such offer as aforesaid, shall be deemed guilty of misdemeanor, Punishm'nt. and may be prosecuted therefor, and on conviction, shall be punished by a fine not exceeding one thousand dollars, or imprisonment in the State Prison not exceeding one year, or both, at the discretion of the court.

Terms of office. (§ 15.) SEC. 13. The Water Commissioners shall hold their respective offices for the term of five years,[f] the Controller and Superintendent of the House of Correction

[f] See Section 203.

for the term of three years, the Recorder for the term of six years, the Mayor, Aldermen, School Inspectors, Treasurer, City Clerk, Attorney, Marshal, City Surveyor, Director of the Poor, and Receiver of Taxes for the term of two years, and all other officers who are elected or appointed, shall hold for the term of one year: *Provided, however*, That all officers, whether elected or appointed, shall hold their offices respectively until their successors shall be duly elected or appointed and qualified, and shall enter upon the discharge of their duties. [*As amended by Law of* 1861, *p.* 181.]

Stadler vs. City of Detroit, 1 th Mich., 346.

Proviso.

(§ 16) SEC. 14. The official terms of all officers who are elected, shall commence on the second Tuesday of January, after the annual city election at which they may have been elected, on which day there shall be a meeting of the Common Council; and the official terms of all officers who are appointed shall commence and expire on the third Tuesday of January, (on which day there shall also be a meeting of the Common Council,) except the Water Commissioners, whose official terms shall commence and expire as provided for in the act incorporating "The Board of Water Commissioners of the City of Detroit," approved February 14th, 1853, and the Controller, whose official term shall commence and expire on the first Tuesday in April.

Commencement of official terms.

(§ 17.) SEC. 15. Every officer, appointed or elected under this act, before entering on the duties of his office, shall take and subscribe the following oath of office: "I do solemly swear (or affirm) that I will support the constitution of the United States and of this State, and that I will faithfully discharge the duties of such office to the best of my ability;" and shall file said oath,

Oath of office.

duly certified by the officer before whom it was taken, in the office of the Clerk of said city.

Oaths, before whom taken. (§ 18.) SEC. 16. Officers, who are elected at the annual city election, shall take and subscribe the oath of office before the City Clerk, file their official bonds, and enter upon their official duties, on the second Tuesday of January next ensuing their election, or within ten days thereafter; and officers who are appointed for full terms, shall take and subscribe the oath of office, file their official bonds, and enter upon their official duties on the third Tuesday of January, or within ten days thereafter; but officers who are either elected at a special election, or appointed to fill the unexpired portion of a term, shall take and subscribe the oath of office, file their official bonds, and enter upon their duties within ten days next ensuing notice of their election or appointment, except Justices of the Peace.

Discontinuing office. (§ 19.) SEC. 17. Any office hereby authorized, but not specially named, may at any time be discontinued by the Common Council, and if there be an incumbent in such office, such continuance shall, on notice thereof, discharge him from the office and a further execution of its duties, and his office be deemed vacant.

Recorder subject to impeachm't (§ 20.) SEC. 18. The Recorder shall be subject to impeachment and removal from office for corrupt conduct in office, or for crimes and misdemeanors, in the same manner as judicial officers, pursuant to the provisions of the constitution of this State.

Expulsion from office. (§ 21.) SEC. 19. The Common Council may expel or remove from office any of its own members, or any other officer holding office by election, except the Mayor and Recorder, for corrupt or willful malfeasance or misfeasance in office, or for willful neglect of the duties of his office, by a vote of two-thirds of all the Aldermen elect, and in such case the reasons for such expulsion or removal shall be entered on the records of the Common Council, with the names and votes of the members voting on the question. No officer holding office by election shall be expelled or removed by said Common Council, unless first furnished with a copy of the charges in writing, and allowed to be heard in his defense, with aid of counsel, and for the purposes hereof the Common Council shall have power to issue subpœnas, to compel the attendance of witnesses and the production of papers, when necessary, and shall proceed, within ten days after service of a copy of the charges, to hear and determine upon the merits of the case. If such officer shall neglect to appear and answer to such charges, his default may be deemed good cause for removal from office. The Mayor shall have power to suspend or remove from office the Marshal, Street Commissioners, Deputy Marshal, Constables, Overseers of Highways and officers of the Police;[g] and in case of such suspension or removal he shall report the same, with the reasons therefor, to the Common Council.

Mayor may suspend officers.

(§ 22.) SEC. 20. Any officer holding office by appointment, unless otherwise provided by law or ordinance, may be removed at any time by the Common Council, without charges, and a trial thereof, by a vote of the majority of the Aldermen elect, except the Controller, Receiver of Taxes, and Superintendent of the House of

Removal of officers.

Stadler vs. City of Detroit, 13th Mich., 346.

---

[g] The Mayor's power to remove police officers is superseded by the Police Act of 1865. See Section 338 *et post*.

Correction, who may be removed for the same causes and on the same proceedings as a member of the Common Council. [*As amended by Laws of* 1861, *p.* 182.

Temporary suspension from office. (§ 23) SEC. 21. Any officer holding office by election, except the Recorder, against whom charges shall be preferred, may be suspended from office by a majority vote of all the Aldermen elected, until such charges shall be heard and determined; and any officer holding office by appointment, may be suspended temporarily from office, at any time, by the like vote.

Vacancies. (§ 24.) SEC. 22. In case of expulsion or removal from office, death, resignation or permanent disability of any officer, his office shall thereby become vacant, and may be so declared by the Common Council.

Resignati'n. (§ 25.) SEC. 23. Resignations of office shall be made to the Common Council, in writing, and be subject to their approval and acceptance.

Filling vacancies in appointed offices. (§ 26.) SEC. 24. If any office of appointment shall become vacant, the Common Council may appoint a successor to serve for the unexpired portion of the official term.

Vacancies in office of Mayor or Aldermen—how filled. (§ 27.) SEC. 25. If a vacancy occurs in the office of Mayor or Alderman more than six months before the time for holding the next succeeding annual city election, the Common Council shall order a special election to fill such vacancy for the residue of the official term; if it occurs within six months before the time for holding such election, the Common Council may, in its discretion, order a special election to fill such vacancy for the residue of the official term.

Vacancies in other elective offices; how filled. (§ 28.) SEC. 26. If a vacancy occurs in any elective office, other than that of Mayor, Recorder or Alderman, the Common Council shall appoint some person, eligible under this act, to serve in such office until the next annual election, when the vacancy shall be filled for the residue of the official term. The People vs. Witherell. 14 Mich. 48.

(§ 29.) SEC. 27. The Controller, Treasurer, Clerk, Attorney, Receiver of Taxes, Superintendent of the House of Correction, Collectors, Marshal, Clerk of the Markets, Street Commissioners, and Constables, shall, *respectively*, before they enter upon the duties of their respective offices, and such other officers as the Common Council may direct, file in the Clerk's office an official bond, in such sum and with such sureties as the Common Couucil shall direct and approve. [*As amended by Laws of* 1861, *p.* 182.] Official bds.

(§ 30.) SEC. 28. The official bond of every officer shall be conditioned that he will faithfully perform the duties of his office, and will, on demand, deliver over to his successor in office, or other proper officer or agent of the corporation, all books, papers, moneys, effects and property belonging to the corporation, or appertaining to his office, which may be in his custody as an officer; and such bond may be further conditioned as the Common Council shall prescribe. The official bond of every officer whose duty it may be to receive or pay out money, besides being conditioned as above required, shall be further conditioned that he will, on demand, pay over or account for to the corporation, or any proper officer or agent thereof, all moneys received by him as such officer. Conditi'n of official bds.

(§ 31.) SEC. 29. Every person elected to the office of constable in said city, before entering on the duties of his office, shall, with two or more sureties, to be approved by the Common Council, execute and file with the City Clerk a bond or instrument, in writing, to the Constables' bonds.

City of Detroit, in the penal sum of two thousand dollars, conditioned well and faithfully in all things, to execute and perform the duties of his office during the continuance therein, and to pay to each and every person who may be entitled thereto, all sums of money which said constable may become liable to pay on account of any execution or process for the collection of money which shall be delivered to him; and further conditioned as the Common Council may prescribe. [*As amended by Laws of* 1861, *p.* 182.]

Condition.

Renewal of official bds.

(§ 32.) SEC. 30. The Common Council may at any time require any officer, whether elected or appointed, to execute and file with the Clerk of the city new official bonds in the same or in such further sums, and with new or such further sureties as said Council may deem requisite for the interest of the corporation.

Notice of election to office.

(§ 33.) SEC. 31. The Clerk of the city shall cause every officer, whether elected or appointed, as soon as practicable after his election or appointment, to be served with a written notice thereof and of the amount of his official bond; and if such officer shall neglect to take and subscribe his oath of office, or to file his required official bond within the time prescribed therefor by this act; or if any officer, required to execute and file a new official bond, as provided in the preceding section, shall not comply with such requirement within ten days after notice thereof from the City Clerk, the Common Council may declare the office in such case vacant, and such vacancy may be filled as heretofore provided in this act.

Neglect to qualify.

Sureties in official bds. may be requr'd to justify on oath.

(§ 34.) SEC. 32. The Common Council, or such officer as the Common Council shall by resolution or ordinance prescribe, may examine into the sufficiency of the proposed sureties in any official bond, or instrument, in writing, required by this act, or in any contract, in writing, to which the corporation or any officer or board under this act shall be a party in interest, and may require such sureties to submit to an examination, under oath, as to their property and responsibility. The depositions of the surety shall be reduced to writing, be signed by him, certified by the person taking the same, and annexed to and filed with the bond, or instrument in writing, to which it relates.

City Cl'k to rep'rt delinquents to Council.

(§ 35.) SEC. 33. The Clerk of the city shall report the name of any person elected or appointed to any office, who shall have neglected to file his official bond and oath of office, as required by this act, to the Common Council, at its next meeting after such default.

Aldermen may exercise powers of policem'n

(§ 36.) SEC. 34. The Aldermen of said city shall, by virtue of their office, be vested with and may exercise all the powers of Policemen of said city.[h] [*As added by Laws of* 1861, *p.* 183.]

[h] See Section 338.

CHAPTER III.

ELECTIONS: HOW CONDUCTED.

SECTION
37. Annual city election: time, place and notice; special elections.
38. Council may divide wards into election districts; Inspectors, how appointed; Board of Registration; where electors shall vote; residence defined.
39. Inspectors of election: how chosen; oath of Inspectors.
40. Clerks of Election: how appointed.
41. Ballot box.
42. Time for opening and closing polls.
43. Qualification of voters.
44. Challenge and oath.
45. Perjury and punishment.

SECTION
46. Punishment for voting more than once.
47. State law applicable, unless otherwise provided.
48. Manner of certifying returns of election; canvass.
49. Special elections: how conducted.
50. Ballots for vacancy or residue of term: what to state.
51. Plurality to elect.
52. Proceedings in case of tie.
53. Mode of conducting State, District and county elections.
54. Privilege from arrest on election day.
55. First election under act: time of; officers holding office to continue.

Annual city election; time, place, and notice.

(§ 37.) SECTION 1. The annual city election shall be held on the first Tuesday after the first Monday of November in each year, at such places in the several wards as shall be designated by an order of the Common Council, at least twenty days previous thereto, notice of which, specifying, also, the officers to be elected and the time for opening and closing the polls, shall immediately, or within three days after the date of such order, be given by the City Clerk, by publication in two or more daily newspapers published in said city. The time and place for holding a special election shall be designated, and the notice thereof given in the same manner, and to the same effect.

People vs. Hartwell, 12 Mich., 508.

Special elections.

ELECTIONS: HOW CONDUCTED. CHAPTER III.

(§ 38.) SEC. 2. Each ward shall be an election district by itself; but it shall be lawful for the Common Council, in its discretion, at any time before the first day of October next preceding any charter or general election, to divide the several wards of the city, or either of them, into convenient election districts for the holding of general and special elections;[a] and in case any ward or wards shall be so divided, the provisions of the general laws of the State, and of this act, relating to elections other than in towns, shall be applicable to such election districts. The Common Council shall, at least twenty days prior to any general or special election, appoint two Inspectors of Election for each ward so divided into election districts, and one of the Inspectors so appointed, with one of the Aldermen of the ward so divided, shall act as a Board of Registration in each of said election districts; and with one Inspector to be elected by a *viva voce* vote of the electors of the district, on the opening of the polls at any election, shall form a Board of Inspectors for said election. Vacancies in any Board of Inspectors, may be filled by the electors present, as in other cases of such vacancies. Any election district so made, shall remain an election district by itself until changed by the Common Council. Every elector shall vote in the ward and district in which he resides, as provided by law.[b] The residence of an elector shall be the ward and district in which his family resides, or in which is his regular boarding house. [*As amended by Laws of* 1861, *p.* 183.]

Co'ncil may divide war's into electi'n districts.

Inspectors: how appointed.

Board of Registrat'n.

Board of Inspectors.

Where electors shall vote.

Residence defined.

[a] See Section 506.

[b] Const., Art. VII, Section 1. Also, Section 43, *post*.

Inspectors of election.

(§ 39.) SEC. 3. At every election, the Inspectors of Election for the ward or district in which such election may be held, in case the ward has not been divided into election districts, shall consist of the Aldermen of the ward and a third person, to be chosen *viva voce* by the electors present, from their number, at the time of opening the polls; and in case the ward has been divided into election districts, the Inspectors of Election shall consist of one Alderman of the ward, one of the persons appointed by the Common Council for that purpose, and one elector of the ward and district, chosen by a *viva voce* vote of the electors present, at the time of opening the polls; and if, from any cause, either or both of the Aldermen, or of the Inspectors appointed by the Common Council, shall fail to attend such election, his or their places shall be supplied by the electors present, who shall elect any of their number *viva voce.* Said Inspectors, before entering upon their duties, shall each take the same oath of office prescribed for other officers under this act.[c] [*As amended by Laws of* 1861, *p.* 184.]

Oath of Inspectors.

Clerks of elect'n; how appointed.

(§ 40.) SEC. 4. The Inspectors of each ward, if not divided into election districts, and in each district, if so divided, shall appoint two competent Clerks of the election, who shall take the same oath as the Inspectors, which oath either of the Inspectors may administer. [*As amended by Laws of* 1861, *p.* 184.]

Ballot box.

(§ 41.) SEC. 5. One suitable ballot box, with lock and key, shall be provided and kept by the City Clerk, at the expense of the city, for each ward or district;

[c] Section 17, *ante*.

and it shall be the duty of the City Clerk to deposit such box, with the key, in the hands of the Inspectors of each ward or district, prior to the opening of the polls. [*As amended by Laws of* 1861, *p.* 184.]

(§ 42.) SEC. 6. The polls of election shall be opened at eight o'clock in the forenoon, or as soon thereafter as may be, on the day of election, and shall be continued open until five o'clock in the afternoon of the same day, and no longer. **Opening and closing polls.**

(§ 43.) SEC. 7. The qualifications of electors, under this act, shall be those prescribed in the first section of the seventh article of the constitution of this State, which is as follows: "In all elections, every white male citizen, every white male inhabitant residing in the State on the twenty-fourth day of June, one thousand eight hundred and thirty-five; every white male inhabitant residing in this State on the first day of January, one thousand eight hundred and fifty, who has declared his intention to become a citizen of the United States, pursuant to the laws thereof, six months preceding an election, or who has resided in this State two years and six months, and declared his intention as aforesaid, and every civilized male inhabitant, of Indian descent, a native of the United States, and not a member of any tribe, shall be an elector, and entitled to vote; but no citizen or inhabitant shall be an elector, or entitled to vote at any election, unless he shall be above the age of twenty-one years, and has resided in this State three months, and in the township or ward in which he offers to vote, ten days next preceding such election." **Qualificat'n of voters.**

(§ 44.) SEC. 8. If, at any election, a vote shall be challenged, either of the Inspectors of Election shall be **Challenge and oath.**

authorized to swear or affirm the person whose vote is challenged, to answer such questions as may be put to him touching his qualifications as an elector, and said Inspectors shall decide from such examination as to the legality of such vote.[d]

Perjury. (§ 45.) SEC. 9. If any person, thus sworn or affirmed, shall willfully swear or affirm falsely, as to any material matter concerning his qualifications as an elector of said city, he shall be deemed guilty of perjury, and may be Punishment prosecuted therefor; and, on conviction thereof, be punished by a fine not exceeding one thousand dollars, or imprisonment at hard labor in the State Prison for a period not exceeding five years, or both, in the discretion of the court.[e]

Punishment for voting more than once. (§ 46.) SEC. 10. If any person shall vote in more than one ward or district, or more than once in the same ward or district, at any election in said city, he may be prosecuted therefor, and, on conviction, shall be punished by a fine not exceeding five hundred dollars, or imprisonment at hard labor in the State Prison for a period not exceeding three years, or both, in the discretion of the court. [*As amended by Laws of* 1861, *p.* 185.]

Conducting elections. (§ 47.) SEC. 11. The manner of conducting and voting at elections to be held under this act, the keeping of the poll lists, canvassing of the votes, certifying the returns, and all other proceedings connected with such elections, shall be the same, as nearly as may be, as is now, or hereafter may be provided for by the laws of

---

[d] See Section 483.

[e] For penalty of illegal voting, see Compiled Laws, section 5915; also *post*, sections 484 and 481.

this State, applicable to general State elections, except as may be otherwise provided in this act.

(§ 48.) SEC. 12. On canvassing the votes, the Inspectors shall certify a full and true return thereof, under their hands, to the Clerk of the city, carefully sealed up, together with the poll lists and ballots, within seventy-two hours after the closing of the polls; and the Inspectors of each election district shall thereupon choose one of their number to represent such election district, in the Board of City Canvassers, and the persons so chosen shall form the Board of Canvassers for the city, and shall, on the Saturday next after election, at three o'clock in the afternoon, meet at the City Clerk's office, or in the Common Council chamber, and proceed to open and canvass the said returns, and declare the result of the election. [*As amended by Laws of* 1861, *p.* 185.]

Certifying returns of election.

Canvass.

(§ 49.) SEC. 13. Special elections shall be conducted, as near as may be, in the same manner as general elections,[f] but in such cases the returns of the Inspectors shall be opened and canvassed, and the result declared by the Common Council, at its first meeting after the making of said returns.

Conducting special elections.

(§ 50.) SEC. 14. If any person be voted for at any election, to fill a vacancy, or residue of a term, the ballots of the electors shall designate such vacancy or residue.

Ballots for vacancy.

To designate vacancy.

(§ 51.) SEC. 15. In the canvass of votes, any person who has received a plurality of the votes for any office, shall be declared duly elected to such office.

Plurality to elect.

(§ 52.) SEC. 16. When two or more persons shall have an equal number of votes for the same office, the

Proceedin's in case of tie

[f] As to review of Registration in such case, see section 502.

election shall be determined by the drawing of lots in the presence of the Common Council. The names of each of such persons shall be written on separate slips of paper and deposited in a box, or other proper place, and the President of the Common Council shall draw out of said box, or other place, in the usual manner of determining by lot, one of said slips, and the person whose name is thereon, shall be deemed entitled to hold the office for which he received said votes, in the same manner as other officers duly elected.

Mode of conducting state, district, and county elections.

(§ 53.) SEC. 17. The mode of conducting all State, district and county elections in said city, shall be in the manner herein provided for the election of city officers, except that the returns thereof shall be made to the County Clerk, and the same proceedings had, as near as may be, as are now or hereafter may be provided by law for the return of votes by township Inspectors of Election.

Privilege from arrest.

(§ 54.) SEC. 18. No person, entitled to vote at any election held under this act, shall be arrested on civil process, within said city, on the day on which such election is held.[g]

First election; time of.

(§ 55.) SEC. 19. The first election, under this act, shall be held on the first Tuesday after the first Monday in November, 1857, and all officers now holding offices, by election, in said city, which are made elective by the people, under this act, shall continue to hold their respective offices until the second Tuesday of January, 1858. The Aldermen of said city, who were elected in the year 1855, shall continue in office until the

[g] Constitution, Art. VII, sec. 4, Compiled Laws, sec. 117.

Officers holding office to continue.

second Tuesday in January, 1858, and shall be succeeded in office by the Aldermen who are elected in November, 1857, and the Aldermen who were elected in the year 1856, shall continue in office until the second Tuesday in January, 1859, and shall be succeeded in office by the Aldermen who are elected in November, 1858. In all cases where any new office is created, or where any vacancy may occur, under the provisions of this act, the Common Council may appoint persons to fill the same until the second Tuesday in January, 1858, when their successors shall be appointed, except the Assessor, who shall be appointed for his full term, as herein provided. The present Recorder of said city shall continue to hold his office until the second Tuesday in January, 1858, and shall possess and exercise the powers and duties now possessed and exercised by him, under the present charter of said city, and shall also be President of the Common Council, and shall possess and exercise the powers and duties of that office, as herein provided, until the expiration of his term of office, and shall receive such salary as the Common Council may prescribe. The present Controller of said city shall continue to hold his office until the first day of April, 1859. The office of Ward Assessor is hereby abolished.

CHAPTER IV.

OFFICERS: THEIR RIGHTS, POWERS AND DUTIES.

SECTION
56. Mayor: his duty.
57. Salary of Mayor; who to act as Mayor in certain cases.
58. President of Council.
59. In certain cases President *pro tempore* to preside; powers of.
60. Duties of Attorney.
61. Duties of Clerk.
62. Duties of Controller.
63. Further duties of Controller.
64. Recorder, and Clerk of Recorder's Court.
65. Duties of Treasurer.
66. Powers and duties of Marshal.
67. Assistant Marshal.
68. Powers and duties of Surveyor.
69. Powers and duties of City Collector.
70. Duties of Assessor.
71. Duties of Street Commissioners relative to streets.
72. Duties of Overseers of Highways.

SECTION
73. Duties of Ward Collectors, etc.
74. Books, papers, etc., to be delivered to successor.
75. General powers and duties of officers.
76. Who may administer oaths; Controller may take acknowledgement of deeds.
77. Mayor may entertain complaints against persons to whom licenses have been granted for violation of ordinances.
78. Chairmen of Committees may administer oaths respecting matters pending before them.
79. Unsafe buildings; powers of Council.
80. Claims against city.
81. Clerk to countersign all licenses granted by the Mayor.

Mayor; his duty.

(§ 56.) SECTION 1. The Mayor shall be the chief executive officer of the City of Detroit, and conservator of its peace. It shall be his duty to keep an office in in some convenient place in said city, to be provided by the Common Council; to see that all officers of said city faithfully comply with and discharge their official duties; to see that all laws pertaining to the municipal government of said city, and all ordinances and resolutions of the Common Council be faithfully observed and executed; and he shall have power in his discretion, to report to the Common Council any violations thereof. He shall, from time to time, give to the Common Council such information, and recommend such measures as he shall deem necessary or expedient.

(§ 57.) SEC 2. The Mayor shall be paid a salary of twelve hundred dollars *per annum*. In case of a vacancy in the office of Mayor, or of his being unable to perform the duties of his office, by reason of sickness, absence from the city, or other cause, the President of the Common Council shall be acting Mayor; and in case, at the same time, there shall also be a vacancy in the office of President of the Common Council, or he shall be unable to perform the duties of his office, by reason of sickness, absence from the city, or other cause, the President *pro tempore* of the Common Council shall be acting Mayor; and such acting Mayor shall be vested with all the powers, and shall perform all the duties of Mayor, until the vacancy or vacancies aforesaid be filled, or the Mayor or President of the Common Council, as the case may be, shall resume his office.

Salary of Mayor.

Who is to be acting Mayor in certain cases.

(§ 58.) SEC. 3. The Common Council shall, at its first meeting in January in each year, select from their number a President for the year,[a] and in case of a vacancy, or his temporary absence, supply his place by the election of a President *pro tempore*.

President of Com. Council.

(§ 59.) SEC. 4. The President *pro tempore* of the Common Council shall preside at its meetings, in case of a vacancy in the office of President of the Common Council, or of his being unable, from any cause, to be present and preside. In such case, the President *pro tempore* shall be invested with all the powers, and shall perform

In certain cases President *pro tempore* to preside.

Powers of.

[a] See Section 84.

all the duties of President of the Common Council until he shall resume his office, or the vacancy therein be filled.

Duties of Attorney. (§ 60.) SEC. 5. The Attorney shall appear in and conduct all suits, prosecutions and proceedings in the Recorder's Court, to which the city of Detroit is a party, to the end thereof, subject to the rules and practice of said court, and if the same be removed to any other tribunal, by writ of error, *habeas corpus*, or otherwise, he shall conduct the case before such tribunal.

Duties of Clerk. (§ 61.) SEC. 6. The Clerk of the corporation shall keep the corporate seal, and all papers filed in or pertaining to his office, and shall be Clerk of the Common Council, shall attend its meetings, and shall make and preserve a record of all its ordinances, resolutions, and other proceedings, in proper books to be provided therefor, and when requested, shall duly certify, under the corporate seal, copies thereof, and of all papers duly filed in his office pertaining to the same, and shall possess and exercise the powers of Township Clerks.

Duties of Controller. (§ 62.) SEC. 7. It shall be the duty of the Controller to countersign all bonds which the corporation or Common Council is authorized to issue, pledging the faith and credit of said city; to receive all accounts and demands against the corporation, examine them in detail, audit and allow them, or such parts thereof as to the correctness of which he has no doubt, and which the claimant is willing to accept in full discharge thereof, File vouchers. file and number them as vouchers, in the order of their allowance, register them, with the amount allowed and date of allowance, in the same order, in a proper book provided for such purpose, and, on their being properly Draw warrants. discharged, in writing, to draw and sign his warrant therefor, upon the Treasurer, when the same is ordered to be paid by the Common Council. If he shall have any doubt concerning their correctness, he shall register them in a separate list and return them to the Common Council, with his objections. If the same be allowed by the Common Council, in pursuance of their authority under this act, on their return to the Controller, with a certificate of the Clerk endorsed thereon that they have been allowed by the Common Council, he shall then file and register them in the list of allowed claims, in the same manner as above provided for the registering of claims audited and allowed by him, and, on their being properly discharged, in writing, shall draw and sign his warrant therefor on the Treasurer. It shall also be the duty of the Controller to lay before the Common Council, once in each year, in the month of April, or oftener if directed by the Common Council, a schedule of all accounts audited and allowed by him, and of all leases of the property of the corporation, specifying the names of the lessees, the rates of rent, and the period when the leases will terminate. It shall also be the duty of the Controller to examine the tax rolls and returns of the city officers, and take general supervision of the financial concerns of the corporation; to keep a complete set of books, exhibiting the financial condition of the corporation in its various departments and funds, its resources and liabilities, with a proper classiffication thereof, and each fund or appropriation for any distinct object of expenditure, or class of expenditures. When any such fund or appropriation has been exhausted by warrants already drawn thereon, or by appropriations, liabilities, debts, and expenses actually made, incurred, or contracted

Register doubtful accounts and return to Com, Council.

To present to Council schedule of acc'nts, etc.

To examine tax rolls and returns of city officers.

To advise Com. Council wh'n any fund is exhausted.

for, and to be paid out of such fund or appropriation, the Controller shall advise the Common Council thereof at its next meeting.

To open an acco't with Treasurer.

(§ 63.) SEC. 8. The Controller shall also open an account with the Treasurer, in which he shall charge said Treasurer with the whole amount of taxes, general and special, levied in said city, also the whole amount in detail of all bonds, notes, mortgages, leases, rents, interest, and other moneys receivable, in order that the value and description of all personal property belonging to the corporation may, at any time, be known. He shall also keep a list of all the property, real, personal, and mixed, belonging to the corporation, and of all its debts and liabilities, in order that the amount of the moneys and liabilities of the corporation may at any time be known at his office. The Controller shall also perform such other duties as are prescribed by this act, or may be prescribed by the Common Council, subject to the provisions hereof. The Controller shall also open accounts with the Treasurer, in which he shall charge him with all moneys appropriated, raised, or received for each of the several funds of the corporation, and credit him for all the warrants drawn thereon, keeping a separate account of debit and credit for each fund, charging every warrant drawn to the account of the particular fund constituted or raised for the specific purpose for which such warrant is drawn, in order that it may be known, at the Controller's office, when each fund has been or may be exhausted, and what balance, if any, may remain therein.

To keep a list of property of corporation.

Powers and duties of Recorder and Clerk of Recorder's Court.

(§ 64.) SEC. 9. The Recorder of the city, and the Clerk of the Recorder's Court, shall possess and exercise the powers and duties elsewhere prescribed in this act.[h]

(§ 65. SEC. 10. The treasurer shall have the custody of all moneys, bonds, mortgages, notes, leases, and evidences of value belonging to the corporation. He shall receive all moneys belonging to and receivable by the corporation, and keep an accurate account of all receipts and expenditures thereof. He shall pay no money out of the Treasury, except in pursuance of and by authority of law, and on a warrant signed by the Controller, which shall specify the purpose for which the amount thereof is to be paid. He shall keep an accurate account of, and be charged with, all taxes and moneys appropriated, raised, or received for each fund of the corporation; shall keep a separate account for each fund, and shall pay every warrant out of the particular fund constituted or raised for the purposes for which said warrant was issued, and having the name of such fund indorsed thereon by the Controller. He shall exhibit to the Common Council annually, and as often and for such period as may be required, a full and detailed account of all receipts and disbursements since the date of his last annual report, classifying them by the fund to which such receipts are credited, and out of which such disbursements are made; shall report to the Controller, at the end of each month, the amount received and credited by him to each fund, and on what account received; and shall also, when required, exhibit a general statement showing the financial condition of the treasury; Duties of Treasurer.

[h] See section 108, 109, 121, 122. See also, section 568. The Laws of 1867, Vol. I, p. 88, also confers jurisdiction on the Recorder in cases of "forcible or unlawful entry and detainer,"

which account, report, and statement shall be filed in the office of the Controller.

Powers and duties of Marshal.

(§ 66.) SEC. 11.[i] The Marshal shall possess and exercise the powers and duties, as a conservator of the peace, which township constables, under the general laws of this State possess and may exercise, and shall possess and exercise such other powers and duties as shall be prescribed by the Common Council for the preservation of the public peace, and shall possess and exercise the same powers for the service and execution of all writs, process, and warrants issuing out of the Recorder's Court, in cases arising under the ordinances of the city, which Sheriffs now have, or may have by law, for the service and execution of writs and process issuing from the Circuit Courts of this State. He shall obey and execute all lawful precepts and commands of said Common Council, and of said Recorder's Court; shall attend the sittings of said court, and he, or one of his deputies, shall attend the meetings of said Common Council.[j]

Assistant Marshal.

(§ 67.) SEC. 12. Assistant Marshals shall have and exercise the same powers and duties as the Marshal.[j]

Surveyor's powers and duties.

(§ 68.) SEC. 13. The Surveyor shall have power, and it shall be his duty, to survey within the corporation limits. He shall have the same power to make surveys and plats within the corporation limits, as are now or may hereafter be given, by law, to county surveyors, and the like effect and validity shall be given to his official acts, surveys, and plats, as are or may hereafter be given, by law, to the official acts, surveys, and plats

[i] By Session Laws of 1857, p. 89, sections 11 and 12, are both numbered as section 12.

[j] Office of Marshall and assistants abolished by section 373.

of county surveyors. He shall make out the assessment rolls for paving, for side and crosswalks, for lateral sewers, and for all other special assessments, and shall survey for the city.

(§ 69.) SEC. 14. It shall be the duty of the Collector of the corporation to collect all special assessments imposed and levied by the Common Council, except such as shall be paid by the person assessed to the Receiver of Taxes, prior to the issue of the warrant for the collection of the same, as is or may be provided by the ordinances of said city. [*As amended by Laws of* 1861, *p.* 185.] Collector's duties.

(§ 70.) SEC. 15. The Assessor shall assess all the property liable to assessment, for the purpose of levying the taxes lawfully imposed thereon, as hereinafter more particularly provided. The Assessor shall also prepare and return a list of persons to serve as jurors, as hereinafter provided in this act. Assessor's duties.

(§ 71.) SEC. 16. The Street Commissioners, within their respective districts, under the direction of the Common Council, shall superintend the construction, repairs, and cleaning of pavements, sidewalks, crosswalks, culverts, and bridges, and direct the working, cleaning, and improving the highways, streets, alleys, and public places in said city. They shall keep an accurate record of the names of persons, together with the number of horses, carts, and wagons employed by them in the several wards, and render, under oath, to the Controller, a true account of the time of each, and the expenses thereof. [*As amended by Laws of* 1861, *p.* 185.] Street Commissioners to superintend construction and clean'g of pavem'ts, etc.

(§ 72.) SEC. 17. The Overseer of Highways for each ward shall, under the superintendence and control of the Duties of Overseers of Highways.

Street Commissioner, and when directed by him, work and improve the highways, streets, alleys, and public places of said city, in the ward for which he is elected: *Provided*, That nothing in this act contained shall be construed to prevent the Common Council, in its discretion, from paving, graveling, macadamizing, or otherwise improving and cleaning the streets, alleys, and public places of said city by contract; in which case such contract or contracts shall be awarded to the lowest qualified and responsible bidder, after due notice of the time of letting the same, in one or more of the daily newspapers published in said city. [*As amended by Laws of* 1861, *p.* 186.]

Duties of Ward Collectors.

People vs. Smith, 9th Mich., 193.

(§ 73.) SEC. 18. The Collector for each ward shall collect all State and county taxes assessed and imposed upon the real and personal property of such ward,[k] and such city, highway, sewer, and school taxes as shall be placed in his hands for collection, by the Receiver of Taxes, or other proper officer of said city, and shall account for and pay over the same as required by law, or by ordinance, or resolution of the Common Council of said city. The director of the poor and constables shall have the power and perform the duties of such township officers, elected under the general laws of the State, subject to the provisions of this act. [*As amended by Laws of* 1861, *p.* 611.]

Director of the poor and constables, powers and duties of.

Books, etc., to be delivered to successors in office.

(§ 74.) SEC. 19. Whenever any officer shall resign, or be removed from office, or the term for which he shall have been elected or appointed shall expire, he shall, on demand, deliver over to his successor in office

[k] See section 461.

all the books, papers, moneys, and effects in his custody, as such officer, and in any way appertaining to his office, and every person violating this provision, shall be deemed guilty of misdemeanor, and may be proceeded against in the same manner as public officers generally for the like offense, under the general laws of this State, now or hereafter in force and applicable thereto; and every officer, appointed or elected under this act, shall be deemed an officer within the meaning and provisions of such general laws of the State.

Penalties for violat'n.

Gen'l powers and duties of officers.

(§ 75.) SEC. 20. In addition to the rights, powers, duties, and liabilities of officers prescribed in this act, all officers, whether elected or appointed, shall have such other rights, powers, duties, and liabilities, subject to and consistent with the provisions of this act, as the Common Council may deem expedient, and shall prescribe by ordinance or resolution.

Who may administer oath.

(§ 76.) SEC. 21. The Mayor, Recorder, and members of the Common Council, Clerk, Controller, and Clerk of the Recorder's Court, are hereby authorized generally to administer oaths, and to take affidavits; but neither of said officers shall receive any fees therefor, except said clerks. The Controller shall have the power to take acknowledgments of deeds under the laws of this State.

Controller may take acknowledg't of deeds.

Mayor may entertain complaints against pers'ns to wh'm a license has be'n grant'd for violati'n of ordinances.

(§ 77.) SEC. 22.[1] The Mayor may issue process, and hear, in a summary way, any complaint against any person to whom a license of any description has been granted in pursuance of this act, for any violation of the laws of the State, or the ordinances of the corporation, and

---

[1] By Laws of 1861, p. 186, this and the four following sections are ordered to stand as sections 23, 24, 25, 26 and 27.

may issue subpœnas and compel the attendance of witnesses, on the hearing of such complaint, in the same manner as Justices of the Peace, in the trial of civil cases, and on such hearing, may annul such license, or suspend it for any certain time. Every determination on such complaint shall be forthwith filed with the Clerk of the city, who shall serve a certified copy thereof on the person holding a license, affected by such determination, either personal, or by leaving the same at his or her usual place of abode; and from the time of such service, such license shall be annulled or suspended, according to the tenor of such determination. [*As added by Laws of* 1861, *p.* 187.]

Chairmen of committees may administer oaths respecting matters pending before them.

(§ 78.) SEC. 23. The chairman of any committee, or special committee, or of any board established by this act, may administer any oath, or take any affidavit in respect to any matter pending before them respectively. [*As added by Laws of* 1861, *p.* 187.]

Unsafe b'ldings, powers of Council.

(§ 79.) SEC. 24. Whenever, in the opinion of the Common Council, any building, fence, or other erection of any kind, or any part thereof, is liable to fall down and endanger persons or property, they may order any owner or occupant of the premises on which such building, fence, or other erection stands, to take down the same, or any part thereof, within such time as they may direct. In case the order be not complied with, they may cause the same to be taken down at the expense of the city, on account of the owner of the premises, and assess the expense on the land on which it stood. The order, if not immediate in its terms, may be served on any occupant of the premises, or be published in the city paper, as the Common Council shall direct. [*As add.d by Laws of* 1861, *p.* 187.]

(§ 80.) SEC. 25. The Common Council shall audit and allow all accounts chargeable against the city; but no unliquidated account, or claim, or contract, shall be received for audit or allowance, unless it be accompanied with an affidavit of the person rendering it, to the effect that he verily believes that the services or property therein charged, have been actually performed or delivered for the city; that the sums charged therefor, are reasonable and just, and that, to the best of his knowledge and belief, no set-off exists, nor payment has been made on account thereof, except such as are included or referred to in such account or claim. It shall be a sufficient bar and answer to any action or proceeding, in any court, for the collection of any demand or claim against said city that it has never been presented to the Council for audit or allowance, or if on contract, that it was presented without said affidavit, and rejected for that reason, or that the action or proceeding was brought before the Council had a reasonable time to investigate and pass upon it. [*As added by Laws of* 1861, *p.* 187.]

Claims ag'st city.

What sufficient bar to action ag'st.

(§ 81.) SEC. 26. The City Clerk shall countersign all licenses granted by the Mayor, or any other officer thereto authorized, and shall enter, in proper books, full minutes of all such licenses, and no license shall be valid unless so countersigned. [*As added by Laws of* 1861, *p.* 188.]

Clerk to countersign licenses.

CHAPTER V.

COMMON COUNCIL: POWERS AND DUTIES.

SECTION
82. Aldermen to constitute Common Council. Absent Aldermen.
83. City Clerk to be Clerk of.
84. Council to appoint President. — Term of office. Clerk to call first meeting to order and preside.
85. Sessions of Council.
86. Special sessions—how called. Notice of.
87. What ordinances and resolutions to be presented to Mayor for his approval. His duty, if he approve or disapprove.
88. Mayor's veto.
89. Duty of Council to reconsider the vote.
90. Clerk's certificate of presentation, and recording same.
91. Ordinances to be recorded.
92. Publication of Council proceedings.

SECTION
93. Style of ordinances.
94. Council meetings to be public.
95. Right of petition.
96. Council judge of qualification of members.
97. Council powers over city property.
98. What resolutions or ordinances not to pass at time introduced. Yeas and nays — when to be taken, and how demanded.
99. Aldermen interested not to vote.
100. Appointments and removals—how made.
101. Standing committees.
102. Powers of chairmen thereof.
103. Enumeration of general powers.
104. Further enumeration of powers.
105. Same.
106. When re-assessment of taxes may be ordered.

Com. Council quorum.

Absent aldermen sent for.

(§ 82.) SECTION 1. The Aldermen of the city shall constitute the Common Council thereof, and a majority of all the Aldermen elected shall be a quorum for transaction of business, but a smaller number may adjourn from day to day; and upon a call of the Council by any member thereof, if supported by a majority of the members present, whether a quorum or not, the President shall have power to send a Sergeant of Police, or any other member of the police force of the city, to bring the absent alderman forthwith before said Common Council. [*As amended by Laws of* 1867, *Vol. II, p.* 1115.]

(§ 83.) SEC. 2. The Clerk of the city shall be Clerk of the Common Council. City Clerk to be Clerk of.

(§ 84.) SEC. 3. The Common Council, at its first meeting after the annual city election, and after the newly elected Alderman or a majority thereof shall have entered into their offices, shall appoint, by ballot, one of their number president, who shall serve until the first meeting of the Common Council after the next annual election, unless sooner removed by death or otherwise, and shall have the powers and duties prescribed in this act.[a] And the Clerk of said city shall call the first meeting of such newly elected aldermen to order, and shall preside over the same, and each of their subsequent meetings, until a President of such Common Council shall be elected, and no other business shall be transacted by said Council until a President thereof shall have been chosen. [*As amended by Laws of* 1867, *Vol. II, p.* 38.] President; appointm'nt of. Term of office. First meeting.

(§ 85.) SEC. 4. The Common Council shall hold regular sessions at such times and places as they shall, by ordinance or resolution direct, and may adjourn regular sessions from time to time, as may be deemed expedient. Sessions of Council.

(§ 86.) SEC. 5. Special meetings of the Common Council may be called at any time by the Mayor; or, if one-third of all the Aldermen elected shall, in writing, request the President of the Common Council to call a special meeting, stating therein the time and objects thereof, and he shall refuse or neglect, for twenty-four hours, to call such meeting, a copy of such request to the President, may be filed with the Clerk of the Spec'l meetings; by whom cal'd.

[a] See section 58, *ante*. Sec 101.

city, with the certificate of any Alderman indorsed thereon, showing the presentation thereof to the President, and his refusal or neglect as aforesaid, and thereupon such special meeting shall be held, and the Clerk of the city shall cause notice thereof, and of its time and place, to be served on each of the members of the Common Council personally, or by leaving the same at their usual place of abode, and the proceedings of said meeting shall be limited to the objects thereof, as set forth in such request to the President. Special meetings may be adjourned from time to time, as may be deemed necessary, in order to dispose of the business which they are called to consider.

Notice of spec'l meetings.

May be adjourned.

Ordinances and resolutions to be presented to Mayor for approval.

(§ 87.) SEC. 6. Every ordinance, resolution, or proceeding of the Common Council, imposing taxes or assessments, or originating the expenditure or disposal of money or property, or whereby the corporation, or any board of officers under this act, may incur any debt or liability, and every ordinance and resolution, except resolutions making appointments to or removal from office, and except ordinances and resolutions for the fixing of salaries, and for the payment of debts and liabilities, previously and lawfully contracted, shall, before it takes effect, be presented by the Clerk to the Mayor. If the the Mayor approve thereof, he shall thereon write his approval with the date thereof, and sign the same, and thereupon such ordinance, resolution, or proceeding shall go into effect; and such as he shall not so approve and sign, he shall return to the Common Council, with his objections thereto, in writing, under cover, sealed and addressed to said Common Council.

If Mayor approves, he shall write and sign his approval.

If Mayor shall not approve, he shall return with his objections.

Mayor's veto.

(§ 88.) SEC. 7. If the Mayor shall neglect to approve, as aforesaid, any ordinance, resolution, or proceeding, or return the same, as aforesaid, to said Common Council, with his objections, at its next regular meeting after the same shall have been presented to him by the Clerk, as before provided, the same shall go into effect.

(§ 89.) SEC. 8. Upon the return, as aforesaid, of any ordinance, resolution, or proceeding, the Common Council shall proceed to reconsider the vote by which the same was passed and adopted; and if, after such reconsideration, two-thirds of all the members elected shall agree by ayes and noes, which shall be entered of record, to pass or adopt the same, it shall go into effect.

Reconsideration of vetoed resolutions, etc.

(§ 90.) SEC. 9. The Clerk of the city shall, at the time of presenting any ordinance, resolution, or proceeding of the Common Council to the Mayor, for his approval or disapproval, make a certificate, to be indorsed thereon or attached thereto, in which he shall specify the day on which the same was so presented; and such certificate shall be recorded with the proceedings of the Common Council.

Clerk's certificate of presentat'n.

Recording certificate.

(§ 91.) SEC. 10. All ordinances, resolutions, and written proceedings of the Common Council shall be deposited in the office of the Clerk of the city, who shall safely keep the same, and they shall be recorded in proper books, to be provided therefor. He shall keep a journal record of the proceedings of the Common Council, and also a record of every ordinance enacted, and of the time of its first publication, which record shall be signed by the Clerk, and by the President of the Common Council.

Ordinances, etc., deposited with the clerk and recorded.

Clerk to keep journ'l and record.

(§ 92.) SEC. 11. All proceedings of the Common Council shall be published in some daily newspaper

Publication of proceedings.

published in said city.[b] All ordinances shall be published for six successive days in the official daily newspaper of said city, and in one other daily newspaper published in said city, and shall take effect in ten days after their enactment: *Provided, however*, That the Common Council may fix and prescribe therein, a different period, and that no ordinance shall take effect before at least one publication thereof.

Proviso.

Style of ordinances.

(§ 93.) SEC. 12. The style of ordinances shall be: "It is hereby ordained by the Common Council of the City of Detroit."

Council meetings to be public.

(§ 94.) SEC. 13. All meetings of the Common Council shall be public, and its proceedings and records shall be open to public inspection, at reasonable times.

Right of petition.

(§ 95.) SEC. 14. The inhabitants of said city shall have the right to petition the Common Council.

Powers of Com. Council.

Proviso.

Compensation of members.

(§ 96.) SEC. 15. The Common Council shall be the judge of the election and qualifications of its own members, and shall have the power to determine contested elections; to fix the compensation of its members: *Provided*, The *per diem* allowed shall not exceed one dollar and fifty cents to each member for actual attendance at each regular session of the council; to compel the attendance of absent members, to determine the rule of its proceedings, and pass all by-laws and rules necessary and convenient for the transaction of business, and not inconsistent with the provisions of this act. [*As amended by Laws of* 1867, *Vol. II*, *p.* 1111.]

Council's powers over city property.

(§ 97.) SEC. 16. The Common Council shall have the general management and control of the finances, and all

[b] The publication furnishes a presumption of notice. People vs. Hartwell, 12 Mich., 503. See also Williams vs. Mayor, etc., of Detroit, 2 Mich., 560.

the property, real, personal, and mixed, belonging to the corporation, whether lying within or beyond the limits of said city, with full power to lease, sell, convey, transfer and dispose of the same absolutely; and shall have power to make all necessary regulations for preserving and protecting the same from destruction, decay, or injury, and concerning the management thereof.

Money resolution, etc., not to be passed at same meeting at which it is introduced.

(§ 98.) SEC. 17. No resolution, ordinance, or proceeding of the Common Council, imposing taxes or assessments, or requiring the payment, expenditure, or disposal of money or property, or creating a debt or liability therefor, and no other ordinance, shall be passed at the same meeting at which it was introduced, unless by unanimous consent, or at a special meeting called therefor; and every such ordinance, resolution, or proceeding, shall be passed by yeas and nays, to be entered on the record; and, upon the demand of one-fourth of the members present, the yeas and nays shall be taken on any question and entered on the record.

Exception.

Yeas and Nays.

Aldermen interested not to vote.

(§ 99.) SEC. 18. No Alderman shall vote on any question in which he is interested; on all other questions every Alderman present shall vote, and in all cases of a tie vote, the question shall be lost.

Appointm'ts and removals by a majority vote.

(§ 100.) SEC. 19. All appointments to office shall be made by a majority vote of all the Aldermen elected, and removals from office shall be made by the like vote, except in cases where, by this act, a different vote may be required.

Standing Committees

(§ 101.) SEC. 20. The President of the Common Council shall appoint such committees as the Common Council may deem necessary. The duties of standing committees shall be prescribed by general ordinance.[c]

[c] Revised Ordinances of 1863, p. 44.

Powers of Chairman of Committees

(§ 102.) SEC. 21. The chairman of any committee, and the members of any board, established by or under this act, may administer oaths and take affidavits in respect to any matter pending before such committee or board; such committees or board shall have power to subpœna witnesses, to compel their attendance, and the production of necessary papers in all examinations pending before them, and to that end the Common Council may prescribe and regulate the necessary proceedings, and confer upon the Marshal, or other officer of the corporation, all needful powers for the purposes aforesaid.

Powers of Council.

(§ 103.) SEC. 22. The Common Council, in addition to its other powers under this act, and subject to and consistently with its provisions, shall have power within the limits and jurisdiction of the corporation:

Compensation of officers.

1st. To determine and regulate the compensation of all officers elected or appointed under this act, except as is herein otherwise provided; but the compensation of no officer, fixed by an annual or periodical salary, shall be diminished during the term for which he was elected or appointed.

Salary.

The salary of no officer shall be increased during his term of office, unless by a two-thirds vote of the Common Council.

Appointm'ts and removals.

2d. To provide for and regulate the election and appointment of all officers, and for their removal from office, and for the filling of vacancies, subject to this act.

Fees and costs.

3d. To authorize and regulate the demand and receipt, by officers, of such fees and costs, and in such cases as the Common Council may deem reasonable.

Fees of jurors and witnesses.

4th. To fix and regulate the fees of jurors and witnesses, in any proceeding under this act, or under any ordinance of the Common Council.

5th. To provide for and preserve the purity and salubrity of the waters of the Detroit River; to prohibit and prevent the depositing therein of all filthy and other matter tending to render said water impure, unwholesome, or offensive; to preserve and regulate the navigation of the said river, within the limits of said city; to prohibit and prevent the depositing or keeping therein any structure, earth, or substance, tending to obstruct or impair the navigation thereof, and remove all obstructions that may, at any time, occur therein; and to direct and regulate the stationing, anchoring, and mooring of vessels, and laying out of cargoes and ballast from the same. Detroit River.

6th. To license, continue, and regulate so many ferries from within said city, to the opposite shore of the Detroit River, for carrying and transporting persons and property across said river, in such manner as shall seem most conducive to the public good. Ferries. Chilvers vs. People, 11th Mich., 43.

7th. To erect, repair, and regulate public wharves and docks at the ends of streets, and on the property of the corporation; to regulate the erection and repair of private wharves and docks, so that they shall not extend into the Detroit River, beyond a certain line to be established by the Common Council; and to prohibit the encumbering of all public wharves and docks, with boxes, carriages, carts, drays, sleighs, sleds, or other vehicle or thing whatsoever. Wharves and docks.

8th. To lease the wharves and wharfing privileges at the ends of streets, on the Detroit River, in said city, upon such terms and conditions, and under such covenants, and with such remedies, in case of non-performance, as the Common Council may direct; but no buildings shall Leases of wharves.

be erected thereon. No lease thereof shall be executed for a longer period than three years, and a free passage at all times, for all persons, with their baggage, over said public wharves.

Highways and streets. 9th. To work and improve all highways, avenues, streets, lanes, alleys, and public spaces within said city; to assess and levy upon all taxable property within said city, and expend such highway taxes as may be necessary therefor, and to elect whether the same shall be collected in money or labor, in such amount as the Common Council shall prescribe for each ward respectively: Proviso. *Provided*, Such highway taxes shall not in amount exceed the rates now fixed by law, and the same shall be collected, assessed, and levied as other taxes.[d]

Public p'rks etc. 10th. To make, grade, improve, and adorn the public parks, squares, spaces, and all grounds in said city, belonging to or under the control of the corporation, and to control and regulate the same consistently with the purposes and objects thereof.

Opening of streets, etc. 11th. To establish, open, widen, extend, straighten, alter, vacate and abolish highways, streets, avenues, lanes, alleys, and public grounds or spaces within said city;[e] Hinchman vs. City of Detroit, 9th Mich., 110. and to grade, pave, repair, and otherwise improve the highways, streets, avenues, lanes, alleys, or interior public spaces, created by the intersection of streets, crosswalks, and sidewalks in said city, with stone, wood, brick, or other material; and the Common Council shall have Pay'g costs and expenses. full power and authority to provide for paying the costs and expenses thereof, by assessment on the owner of the

[d] Comp. Laws, Section 1,017.

[e] See Section 157, *post*.

lot or premises in front of or adjacent to which such highways, streets, avenues, lanes, alleys, interior or public spaces, crosswalks or sidewalks, may be directed to be graded, paved, re-paved, or otherwise improved: *Provided*, That the cost of such grading, paving, repairing, or improving such interior or public spaces shall be assessed to each block, in such proportion as the Common Council shall deem just and equitable. *Provided, further*, That each block shall only be assessed to the center of such interior or public spaces, each way; which assessment shall be a lien, until paid, on such lot or premises in front of or adjacent to which such grading, paving, repairing, and improving may be directed, and shall be collected in the same manner as other assessments or taxes imposed by authority of the Common Council. Whenever such grading, paving, repairing, and improving shall be at the intersection of two or more avenues or streets, and in front of or adjacent to the point of a triangular block, such portion of the costs and expenses thereof shall be assessed to and paid by the City of Detroit, as the Common Council shall deem just.

Proviso.

2d Proviso.

12th. To sell, or otherwise provide for disposing of all dirt, filth, manure and cleanings, lying in or gathered from highways, streets, avenues, lanes, alleys, and public spaces, and all earth to be removed therefrom, or from the public squares and grounds of said city, in grading, paving, or otherwise improving the same.

Dirt, etc.

13th. To clean the highways, streets, avenues, lanes, alleys, public grounds and squares, crosswalks and sidewalks, in said city, of filth, mud, and other substances; to prohibit and prevent the incumbering thereof with boxes, signs, posts, and all other materials or things

Cleaning streets, etc.

whatsoever, and to remove the same therefrom; to prevent the exhibition of signs on canvas, or otherwise, in and upon any vehicle, standing or traveling, upon the streets of said city; to control, prescribe, and regulate the mode of constructing and suspending awnings, and the exhibition and suspension of signs therein; to compel the occupants of lots to clear the sidewalks in front of and adjacent thereto, of snow, ice, dirt, mud, boxes, and every incumbrance or obstruction thereon; to control, prescribe and regulate the manner in which the highways, streets, avenues, lanes, alleys, public grounds, and spaces, within said city, shall be used and enjoyed; to direct and regulate the planting, and provide for the preservation of ornamental trees therein; to provide for and regulate the lighting of the same, and the erection of lamps and lamp-posts therein; to prohibit and prevent racing, and fast or dangerous driving and riding therein; to prohibit and prevent the flying of kites, and all practices, amusements, and doings therein, having a tendency to frighten teams and horses, or dangerous to life or property; to remove, or cause to be removed, all walls and other structures that may be liable to fall therein, or otherwise, so as to endanger life or property.

Riots, etc. 14th. To prohibit and prevent any riot, rout, disorderly noise, disturbance, or assemblage, or the crying of any goods in the streets, or elsewhere in said city.

Quiet on docks and streets. 15th. To preserve quiet and order on the docks, and in the streets of said city, at the arrival and departure of rail road cars, steamboats, and other vessels, and prescribe and regulate the manner and places in which drivers, porters, runners, solicitors, agents, and baggage collectors for hotels or public houses, or express companies, draymen, cabmen, cartmen, hackmen, omnibus drivers, and solicitors for passengers, or for baggage, with their drays, carts, cabs, carriages, sleighs, or other vehicles, shall stand, and to prohibit or prevent them from entering or driving within any rail road depot, or upon any wharf or dock, or entering upon any steamboat, or other vessel, to solicit passengers, or for baggage.

Stands for vehicles.

16th. To prescribe places or stands in the streets of said city, within which drays, carts, cabs, hacks, coaches, carriages, sleighs, sleds, and other vehicles may stand and be kept for hire, and within which loads of wood, coal, hay, and other articles may be kept for sale, and to regulate such stands and places.

Fireworks.

17th. To prohibit and prevent the exhibition of fireworks, and firing of cannon, or any fire-arms, which the Common Council may deem dangerous to life or property.

Paving sidewalks.

18th. To permit any person to pave or plank the sidewalks in front of the premises owned or occupied by such person, in said city, under the direction of the Street Commissioners, or some other officer of the corporation, and according to such regulations as the Common Council shall prescribe; and whenever any street shall have been paved, graveled, planked, or macadamised by the Common Council, and the assessment for the costs and expenses thereof has been duly paid to the corporation, such person shall not be assessed or compelled to pay any district, road or highway tax on the premises in front of which such pavement shall have been made, so long as he shall keep the same in repair, to the satisfaction of the Common Council.

Indecent exposure of person, etc.

19th. To prohibit and prevent, in the streets or elsewhere in said city, indecent exposure of the person, the show, sale, or exhibition for sale, of indecent or obscene pictures, drawings, engravings, paintings, and books or pamphlets, and all indecent or obscene exhibitions, and shows of every kind.

Cattle at large in sts. 20th. To prohibit and prevent, or regulate the leading and driving, or running at large, of cattle, horses, asses, mules, swine, sheep, goats, geese, and domestic fowls, in the streets, or elsewhere in said city, and to impound the same, when running at large, in one or more sufficient pounds, to be provided and maintained by the city, and to sell the same to pay the costs of proceedings, and any penalty thereby incurred, rendering the surplus, if any, to the owner.

Dogs. 21st. To prohibit and prevent, or regulate the running at large of dogs, to require them to be muzzled, and to authorize their destruction when running at large in violation of any ordinance of the Common Council; Securing teams. to compel persons to fasten or secure their horses, oxen, or other animals, attached to vehicles, or otherwise, while standing or remaining in the streets, lanes or alleys of Driving on sidewalks. said city; to prohibit and prevent persons from driving in vehicles, or otherwise, upon or across the sidewalks of said city.

Bridges, culverts, sew'rs and drains. 22d. To establish, construct, maintain, repair, enlarge, and discontinue, within the highways, streets, avenues, lanes, alleys, and public spaces of said city, such bridges, culverts, sewers, drains, and lateral drains and sewers, as the Common Council may see fit, with a view to the proper sewerage and drainage of said city; to compel the owners of all occupied lots, premises, and subdivisions thereof, within said city, to construct private drains or sewers therefrom, to connect with some public sewer or drain. Said private drains and sewers shall be constructed in such manner, and of such form and dimensions, and under such regulations, as the Common Council shall prescribe.

23d. To assess, levy, and collect an annual assessment, or tax, on all lots and subdivisions thereof, and on all cellars, drained by private drains or sewers, connected with any public sewer or drain, as hereafter further provided.[f] Assessment on cellars, lots, etc.

24th. To survey, ascertain, and establish the boundaries of the city, and of all highways, streets, avenues, lanes, alleys, public parks, squares, and spaces in said city; to prohibit and remove all encroachments upon the same, by buildings, fences, or in any other manner; and to number the buildings, the expense of such numbering to be assessed against and collected of the owner or occupant. Boundaries of city and streets. Number buildings.

25th. To provide for the draining of any swamp, marsh, wet or low lands, in said city, or within the distance of three miles therefrom, by the opening of ditches; but a jury, of not less than six disinterested freeholders, of the County of Wayne, before any proposed ditch can be opened, shall ascertain that the opening thereof is necessary or proper; also, whether the benefits which will accrue to the owner or owners of any lands, from the opening of the ditch, will or will not be equal to any damages he or they will sustain thereby. If such benefits are exceeded by the damages, they shall ascertain and certify the damages to which the owner or owners will be entitled, after deducting Draining swamps.

---

[f] See Section 202.

therefrom the amount of benefits their lands will receive, from the opening of the proposed ditch. On payment, or tender of the damages thus ascertained and certified, the Common Council shall have power to enter upon any land through which the proposed ditch will run, with the necessary agents, teams, and implements, to cut and open said ditch, to protect, clean, and scour it from time to time, so as to preserve its original dimensions, and to prohibit and prevent all obstruction thereof, or injury thereto.

Markets. 26th. To erect and maintain market houses, establish markets and market places; to lease market stalls, booths, and stands; to provide fully for the good government and regulations thereof, and to prohibit, prevent, and punish forestalling and regrating.

The Public health. 27th. To provide for the preservation of the general health of the inhabitants of said city; to make regulations to secure the same; to prevent the introduction or spreading of contagious or infectious diseases; to prevent and suppress diseases generally, and, if deemed necessary, to establish a Board of Health, and prescribe and regulate its powers and duties.

Abatement of nuisances 28th. To prohibit, prevent, abate, and remove all nuisances in said city, or within the distance therefrom of half a mile, and to punish the authors or maintainers thereof, and authorize and direct the speedy or immediate abatement or removal of nuisances, by some officer of said city. If, in order to abate or remove any nuisance, the Common Council shall deem it necessary to fill up, level, or drain any lot or premises, they shall have power so to do; to assess the cost and expenses of such filling, leveling, or draining, and impose the same as an assessment or tax on said lot or premises, which shall be a lien thereon, till paid, and shall be collected in the same manner as other taxes and assessments, levied and imposed by authority of the Common Council.

29th. To compel the owner or occupant of any grocery, cellar, tallow-chandler's shop, soap, candle, starch, or glue factory, tannery, butcher's shop, or stall, slaughter house, stable, barn, privy, sewer, or other unwholesome or nauseous house, or place, to cleanse or abate the same, whenever necessary for the health, comfort, or convenience of the inhabitants of said city. Nuisances.

30th. To prohibit and prevent any person from burying, depositing, or leaving within the limits of said city, or within one mile distant therefrom, or keeping, or having, on the premises owned or occupied by him, in said city, any dead carcass, putrid or unsound beef, pork, fish, hides and skins, and any article, substance or thing that is unwholesome, or nauseous, and to compel and authorize the removal thereof by some officer of said city; or to compel any person so bringing, depositing, or leaving the same within the limits of said city, or one mile distant therefrom, or having or keeping the same on the premises owned or occupied by him, in said city, to remove the same. Nuisances.

31st. To direct and regulate the construction of cellars, slips, barns, private drains, sinks, and privies; to compel the owner or occupant to fill up, drain, cleanse, alter, relay, or repair the same, or to cause the same to be done by some officer of the corporation, and assess the expenses thereof on the lot or premises having such cellar, slip, barn, private drain, sink or privy thereon, Cellars.

which assessment shall be a lien on such lot or premises, and be collected in the same manner as other assessments, imposed by authority of the Common Council. To direct and regulate the construction of lateral sewers, or drains, for the purpose of more effectually draining all lots, or cellars, yards, and sinks, within the limits of said city, whenever, in their opinion, the same shall be necessary: *Provided*, Such lateral sewers or drains shall be laid or constructed through any of the streets and alleys adjoining, or in front of the premises through which sewers or drains shall be ordered constructed, and assess the expense thereof on such lots or premises benefitted thereby, which assessment shall be a lien on such lots or premises, until paid, and be collected in the same manner as other assessments, imposed by authority of the Common Council.

Proviso.

Fire department.

32d. To establish a fire department; to provide for the prevention and extinguishment of fires, and to establish, organize, and regulate fire companies, in the manner elsewhere prescribed in this act.

Powder or other factr'y or buildings

33d. To prohibit and prevent, within certain limits in said city, to be determined by the Common Council, the location or construction of buildings for storing powder, powder factories, tanneries, distilleries, buildings for the manufacture of turpentine, camphene, and dangerous or easily inflammable, or explosive substances, slaughter houses and yards, butchering shops, soap, candle, starch, and glue factories, establishments for steaming or rendering lard, tallow, offal, and such other substances as can be rendered into tallow, lard, or oil, and all establishments where any nauseous, offensive, or unwholesome business may be carried on. And such buildings, factories, shops, and establishments as aforesaid, now or hereafter to be constructed, in said city, whether within or without the limits, to be determined as aforesaid, together with blacksmith shops, foundries, cooper shops, steam boiler factories, carpenter shops, planing establishments, breweries, and all buildings and establishments usually regarded as extra-hazardous in respect to fire, shall be subject to such regulations in relation to their construction and management, as the Common Council may make, with a view to the protection of any property from injury by fire, or to the health and safety of the inhabitants of said city, and to prevent their becoming in any way nuisances.

34th. To regulate the keeping and conveyance, in said city, of powder and other combustible or dangerous articles, and the use and kind of lights or lamps to be used in barns, stables, and all buildings and establishments usually regarded as extra-hazardous, in respect to fire. Safe-guards against fire.

35th. To prohibit and prevent the location or construction of any wooden or frame house, store, shop, or other building, on such streets, alleys, and places, or within such limits in said city as the Common Council may, from time to time, prescribe; to prohibit and prevent the removing of wooden or frame buildings from any part of said city, to any lot on such streets, alleys, and places, or within said limits, and the rebuilding and repairing of the same; to prevent the rebuilding or repairing of wooden buildings on said streets, alleys, and places, or within said limits, when damaged by fire, or otherwise. Wooden buildings, construct'n, removal and re-building. May be prohibited. Brady vs. North West Ins. Co. 11th Mich., 425.

36th. To regulate the construction of partition fences, and of partition and parapet walls, the thickness of walls,[g] Partition fenc's, walls, chimneys, etc.

[g] See Section 104, *post*.

and the size of brick; to regulate the construction of chimneys, hearths, fire-places, fire-arches, ovens, and the putting up of stoves, stove-pipes, kettles, boilers, or any structure or apparatus that may be dangerous in causing or promoting fires; to prohibit and prevent the burning out of chimneys and chimney flues; to compel and regu late the cleaning thereof, and fix the fees therefor; to compel and regulate the construction of ash-houses, or deposits for ashes; to compel the owners of houses, and other buildings, to have scuttles upon the roofs thereof, and stairs or ladders leading to the same; to appoint one or more officers to enter into all buildings and enclosures, to discover whether the same are in a dangerous state, and to cause such as are in a dangerous state to be put in a safe condition; to authorize any of the officers of the city to keep away from the vicinity of a fire, all idle or suspicious persons, and to compel all officers of the city, and other persons, to aid in the extinguishment of fires, and in the preservation of property exposed to danger therefrom.

Safe-guards against fire.

Officers at fires.

Bathing.

37th. To prohibit and prevent, or to regulate bathing and swimming in any of the waters in and adjoining said city, determine the times and places thereof, and prohibit and prevent any obscene or indecent exhibition, exposure, or conduct thereat.

Houses of ill-fame and assignation.

38th. To prohibit, prevent, and suppress the keeping of houses of ill-fame, or assignation, or for the resort of common prostitutes, disorderly houses, and disorderly groceries; and to restrain, suppress and punish the keepers thereof; to punish, restrain and prevent common prostitutes, vagrants, mendicants, street beggars, drunken or disorderly persons; to prohibit, prevent, and suppress

Games.

mock auctions, and every kind of fraudulent game, devise, or practice, and punish all persons managing, using, practicing, or attempting to manage, use, or practice the same, and all persons aiding in the management, use, or practice thereof.

39th. To prohibit, prevent, and suppress the sale of every kind of unsound, nauseous, and unwholesome meat, poultry, fish, vegetables, or other articles of food and provisions, and impure or spurious wines and spiritous liquors, and to punish all persons who shall knowingly sell the same, or offer or keep the same for sale. Unsound meats.

40th. To prohibit, restrain, and prevent persons from gaming for money, with cards, dice, billiards, nine or ten pin alleys, tables, ball alleys, wheels of fortune, boxes, machines, or other instruments or devices whatsoever, in any grocery, store, shop, or any other place in said city; to punish the persons keeping the building, instruments, or means for such gaming, and compel the destruction of the same. Gaming.

41st. To prohibit, prevent, and suppress all lotteries for the drawing or disposing of money, or any other property, whatsoever, and to punish all persons maintaining, directing, or managing the same, or aiding in the maintenance, direction, or management thereof. Lotteries.

42d. To prohibit and prevent persons from selling or giving away ardent spirits, or other intoxicating liquors, to any child, apprentice, or servant, without the consent of his or her parent, guardian, master, or mistress; to license and regulate the selling or giving away of any ardent spirits, or other intoxicating liquors, by any shopkeeper, trader, grocer, inn, hotel, or tavern-keeper, keeper of any ordinary, saloon, recess, victualing, or other house, Intoxicat'g liquors.

or by any other person, in case the selling or giving away of ardent spirits, and other intoxicating liquors, and licensing the sale thereof, shall hereafter be authorized by the laws of the State.

To license porters and runners.

43d. To license and regulate solicitors of passengers or for baggage for the benefit of any hotel, tavern, public house, boat or railroad, also draymen, carmen, truckmen, porters, runners, drivers of cabs, hackney coaches, omnibusses, carriages, sleighs, express vehicles and vehicles of every other description used and employed for hire, and to fix and regulate the amount and rates of their compensation.

Auctioneers peddlers, etc

44th. To license and regulate auctioneers, hawkers, peddlers and pawn-brokers, and regulate auctions, hawking, peddling and pawn-brokerage; to license and regulate the peddling and hawking of fruits, nuts, cakes, refreshments, jewelry, merchandise, goods and other property whatsoever, by hand, hand-cart, show-case, show-stand or otherwise in the public streets.

Public exhibitions.

45th. To prohibit and prevent, or license and regulate the public exhibition by itinerant persons, or companies, of natural or artificial curiosities, caravans, circuses, menageries, theatrical representations, concerts, musical entertainments, exhibitions of common showmen, and shows of any kind.

Hotels, etc.

46th. To license and regulate the keepers of hotels, taverns and other public houses, grocers and keepers of ordinaries, saloons, and victualling, or other houses or places for furnishing meals, food or drink.

Butchers, provision dealers, etc.

47th. To license and regulate butchers; to license and regulate or suppress hucksters, and to license and regulate the keepers of shops, stalls, booths or stands at markets or any other place in said city, for the sale of any kind of meat, fish, poultry, vegetables, food or provisions. Ash vs. People, 11 Mich. 351.

48th. To license and regulate keepers of billiard tables, pin alleys, nine or ten pin alleys, but not for the purpose of gaming. Billiards and pin alleys.

49th. To license and regulate public bath houses or bath rooms on land, and any public floating bath houses, bath rooms or vessels on the Detroit River. Bath houses

50th. To establish and regulate an efficient system of police for the good government of said city; to appoint, on the recommendation of the Mayor, or acting Mayor, policemen and watchmen, who shall possess and exercise the same powers, as conservators of the peace, which township Constables, under the general laws of this State, possess, and to prescribe and regulate their further powers and duties, and fix their compensation. Said policemen and watchmen may be removed at any time by the Common Council, on the recommendation of the Mayor or acting Mayor. Police. Removal of policemen.

51st. To appoint one or more inspectors, measurers, weighers and gaugers of articles to be measured, inspected, weighed and gauged; to prescribe and regulate their powers and duties, fees and compensation. Weighers and gaugers

52d. To direct and regulate the weight and quantity of bread, the size of the loaf, and the inspecting thereof. Bread.

53d. To direct and regulate the inspecting and measuring of wood, lumber, shingles, timber, posts, stones, heading and all building materials; the inspecting, measuring and weighing of coke, and all kinds of coal; the inspecting and weighing of hay; the inspecting of vegetables, fresh, dried, smoked, salted, pickled, and other Inspection of wood, etc.

meat, or fish, poultry, butter, lard, and other food or provisions to be sold at wholesale or retail; the inspecting and weighing of flour, meal, pork, beef, and all other food or provisions, and salt, to be sold in half-barrels, barrels, casks, hogsheads, boxes, or other packages; and the inspecting and gauging of oils, wines, whisky, and other spirituous liquors, to be sold at wholesale or retail, or in kegs, half-barrels, barrels, casks, hogsheads, or other vessels: *Provided*, That nothing herein contained shall be construed to authorize the inspecting, measuring, weighing, or guaging of any article herein enumerated, which is to be shipped beyond the limits of this State, except at the request of the owner thereof, or of the agent having charge of the same.

Proviso.

Weights and measures.

54th. To regulate the weights and measures to be used in said city, and compel every merchant, retailer, trader and dealer in merchandise, groceries, provisions or property of any description which is sold by measure or weight, to use weights and measures to be sealed by the City Sealer, and to be subject to his inspection and alteration, so as to be made conformable to the standard of weights and measures established by the general laws of the State.[h]

Paupers.

55th. To provide for the protection and care of paupers, and to prohibit and prevent all persons from bringing, in vessels or in any other mode, to said city, from any other port or place, any pauper or other person likely to become a charge upon said city, and to punish therefor.

Burial of paupers, etc.

56th. To provide for the burial of strangers and poor deceased persons; to regulate the burial of the dead

[h] See Vol. I., Compiled Laws, Chap. XXX., p. 403. Laws of 1863, p. 378. Laws of 1867, Vol. I., p. 221.

and the registrations of births and deaths, and to order and compel the keeping and returning of bills of mortality by physicians, sextons and others. Births, d'ths, etc.

57th. To provide for taking a census of the inhabitants of said city, whenever the Common Council may see fit, and to direct and regulate the same; to provide for calling meetings of the inhabitants of said city by public notice thereof, fixing the time and place of meeting, and to regulate the ringing of bells. Census. Public meetings.

58th. To erect and provide for the erection of a City Hall and all needful buildings and offices for the use of the corporation or of its officers, and to control and regulate the same. Public b'ldings.

59th. To establish, organize and maintain an Alms House Department, to purchase the necessary grounds, and erect and provide for erecting the necessary buildings therefor, either within or without the city limits. Alms House Departm'nt.

60th. To establish and build jails, work houses, and houses of correction, for the confinement of offenders; to erect and provide for erecting the necessary buildings therefor, and control and regulate the same; to appoint all necessary officers for taking charge of the same and of persons confined therein; to prescribe their powers and duties, and provide for their removal from office and the filling of vacancies. Jails, work-houses and houses of correction.

61st. To imprison and confine in said jails, work houses and houses of correction, at hard labor or otherwise, all persons liable to be imprisoned or confined under this act or any ordinance of the Common Council, or lawfully committed thereto by any court or magistrate, as herein provided. Any court or magistrate in the City of Detroit or the County of Wayne may Imprisonment.

commit to any work house or house of correction of said city, instead of the jail of Wayne County, any person convicted of an offense against the general laws of the State, now or hereafter punishable by imprisonment in the jail of Wayne County. Any court of competent jurisdiction of the State of Michigan may, in its discretion, commit any male under sixteen, or female under fourteen years of age, to any work house or house of correction of said city, instead of the State prison, who shall be convicted of any crime now or hereafter punishable by imprisonment in the State prison, whenever in the opinion of the court the welfare of the public and of the convict will be promoted thereby. All expenses attending the confinement of any person sentenced to be committed to any work house or house of correction of said city for any offense against the general laws of this State, now or hereafter punishable by imprisonment in the State prison, shall be paid by the State Treasurer quarter-yearly, on the certificate of the City Controller that such expenses have been incurred. All expenses attending the confinement of any person sentenced to be committed to any work house or house of correction of said city for any offense against the general laws of the State, now or hereafter not punishable by imprisonment in the State prison, shall be paid quarter-yearly by the Treasurer of the County in which the offender was tried and convicted, upon the certificate of the City Controller that such expenses have been incurred.

The speed of cars.

62d. To prescribe and regulate the speed of cars and engines on railroads within the limits of said city.

Licenses by Mayor.

63d. To authorize the Mayor to grant, issue and revoke licenses in all cases where licenses may be granted and issued under this act and the ordinances of the Common Council; to direct the manner of issuing and registering the same, and to prescribe the sum of money to be paid therefor into the treasury of the corporation.[1] No license shall be granted for more than one year, and the person receiving the same shall, before the issuing thereof, execute a bond to the corporation in such sum as the Common Council may prescribe, with one or more sufficient sureties, conditioned for a faithful observance of the charter of the corporation and the ordinances of the Common Council, and otherwise conditioned as the Common Council may prescribe. The Mayor may inquire into the sufficiency of the sureties in such bond by an examination under oath as to their property and responsibilty, which oath may be administered by him. The depositions of the sureties shall be reduced to writing, be signed by him, certified by the Mayor, annexed to and filed with the bond to which it relates, in the office of the Clerk of the city.

Chilvers vs. People, 11th Mich., 43, 49.

64th. To assess, levy, and collect taxes for the purposes of the corporation upon all property made taxable by law for State purposes, which taxes shall be liens upon the property taxed till paid; to make regulations for assessing, levying and collecting the same, and to sell the property taxed to pay the taxes thereon.

Taxes.

Chilvers vs. People, 11th Mich., 43, 49.

65th. To appropriate money, provide for the payment of the debt and expenses of the said city, and make regulations concerning the same.

Appropriation of money.

---

[1] Construction of the term "license." See Chilvers vs. People, 11 Mich., 43; Ash vs. People, 11 Mich., 347.

Punishment of offenders.

66th. To punish all offenders for violations of, or offenses against this act, or any ordinance of the Common Council enacted under this or any other act of the Legislature, by holding to bail for good behavior, by imposing fines, penalties, forfeitures and costs, and by imprisonment in the jail of Wayne County, any jail, work house, house of correction, or alms house of said city, or by either, in the discretion of the court or magistrate before whom conviction may be had. If only a fine, penalty or forfeiture be imposed, together with the costs, the offender may be sentenced to be imprisoned until the payment thereof, for a term not exceeding six months. All punishments for offenses against the ordinances of the Common Council shall be prescribed in the ordinance creating or specifying the offense to be punished; and no penalty or forfeiture shall exceed one thousand dollars, no fine shall exceed five hundred dollars, and no imprisonment shall exceed the period of two years.[j]

Employme't of prisoners.

67th. To employ all persons confined for the non-payment of any fine, penalty, forfeiture or costs, or for any offense under this act or any ordinance of the Common Council, in the jail of Wayne county, or any jail, work house, house of correction, or alms house of said city, at work or labor, either, within or without the same, or upon the streets of said city, or any public work under the control of the Common Council; to allow any person thus confined for the non-payment of any fine,

[j] "When a Charter specifically enumerates various powers which the Council may render effectual by means of penal prosecution, this enumeration is an implied exclusion of the right to impose penalties in other cases." City of Grand Rapids vs. Hughes, 15 Mich., 54.

penalty, forfeiture or costs, to pay and discharge the same by such work or labor, and to fix the value and rates of such work and labor.

68th. To provide for printing and publishing all matters required to be printed and published under this act, or by order of the Common Council, in such manner as said Common Council may prescribe. Printing.

69th. To provide for maintaining the peace, order and good government of the city of Detroit. The Common Council shall have power to subdivide the city of Detroit into wards.[k] The public peace. Wards.

70th. The Common Council shall have power to purchase and sell real estate for the use of said corporation, for corporate purposes, and to execute mortgages on the same, for any balance which may remain unpaid on the purchase money paid for such real estate. They shall also have power to purchase and control land for cemetery purposes, either within or without the corporation limits of said city. Purchase of real estate.

(§ 104.) SEC. 23. The Common Council shall also have power:

1st. To regulate the construction of stone or brick buildings, the thickness of walls, and the size of brick.[l] To regulate constructi'n ofbuildings.

2d. To adopt such measures as may be deemed expedient to perpetuate evidence of title of real estate, by the preservation of maps, plats, records, and papers relating thereto.[m] To perpetuate evid'nce of title.

---

[k] See Section 506.

[l] See first subdivision of next section.

[m] See second subdivision of next section.

6

To appoint policemen and watchmen.

3d.[n] To appoint, on the nomination of Police Commissioners, Policemen and Watchmen, who shall hold their office during the pleasure of the Common Council, unless sooner removed by said Board, as aforesaid. The Policemen so appointed, shall have power to serve any summons, subpœna, warrant, order, notice, paper, or process whatever, issued or directed by any Justice of the Peace, Judge, Court, or officer whatever, in the execution of the laws of the State, for the prevention of crimes, and the punishment of criminal offenders, or of the police laws, and regulations of the State or city, in any proceeding collateral to, or connected with the execution of such general laws, and police laws and regulations. They shall have power to serve any process for any violations of the city ordinances, and generally shall have and exercise the powers, as conservators of the peace, which Township Constables, under the general laws of the State possess; but such Policemen shall have no power to serve any paper or process in any civil action, or any paper connected therewith. The Mayor, or acting Mayor, shall make no nomination of Policemen, or Watchmen, unless thereto requested by the Police Commissioners. [*As added by Laws of* 1861, *p.* 188.]

Powers of policemen.

Powers of Com. Council.

(§ 105.) SEC. 24.[o] The Common Council shall have power:

Walls, etc.

1st. To regulate the construction of stone or brick buildings, the thickness of walls and the size of bricks.

---

[n] This subdivision is superseded by the "act to establish a police government for the city of Detroit." Laws of 1865, p. 99. See sec. 338, *et post.*

[o] By Laws of 1865, p. 678, this Section is ordered to stand as Section 23; there being no Section 24 provided for, the compiler has numbered this Section 24.

2d. To adopt, by ordinance or otherwise, such measures as may be deemed expedient to perpetuate the evidence of the title to real estate in said city, by the preservation of maps, plats, records and papers relating thereto, or by duly certified copies of such maps, plats, records and papers, and which, certified and filed as such ordinances shall prescribe, shall be received in evidence in all courts. Maps, plats, etc.

3d. To provide and ordain by ordinance, that whenever any sidewalk requires to be built or repaired, the Common Council, or any Alderman, may direct the Street Commissioner to notify the owner, agent or occupant of any lot in front of, or adjacent to which such walk is required to be built or repaired, to build or repair the same, and that if such agent, owner or occupant shall neglect, for a time to be specified in the ordinance, to do such building or repairing, it shall be the duty of the Street Commissioner to at once do or cause the same to be done, and the expenses thereof shall be a lien upon the lot, to be assessed therein and collected in a manner to be prescribed in such ordinance, and further to provide that the owner, agent or occupant so neglecting to build or repair, shall be liable to the city for all damages which shall be recovered against the city for any accidents or injuries occurring by reason of such neglect, and also to prosecution in the Recorder's Court, and on conviction, to be fined not to exceed fifty dollars; and that if the Street Commissioner neglect, when required to give such notice, or to have such walk built or repaired within such time as such ordinance shall prescribe, he also shall be liable to similar prosecution and fine. Repairing sidewalks.

Tax illeg'lly collected to be refund'd.

4th. To provide and ordain by ordinance, that whenever it shall appear that any taxes or assessments have been illegally assessed or collected, the Common Council may, by a vote of two-thirds of all members elected, direct and cause the amount so collected to be refunded out of the contingent fund, or in case it has not been collected, to vacate the assessment and fix upon an amount to be received in full of such tax or assessment, and no such action on the part of the Council under such ordinance shall in any way affect or invalidate any other tax or assessment assessed, levied or collected in said city.

Tax upon insurance companies.

5th. To impose a tax upon all insurance companies who do business and have agencies in said city, and to provide by ordinance for the assessing and collecting of the same, in the same manner in which other city taxes are collected, and also for compelling the agents or officers of such companies, under penalty of prosecution in the Recorder's Court, and fine or imprisonment, within a term to be herein prescribed, to deliver to the city Assessor a statement, under oath, of the gross amount received by their respective companies for premiums for policies issued during the preceding year upon property:

Proviso.

Provided, The said tax shall in no case exceed one per cent. upon the amount of such premiums, and that no such tax shall be levied upon premiums for insurance upon property owned and situated without the limits of said city, at the date when such policy issued, or such premium was paid or contracted to be paid; all taxes collected under these provisions shall be credited to the fire department fund, and paid into the same. [*As added by Laws of* 1865, *p.* 678.]

(§ 106.) SEC. 25. The said Common Council shall also have power to provide by ordinance that whenever any lots or premises were or hereafter shall be legally liable to be assessed for the costs and expenses of any paving, or other public work or improvement, that if it should appear that the amount originally assessed upon such lots or premises, was not sufficient to pay in full the costs and expenses of such improvement, that a new or re-assessment for the amount of deficiency may be made upon such lots or premises; and also to provide, that if any illegality or deficit against any such special assessment for the costs and expenses of the making of any such improvement shall be sanctioned by any court of competent jurisdiction, that the Common Council may order, and there shall be made and collected in the manner provided by law, a new or re-assessment upon such lots or premises for the amount of such costs and expenses; the Common Council may, by ordinance, limit the time within which such new or re-assessment shall be made, and prescribe all necessary rules and regulations in reference to the making and collecting of the same. [*As added by Laws of* 1867, *Vol. II, p.* 1111.]

Re-assesm't of property to supply deficiency.

Illegality of assessment.

Time for re-assessment.

CHAPTER VI.

RECORDER'S COURT.

SECTION
107. Court established; Court of Record.
108. Recorder to be Judge thereof.
109. Powers and duties of Clerk thereof.
110. Sheriff to attend.
111. Jurisdiction.
112. Prosecutions; how commenced.
113. Form of information; contents; joinder of offenses; Rights of defendants.
114. Information in certain cases.
115. Degrees of offenses.
116. General laws of State to apply.
117. Jurisdiction to enforce recognizances.
118. Form of recognizances.
119. Indictments from Wayne Circ't C't; proceedings upon.
120. Duty of Prosecuting Attorney.
121. Habeas corpus; power of Recorder.
122. Power of Judge at Chambers.
123. Rules of court; how made.
124. Seal of court.
125. Writs; to whom directed and how served.
126. Prosecutions; how commenced.
127. Proceedings in case of vacancy in office of Attorney.
128. Terms of Court.
129. Exclusive cognizance of offences against Ordinances.
130. Writ of Error to Supreme Court.

SECTION
131. Attorney to collect fines.
132. Records open to inspection.
133. City liable for board of prisoners in certain cases.
134. Salary of Recorder.
135. Prisoners may be imprisoned in the Wayne county jail.
136. General laws to apply.
137. Punishments; how prescribed.
138. Challenges.
139. Trial by jury.
140. Assessor to furnish list of persons for jurors; penalty for neglect to furnish.
141. Clerk's duties on receiving list.
142. To destroy old ballots.
143. Drawing jury.
144. Judge and Sheriff to attend drawing.
145. Proceedings thereupon.
146. Venire facias; who to serve.
147. How served and returned.
148. Fine against jurors.
149. Proceedings, when excused.
150. Ballots to be put in box, etc.
151. How panel filled.
152. Duties of Sheriff.
153. Talesmen.
154. General laws applicable.
155. Clerk to report to Council.
156. When provisions of this chapter to go into effect.

Recorder's Court, Court of Record.

(§ 107.) SECTION 1. There shall be a Municipal Court in and for the city of Detroit, to be called "The Recorder's Court," which shall be a court of record.

Recorder to be judge, etc.

(§ 108.) SEC. 2. The Recorder of said city shall be the Judge of said court, but in case of his absence from the city, inability to attend, or a vacancy in his office, one of the Judges of the Circuit Court, to be previously designated by the Recorder, or the Common Council, shall be the Judge of said court, and, as such Judge, have and exercise all the powers and duties of said Recorder, until he shall resume his office, or such vacancy be filled.

(§ 109.) SEC. 3. There shall be a Clerk of said court, as before provided in this act, whose duty it shall be to keep a true record of the proceedings of said court, in proper books to be provided therefor, and file and safely keep all books and papers belonging or pertaining to said court. He shall sign and seal all writs and process issuing from said court, and shall have power generally, to administer oaths and take affidavits. Clerk of C't, his duty and powers.

(§ 110.) SEC. 4. The Sheriff of Wayne county, and his deputies, shall attend the sittings of said court, and it shall be their duty, and they shall have power to execute, under the direction of the Sheriff, all lawful precepts and commands of said court, and serve and execute all lawful writs and process issuing therefrom. Sheriff and deputy to attend Recorder's Court.

(§ 111.) SEC. 5. The said Recorder's Court shall have original and exclusive jurisdiction of all prosecutions and proceedings in behalf of the people of this State, for crimes, misdemeanors, and offenses arising under the laws of this State, and committed within the corporate limits of the city of Detroit, except in cases cognizable by the Police Court of the city of Detroit,[a] or by the Justices of the Peace of the said city; and shall have power to issue all lawful writs and process, and to do all lawful acts which may be necessary and proper, to carry into complete effect the powers and jurisdiction given by this act, and especially to issue all writs and process, Jurisdiction of Recorder's Court.

[a] See Section 382.

and to do all acts which the Circuit Courts of this State' within their respective jurisdictions, may, in like cases, issue and do, by the laws of this State:[b] *Provided*, That this section shall not be construed to prevent the grand jury for the county of Wayne from inquiring into and presenting indictments, as heretofore, for crimes and offenses committed within the limits of said city: *Provided, further*, That this act shall not in any way affect the jurisdiction of the Circuit Court for the county of Wayne, over any case now pending in said court, nor the validity of any recognizance, as heretofore made to said court.[c]

Proviso. 2d Proviso.

Prosecut'ns how commenced.

(§ 112.) SEC. 6. Prosecutions in the Recorder's Court, for crimes, misdemeanors, and offenses, arising under the laws of this State, and within the jurisdiction of said court, may be either by information, complaint, or indictment.

Form of information and complaints.

(§ 113.) SEC. 7. Such informations and complaints shall be in the name of the People of the State of Michigan, shall be signed by the Prosecuting Attorney, shall be certified by the oath of the prosecuting, or of some complaining witness, and shall have thereon indorsed the names of witnesses, as is required in cases of indictments, and shall have, in the statement of the offense or offenses charged, the same preciseness and fullness in matters of substance, as is required in indictments in like cases, in the courts of this State, and the same may be amended in like manner as is provided in cases of indictment. Different offenses, or different degrees of the

Contents. Joinder of offences.

---

[b] May issue capiases for witnesses. Section 392.

[c] Under the Registry Act, jurisdiction of offenses against it is specially conferred. See Section 492. Also, under the prohibitory Liquor Law, jurisdiction is conferred upon municipal courts. Comp. Laws, sec. 1666.

same offense, may be joined in one information, or complaint, in all cases where the same might be joined by different counts in one indictment; and in all cases, a defendant, or defendants, shall have the same rights in all subsequent pleadings and proceedings, as he or they would have, if prosecuted for the same offense by indictment. Rights of defendants.

(§ 114.) SEC. 8. No information or complaint shall be filed against any person, for either the crimes of treason, murder, arson, rape, or perjury, unless the same shall first be laid before the judge of said court, and he shall thereon indorse a direction that the same be filed. Information or compl'nts in certain cases.

(§ 115.) SEC. 9. Where an offense consists of different degrees, the defendant, or defendants may be found guilty of any degree of the offense, inferior to the one charged in the information or complaint, or of any attempt to commit the same.[d] Degrees of offences.

(116.) SEC. 10. All provisions of law, relative to the joinder of persons or offenders, in one indictment, and relative to subsequent pleadings and proceedings in cases of indictment, in either the court of original or appellate jurisdiction, or in the execution of any sentence,[e] shall be applicable, so far as may be, to prosecutions by information or complaint, under this act, for offenses against the laws of this State. Gener'l laws of State to apply.

(§ 117.) SEC. 11. Said Recorder's Court shall have full jurisdiction and authority to control and enforce all recognizances, lawfully taken by said court, or by the Jurisdiction of recognizance.

---

[d] See Compiled Laws, Section 5953.

[e] See Section 393, *post*.

Judge thereof, or by any other court, judge, or magistrate, in the course of any prosecution or proceeding pending in said court, or lawfully taken by any court, judge, or magistrate, to compel any person or persons to appear before said Recorder's Court, and there to answer and do according to the terms thereof, and whenever default shall be made in any such recognizances, such default shall be duly entered of record in said Recorder's Court, and thereafter said court shall, upon the motion of the Prosecuting Attorney, summarily enter judgment against all the parties liable on said recognizance, for the full amount thereof: *Provided, however*, That any person against whom such judgment may have been entered, shall have the right to apply to the court within twenty days after the rendition of such judgment, for the vacation of the same, for good cause shown, and said court may thereupon, in its discretion, vacate such judgment on such terms as it may deem just. Execution shall be awarded and executed upon said judgment in like manner as is provided in personal actions.

Proviso.

Form of recognizance.

(§ 118.) SEC. 12. All such recognizances as are mentioned in the preceding section, may be in the usual form, or may contain a further clause, authorizing said Recorder's Court, upon default in said recognizances, summarily to enter judgment upon the same, against the several parties liable thereon, for the full amount of such recognizance.

Indictments presented to CircuitCor't for Wayne County to be certified to Recorder's Court.

(§ 119.) SEC. 13. All indictments for offenses committed within the limits of the city of Detroit, which may be found and presented to the Circuit Court for the County of Wayne, by the grand jury of said county, shall be forthwith certified and transmitted by the Clerk of said Circuit Court, to said Recorder's Court, and thereupon said Recorder's Court shall have a full and complete jurisdiction of said indictments, as if the same had been originally presented to said Recorder's Court, and shall have full power to take all further proceedings thereon.

(§ 120.) SEC. 14. The Prosecuting Attorney for the county of Wayne shall appear and act for the people of the State of Michigan, in said Recorder's Court, in all cases arising under the laws of this State, and he shall render to said court, in writing, and on oath, at the last term thereof in each year, an annual account of all moneys collected or received by him as the prosecuting officer of said court.

Prosecuting Attorney for Wayne County to act for the People in Recorder's Court.

To render account.

(§ 121.) SEC. 15. The Judge of said Recorder's Court shall possess the same power to grant writs of *habeas corpus*, returnable before himself, and to adjudicate thereon, and do all acts in vacation touching any suit or proceeding in said court, as is now, or may be possessed by the Circuit Courts of the State, in matters before said Circuit Courts.

Recorder's powers in case of *habeas corpus*.

(§ 122.) SEC. 16. The Judge of the Recorder's Court shall have all such powers and authority at chambers, touching any suits or proceeding in said Recorder's Court, as the Judges of the Circuit Courts now have, or may have, in like suits or proceedings before said Circuit Courts.[f]

Powers of Judge at Chambers.

(§ 123.) SEC. 17. The said Recorder's Court shall have power to make rules for regulating the practice,

Rules of Court, how made.

[f] See Section 568, as to certain powers of the Recorder.

and conducting the business thereof, and to alter, amend, or repeal the same, in its discretion.

Seal.

(§ 124.) SEC. 18. Said Recorder's Court shall devise its own seal, at the expense of said city, and a description thereof, attested by the Clerk of said court, shall be deposited in the office of the Controller.

Writs, to whom directed and by whom and when serv'd form of, etc.

(§ 125.) SEC. 19. All writs and process, issuing from said Recorder's Court, on complaints under the city ordinances, shall be directed to the Marshal, or any Constable of said city, and may be served and executed by the officers to whom the same are directed, at any place within the limits of this State;[g] and all writs and process for offenses under the general laws of the State, shall be directed to the Sheriff, shall run "In the name of the People of the State of Michigan," be sealed with the seal of the court, signed by the Clerk of said court, dated on the day on which the same may issue, and tested in the name of the Recorder of said city.

Constitut'n, Art. VI, Sec. 35.

Prosecut'ns, how commenced.

(§ 126.) SEC. 20. All prosecutions for offenses in said Recorder's Court, arising under this act, or under any ordinance or regulation of the Common Council, shall be in the name of the People of the State of Michigan, and be commenced by filing with the Clerk of said court a complaint, in writing, in the form of an affidavit, duly sworn to before said Clerk, and subscribed by the person making the complaint, and having indorsed thereon the proper jurat of said Clerk; and it shall be deemed sufficient to set forth, in said complaint, the offense complained of according to its substance. The trial shall be had and determined upon said complaint, and upon

Trial.

[g] See Section 350.

pleadings, which may be amended, in the same manner as indictments and pleadings under the general laws of the State.

(§ 127.) SEC. 21. In case of a vacancy in the office of Attorney, his absence or inability to attend, said Recorder's Court may designate a suitable person to discharge the duties of said Attorney, until such vacancy be filled, according to the provisions of this act, or he shall resume his office; and the person thus designated shall receive for his services a reasonable compensation, to be paid by the county of Wayne, and fixed and determined by the Board of Auditors of said county. Proceedi'gs in case of vacancy in office of Attorney.

(§ 128.) SEC. 22. There shall be a term of said Recorder's Court once in each month, which shall commence on the first Monday thereof, and may be continued or adjourned from time to time, as long as said court may deem necessary for the transaction of its business; and if, from any cause, the Judge of said court shall be unable to hold the same on the first day of a term, or on any other day to which said court is adjourned, the Clerk thereof shall have power to open said court and adjourn it from time to time, until the Judge shall be able to attend; and in such case all prosecutions, proceedings and matters pending in said court, shall stand continued, until said Judge can hold said court. [*As amended by Laws of* 1865, *p.* 681.] Terms of Recorder's Court. Adjournm't and continuance.

(§ 129.) SEC. 23. Said Recorder's Court shall also have exclusive cognizance of all offenses against any ordinances of the Common Council of the City of Detroit. Exclusive cognizance of.

(§ 130.) SEC. 24. All the proceedings of said Recorder's Court, at any time before or after final judgment or sentence, may be removed to the Supreme Court Writ of error to Supreme Cor't.

by writ of error or other process, in the same manner that like proceedings may, by law, be removed to the Supreme Court from the Circuit Courts of the State, and the Supreme Court shall proceed to adjudicate thereon in the same manner as on proceedings removed from said Circuit Courts.

City Attorney to collect fines and penalties.

(§ 131.) SEC. 25. It shall be the duty of the City Attorney to collect all fines and penalties imposed for offenses under this act or any ordinance or regulation of the Common Council of said city, which shall be reported in writing by the Clerk of said court, at the close of each term thereof, to said Common Council, and immediately after their collection or receipt by the City Attorney, shall be paid by him to the Treasurer of said city.

Records open for inspection.

(§ 132.) SEC. 26. The Common Council of said city and the Board of Auditors of Wayne County, or any committee thereof appointed for the purpose, may at all reasonable times inspect the records and papers of said Recorder's Court, and the Clerk thereof shall give them, when requested, any information within his power or knowledge concerning such records and papers, and concerning all fines and penalties imposed by said court.

City liable for expense of Board of Prisoners in cert'in cases

County liable for expenses in other cases.

(§ 133.) SEC. 27. The City of Detroit shall be liable for all reasonable costs and expenses, and board of prisoners incurred in prosecutions for offenses and proceedings in said Recorder's Court, arising under this act, or any ordinance or regulation of the Common Council of said city; and the County of Wayne shall be liable for all reasonable costs and expenses, and board of prisoners incurred in prosecutions for offenses and proceedings in said court, arising under the general laws of the State;

but if there be a conviction and sentence of confinement in any work house, or house of correction of said city, for any offense now or hereafter punishable by imprisonment in the State Prison, the expenses attending the confinement of the prisoner after sentence shall be paid by the State Treasurer quarter-yearly, on the certificate of the City Controller that such expenses have been incurred.

(§ 134.) SEC. 28. The salary to be paid to the Recorder shall be [the] same as is allowed, or may be from time to time allowed to the circuit judges of the State, and shall be paid by the State in the same manner as the circuit judges are paid; and the Common Council of the City of Detroit are authorized, directed and required to pay the said Recorder in the same manner as other officers of said city are paid, the sum of five hundred dollars as salary for his sevices. The Clerk of the Recorder's Court shall be paid by the City of Detroit such salary as the Common Council may prescribe. [*As amended by Laws of* 1867, *Vol. II, page* 1112.]

Salary of Recorder, how paid.

Salary of Clerk.

(§ 135.) SEC. 29. Any person liable to be imprisoned or confined under this act or any ordinance or regulation of the Common Council of said city, may be so imprisoned or confined in the jail of Wayne County, and it shall be the duty of the keeper of said jail to receive and safely keep therein all persons thus subject to imprisonment or confinement, until legally discharged therefrom.

Prisoners may be imprisoned in county jail.

(§ 136.) SEC. 30. Any law of this State for the safe keeping of prisoners in a county jail, or for preventing or punishing their escape or the aiding of them to

Gene'l laws to apply.

escape, or any other act detrimental to their safe keeping in a county jail, shall apply to any jail, work house, or house of correction, established and provided under this act by the City of Detroit for the imprisonment or confinement of offenders, in the same manner and to the same effect as to a county jail.

Certain punishments to be prescribed by Common Council.

(§ 137.) SEC. 31. Punishments not herein prescribed for offenses against this act, and for offenses against the ordinances and regulations of the Common Council, shall be prescribed by said Common Council.

Challenges of jurors.

(§ 138.) SEC. 32. In all jury trials in said Recorder's Court, the person or persons on trial shall have the same right of challenge[h] and other rights and benefits extended by law to persons on trial, by a jury in criminal cases before the Circuit Courts of the State, subject to the provisions of this act.

Trial by jury.

Smith v. The People, Sup. Court, April Term, 1861.

(§ 139.) SEC. 33. In all trials upon indictments, the person or persons on trial shall be tried by a jury, unless the right to a trial by jury be, with consent of the court, waived.[i] In all trials for offenses against this act or any ordinance or regulation of the Common Council of said city, the person or persons on trial shall be tried by the court, unless he or they shall request to be tried by a jury. Juries shall be obtained, summoned, drawn and sworn as hereinafter provided.

Selection of persons to serve as jurors.

(§ 140.) SEC. 34. The Assessor of said city, at the time herein appointed to review the assessment rolls in each year, shall select from them, when completed, a list of three hundred persons to serve as jurors in all cases

---

h Challenge allowed against a person who has served on any other panel of jurors within the year in the Recorder's Court, Section 394.

i See Constitution, Article VI, Section 27.

where juries may be required under this act or any ordinance or regulation of the Common Council; and the persons thus selected shall be qualified electors of the City of Detroit, shall be of fair character and sound judgment and understanding, and, so far as practicable, such as were not actually drawn, or did not serve as jurors during the preceding year.[j] Said list shall be signed by said Assessor, returned to the Clerk of said Recorder's Court and filed in his office. If said Assessor shall refuse or neglect to return the list of jurors, as above provided, the Judge of the Recorder's Court shall have power to compel him to make such return. For every day that said Assessor shall neglect or refuse to make such returns, after the time prescribed in this section, he shall forfeit the sum of one hundred dollars.

Penalty on Assessor for neglect to return a list of jurors.

(§ 141.) SEC. 35. The Clerk of said court, on receiving said list, shall file it in his office, shall write the names of the persons thus selected on separate strips of paper of the same size and appearauce, as nearly as may be, shall fold up each of said strips of paper in the same manner, so as to conceal the name thereon, and deposit and preserve the same in a box, to be called and labelled "jury box," and the persons whose names are thus returned and deposited in said jury box, shall be liable to serve as jurors for one year, and until another list shall be selected, returned and filed with said Clerk, and the names thereon deposited in said jury box in the manner aforesaid.

Clerk's duties on receiving list.

(§ 142.) SEC. 36. Before depositing in said jury box the names contained in any new list, the ballots deposited

Old ballots to be destroyed.

---

[j] See Section 394.

therein for the preceding year shall be taken out and destroyed, and it shall be the duty of the Judge of said court to attend and be present with the Clerk, when the ballots, containing the names of persons to serve as jurors, are deposited in said jury box or taken out to be destroyed.

New ballots to be put in jury box.

Drawing petit jurors.

(§ 143.) SEC. 37. At least ten days before any term of said Recorder's Court, at which jury trials may be had as above provided, the Clerk of said court shall draw from the jury box the names of as many persons as the Judge of said court may deem necessary, not less than fourteen, nor more than twenty-four, to serve as petit jurors in said court; and at least two days before such drawing, the said Clerk shall give notice to the Judge of said court and to the Sheriff, of the day and hour when such drawing shall take place.

Judge and Sheriff of Wayne Co. to attend drawing.

(§ 144.) SEC. 38. At the time so appointed, it shall be the duty of said Judge, and of the Sheriff of Wayne County, or some Deputy Sheriff, to attend at the Clerk's office and witness said drawing of jurors, and if neither said Judge, Sheriff, or Deputy Sheriff be present at the appointed time, the Clerk may adjourn such drawing to some certain hour on the next day, of which adjournment he shall forthwith give notice to said Judge and Sheriff.

Proceedin's on drawing jurors.

(§ 145.) SEC. 39. If at the time first appointed for such drawing, or at the adjourned time therefor, either said Judge, Sheriff, or Deputy Sheriff shall be present, the Clerk shall proceed in such drawing as follows: he shall shake the jury box, so as fairly to mix the slips of paper deposited therein; shall then draw from said box publicly and in the presence of the officer or officers attending, as many strips of paper, containing the names of jurors written thereon, as may have been ordered by said Judge, and one of the attending officers shall keep a minute of such drawing, in which he shall enter the name on every strip of paper drawn, before any other such strip be drawn. If, after drawing the whole number required, the name of any person shall appear to have been drawn who is insane or dead, or has removed from the City of Detroit, to the knowledge of said Clerk or any attending officer, an entry of such fact shall be made on the minute of the drawing, the strip of paper containing his name shall be destroyed and another name shall then be drawn in the place of that destroyed, and entered on the minute of the drawing, and like proceedings shall be had as often as necessary, until the whole number of jurors required shall be drawn.

Minute of drawing jurors to be filed.

(§ 146.) SEC. 40. The said minute of the drawing shall then be signed by the Clerk of said court and the attending officers, and filed by the Clerk in his office, and he shall immediately make out a *venire facias* and deliver the same to the Sheriff of Wayne County, which shall command him or any of his deputies to summon the persons therein named to be and appear in said court, at the terms thereof for which they were drawn, to serve as petit jurors, and not depart the same until discharged, under such penalty as the court may impose.

Venire facias.

Who to serv.

Venire facias, how served and returned.

(§ 147.) SEC. 41. Said *venire facias* shall be served at least three days before the term of the court therein specified, by giving personal notice to each person therein named, or by leaving a written notice at his place of residence, with some person of proper age, and return thereof shall be made to said court at its opening, specifying those who were summoned, and the manner in which each person was notified.

Fines for neglect of jurors to attend. (§ 148.) SEC. 42. Said court shall impose a fine on each person duly summoned to attend as a juror, who shall, without reasonable cause, neglect to attend, not exceeding five dollars for each day's non-attendance and neglect; but all persons who, under the general laws of Exemption. the State, are exempted or may be excused from serving as jurors in the Circuit Courts, shall be exempted[1] and may be excused from serving as jurors in said Recorder's Court.

Proce'dings when jurors excused. (§ 149.) SEC. 43. The Clerk of said court shall destroy the ballots of all persons excused from serving as jurors, on the ground of being exempted by law from such service; and the ballots of persons who did not appear and serve, which shall not have been destroyed, shall be returned to the jury box.

Ballots of persons attending as jurors to be deposited in box. (§ 150.) SEC. 44. The ballots of persons who shall attend and serve as jurors, shall be inclosed by the Clerk in an envelope, under seal, or deposited by him in a separate box and preserved; and if, at any subsequent drawing of a jury, a sufficient number of ballots shall not remain in the jury box to furnish the number of jurors required, after having drawn all the ballots therein, the ballots preserved by the Clerk as aforesaid shall be returned by him to the jury box and drawn in like manner as required above, until the required number of jurors is obtained.

Drawing jurors forthwith in certain cases. (§ 151.) SEC. 45. Whenever, for any cause, petit jurors shall not have been drawn or summoned to attend

---

[1] See Sections 262, 365, 394, 395, 438. See also, Compiled Laws, Sections 666, 1623, 4367, 4368.

any term of said Recorder's Court, or a sufficient number of qualified jurors shall fail to appear, such court may, in its discretion, order a sufficient number of petit jurors to be forthwith drawn and summoned to attend such court; or said court may, by an order to be entered in its minutes, direct the Sheriff forthwith to summon so many good and qualified men of said city to serve as jurors, as the case may require.

(§ 152.) SEC. 46. The Sheriff, on receiving a list of jurors drawn pursuant to the preceding section, or a copy of the order therein mentioned, shall proceed, as soon as possible, to summon such jurors forthwith to attend such court, and make return to said court of his doings, in the same manner as in the case of a *venire facias*. Duties of Sheriff in summoning jurors and making return.

(§ 153.) SEC. 47. When there shall not be jurors enough present to form a panel to any case, said court may direct the Sheriff to summon a sufficient number of persons having the qualifications of jurors, to complete the panel, from among the by-standers or the neighboring citizens; and the Sheriff shall immediately summon the number so ordered and return their names to said court. Talesmen.

(§ 154.) SEC. 48. In all further proceedings touching jury trials, their incidents and all matters connected therewith, said Recorder's Court shall be governed in the same manner as the Circuit Courts of the State, by the general laws thereof, which, so far as the same may apply, are hereby made applicable to said Recorder's Court, its officers and all proceedings therein, subject to the provisions of this act. Gene'l laws ap'licable to further proceedings.

Clerk to report to Common Council.

(§ 155.) SEC. 49. The Clerk of said court, on the first day of January in each year, or as soon thereafter as practicable, shall make to the Common Council a report, in writing, duly certified by him, showing the whole number of prosecutions by indictment, which number shall be also classified by the name or description of the offense; the whole number of prosecutions for offenses against this act or the ordinances and regulations of the Common Council, which shall be also classified in like manner, so far as practicable; the whole number of prosecutions, convictions, acquittals, cases dismissed and discontinued, and cases pending; the whole number of sentences passed; the whole number punished by fines and penalties; the whole number punished by imprisonment and confinement, which shall also be classified according to the prison, jail or other place of imprisonment or confinement; and the whole number held to bail for good behavior, and to keep the peace; and said report shall be published in the daily newspaper published by the printer for the city.

Repo't, what to contain.

Provisions of this chapter to go into effect on the second Tu'sday in January, 1858.

(§ 156.) SEC. 50. The provisions of this chapter shall not go into effect until the second Tuesday in January 1858; and the provisions of the present Charter of said city, relative to the Mayor's Court, shall continue in full force and effect until the Recorder's Court is organized, under this act.

CHAPTER VII.

OPENING, ALTERING AND CLOSING STREETS.

SECTION
157. Powers of Council as to streets.
158. Proceeding to open, etc.; how commenced.
159. Notice; how given.
160. Duty of City Clerk.
161. Jurors; duty of Marshal.
162. Summoning jurors.
163. Drawing jury.
164. When jurors exempt, set aside, or excused; how panel filled.
165. First twelve approved to constitute jury.
166. Jury to view property.
167. Duties of jury.
168. Assessment of damages on lots benefited; "alley" defined.
169. Report of jury.
170. What to contain.
171. What further to contain.
172. Confirmation of report.
173. Objections to matters of form not to vitiate.
174. If no objection, report to be confirmed; proceedings if objections are filed.
175. New jury; when to be called.
176. Vacancy in jury; how supplied.

SECTION
177. Appeal; how made.
178. Return to appeal.
179. Duties of Supreme Court.
180. Remanding proceedings in certain cases.
181. Common Council may elect to pay damages in certain cases.
182. Confirmation of report to be final.
183. Certified copy of proceedings to be filed and recorded.
184. Awards to be paid by City Treasurer.
185. Damages to be tendered within sixty days.
186. Upon payment to become highway.
187. Leases upon land taken.
188. Compensation of jury.
189. Commissioners on plan of city.
190. City Clerk clerk thereof.
191. Plans not properly recorded of no validity until approved.
192. Vacancies; how filled.
193. Compensation of Commissioners.
194. Juries to assess and deduct benefits from damages in opening streets.
195. Assessment of damages to estates of deceased persons.

Powers of Com. Council as to sts.

Hinchman vs. City of Detroit, 9th Mich.

(§ 157.) SECTION 1. The Common Council of the City of Detroit shall have full power to lay out, establish, open, extend, widen, straighten, alter, close, vacate, or abolish any highways, streets, avenues, lanes, alleys, public grounds, or spaces in said city, whenever they shall deem it a necessary public improvement,[a] and pri-

[a] Where *public property* is taken, the resolution of the Council need not specify the use to which the property is to be put, nor need a jury pass upon the necessity of using the same. Hinchman vs. Detroit, 9 Mich., 103.

vate property may be taken therefor; but the necessity for using such property, the just compensation to be made for the same, and the damages arising to any person from the making of said improvement, shall be ascertained by a jury of twelve freeholders, residing in said city.[b]

Williams vs. Mayor, etc., of Detroit, 12 Mich., 560.

Resolution declaring improvem't necessary; what to contain.

(§ 158.) SEC. 2. Whenever the Common Council shall deem any such improvement necessary, they shall so declare by resolution, which shall be drawn by the City Attorney, and in said resolution shall describe the contemplated improvement; and if they intend to take private property therefor, they shall declare such intention, and describe such property, in said resolution, with particularity sufficient for an ordinary conveyance thereof; and further declare that they will, on some day to be named in said resolution, apply to the Recorder's Court of said city for the drawing of a jury, to ascertain the necessity for using the property intended to be taken, if it be intended to take any for such improvement, to ascertain the just damages and compensation which any person may be entitled to, if such intended improvement be made, and to apportion and assess such damages and compensation to and upon all lots, premises and subdivisions thereof, which will be benefited by such improvement;[c] and the time to be named for applying to said court, shall be on a day subsequent to the required publication of said resolution.

Notice of intended improvement; how given.

(§ 159.) SEC. 3. The Common Council shall give notice of the intended improvement, and of their intended

[b] See Constitution, Article XV., Sections 15, 9; Article XVIII., Sections 2, 14. Also, Williams vs. Mayor, etc., of Detroit, 2 Mich., 560.

[c] See latter part of Section 167. See also Campau vs. City of Detroit, 11 Mich., 276 and 283, relative to payment of damages in cases of street openings.

application to said court, by causing a copy of said resolution, certified by the Clerk of the city, to be published for four successive weeks in the official daily newspaper of the city, and one other daily newspaper, published in said city, and the Marshal shall also give notice of said resolution, by delivering a notice thereof, with a copy of the same annexed, to the owner, or owners, or agent of any private property intended to be taken, if they can be found in said city, which notice shall be directed to them, or, if they cannot be found, by leaving the same at their place of residence in said city, with some person of proper age. If they or their place of residence cannot be found, and such property be occupied, said notice and copy of said resolution shall be served by delivering the same to the occupant or occupants, or by leaving the same at their place of residence, within said city, with some person of proper age; but if the owner, or owners, or agent of such property, or their place of residence, cannot be found, and it be not occupied, but they, their place of residence, and that of the occupant or occupants cannot be found, or if the owner or owners, occupant or occupants, be unknown, or non-residents of said city, then, in either of such cases, notice of said resolution may be given by posting the same, with the copy of said resolution, in some conspicuous place upon the property intended to be taken. The Marshal shall give notice of said resolution,[d] as above directed, and make return of his doings, and of the manner of giving said notice as soon as practicable after

Upon whem served.

Return of services.

Campau vs. City of Detroit, 14th Mich., 276, 283.

[d] As to time of service of notice of the resolution, see Campau vs. City of Detroit, 14 Mich., 276.

When and where made

the passage thereof, which return shall be made to said Recorder's Court, at least six days before the day appointed in said resolution for the hearing of said application, and all persons interested therein, after notice given in the manner aforesaid, shall take notice of, and be bound by all subsequent proceedings, without any further notices, except as herein otherwise provided.

Certified copy of resolution to be served on City Attorney.

(§ 160.) SEC. 4. The Clerk of the city shall deliver to the City Attorney a certified copy of said resolution of the Common Council, whose duty it shall be to appear in said court, and make the application therein referred to, and conduct all further proceedings thereon in behalf of the Common Council.

Jurors.

(§ 161.) SEC. 5.[e] Upon the day designated in said resolution, or some other day, to be appointed by the

---

[e] By the Laws of 1865, pp. 680, 681, Sections 5, 6, 9, of this chapter were amended so as to read as follows:

"SEC. 5. Upon the day designated in said resolution, or some other day to be appointed by the Court, and on filing a copy of said resolution and affidavit, showing the required publication thereof, the Marshal shall attend said Court, and write down the names of *twelve* disinterested freeholders, residing in said city, and who shall be approved by the Court as such disinterested freeholders and residents, and as qualified to act as such."

"SEC. 6. Said Court shall then issue a writ of summons, commanding the Marshal to summon said *twelve* persons to be and appear in said court, to serve as jurors, on some day to be therein named, which shall not be less than seven days after the issuing thereof. The Marshall shall serve such summons at least three days before the return day thereof, and make return in the same manner as in the case of a summons for petit jurors of said court, and the persons thus summoned shall be bound to attend said court and serve until discharged; and said court shall impose upon them a fine not exceeding five dollars for each day's non-attendance in court, or neglect to serve, but they may be exempted and excused by the court from serving for the same reasons for which petit jurors may be exempted or excused."

"SEC. 9. The first *six* persons who shall appear as their names are drawn and called by the Clerk, or who are called by him when all the ballots have been drawn from the box, and shall be approved by the court as qualified, shall be the jury, and be sworn to discharge their duties faithfully and according to the best of their abilities. Said court shall then instruct said jury as to their duties, and the law applicable to the case, and deliver to them a copy

court, and on filing a copy of said resolution, and an affidavit showing the required publication thereof, the Marshal shall attend said court, and write down the names of twenty-four disinterested freeholders, residing in said city, and who shall be approved by the court as such disinterested freeholders and residents, and as qualified to serve.

Campau vs. City of Detroit, 14th Mich., 276, 284.

(§ 162.) SEC. 6. Said Court shall then issue a writ of summons, commanding the Marshal to summon said twenty-four persons to be and appear in said court, to serve as jurors, on some day to be named therein, which shall not be less than seven days after the issuing thereof. The Marshal shall serve such summons at least three days before the return day thereof, and make return in the same manner as in the case of a summons for petit jurors of said court;[f] and the persons thus summoned shall be bound to attend said court, and serve until discharged, and said court shall impose upon them a fine not exceeding five dollars for each day's non-attendance in court, or neglect to serve; but they may be exempted and excused by the court from serving, for the same reasons for which petit jurors may be exempted or excused.[g]

Summoning jurors.

Campay vs. City of Detroit, 14th Mich., 270, 284.

(§ 163.) SEC. 7. The names of the jurors in attendance, and who do not claim to be exempted, or are

Drawing jury.

of the resolution of the Common Council, as filed in said court, certified by the Clerk of said court; and the City Attorney shall give said jury legal advice and counsel concerning their duties, whenever requested."

In the case of Campau vs. the City of Detroit, 11 Mich., 276, the Supreme Court declared these amendments void, as being in conflict with Article XV, Section 15, and Article XVIII, Section 2, of the Constitution.

[f] See Section 147, *ante*.

[g] See note, Section 148, *ante*, as to exemptions.

not excused from serving, shall then be written by the Clerk of the Court on separate slips of paper, of equal size and appearance, as near as practicable, and be deposited by him in a box having a lid, or cover. He shall then shake said box, so as thoroughly to mix said slips of paper, and shall then draw impartially, openly, and in the presence of the court, so many of the slips of paper, or ballots, containing names written thereon, one after another, as shall be sufficient to form a jury. The right of challenge shall be allowed, as in civil cases, under the laws of this State.

In case of insufficiency of ballots other persons to be summoned.

(§ 164.) SEC. 8. If, in consequence of jurors being exempted, excused, or set aside, there shall not be in the box any ballots, or a sufficient number of ballots from which to draw the jury, the Marshal shall forthwith, under the order of the court, summon such number of persons as the court shall deem necessary, and may order to be and appear in said court, to serve as jurors, and the persons thus summoned shall be returned, be bound to attend said court and serve, and be competent to form the jury, in the same manner, and to the same effect as those first summoned.

First twelve appearing and approved to be jury and sworn.

Campau vs. City of Detroit, 14th Mich., 276, 284.

Instructions to jury by Court and Attorney.

(§ 165.) SEC. 9. The first twelve persons who shall appear, as their names are drawn and called by the Clerk, or who are called by him when all the ballots have been drawn from the box, and shall be approved by the court as qualified, shall be the jury, and be sworn to discharge their duties faithfully, and according to the best of their abilities. Said court shall then instruct said jury as to their duties, and the law applicable to the case, and deliver to them a copy of the resolution of the Common Council, as filed in said court, certified by the Clerk of said court; and the City Attorney shall give said jury legal advice and counsel concerning their duties whenever requested.

(§ 166.) SEC. 10. The jury shall go to the place of the intended improvement, and upon or as near as practicable to any property intended to be taken, and described in said resolution, or as the case may be, which will be damaged or benefited, if the intended improvement be made. Jury to view

(§ 167.) SEC. 11. Said jury shall then ascertain the necessity for using the property intended to be taken, if it be intended to take any for such improvement, and if they shall find in the affirmative, they shall next determine the just damages and compensation to be paid to the owner or owners of any property intended to be taken for, or that they may be damaged by, the intended improvement, and award to the owner or owners thereof, such damages and compensation as they shall deem just:[h] If such property shall be subject to a valid mortgage, lease, and agreement, or to either, and such facts shall be made to appear to the jury, then said jury shall apportion and award to the owners of such property, the parties in interest to such mortgage, lease, and agreement, or to either of them, such portions of the damages and compensation as they shall deem just. And in all cases where any such damages shall be awarded, except for the laying out, establishing, opening, widening, altering, or vacating an alley, or alleys, such damage shall be payable out of the city treasury, and Duties of jury. Cert'in damages payable out of City Treasury. Campau vs. City of Detroit, 14th Mich., 276, 283.

---

[h] See Section 194, *post*, relative to determining the benefits to, or enhanced value of property.

the means therefor shall be raised from time to time, as may be necessary, with the general city taxes.

Apportionment of expenses. (§ 168.) SEC. 12. In case of laying out, establishing, opening, widening, altering or vacating an alley or alleys, said jury shall further proceed to apportion the total damage and compensation to be paid for the proposed improvement, among the lots of land, premises or subdivisions thereof, within the block in which the alley in question is situated, and which will be benefited by the proposed improvement, apportioning and assessing the same upon the said lots, premises or subdivisions thereof, as near as may be, in proportion as the same will be benefited by said improvement. Contingent fund. The benefits assessed under this section shall, when collected, be paid into the city treasury, and by the treasurer placed to the credit of the contingent fund, and all damages awarded by the jury shall be paid out of said contingent fund.[1] [*As amended by Laws of* 1867, *Vol. II*, *p.* 1112.

Report of jury. (§ 169.) SEC. 13. Said jury, after completing the aforesaid duties, shall then make, in writing, and each shall sign the report to said court, of their doings, inclose the same in a sealed envelope, and file it in the office of the Clerk of said court, within thirty days after they were sworn.

Rep'rt. what to contain. (§ 170.) SEC. 14. In cases where said jury shall find such improvement to be necessary, they shall state, in their report, the just damages and compensation ascertained and awarded by them to the owner of any private property, or to any person claiming an interest (Hinchman vs. City of Detroit, 7th Mich., 103.)

[1] See Section 171, *post*.

therein, by virtue of any valid mortgage, lease, or agreement, to which such property may be subject, together with the names of such owner, or claimant, if known, and a description of the property intended to be taken. In case any damages and compensation be awarded to any person claiming an interest in such property, by virtue of a valid mortgage, lease, or agreement, to which such property may be subject, it shall be sufficient to state further, in such case, the name of such claimant, the date of such mortgage, lease, or agreement, or assignment thereof, if there be any, by virtue of which such claimant has an interest in the property intended to be taken.

(§ 171.) SEC. 15. Said jury shall also, in the case provided by section twelve, state in their report what portions in amount of the total ascertained damages and compensation they have apportioned to and assessed upon any lot, premises, or subdivision thereof, which will be benefited by the intended improvement, together with the names of the owners thereof, if known, and a description of the same, and also what portion, if any, of the ascertained damages and compensation they have apportioned and assessed to the City of Detroit, in the case above provided for. What further to contain.

(§ 172.) SEC. 16. Said report may be confirmed by said court, at any term thereof, and the court shall appoint some day when it will consider said report and objections against the confirmation thereof, on the part of all persons interested therein, whereof the City Attorney shall give notice, by publishing the same in the official daily newspaper of said city, and in one other daily newspaper, published in said city, for six successive Confirmat'n of report.

days, and he shall file in said court an affidavit of such publication, before the time appointed for considering said report. Said objections shall be filed with the Clerk, in writing, but may be argued, and the consideration of said report and objections may be adjourned, from time to time, until said report be confirmed, or otherwise disposed of, as herein provided.

Objection.

Report not to be annulled for matters of form.

(§ 173.) SEC. 17. Said report shall not be annulled for objections as to matters of form; all objections shall be objections of law, and to matters of substance, but the damages and compensation to be paid to any person, or the portions thereof apportioned to, and assessed upon any lot of land, premises, or subdivision thereof, may be inquired into, if objected to as being excessively large or small.

If no objections filed, report to be confirmed.

(§ 174.) SEC. 18. If no objections be filed, said report shall be confirmed; but if objections be filed, said court, after considering the same, shall, in its discretion, confirm or annul said report, or may refer it back to the same jury, for the purpose of reviewing all matters, and correcting all errors therein contained, and making any alteration thereof which said court may direct, or said jury may deem just or necessary, and thereon said jury shall review, correct, or alter said report, in manner aforesaid, and shall return and file the same, with the Clerk of said court, within five days after said report was referred back to them as aforesaid, and thereupon said court shall confirm or annul said report.

Proceedin's if objections are filed.

New jury to be summoned in certain cases.

(§ 175.) SEC. 19. If said report be annulled, or the jury cannot agree, or from death, sickness, or any other cause, shall fail to make a report within the thirty days required above, the court may, on the application of the

City Attorney, designate some day in term, when another jury may be had, and such jury shall be obtained, drawn, summoned, returned, bound to attend and serve, have the same qualifications, be sworn, and when sworn, have the same powers and duties as the first jury. The same proceedings, after they are sworn, shall be had by them, and by and in said court, as provided for above, after the first jury is sworn.

(§ 176.) SEC. 20. If any juror, after being sworn, shall die, or from sickness be unable to discharge his duties, the court may appoint another person to serve in his place, who shall be sworn, and shall have the like qualifications, powers and duties as those already sworn. Vacancy in jury, how supplied.

(§ 177.] SEC. 21. Any person, to whom damages and compensation may be awarded for any of his property, intended to be taken, or on account of the intended improvement, or to and upon whose property any portion of such damages and compensation may be apportioned and assessed, considering himself aggrieved, may appeal from the judgment of the Recorder's Court, confirming the report of the jury, to the Supreme Court, by filing, in writing, with the Clerk of said Recorder's Court, a notice of such appeal, and specification of the errors complained of, within five days after the confirmation, and serving, within the same time, a copy of said notice and specification of errors, on the City Attorney, and filing a bond in said Recorder's Court, to be approved by the Recorder, conditioned for the prosecution of said appeal, and the payment of all costs that may be awarded against the appellant, in case the judgment of confirmation of the Recorder's Court be affirmed. Appeal. Notice of specificati'n of errors. Bond on appeal. Condition.

Return to appeal. (§ 178.) SEC. 22. In case of appeal, as above, it shall be the duty of the Clerk of said Recorder's Court, forthwith, or as soon as practicable, to transmit to the Supreme Court a certified copy of all the proceedings in the case, which may be filed in the office of any clerk of said court.[j]

Duties of Supreme Co'rt on appeal. (§ 179.) SEC. 23. The Supreme Court, at any term thereof, shall, with the least practicable delay, hear and try the matter of said appeal, and may affirm or reverse the judgment of the Recorder's Court, confirming the report of the jury; but the same shall not be reversed for matter of form, nor for any errors, except errors of law, and only in regard to the appellant, or appellants. The court shall give judgment for reasonable costs and expenses in the matter of said appeal, and proceedings thereon to be taxed, and all costs and expenses awarded to the City of Detroit, in case of affirmation, shall be applied on and deducted from the damages and compensation, if any, to be paid to the appellant or appellants. (Duffield vs. City of Detroit, 15th Mich., 474.)

Remanding proceedings in certain cases. (§ 180.) SEC. 24. If there be a reversal for any errors, which it is practicable for the Recorder's Court or said jury to correct, with due regard to the public interest and rights of individuals, the proceedings shall be remanded to said Recorder's Court, with direction that such error be corrected. Said Recorder's Court, at any term thereof, or (as the case may be) said jury, under the direction of said court, shall correct such error, and thereupon the report of the jury shall be confirmed by said Recorder's Court, without any further right of appeal.

[j] In Duffield vs. City of Detroit, 15 Mich., 474, 481, it was held, *per* Cooley J., that this section made it imperative upon the Recorder to put his rulings in this class of cases in writing.

(§ 181.) SEC. 25. In every case of annulment of the report of the jury, by the Recorder's Court, or reversal by the Supreme Court, the Common Council, in behalf of said city may, by resolution, elect to pay the damages and compensation claimed by, or the assessment made upon the property of the objector, appellant or appellants. On filing a certified copy of said resolution, in the Recorder's Court, within twenty days after the annulment or reversal, the report of said jury shall be reviewed and confirmed by said Recorder's Court, as to all persons interested therein, except the objector, appellant, or appellants, and without further right of appeal. If the Common Council do not elect, as above provided, all the proceedings shall be null and void, and no further proceedings shall be had, except in a case of reversal, when the proceedings may have been remanded to the Recorder's Court for the correction of certain errors, in which case such errors shall be corrected, and the report of the jury confirmed, as above provided.

Com. Council may elect in certain cases to pay damages.

(§ 182.) SEC. 26. If the report of the jury be confirmed by the Recorder's Court, in any case above provided for, or if the judgment of confirmation be affirmed, on appeal to the Supreme Court, such confirmation shall be final and conclusive as to all persons interested therein; and the damages and compensation apportioned to, and assessed upon any lot of land, premises, or subdivision thereof, according to said report, as confirmed, shall be a lien thereon, from the time of the aforesaid confirmation, until they are paid and satisfied.

Confirmat'n of report to be final.

(§ 183.) SEC. 27. When the report of the jury shall have been thus finally confirmed, or the judgment of confirmation affirmed by the Supreme Court, the Clerk

Certified copy of proceedings to be filed and recorded.

of the Recorder's Court shall prepare a certified copy, under the seal of the court, of the report of the jury, as confirmed by the Recorder's Court, and of the order of the court, confirming the same, and the Clerk shall file said certified copy in the office of the Clerk of the city, who shall record the same at length, in a book to be provided, used and known as a book of street records. Such certified copy, such record, or a like copy, made and certified by the Clerk of the Recorder's Court, shall, in all courts and places, be presumptive evidence of the matters therein contained, and of the regularity of all proceedings, from the commencement thereof to the order of the court confirming the report of the jury.

Amounts to be paid to City Treasurer.

(§ 184.) SEC. 28. The amounts apportioned to and assessed upon all lots of land, premises, or subdivisions thereof, for the benefits they will receive, shall be paid to the Treasurer of said city, in case of confirmation of the report of the jury, as above provided, or in case the judgment of confirmation be affirmed by the Supreme Court, and may be collected, and said lots, premises, or subdivisions thereof may be sold therefor, in the same manner as in the case of collection or sale for assessments to pay the cost and expenses of paving streets.

Damages to be paid or tendered in sixty days.

(§ 185.) SEC. 29. Within sixty days after the confirmation of the report of the jury, or after the judgment of confirmation shall, on appeal, be affirmed, the Common Council shall pay, or tender to the respective persons the several amounts of damages and compensation awarded to them, according to the report of the jury as confirmed, or elected as above provided for, to be paid by the Common Council; and in case any such person shall refuse the same, be unknown, or a non-resident of said city, or for any reason incapacitated from receiving his or her amount, or the right thereto be disputed or doubtful, the Common Council may deposit the amount awarded in such case, or elected to be paid by the Common Council, in the treasury of the city, to the credit of any person entitled thereto, and shall, on demand, pay the same over to any person competent and entitled to receive it.[k]

Damages to be deposited in certain cases with Treasurer.

(§ 186.) SEC. 30. Upon such payment, tender, or deposit in the city treasury, the same shall become a public highway, and the Common Council may enter upon, take possession of, and convert the same to the uses and purposes for which it has been taken. A certificate of the City Treasurer of such tender, payment, or deposit, or record thereof, in the book of street records, or certified copy of such record, shall, in all courts and places, be presumptive evidence of the facts therein stated, of the vesting of the fee of the property taken in the City of Detroit, and of the right of the Common Council to take possession of and convert the same to the uses for which it has been taken.[l]

Upon payment, tender or deposit, to become public highway.

(§ 187.) SEC. 31. In all cases where any real estate, subject to any lease or agreement, shall be taken as aforesaid, all the covenants and stipulations contained therein shall cease, determine, and be discharged, upon the final confirmation of the report of the jury, or upon the affirmation by the Supreme Court of the judgment of confirmation. If a part, only, of such real estate be

Upon confirmation of report, stipulations in lease or agreements to cease.

---

[k] See Section 195, *post.*

[l] See Section 195, *post.*

taken, said covenants and stipulations shall cease, determine, and be discharged only as to such part; and the Recorder's Court, on application of any party in interest to such lease or agreement, and after a notice thereof of eight days, in writing, to the other parties in interest, may appoint three disinterested residents and freeholders of said city, commissioners, to determine the rents and payments to be thereafter paid, and the covenants, stipulations, or conditions thereafter to be performed under such lease or agreement, in respect to the residue or part of such real estate not taken. Said commissioners shall, before entering on their duties, take and subscribe an oath, to be administered by the court, faithfully to discharge their duties, which oath shall be filed in said court. Said three commissioners shall make and sign a report, in writing, of their doings, to said court, which shall be filed therein within thirty days after their appointment, and said report, on being confirmed by the court, shall be binding and conclusive on the parties in interest to such lease or agreement.

Commis'ioners to apportion rents in certain cases.

Duties of Commi'sioners.

(§ 188.) SEC. 32. The Common Council shall pay said jury such compensation for their services as they may deem just, and they shall have power to abandon or discontinue proceedings, under this chapter, in said Recorder's Court, at any time before the final confirmation of the report of the jury.

Compensation of jury.

Com. Council may abandon proceedin's.

(§ 189.) SEC. 33. For the purpose of introducing a greater uniformity in the laying out the land in said city into public streets and blocks, and to restrain persons from laying out such streets and blocks in a manner prejudicial to the interest of the city, there shall be constituted a Board of Commissioners, upon the plan of

Commission on plan of city.

the city, consisting of three persons, to be appointed by the Common Council, on the nomination of the Mayor, and no land within the limits of said city shall be laid out into blocks and public streets, without the consent and approval of a majority of said Commissioners, in writing, entered upon a plan of said land so laid out, which plan, duly acknowledged, and with said approval, in writing, thereon indorsed, shall be recorded in the Register's office for the County of Wayne: *Provided, however*, In cases where a parcel of land lies between parcels of land duly laid out by plats, now on record, whose streets do not correspond in direction or size, the power of control shall not be so exercised over the platting of such intermediate parcel in order to produce such correspondence, as to essentially diminish their value.

Land not to be laid out into blocks and streets without consent of Commissioners.

Proviso.

(§ 190.) SEC. 34. The City Clerk shall act as the Clerk of said Board, and plans for the approval of said Commissioners, may be deposited with said Clerk for their action thereon, and if approved, a copy thereof shall be filed with said Clerk, by the person making or laying out the same.

Clerk of Board; plan to be deposited with Clerk.

(§ 191.) SEC. 35. Any plans for laying out into public streets and blocks, now existing in said city, and not acknowledged and recorded according to law, shall be of no validity until they receive the approval of said Commissioners, as hereinbefore provided. But the platting and recording of any blocks, lots, squares, lanes, alleys, parks, or public places within said city, shall be a full and irrevocable dedication of the same to the public for the uses and purposes specified or named upon any such record, plat, or plan; any such plats or plans, now of

Plans not ackno'leged and recorded to be of no validity without approval of commi'sioners.

record, shall be, and be evidence of dedication, as hereinbefore provided, unless reclaimed of record within thirty days after this act shall take effect. [*As amended by Laws of* 1861, *p.* 189.]

Vacancies, how filled.

(§ 192.) SEC. 36. If a vacancy occurs in the office of said Commissioners, or either of them, it may be filled by the Common Council, on the nomination of the Mayor.

No compensation.

(§ 193.) SEC. 37. Said Commissioners shall receive no compensation for their services.

Jury to deduct amo'nt of benefit from damages.

Duffield vs. City of Detroit, 15 M., 474.

(§ 194.) SEC. 38. In assessing the damages and compensation mentioned and provided for in section eleven, in cases where only a portion or portions of a lot or lots are taken, the court may instruct the jury to, and in case of such instruction, the jury shall determine the benefits or enhanced value that will accrue from the improvements to the portion or portions not taken, and deduct the same from the damages or compensation they would otherwise award to the owner or owners.[m] [*As added by Laws of* 1865, *p.* 681.

Assessm'nts of damages to estates of deceased persons.

(§ 195.) SEC. 39. Whenever any jury acting under the provisions of this chapter shall find in favor of taking and using any property belonging to the estate of any deceased person, or that such estate will be damaged by the intended improvement, the just damages and compensation determined upon by them shall be awarded to the estate of such deceased person, and the amount thereof shall be paid or tendered to any executor

[m] Where the jury, under this section, are instructed to determine the "benefits or enhanced value," as to the portion or portions of the land not taken, they must make separate findings of the respective amounts of the damages and of the benefits or enhanced value, concurring on both items, and report the same to the court. Duffield vs. City of Detroit, 15 Mich., 474.

or administrator of such estate; if there be no executor or administrator, or if he cannot be found, or refuse to accept the same, the amount shall be deposited into the city treasury, to the credit of such estate, and shall on demand, be paid to such executor or administrator, or other person entitled to receive the same; such payment, tender or deposit, shall be made within the same time, and shall be of like effect, and may be evidence in the same manner as other payments, tenders or deposits, as provided for by sections twenty-nine and thirty, of said chapter seven. [*As added by Laws of* 1867, *Vol. II*, *p.* 1113.]

Payment of damage.

CHAPTER VIII.

TAXATION AND FINANCE.

SECTION
196. Into what funds revenues divided.
197. Powers of Council to collect taxes for different funds.
198. For district road fund.
199. For sewer fund.
200. Controller to present estimate; public meeting to vote taxes.
201. Taxes for interest fund.
202. Special sewer tax.
203. Paving assessment and tax.
204. Loans for public building fund.
205. Consent of citizens required before issue of bonds for said fund.
206. Public works not provided for; when and how let.
207. Contracts over $200 let to the lowest bidder.
208. Evidences of debt; for what issued.
209. Council may authorize Controller to borrow money.
210. New bonds; what to show and how issued.
211. Refunded bonds to be destroyed.
212. Bonds; when void.
213. No illegal claim to be paid.
214. No money to be paid from treasury, except on warrant.

SECTION
215. Affidavit to accompany claim.
216. Drafts on funds limited.
217. Officers not to be interested in contracts.
218. When ordinances and resolutions may be passed at session when introduced.
219. Fiscal year; Controller's report, what to contain.
220. Controller and Council may require estimates from officers and boards.
221. Money to be put in bank at interest.
222. Committee for negotiating loans.
223. Taxes; to what fund credited.
224. Moneys; how applied.
225. Moneys not transferable from one fund to another.
226. Sinking fund; Board of Commissioners.
227. Meetings of Board.
228. Treasurer custodian of sinking fund.
229. Pledge for payment of moneys borrowed.
230. Officers converting moneys; penalty.
231. Plank crosswalks; how paid for.

Funds. (§ 196.) SECTION 1. The revenues and moneys of the corporation shall be divided into the following funds, viz.:

Gen'l Fund. 1st. General Fund, which shall be appropriated to defray the expenses of the City of Detroit, for the payment of which out of some other fund, no provision is herein made.[a]

Contingent. 2d. Contingent Fund, to defray the contingent expenses of said city.

---

[a] See section 223, *post*.

3d. Interest Fund, to pay the interest on the funded debt of the city.[b] Interest.

4th. Sinking Fund, to pay the funded debt of said city.[c] Sink. Fund.

5th. Fire Department Fund, to defray the expenses of purchasing lots, erecting engine houses thereon, purchasing engines and other fire apparatus, and all other expenses necessary to maintain the Fire Department of said city.[d] Fire Department Fund.

6th. Poor Fund, to defray the expenses of providing for and taking care of the poor of said city. Poor Fund.

7th. General Road Fund, to defray the expenses of repairing paved streets and alleys, and of grading, paving and improving the highways, streets and alleys of said city, in front of or adjacent to the property of the corporation. Gen'l Road Fund.

8th. District Road Fund for each ward of the city, to defray the expenses of working, repairing, cleaning, and improving the highways, streets and alleys, in the ward for which such District Road Fund is constituted and raised.[e] Distr't Road Fund.

9th. Sewer Fund, to defray the expenses of constructing sewers in said city. Sewer Fund.

10th. Street Opening Fund, to defray the expenses of opening, widening, vacating, altering, straightening, extending or abolishing any highways, streets or avenues in said city, under the provisions of chapter seven of this act. Street Opening Fund.

---

[b] See Section 201, *post.*

[c] Various provisions relative to the Sinking Fund are found in sections 201, 224, 226, 227, 228.

[d] Section 433 provides for the Detroit Fire Commission Fund.

[e] See Section 231, relating to this fund.

Street Paving Fund.

11th. Street Paving Fund,[f] to defray the expenses of grading, paving and graveling, macadamising or planking highways, streets, alleys, sidewalks and crosswalks in front of or adjacent to private property, and of putting curbstones and culverts therein.

Public B'ilding Fund.

12th. Public Building Fund,[g] for purchasing any real estate for the erection thereon of any public buildings, and to defray the expenses of erecting, repairing and preserving such public buildings as the Common Council is authorized to erect and maintain, and are not herein otherwise provided for, which fund shall, from time to time, be divided into Special Building Funds, to defray the expenses of erecting, repairing and preserving the particular building or buildings for which such Special Building Fund may be constituted or raised.

Recorder's Court Fund.

13th. Recorder's Court Fund, to maintain the Recorder's Court.

Other Funds

14th. Such other funds as the Common Council may constitute for special purposes, not inconsistent with, nor to be taken from any of the funds above constituted or raised.[h]

Powers of Council to collect.

(§ 197.) SEC. 2. The Common Council shall have power annually to levy, assess and collect taxes, not exceeding one per cent. on the assessed value of all real and personal estate in said city, made taxable by the

---

[f] 11th subdivision of Section 103, *ante*, p. 54. Also Section 203, *et post.*

[g] See Sections 204, 224.

[h] For provisions as to Library and School Fund, see Public Schools, Part II, Chapter IX. As to tax to pay interest on bonds of Water Commissioners, see Section 330. As to tax to pay interest on Bounty Fund, see Sections 465, 466.

laws of this State,[i] in order to defray the expenses, and for the purposes for which the General Fund, Contingent Fund, Fire Department Fund, Poor Fund, General Road Fund and Recorder's Court Fund are constituted as above. Taxes for cert'n funds.

(§ 198.) SEC. 3. The Common Council shall also have power annually to levy, assess and collect taxes on the assessed value of all real and personal estate in each ward of said city, made taxable by the laws of this State, in order to defray the expenses, and for the purposes for which the District Road Fund is constituted as above: *Provided*, That such taxes shall not exceed in amount, the rates of township road or highway taxes as now or hereafter established by the laws of this State.[j] For District Road Fund.

(§ 199.) SEC. 4. The Common Council shall also have power annually to levy, assess and collect taxes, not exceeding fifty thousand dollars on the assessed value of all the real and personal estate in said city, made taxable by the laws of this State, in order to defray the expenses of constructing sewers, and for the purpose for which the Sewer Fund is constituted as above. [*As amended by Laws of* 1867, *Vol. II, p.* 1113.] Tax for expense of sewers.

(§ 200.) SEC. 5. Before any taxes shall be levied, as aforesaid, for the purposes of the General Fund, Contingent Fund, General Road Fund, Street Opening Fund, District Road Fund, Fire Department Fund, Poor Fund, Sewer Fund, and Recorder's Court Fund, the Controller shall present to the Common Council, in writing, his Controller to present estimate.

---

[i] For what is taxable property; Comp. Laws, Sections 782, 783, 784. For what is exempt from taxation; Comp. Laws, Sections 786, 944, 1515. See also 64th Subdivision of section 103, p. 71.

[j] See 9th Subdivision of Section 103 *ante*, p. 54.

estimate of the amount of taxes, which, in his opinion, it may be necessary to raise for the ensuing year, for the purposes of said fund; shall state therein the amount estimated for the purposes of each of said funds, and also an estimate of the entire proposed expenditures for said year, whether the same is to be raised by tax, by loan, or by special assessment, and said estimate shall be published in the official paper of the city, and shall, at the same time, give to the Common Council any information in his power, and which they may request, concerning the finances of said city. The Common Council, after revising or altering said estimate, but not so as to exceed the aggregate taxes hereby authorized to be levied, shall direct the Mayor or acting Mayor to call a public meeting of citizens of said city, to take into consideration the taxes proposed to be raised and specified in said estimate, by publishing notice thereof in one or more daily newspapers published in said city, for not less than three successive days, and posting the same in conspicuons places in said city, at least three days prior to the time of the meeting, which notice shall contain the substance of said estimate. Said meeting shall transact the business for which it was called. If a majority of the citizens present shall consent to the levying of the taxes specified in said estimate, then the Common Council shall proceed to levy, assess and collect the same, or such part thereof as may have been consented to; but if said meeting shall not consent to the levying of said taxes, the said Common Council may call a second meeting of said citizens in the same manner, and which shall have the same power as the first meeting hereinbefore provided for.

Publicmeetings to vote taxes.

Sec'ndmeeting.

(§ 201.) SEC. 6. The Common Council shall annually levy, assess and collect on the assessed value of all the real and personal estate in said city, made taxable by the laws of this State, taxes for the purposes of the interest fund, not exceeding, in amount, a sufficient sum to pay the interest, accrued or to accrue on the funded debt of said city, for the year for which such taxes are levied; and also taxes not less than five, nor more than ten thousand dollars, for the purposes of the sinking fund.[k] Taxes for Interest Fund.

(§ 202.) SEC. 7. The Common Council shall also have power annually to levy, assess and collect a tax or assessment on all lots, premises and subdivisions, thereof drained by private sewers or drains, leading into or connected with any public sewer, or drain, which tax shall be one dollar and fifty cents on every lot, premises or subdivision thereof having a cellar, fifty cents if there be no cellar thereon, and such sums as the Common Council may fix for all lots and establishments drained as aforesaid, and requiring an unusual or extraordinary amount of drainage.[l] Said tax or assessment shall be credited to the sewer fund, and applied to the repairing of sewers and drains, and if the same be more than is required for such purpose, the surplus may be applied to the construction of sewers and drains. Special Sewer Tax.

(§ 203.) SEC. 8. The Common Council shall also have power from time to time to levy, assess and collect a Tax for grading, paving etc.

---

[k] See 3d subdivision of Section 196; also, 4th subdivision of the same section.

[l] Held that the payment of such tax created no liability of the City to pay damages resulting from use of the sewer, even if defective. Dermont vs. City of Detroit, 4 Mich., 435.

Wo'dbridge vs. Detroit, 8 Mich., 272. tax or assessment on all lots, premises or subdivisions thereof, sufficient to defray the expenses of grading and paving, graveling, macadamizing or planking any highway, avenue, street, lane, alley, or cross-walk in said city, in front of or adjacent to such lots, premises or subdivisions thereof, and of putting curb-stones and culverts therein, the proceeds of which tax or assessment shall be credited to the street paving fund:[m] *Provided*, That such tax or assessment shall not, in any one year exceed, in the aggregate, the sum of fifty thousand dollars, except upon the petition of the holders of a majority of the property upon any alley, street, block or square which the petitioners may desire paved; such grading, paving, graveling, macadamizing and putting in of curb-stones and culverts shall be commenced and completed, and all contracts therefor shall require the same to be commenced and completed within the six months next preceding the first day of December of the year in which such contract shall be made, but it shall be lawful for the Common Council to extend the time for the completion of any such contract for work which may have been commenced in good faith and not fully completed by the time above mentioned. [*As amended by Laws of* 1861, *p.* 189.]

Proviso.

Loans for public building fund. (§ 204.) SEC. 9. The Common Council shall also have power to provide money for the public building fund, by loaning, upon the faith and credit of said city, and upon the best terms that can be made, a sum of money not exceeding three hundred thousand dollars, and to

---

[m] See cases of Lefevre vs. Mayor. etc. of Detroit, 2 Mich., 286; Williams vs. Mayor, etc. of Detroit, 2 Mich., 560.

issue the bonds of said city to an amount not exceeding that sum, pledging its faith and credit for the payment of the principal and interest, but said bonds shall not be negotiated at less than their par value. Said bonds shall be denominated "Public Building Stock of the City of Detroit," shall be regularly dated and numbered in the order of their issue; shall be for sums not less than five hundred dollars each; shall bear interest not exceeding seven per cent. per annum; shall be payable in not less than twenty years from date; shall be issued under the seal of the corporation, signed by the Mayor, and countersigned by the Controller. The Controller shall keep an accurate record of said bonds, showing the class of indebtedness to which they belong, the number, date, and amount of each bond, its rate of interest, when and where the same is payable, and the person to whom it is issued. The proceeds of said bonds shall be paid to the Treasurer, and be credited to the public building fund, and applied exclusively to the purposes for which said fund is constituted as above. [*As amended by Laws of* 1861, *p.* 190.]

Consent of public meeting requir'd for issue of bonds for public b'ild-ing fund.

(§ 205.) SEC. 10. No bonds shall be issued as aforesaid for the purposes of the public building fund, until a public meeting of the citizens of said city shall have been called and held to consider the subject of constructing a public building for such purpose as the Common Council may propose, which meeting shall be called and may be held in the manner above prescribed for calling and holding in relation to the levying of taxes. The Common Council shall cause to be presented to said meeting, by the Controller, an estimate of the necessary cost of purchasing the necessary real estate for the erection

9

thereon of any building and expense of the building proposed to be constructed. If a majority of the citizens present shall consent to the purchase of such real estate, and construction of a building for the purpose proposed, and to the estimate presented, or any part thereof, the Common Council shall then be authorized to contract for the purchase of such real estate and for the construction of said building, at a cost and expense not exceeding in amount, the estimate or part thereof thus consented to, and to expend thereon, borrow money and issue bonds as above provided. [*As amended by Laws of* 1861, *p.* 191.]

Pub. works not provid'd for; how and when to be let.

(§ 206.) SEC. 11. No contract shall be let or entered into for the construction of any public work within said city,[m] not herein otherwise provided for, and no such public work shall be commenced until it shall have been approved by the Common Council, and a tax or assessment levied to defray the cost and expense thereof; and no such public work shall be paid for or contracted to be paid for, except out of the proceeds of the tax or assessment thus levied.[n]

Williams vs. Mayor, etc., of Detroit, 2 Mich., 560.

No contract for over $200 to be let except to the lowest bidder.

(§ 207.) SEC. 12. No contract for the purchase of any real estate, or for the construction of any public building, sewer, paving, graveling, planking, macadamizing, or for the construction of any public work whatever, or for any work to be done, or for purchasing or furnishing any material, printing or supplies for said

---

[m] See Section 217.

[n] The City cannot make itself responsible for any public work. Payment can only be made from specific funds actually in the hands of the Treasurer. Goodrich vs. City of Detroit, 12 Mich., 279. See Chaffee vs. Granger, 6 Mich., 51, as to contracts made prior to Charter of 1857.

corporation, if the purchase of said real estate, or the expense of such construction, repairs, work, materials, or supplies shall exceed two hundred dollars, shall be let, or entered into, except to and with the lowest responsible bidder, with adequate security,[o] and as to such work or material, requiring mechanical skill, to and with practical mechanics, and as to such other work, supplies or material not requiring mechanical skill, to and with such persons as shall be deemed competent for the performance of any such contract, and not until advertised proposals and specifications therefor shall have been duly published in at least one daily newspaper published in said city, and for such period as the Common Council shall prescribe. And no bids shall be accepted from, or contract awarded to, any person who is in arrears to the corporation upon debt or contract, or who is a defaulter as security, or otherwise, upon any obligation to the corporation, or who shall be in other respects disqualified according to the provisions of this act.

Evidence of debt; for what issued.

(§ 208.) SEC. 13. No loan, bond, or other evidence of debt, not expressly authorized by this act, or any act hereby continued in force, shall be made or issued by the Common Council or any officer of the corporation:[q] *Provided, however*, That the Common Council may issue new bonds for the refunding of bonds and evidences of debt already issued; and the proper officer of the corporation may draw and issue orders on the Treasurer for the necessary and current expenses of the city.

---

[o] See Section 34, *ante*.

[q] See Section 574.

Council may authorize Controller to borrow money.

(§ 209.) SEC. 14. The Common Council shall not have authority to borrow, except as herein before provided, any sums of money whatever, on the credit of the corporation, but may authorize the Controller to borrow, from time to time, on such credit, in anticipation of the revenues of the corporation for the current fiscal year, and not to exceed such revenues in amount, such sums as may be necessary to meet the expenditures under the appropriations for the current fiscal year.

New bonds wh't to show and how issued.

(§ 210.) SEC. 15. All new bonds, issued for the refunding of bonds and evidences of debt before issued, shall show the class of indebtedness to which they belong; be issued on the best terms that can be made; be regularly dated and numbered in the order of their issuance; shall be for sums not less than five hundred dollars each; shall be issued under the seal of the corporation, signed by the Mayor, and countersigned by the Controller. The Controller shall keep an accurate record, showing the class of indebtedness to which they belong, the number, date and amount of each bond, its rate of interest, when and where the same is payable, and the person to whom it is issued, and showing also what bonds or evidences of debt have been thereby refunded.

Controller to keep record.

Refunded bonds to be cancel'd and destroyed.

(§ 211.) SEC. 16. All bonds and evidences of debt, when refunded, shall be canceled and destroyed by the Treasurer, in the presence of the Controller and a special committee of the Common Council appointed for the purpose. He shall record and keep an accurate description of all bonds and evidences of debt thus canceled and destroyed.

Bonds void when issued contrary to this act.

(§ 212.) SEC. 17. All bonds and evidences of debt issued, and all contracts made or entered into contrary to or not authorized by the provisions of this act, shall be absolutely void. The Common Council shall incur no expenses and create or pay no debt or liability contrary to or not authorized by the provisions of this act, and shall not appropriate or use the property or moneys of the corporation, except as authorized by and in pursuance of law.

(§ 213.) SEC. 18. No claim or demand against the corporation shall be allowed or paid, or warrant on the treasury issued therefor, if the same be contrary to, or is not authorized by law, and no additional allowance beyond the legal claim under any contract with the corporation, or for any service on its account, or in its employment, shall be allowed. No warrant on the treasury shall be drawn for any claim or demand for the payment of which there is no money in the treasury raised or received for such purpose, or after the fund constituted and raised therefor has been exhausted by warrants previously drawn thereon, or by appropriations, liabilities, debts and expenses actually made, incurred or contracted for, and to be paid out of such fund.[r]

No illegal claim to be paid.

No warrant to be drawn when there is no money in Treasury.

(§ 214.) SEC. 19. No moneys shall be paid out of the treasury, except upon a warrant signed by the Controller, and approved or authorized by the Common Council in pursuance of law. Such warrant shall specify the purpose for which the amount thereof is to be paid, with sufficient clearness to indicate the particular fund constituted or raised therefor, shall have indorsed thereon the name of the particular fund out of which it is

No money to be paid from treasury except on warrant.

What warrant to contain and how indorsed.

[r] See Section 206.

payable, and shall be paid from the fund constituted for such purpose, and from no other.[8]

Claim to be accompan'd by affidavit.

(§ 215.) SEC. 20. No claim against the corporation shall be audited or paid unless accompanied by the affidavit of the claimant, (if such affidavit be required by the Controller,) that the service, labor or materials upon which such claim is based, have been actually rendered, performed or furnished; that said claim is justly due, and that no part thereof has been paid, except as to the credits, if any, set forth in the account therefor.

Drafts on funds limited.

(§ 216.) SEC. 21. The Common Council shall not, by warrant, draft or order on the treasury, or by any form of contract, create any liability or expense, for the payment of which any particular fund is constituted as above, to a greater amount in the aggregate, for any one year, than the amount of moneys raised for and paid into such fund for the year. All warrants, drafts, orders, and contracts payable under this act, out of any particular fund, and issued or made after the moneys raised for and paid into such fund shall have been exhausted by payments therefrom, or liabilities created and to be paid out of said fund, shall be absolutely void as against the corporation.

Officers not to be interested in any contract with city.

(§ 217.) SEC. 22. No contract or agreement, written or verbal, to which the corporation shall be a party, or to which any officer or board thereof shall officially be a party, for the construction of any pavement, building, sewer, or performance of any public work whatsoever, or contract, or agreement, requiring the expenditure, receipt, or disposition of money or property, by the corporation,

[8] See Section 65, *ante*.

of any officer or board thereof, or creating any debt or liability, shall be let, or entered into, either directly or indirectly, with any member of the Common Council, or other officer of the corporation, either as principal or surety, and any such contract or agreement thus let or entered into, shall be absolutely void:[t] *Provided, however*, That nothing herein contained shall prevent the Overseer of Highways, of any ward, from contracting with the corporation for cleaning, repairing, or improving the streets in their wards respectively. [*As amended by Laws of* 1861, *p.* 191.

Proviso.

No ordinance, etc., to be passed at meeting at which it was introduced.

(§ 218.) SEC. 23. No ordinance, resolution, or proceeding of the Common Council, imposing taxes or assessments, or requiring the payment, expenditure, or disposition of money or property, or creating any debt or liability therefor, and no other ordinance shall be passed at the same meeting at which it was introduced, unless by unanimous consent, or at a special meeting called therefor, and every such ordinance, resolution, or proceeding shall be passed by yeas and nays, to be entered on the record.[u]

Fiscal year.

Controller's report.

(§ 219.) SEC. 24. The Common Council shall determine the fiscal year, and within one month after the end thereof, the Controller shall render to the Common Council a full, complete, and detailed statement, with tabular lists, of all moneys received and expended by the corporation for the preceding fiscal year, showing on what account they were received and expended, to what funds

---

[t] By Section 13 (*ante*) such contract or agreement renders the party guilty of malfeasance in office, and is made punishable by fine or imprisonment, or both.

[u] This section is copied from section 98, *ante*.

they were credited, and out of what funds they were paid, and classifying each receipt and expenditure under its appropriate head. In such statement he shall also give, by tabular lists and otherwise, such general information as may be necessary for an understanding of the pecuniary resources and liabilities of said city, and of the condition of each fund, and may make such recommendations concerning the same, as the interests of said city may require. The Common Council shall cause said statement to be published in the daily newspaper, published by the printer for said city, and in such other paper or papers as the Common Council may direct.

What to contain.

To be published.

Controller or Council may require estimates and acco'nts fr'm officers and boards.

(§ 220.) SEC. 25. The Common Council and the Controller, or either, may, at any time, require from the various officers and boards of the corporation, and it shall be their duty to furnish, when required, and in such form as shall be required, full and particular estimates, in detail, of the expenses of their offices or departments for the current or next ensuing fiscal year, and also full and particular accounts, in detail, of their expenses for any past year, or for any part thereof.

Money may be put in bank.

(§ 221.) SEC. 26. The Common Council shall have power to contract with any safe bank or banks, for the safe keeping of the public moneys, and for the receipt of interest, at a rate not exceeding that established by law, upon such moneys of the corporation deposited with such bank or banks, and to be drawn on account current from such bank or banks, by the corporation, or proper officer thereof, and such interest shall belong and be credited to the sinking fund.

Committee for negotia-ti'n of loans.

(§ 222.) SEC. 27. The Mayor, Controller, and Chairman of the Committee on Ways and Means, shall be a committee for the negotiation of all loans authorized by this act, except as to any loans to be made by the Controller, under the authority of the Common Council, as above provided;[v] and a majority of said committee shall have power to make such negotiation, subject to the approval of the Common Council.

(§ 223.) SEC. 28. All taxes and moneys raised, received, or appropriated for the purpose of any particular fund, shall be paid in and credited to such particular fund; and all taxes and moneys not raised, received or appropriated for the purpose of any particular fund, shall be paid in and credited to the general fund, or such other fund as the Common Council shall direct. *Taxes, to what fund credited.*

(§ 224.) SEC. 29. The moneys belonging to the several funds of the corporation, and all taxes and moneys raised, received, or appropriated for the purposes thereof, shall be applied to the purposes for which said funds are respectively constituted, as above; and for which said taxes and moneys are raised, received, or appropriated: *Provided, however*, That if, from any cause, there shall be, at the end of any fiscal year, a surplus in any other than the public building fund, the district road fund, for each ward, and the sinking fund, over and above the actual or estimated cost of any work for which the money of any fund was specifically raised, such surplus shall be transferred and credited, by the Treasurer, to said sinking fund, at the end of such fiscal year, whenever there shall not be sufficient moneys therein to pay the outstanding funded debt of said city. *Money, how applied.* *Proviso.*

[v] See Section 209.

Moneys not to be transferred from one fund to another.

(§ 225.) SEC. 30. Moneys shall not be transferred from one fund to another, and the moneys received and properly belonging to one fund, shall not be credited to any other, or different fund, except to the sinking fund, as above provided; but the Controller shall have the power to divide the several funds above constituted into special funds, to defray special expenses, belonging to the same class of expenses, for the payment of which said several funds are above constituted.

Funds may be divided.

Board of Commissioners of Sink. Fund.

(§ 226.) SEC. 31. The Mayor, Controller, Treasurer, and Committee on Ways and Means, and their successors in office, by virtue of their offices, shall be a Board of Commissioners of the sinking fund. They shall, from time to time, upon the best terms they can make, purchase or pay the outstanding funded debt of said city, or such part thereof as they may be able to purchase or pay, until the same be fully purchased up, or paid; and all bonds and evidences of debt, thus purchased or paid, shall be delivered to the Treasurer, and shall become and be the property of the Commissioners of the sinking fund, and the interest thereon shall be credited and belong to the sinking fund; and whenever they can not arrange for purchasing or paying the said debt, or any part thereof, they shall, temporarily, and until they can so arrange, invest the moneys belonging to said sinking fund in such securities, paying an interest of not less than seven per cent., as they may deem safe and advisable. Said Commissioners shall, from time to time, and whenever requested by the Common Council, make report of their doings, which report shall be made to the Common Council, referred to and filed with the Controller, and recorded by him in some proper book, to be provided for the purpose.

Duties of Board.

(§ 227.) SEC. 32. Said Board of Commissioners of the sinking fund shall be a board of the corporation, within the meaning of this act, and shall be subject to the provisions of any existing or future ordinances of said city, relative to the sinking fund. They shall meet, from time to time, for the transaction of business, and may adopt rules of proceeding at their meetings. A majority of the whole board shall be a quorum for the transaction of business, but they shall not purchase in, or pay the outstanding funded debt of said city, or invest any of the moneys belonging to the sinking fund, as above provided, except under a resolution for such purpose, passed and approved by the vote of a majority of the whole board, and by yeas and nays, to be entered of record. The Mayor, or, in case of his absence, some member, to be appointed by those present, shall preside at their meetings. They shall appoint one of their members Secretary of the Board, whose duty it shall be to keep a true record of its doings.

Meetings of Board.

Who to preside.

Secretary, his duty.

(§ 228.) SEC. 33. The Treasurer shall have the custody of all moneys, securities, and evidences of value, belonging or pertaining to the sinking fund, and shall pay out the moneys of said fund only by order of the Commissioners, or a majority thereof, and upon the warrant of the Controller.

Treasurer to have custody of Sinking Fund.

(§ 229.) SEC. 34. The faith and property of the City of Detroit shall remain pledged for the final payment of all bonds issued, and of all moneys borrowed by authority of, and in accordance with this or any other act of the Legislature of this State.

Pledge for payment of moneys borrowed.

(§ 230.) SEC. 35. If any officer of the corporation shall, directly or indirectly, appropriate or convert any of the moneys, securities, evidences of value, or any

Officer conv'rting money of corporation to be d'em'd g'lty of malfeasance in office

property whatsoever, belonging to the corporation, or any board thereof, to his own use, or shall, directly or indirectly, and knowingly, appropriate or convert the same to any other purpose than that for which such moneys, securities, evidences of value, or property may have been appropriated, raised, or received, or to any purpose not authorized by law, he shall be deemed guilty of willful and corrupt malfeasance in office, and may be prosecuted, tried, and convicted therefor, and on conviction, may be punished by fine not exceeding one thousand dollars, and imprisonment in the State prison, jail of Wayne County, or jail of said city, not exceeding three years, or either, in the discretion of the court.

Punishm'nt.

Plank crosswalks, how paid for.

(§ 231.) SEC. 36. The expenses of constructing and repairing plank crosswalks, in the several wards, shall be defrayed from the district road fund, mentioned in subdivision eight, of section one of this chapter. [*Added by Laws of* 1861, *p.* 189.

CHAPTER IX.

ASSESSMENT OF TAXES AND THEIR COLLECTION.

SECTION
232. Assessor; term of office.
233. Duties of Assessor.
234. Assessor and Aldermen have power of Supervisors.
235. Manner of assessing.
236. Assessor may demand list of owner.
237. Board of Review; how appointed; session of; powers and duties; compensation.
238. Have same power as Supervisors.
239. Notice to tax payers.
240. Appeal to the Council.
241. Appeals; how considered.
242. May continue hearing.
243. Assessor to extend taxes on rolls; duty of Controller; duty of Receiver; notice; warrants.
244. Powers of collectors.
245. Taxes a lien; delinquent taxes; notice and sale of.
246. Sale for term of years; redemption.
247. Redemption.
248. Taxes paid; how recovered.
249. Interest on redemption.
250. Right to remove buildings.
251. Controller to execute conveyances.
252. When Controller to bid at sale; certificates; sale for special assessments.
253. Conveyances *prima facie* evidence of regularity.
254. Assessment rolls for sewers, sidewalks, and paving; how collected.

(§ 232.) SECTION 1. There shall be an assessor appointed by the the Common Council, upon the recommendation of the Mayor,[a] who shall hold his office for the term of three years, and shall devote his whole time to the service of the city, in connection with the duties of his office, with power to appoint two assistants, and shall receive such compensation as the Common Council may determine. *Assessor; term of office.* *Compensation.*

(§ 233.) SEC. 2. The said Assessor or Assessors shall, between the first day of October, in each year, and the first day of April, in the succeeding year, assess all the real and personal property subject to assessment or taxation *Time for the assessment of property.*

[a] Office of ward assessor abolished. Section 55, *ante*.

by the laws of this State,[b] within the limits of each ward, respectively, of said city; and the said Assessor or Assessors shall so discriminate in assessing said tax as not to impose upon the rural portions those expenses which belong exclusively to the built portion of the city, for which purpose the Assessor or Assessors may, in his or their discretion, distinguish in their assessments what properties are within agricultural or rural portions not having the benefit of highway, watering, watching and other expenditures for purposes exclusively belonging to the built and densely populated portions of the city; and all lands within said agricultural or rural districts, exclusively used for the purposes of cultivation, pasture, meadow, woodland or farming, may, in the discretion of the Assessor, be assessed as farm lands at their cash value; and said Assessor or Assessors shall, within the given period, make out and complete the assessment rolls, one for each ward respectively, in books to be provided for that purpose by the Common Council, and to be delivered to said Assessor on or before the first day of January in each year. The action of the Assessor or Assessors shall at all times be subject to the corrections and revisions of the Board of Review and the Common Council of the city of Detroit, as provided for in the charter of the city. [*As amended by Laws of* 1867, *Vol. II*, *p.* 1114.]

Discrimination b'tween the rural and built portions of the city.

Property assessed as farm lands.

Time to deliver assessment roll.

Action of assessor subject to reviewal.

Assessors and Aldermen to have powers of supervisors.

(§ 234.) SEC. 3. The Assessor, together with the two Aldermen of each ward of the City of Detroit, shall be, and are hereby vested with the powers and duties of Supervisors, as provided by the laws of this State, not inconsistent with the provisions of this chapter, and said Assessor and Aldermen shall attend the

[b] See Section 70, *ante*.

annual session of the Board of Supervisors of the County of Wayne, in October, and all other sessions thereof, and shall represent the interests of this corporation in said Board.[c] [*As amended by Laws of* 1859, *p.* 342.]

(§ 235.) SEC. 4. If any lot or lots shall lie partly in two or more wards, the same shall be assessed in the ward where the greater proportion of such lot or lots is situated, and the said Assessor shall describe all lands, tenements, and subdivisions thereof, subject to assessment or tax in said city, by referring to the number and section of the lot, and the owner or occupant thereof, and if the number and section of any lot, or the owner thereof can not be ascertained, then by such other sufficient description[d] as such Assessor may deem proper; and if, by mistake or otherwise, any person may be improperly designated as the owner of any lot, tenement, or premises, such assessment or tax shall not, for that cause be vitiated, but the same shall be a lien on such lot, tenement, or premises, and collected as in other cases.

Proceedin's where lots lie in two or more wards.

(§ 236.) SEC. 5. The Assessor shall have power and authority to demand of every person owning or having charge, as agent or otherwise, of any property taxable in any ward, a list of such property, with such description as will enable him to assess the same,[e] which demand may be made in writing, and by delivering the same to such person, or by leaving the same at his place of residence, with some person of proper years and discretion, and if the person of whom such demand may be

Assessor may demand list of owner or agent.

---

[c] See Const., Art. X, Sec. 7.

[d] See case of Young Men's Society vs. Mayor, etc., of Detroit, 3 Mich., 172.

[e] For effect of misdescription by the owner, see Hubbard vs Winsor, 15 Mich., 146.

made, shall not, within ten days thereafter, deliver to such Assessor a list of the property in said ward belonging to him or her, or under his or her charge, with a correct description of the same, or if he shall omit any such property in the list delivered, said Assessor shall have power, and it shall be his duty, to assess such property, upon such knowledge or information, as may be satisfactory to him, at its cash value, and according to his best judgment and discretion.

Board of Review; how appointed.

(§ 237.) SEC. 6. A Board of Review shall, on the nomination of the Mayor, be appointed by the Common Council. Said Board shall consist of three resident property holders of said city, who shall hold their office for the term of three years, except that the three persons first appointed, which shall be immediately after this act shall take effect, shall hold their offices respectively for the term of one, two and three years, as shall be determined by lot, on the first meeting of said Board, and thereafter one member of said Board shall be appointed each year, for the term of three years, as hereinbefore provided. The session of the Board of Review shall be held at the Assessor's office, in said city, and shall commence on the first Monday in April, in each year, and continue from day to day until all of said assessment rolls have been fully and carefully reviewed, corrected, and approved, which shall be on or before the fifteenth day of May. The Board of Review shall have power, and it shall be their duty, to equalize, alter, amend, and correct any assessment or valuation, and to place upon the assessment roll of the proper ward, any taxable property, real or personal, not already assessed, held or owned by any person or persons, and to strike from said rolls

Session of: where held.

Powers and duties.

any property, real or personal, wrongfully thereon, but no assessment shall be increased or made by said Board without notice to the person or persons affected thereby, either verbal, or personal, or written, or printed, and left at the usual residence of such person, if a resident, and if a non-resident, by a publication in some daily newspaper published in said city. Any person considering himself aggrieved by reason of any assessment, may complain thereof, verbally or in writing, before the Board of Review, and on sufficient cause being shown by the affidavit of such person, or by other evidence, to the satisfaction of such Board, they shall review the assessment complained of, and may alter or correct the same as to the person charged thereby, the property described therein, and the estimated value thereof. The concurrence of a majority of the Board shall be sufficient to decide any question of altering or correcting any assessment complained of. The Board, or a majority of them, having completed the review and correction of their assessment rolls, shall respectively sign and return the same to the Common Council. The members of said Board shall receive such compensation for their services as shall be prescribed by the Common Council. [*As amended by Laws of* 1861, *p.* 192.]

Compensation.

(§ 238.) SEC. 7. At the meeting of the Board of Review, as required by the preceding section, they shall have the same power to review, correct, and equalize the assessment rolls of the several wards, which Supervisors now or hereafter may have, by law, to review, correct, and equalize the assessment rolls of townships in the respective counties of this State.

Board of Review to have same power as Board of Sup'rvisors.

Notice to ax payers.

(§ 239.) SEC. 8. The City Clerk shall cause a notice to the tax payers of said city to be published in the daily newspaper, published by the printer for the city, and in one other daily newspaper published in said city. for two weeks prior to the time of any meeting of the said Board of Review, stating the time and place of meeting of said Board, and the object for which it will meet, which notice shall be continued on each publication day of said papers, during the session of said Board. [*As amended by Laws of* 1861, *p.* 193.]

Appeal to Common Council.

(§ 240.) SEC. 9. The Common Council, after the expiration of said two weeks, or extended period in which the Board of Review are to sit, as above provided, for reviewing their assessment rolls, shall, at its next regular session, proceed to consider said assessment rolls, and any person aggrieved by the assessment of his property, and the decision of such Board of Review thereon, may appeal to the Common Council at the said regular session. Every appeal shall be in writing, and shall state specially the grounds of the appeal, and the matter complained of, and no other matter shall be considered by the Council. While acting upon said assessment rolls, or appeals, any member of said Board may meet with the Common Council, and make such explanations as they may deem requisite in any case.

Common Council to hear appeals summarily.

(§ 241.) SEC. 10. The Common Council shall hear and determine all appeals in a summary manner, and correct any errors which they may discover in the assessment rolls, and place thereon the names of any persons and the descriptions of any property not already assessed, and assess the same, and may increase or diminish any assessment, as they may see fit: *Provided,*

Proviso.

That they shall not increase any assessment of property without giving a reasonable opportunity to the persons owning or having charge of the same, if known, to appear and object thereto.

Hearing appeals may be continued.

(§ 242.) SEC. 11. The Common Council may continue the consideration of said assessment rolls, and the hearing of said appeals, from session to session, for a period not exceeding sixteen days after the time when they are to be first considered as above provided, and on or before the expiration of said period of sixteen days, they shall be fully and finally confirmed by the Common Council,[f] and shall remain as the basis of all taxes to be levied and collected in the City ot Detroit, according to property valuatión until another assessment shall have been made and confirmed, as above provided for.

Assessor to extend taxes upon rolls.

(§ 243.) SEC. 12. After the assessment rolls shall have been fully and finally confirmed, as provided in the preceding section, it shall be the duty of the Assessor to cause the amount of all taxes, in dollars and cents, authorized to be assessed and collected in each year, to be rateably assessed to each person named, or lots described, upon and according to the aggregate valuation such person or lots shall have been assessed in said assessment rolls or books, prepared for that purpose, to be known as the tax rolls for each ward, in separate columns, showing the amount of highway, sewer, school,[g] and city taxes assessed to each person or lots in each year; and when said tax rolls shall have been completed, the Assessor shall deliver the same to the Controller, who shall cause the same to be delivered to the

Duty of Controller.

[f] See Section 459 as to State and County tax rolls.

[g] See Section 527 as to school taxes.

Receiver of Taxes,[h] and take his receipt therefor, and charge him therewith. Upon the receipt of the tax rolls by the Receiver of Taxes, as hereinbefore provided, the taxes therein stated shall become due and payable, and the Receiver of Taxes shall forthwith, upon the reception of said tax rolls, give six days' notice, by publication in two or more daily papers published in said city, and by posting the same in at least six public places in each ward, which notice shall be a sufficient demand for the payment of all taxes on said rolls;[i] that the general tax rolls have been deposited with him, and that payment of the taxes therein specified may be made to him, at any time before the thirtieth day of December thereafter; that no addition will be made to taxes paid before the first day of August, but that an addition of one per cent. of every unpaid tax will be made thereto on that day, and a like addition of one per cent. every thirtieth day thereafter, until such addition shall amount to six per cent. of such tax. Upon the receipt of any tax, the Receiver shall mark the same paid upon the proper roll, and give a receipt therefor. On the first day of January, next following the time when any tax shall become due and payable, the Receiver shall add to every such tax six per cent. of the amount thereof, as stated in the roll, and the amount of the tax, and of such additions as are hereinbefore specified, shall thenceforth be the unpaid tax, and shall bear interest from that day, at the rate of twelve per cent. per annum, until paid, except as is herein otherwise provided.

Duty of Receiver.

Notice by.

Per centage added.

[h] Special assessment rolls to be delivered to Receiver of Taxes, Sec. 254.

[i] Publication held to be sufficient notice. Williams vs. Mayor, etc. of the City of Detroit. 2 Mich., 560.

On or before the fifteenth day of January, the Receiver shall make, in duplicate, a roll of the unpaid taxes of each ward; such roll shall be a substantial transcript of such portions of the original tax rolls as relate to the unpaid taxes, and shall exhibit the original, and in the last column, the augmented amount of every such tax. Immediately after completing such roll, he shall cause a notice to be published in five successive numbers of at least two daily newspapers published in said city, stating that said roll of unpaid taxes has been made, and that it will remain in his office, where such taxes may be paid, until the first day of February following, after which the property against which such taxes are assessed, shall be advertised and sold, as hereinafter provided. But the Receiver of Taxes, with the advice and consent of the Controller, on or after the first day of August in each year, may cause to be made out, copies of any taxes remaining due and unpaid on said tax or assessment rolls for each ward, and which are assessed wholly or partly against any property or value other than real estate, together with such per centage as shall have been fixed by the Common Council as compensation for the collection of such taxes or assessments, and to be stated in such rolls, and warrants[j] may be issued and annexed to each such tax or assessment roll, signed by the Controller, and under the corporate seal of the corporation, directed to the proper Ward Collector, or Collector of the city, as the case may be, and made returnable upon such day as shall

Notice.

Warrants to Collectors.

Return.

[j] When warrants may issue for collection of assessments for paving, etc., Section 254.

Duty of Collectors.

have been designated by the Common Council, commanding them to collect from the persons named in their respective assessment rolls, the assessment or taxes therein specified and set forth as due from such persons, and for such purpose, if necessary, to levy upon and sell the personal property of such person, occupant, or lessee, refusing or neglecting to pay the same, wherever the same may be found, within the limits of said city, and to pay over and account for the taxes or assessments thus collected, according to law. The Receiver of Taxes shall charge the amount of any such tax or assessment rolls, upon which warrants may be issued, to the Collectors of the proper ward, or of the city, as the case may be, and shall take a receipt therefor.

Warrants may be renewed.

Warrants for the collection of taxes and assessments, may be renewed and extended, from time to time, by the Common Council; but the time for the payment of any general tax shall not be extended beyond the first day of January following the time when such tax shall have become due and payable.

Duty of Assessor as to State and County taxes.

It shall be the duty of the Assessor to make copies of said rolls, as finally confirmed by the Common Council, upon which he shall rateably assess the county and State taxes, as provided by the general laws of the State.[k] [*As amended by Laws of* 1861, *p.* 193.

Powers of Collectors.

(§ 244.) SEC. 13. By virtue of said warrants, the several Collectors,[1] to whom they may be respectively directed, shall have power to levy upon the personal property of persons from whom taxes may be due, or the personal property of the occupant or lessee of any

---

[k] See Section 459 as to duty of Assessor relative to State and County taxes.

[1] Powers and duties of Colletors as to collection of school taxes, Sec. 528.

land or lot on which the tax may have been assessed, wherever the same may be found, within the limits of said city, and shall sell the same in the same manner, and with the same duties and powers of proceeding, as now or hereafter may be provided by the laws of this State, for the collection of State and county taxes, by Township Treasurers or Collectors;[m] and all moneys thus collected, shall be paid over to the Receiver of Taxes, and all moneys received by the Receiver of Taxes, shall be paid over to the Treasurer of said city, as shall be prescribed by the Common Council. [*As amended by Laws of* 1861, *p.* 196.]

Collectors to account to Receiver and Receiver to Treasurer.

(§ 245.) SEC. 14. Every assessment or tax lawfully levied or imposed by the authority of the Common Council, on any lands, tenements, hereditaments, or premises whatsoever, in said city, shall be and remain a lien on such lands, tenements, hereditaments, or premises, from and after the time such taxes shall become due and payable as aforesaid; and the owner or occupants of, or parties in interest in said real estate, shall be liable to pay every such tax or assessment, and if there be a default in paying the same, or any part thereof,[n] or if such person or persons be non-resident of said city, it shall be lawful for said Common Council to cause a notice to be published in the daily newspaper, published by the printer for the city, once a week, for four successive weeks, and posted in three or more public places in each ward, requiring the owners or occupants of, or

Taxes a lien on property.

Delinquent taxes.

Notice.

---

[m] See Section 73, *ante*. See also Compiled Laws, section 821, *et post*.

[n] Under this section it was held, that a part owner may pay so much of his tax as shall be proportioned to his interest. People vs. Treasurer of Detroit, 8 Mich., 14.

parties in interest in such lands, tenements, hereditaments, or premises, to pay such assessment or tax, and that if default be made in making such payment, such real estate will be sold at public auction, at a day and place to be specified in said notice, for the lowest term of years at which any person shall offer to take the same, in consideration of advancing and paying such assessment or tax, with the costs or charges in the premises. [*As amended by Laws of* 1861, *p.* 196.]

Sale at auction.

Sale of real estate for taxes for term of years.

(§ 246.) SEC. 15. If the owners or occupants of, or parties in interest in such real estate, do not pay such assessments or taxes, with the costs and charges, within the period above prescribed for the publication of said notice, then the said Common Council shall have power, without any further notice, to cause such real estate to be sold at public auction for the lowest term of years at which any person shall offer to take the same, in consideration of advancing such assessment or tax, with the costs and charges, and to direct the execution of a proper certificate of such sale to the purchaser thereof; and if such real estate shall not be redeemed within one year after such sale thereof,[o] as hereinafter provided, the Controller shall, in the name of and for the City of Detroit, execute and deliver to such purchaser, or his assignee, a proper deed for the conveyance of such real estate, for the term for which the same was sold, which deed shall in all courts be *prima facie* evidence of the regularity of all the proceedings under which the sale was made, and said deed was executed, up to the date of the deed;[p] and any person who shall under such

Redem'tion.

Controller to execute deed of real estate for term of years.

Deed *prima facie* evidence of regularity of proce'dings.

[o] See Section 247.

[p] See Section 253.

deed enter into any such real estate, and erect or place any building or building materials thereon, shall have the right at any time within three months after the expiration of said term, or in case he shall be ousted before the expiration of such term, by any person claiming adversely to said deed, then within three months after trial, judgment of ouster or ejectment, to remove such building or building materials from said real estate.[q]

Purchaser may erect buildings on premises sold and may remove the same within three months after expiration of term.

(§ 247.) SEC. 16. When any lands, tenements and hereditaments shall be sold according to the foregoing provisions for the payment of any assessment or tax, as aforesaid, if the owners or occupants of or parties in interest in the same shall within one year[r] after such sale deposit with the Treasurer of said city, for the use of the purchaser, the full amount of the assessment or tax for which such real estate was sold, and such interest as the Common Council shall prescribe, as hereinafter authorized, together with the amount of the costs and charges, then the term for which such real estate was sold shall cease and be determined at the time of making such deposit, subject, however, to the right of the purchaser, his heirs, executors, administrators, or assigns, to remove any building or building materials as hereinbefore provided.

Redem'tion.

People vs. Treasurer of Detroit, 8 Mich., 14.

(§ 248.) SEC. 17. Any person in possession of any real estate at the time any tax is to be collected, shall be liable to pay the tax imposed thereon, and in case any other person, by agreement or otherwise, ought to

Taxes paid may be recovered of person who ought to pay the same in action of assumpsit.

---

[q] See Section 250.

[r] See Section 246.

pay such tax or any part thereof, the person in possession who shall pay the same, may recover the amount paid from the person who ought to have paid the same, in an action of assumpsit, as for moneys paid out and expended for his use and benefit.

People vs. City Treasurer of Detroit, 8 Mich. 14.

Interest on redemption.

(§ 249.) SEC. 18. The Common Council shall have power to charge interest at a rate not exceeding twenty-five per cent. per annum, from the time of sale, on the amount of any assessment or tax, for the non-payment of which any lands, tenements or hereditaments may be sold, and upon the amount to be paid upon the redemption of any such real estate and premises so sold. [*As amended by Laws of* 1861, *p.* 197.]

Right to remove buildings.

(§ 250.) SEC. 19. Any person who shall at such sale purchase, for a term of years, any lots, grounds or wharves, shall have the right to remove any building or building materials erected or deposited by, or belonging to him, and situated on said lots, grounds or wharves, at any time within three months after the expiration of the term or time for which the same were sold.[8]

Controller or Mayor may execute conveyances.

(§ 251.) SEC. 20. The Controller, or in his absence, the Mayor, may execute, in the name of the corporation, and under its corporate seal, proper conveyances or certificates of sale of all lands, tenements, or hereditaments sold for assessments or taxes, which, when duly acknowledged and attested by the City Clerk, may be recorded as other conveyances of land under the laws of this State.

Controller to bid where no one offers to bid.

(§ 252.) SEC. 21. It shall be the duty of the Controller, to bid in for the corporation, at any sale of real

[8] See Section 246.

estate for assessments or taxes, every lot of land or premises for which no person shall offer to bid; and if any purchaser shall refuse or neglect to pay the sum or sums bid by him, within the time and under the regulations prescribed by the Common Council, such bid shall enure to the use and benefit of the corporation, if the Common Council so elect. Upon all such bids by the Controller, and all bids as aforesaid, to the use and benefit of the corporation, conveyances and certificates of sale may be executed by the Controller to the corporation, acknowledged and attested by the City Clerk, and recorded in the same manner as provided in other cases of sale for assessment or taxes. But in all cases of sales for special assessments, the property so bid in for the corporation may, at the option of the Common Council, be held in trust for the person or contractor in whose behalf such assessment shall have been made, or his assignee, or upon payment to such person or contractor of the amount for which such property shall have been bid in, the city may, as in case of the general tax, become the owner of the tax title or lease thus obtained, and may dispose of the same as if obtained under a like sale for any general tax. [*As amended by Laws of* 1861, *p.* 197.]

Certificates of sale.

Sales of special assessments.

(§ 253.) SEC. 22. All conveyances, certificates of sale and leases of any lands, tenements or hereditaments, executed by the corporation, or any of its officers, by virtue of this act, shall be taken and received in all courts and proceedings as *prima facie* evidence of the regularity of the proceedings on which such conveyances, certificates of sale, lease, or any title claimed thereby, are founded.[t]

Conveyance to be *prima facie* evidence.

[t] See Section 246.

Assessment rolls for sewers, sidewalks and paving.

(§ 254.) SEC. 23. Assessment rolls[u] to defray the expense of constructing lateral sewers, side and crosswalks, paving, grading, macadamizing, graveling or otherwise improving streets, lanes or alleys, or for defraying the expense of any local improvements properly payable from the proceeds of special assessment, shall be placed in the hands of the Receiver of Taxes, for payment, as may be provided by ordinance or resolution of the Common Council, for the space of thirty days, after which

Warrants.

warrants for the collection of the same may be issued, and such proceedings for the collection thereof be had as are or shall be prescribed by law, or by any ordinance or resolution of the Common Council, and sales of any real or personal estate for any unpaid assessments, shall be made in like manner, and with like effect, as in case of sales for non-payment of the general tax.[v] [*As added by Laws of* 1861, *p.* 198.]

---

[u] These assessments to be made out by City Surveyor. Section 68.

[v] See Sections 245, *et post*.

CHAPTER X.

FIRE DEPARTMENT.[a]

SECTION
255. Council to buy engines.
256. To organize fire companies.
267. Chief engineer and assistants.
258. Fire wardens.
259. Powers and duties of companies and firemen.
260. Meeting of companies.
261. Powers and duties of wardens.
262. Exemption of firemen.
263. Powers of certain officers at fires.

SECTION
264. Power to arrest.
265. Duties of officers at fires.
266. Present companies continued until disbanded.
267. Fire marshal to investigate cause of fires.
268. Testimony taken on investigation.
269. To make complaints.
270. Term of office; how removed.

Common Council to buy engines, etc.

(§ 255.) SECTION 1. The Common Council shall procure fire engines, hose, hooks, ladders and other apparatus and implements used for the extinguishment of fires, for each fire company, pay the expenses of keeping the same in necessary repair, have charge and control of the same, and provide fit and secure engine houses and other places for keeping and preserving the same, and purchase any real estate for the erection of engine houses.

To organize fire companies.

(§ 256.) SEC. 2. The Common Council shall have power to organize engine, hook, hose, ladder, axe and other fire companies, for the prevention and extinguishment of fires, and to dissolve or disband the same,[b] to

---

[a] This Chapter is entirely superseded by Laws of 1867, Vol. II, p. 931, establishing "A Fire Commission in the City of Detroit." See Part II, Chapter VI. As the latter act does not in terms purport to be any portion of the Charter, the Compiler has thought it expedient to retain the original chapter as being an integral portion of the act of revision of 1857.

[b] See 32d subdivision of Section 103, p. 62.

appoint a competent number of able inhabitants of the City of Detroit firemen, to take the care and management of engines, hose, ladders, and other apparatus and implements used and provided for the prevention and extinguishment of fires; to prescribe the duties and powers of firemen and fire companies, make rules and regulations for their government, impose reasonable fines, penalties and forfeitures upon them for a violation of the same, and to remove them for incapacity, neglect of duty or misconduct.[c]

Chief and assistant engineers.

(§ 257.) SEC. 3. There shall be a chief engineer, and two or more assistant engineers,[d] who shall be appointed by the Common Council, upon the nomination of the Mayor, and whose powers and duties shall be prescribed by said Council. [*As amended by Laws of* 1864, *page* 23.]

Fire Wardens.

(§ 258.) SEC. 4. The Mayor, members of the Common Council, Marshal and Deputy Marshals, by virtue of their offices, shall be Fire Wardens, and the Common Council may annually appoint one or more resident electors of each ward, Fire Wardens thereof, who shall hold office until removed, or their successors be appointed and qualified.

Powers and duties of fire companies and firemen.

(§ 259.) SEC. 5. Each fire company shall have power to appoint its own officers, make by-laws and regulations for its good government, not inconsistent with this act or the ordinances and regulations of the Common Council, and may impose and collect such fines for the non-attendance or neglect of duty of any of its

---

[c] This power is now vested in the Fire Commission, Section 443.

[d] See Section 435.

members, as may be prescribed by the by-laws or regulations of said company, and it shall be the duty of each fire company, subject to the control and regulations of the Common Council, to take the care and management of the fire engine, hose, hook, ladder and other fire apparatus and implements of such company, to keep the same in good and perfect repair, and upon any fire alarm or breaking out of any fire within said city, it shall be the duty of each member of a fire company forthwith to repair to the engine house of such company and thence proceed, without delay, with its engine, hose or other fire apparatus and implements, to the place of such fire, and there use the same, and otherwise labor for the extinguishment of such fire, under the direction of the Chief Engineer or other officers present, who may be empowered by the Common Council to give orders and directions at a fire in relation to the extinguishment thereof.

Meetings of companies.

(§ 260.) SEC. 6. It shall also be the duty of each fire company to assemble once in each month, or as often as may be directed by the Common Council, for the purpose of working and examining its engine, hose or other fire apparatus and implements, and putting and keeping them in perfect order and repair.

Powers and duties of Fire Wardens.

(§ 261.) SEC. 7. Fire Wardens appointed for the several wards shall have power, at all reasonable times, and it shall be their duty to enter into and examine all the dwelling houses, out houses, lots and yards in their respective wards; to ascertain how ashes are kept; to direct full obedience to all ordinances of the Common Council, relating to the prevention of fires,[c] and to report

[c] See 36th subdivision of section 103, page 63.

to the Common Council all infractions thereof; and the Mayor, members of the Common Council, Marshal and Deputy Marshals, acting as Fire Wardens, shall have the same powers and perform the same duties within the limits of said city which the appointed Fire Wardens may have and perform within the limits of their respective wards.

Exemption of firemen.

(§ 262.) SEC. 8. Every person, while serving as fireman, or who shall have served as fireman in said city for a term of five years, shall be exempted from serving as a juror and from doing militia duty, except in case of war, invasion or insurrection.[f] A certificate of such service, under the seal of the corporation, signed by the Mayor and Clerk of the city, or as prescribed in the act incorporating "The Fire Department of the City of Detroit," approved February 14th, 1840, shall be, in all courts and places, evidence of such exemption. The Engineers, Assistant Engineers, Fire Wardens appointed for the several wards, and members of engine, hook, hose, ladder and other fire companies lawfully organized, shall be deemed firemen of said city within the meaning of this section.

Powers of certain officers at fires.

(§ 263.) SEC. 9. The Mayor, any member of the Common Council, Engineer or Fire Warden, may order all able-bodied persons present at a fire to assist and labor in the extinguishment thereof and in the preservation of property, and may also order all persons present at a fire, not belonging to the Fire Department or not lawfully employed in its service or in the preservation

---

[f] See Compiled Laws, sec. 1629, exempting Firemen from jury and militia duty. Also, sec. 438, *post*.

and custody of property, to remove from the vicinity of such fire all property exposed by reason thereof.[g]

(§ 264.) SEC. 10. Whenever any person shall refuse to obey any lawful order of the Mayor, any member of the Common Council, Engineer, or Fire Warden at any fire, it shall be lawful for the officer giving such order, to arrest or to direct orally the Marshal, any Deputy Marshal, Constable, Policeman, or any citizen, to arrest such person and confine him temporarily, until such fire be extinguished; and such officers, or any of them, may arrest or direct the arrest and temporary confinement of any person at such fire, who shall be intoxicated or disorderly.

Power of officer at fire to arrest for disobed'nce of order.

(§ 265.) SEC. 11. Upon the breaking out of any fire within said city, the Marshal, Deputy Marshals, Constables and appointed Fire Wardens shall immediately repair to the place of such fire with their staves, and aid and assist in extinguishing such fire, and in removing, securing, preserving and preventing from being stolen, any goods or other property exposed by reason of such fire, and shall in all respects be obedient to the lawful orders of the Mayor, any member of the Common Council or Engineer present.[g]

Duties of officers upon breaking out of fires.

(§ 266.) SEC. 12. Engine, hose, hook, ladder and other fire companies, now organized within the city of Detroit, shall be continued in their organization until dissolved or disbanded, and the present firemen, fire engineers and fire wardens of said city are hereby continued in office until removed; but said companies, firemen and fire engineers shall, in all respects, be

Present fire companies continued until dissolved or disbanded.

[g] See 36th subdivision of section 103, p. 63.

governed by this act in respect to their powers, duties, liabilities, term and tenure of office, and by the ordinances, rules and regulations of the Common Council made pursuant to the provisions of this act.

Fire Marshal. (§ 267.) SEC. 13. The Common Council may, on the nomination of the Mayor, appoint a Fire Marshal,[h] whose duty it shall be to investigate the cause and origin of all fires which shall happen within the city, and for Powers. that purpose he shall have power to administer oaths, and examine witnesses touching such investigations. He shall have power to issue subpœnas requiring the attendance of witnesses. Disobedience to such subpœnas shall render the witness liable to the same penalties as for like disobedience in courts of record. [*As added by Laws of* 1861, *p.* 198.]

Testimony taken on investigation. (§ 268.) SEC. 14. The testimony taken on such investigation shall be reduced to writing, and signed by the witness, when the Marshal shall proceed to determine, Cause of fires. from the circumstances proved before him, the true cause and origin of the fire, and reduce the same to writing, under his hand, and report the same, together with the testimony, to the Common Council. [*As added by Laws of* 1861, *p.* 198.]

To make complaints. (§ 269.) SEC. 15. If in the course of such investigation, or at the close thereof, he shall have good reason to believe that any person or persons willfully set, or caused such fire to be set, he shall forthwith make complaint before some magistrate having jurisdiction in such cases, and cause the parties complained of to be apprehended. [*As added by Laws of* 1861, *p.* 199.]

---

[h] This office is abolished by section 441, and the powers and duties devolved upon the Fire Marshal, created by section 435.

(§ 270.) SEC. 16. The term of the office of Fire Marshal shall be one year from the second Tuesday of January in each year, and until a successor shall be appointed and enter upon the duties of the office. He shall perform such other duties as the Common Council shall direct. He shall be subject to removal in the same manner provided for the removal of other officers appointed by the Common Council. The person first appointed shall hold the office until the second Tuesday in January, 1862, subject to removal as aforesaid. [*As added by Laws of* 1861, *p.* 199.]

Term of.

How removed.

CHAPTER XI.

MISCELLANEOUS PROVISIONS.

SECTION
271. New corporation to pay debts of old.
272. Rights vested in corporation.
273. Actions pending continued.
274. Mayor's Court continued until Recorder's Court established.
275. Removal of Records.
276. Causes of action continued.
277. Certain acts not invalidated.
278. Ordinances to remain in force.
279. Inhabitants not incompetent as jurors in certain cases.
280. Clerk's certificate to be conclusive evidence.
281. Records or certified copies presumptive evidence.
282. Proof of publication of ordinances.
283. Printed ordinances *prima facie* evidence of their enactment.
284. Perjury.
285. Charter a public act.
286. Act may be amended.

New corporation to pay debts of old.

(§ 271.) SECTION 1. The corporation created by this act, shall pay and discharge all the debts, obligations, contracts, and liabilities of "The Mayor, Recorder, Aldermen, and Freemen of the City of Detroit,"[a] and suits may be brought and prosecuted thereon, against said corporation, in law or equity,[b] to the same effect as they could be brought and prosecuted against "The Mayor, Recorder, Aldermen, and Freemen of the City of Detroit," if this act had not been passed.

Rights vested in corporation und'r this act.

(§ 272.) SEC. 2. All property, real, personal, and mixed, and rights of property, in law or in equity, and all debts, fines, penalties, forfeitures, rights, and causes of action, and all rights and powers not inconsistent

[a] See Section 1, *ante.*

[b] In Root vs. City of Ann Arbor, 3 Mich., 433, it was held, that Justices of the Peace had no jurisdiction against municipal corporations. So in Gurney vs. City of St. Clair, 11 Mich., 203. See Comp. Laws, Sec. 3700. Section 1, *ante*, authorizes the Corporation to be sued in any "Court of Record, *and in any other place whatsoever.*"

with the provisions of this act, which belong, have accrued, or may accrue to "The Mayor, Recorder, Aldermen, and Freemen of the City of Detroit," or to the inhabitants of the City of Detroit, in their corporate capacity, shall be, and the same are hereby declared to be fully and absolutely vested in the corporation created by this act, to be held subject to the provisions hereof, and may be prosecuted for, and recovered or claimed, asserted and maintained by said corporation, in its own name, or in any other lawful manner.

(§ 273.) SEC. 3. All writs, prosecutions, actions, and causes of action, now in suit, and instituted or commenced, by or against "The Mayor Recorder, Aldermen, and Freemen of the City of Detroit," shall continue, and may be prosecuted to the end thereof, to the same effect as if this act had not been passed.

Actions pendi'g continued.

(§ 274.) SEC. 4. The Mayor's Court, of the City of Detroit, except as herein otherwise provided, shall continue, with its powers and jurisdiction, as if this act had not been passed, until the organization of the Recorder's Court, under this act, and from and after such organization, its powers and jurisdiction shall cease.[c]

Mayor's court continued until Recorder's court organized.

(§ 275.) SEC. 5. On the organization of the Recorder's Court, all books, records, recognizances, and papers, filed in or pertaining to the Mayor's Court of the City of Detroit and all proceedings, commenced or cognizable therein,[d] shall be removed and transferred to, or commenced in said Recorder's Court, and proceeded with in

Removal of records, etc. to Recorder's court.

---

[c] See Section 156 continuing Mayor's Court until organization of Recorder's Court.

[d] See Sections 328, 519.

conformity with its powers and jurisdiction, to the same effect as if this act had not been passed.

Causes of action continued.

(§ 276.) SEC. 6. All causes of action, rights, and liabilities of individuals of the State, and of bodies corporate, shall continue and remain, as if this act had not been passed, except of "The Mayor, Recorder, Aldermen, and Freemen of the City of Detroit," whose act of incorporation is hereby repealed.

Certain acts not invalidated.

(§ 277.) SEC. 7. This act shall not invalidate any legal act done by "The Mayor, Recorder, Aldermen, and Freemen of the City of Detroit," or by the Common Council, or any officer of said city, now or heretofore in office.

Ordinances to remain in force.

(§ 278.) SEC. 8. All ordinances, by-laws, regulations, resolutions, and rules of the Common Council of the City of Detroit, now in force, and not inconsistent with this act, shall remain in force until altered, amended, or repealed by the Common Council, under this act, and after the same shall take effect.

Inhabitants of Detroit not to be incompetent as jurors, etc.

(§ 279.) SEC. 9. No person shall be an incompetent judge, justice of the peace, or other officer, witness, or juror, by reason of his being an inhabitant or freeholder in the City of Detroit, in any prosecution or proceeding in the Recorder's Court, in any action or proceeding in which the corporation shall be a party in interest, or in any judicial or other proceeding.

Clerk's certificate to be conclusive evidence.

(§ 280.) SEC. 10. The certificate of the Clerk, required by this act,[e] specifying the day on which he may have presented any ordinance, resolution, or proceeding to the Mayor, for his approval or disapproval,

---

[e] See Section 90.

or a copy thereof, certified by such Clerk, under the seal of the corporation, shall, in all courts, places, and proceedings, be conclusive evidence of the facts therein stated.

Records or certified copies to be presumptiv' evidence.

(§ 281.) SEC. 11. The record of any ordinance enacted, and of the time of its first publication, made by the Clerk, as required in this act, or a copy thereof, certified by such Clerk, under the seal of the corporation, shall be presumptive evidence in all courts, places, and proceedings, of the due passage of such ordinance, of its having been duly published, and of the time of its first publication.[f] Copies of all other records and papers, duly filed in and pertaining to the office of the Clerk, certified by him, under the seal of the corporation, shall be evidence in all courts and places, to the same effect as the originals would be, if produced.[g]

Pr'of of publication of ordinances, etc.

(§ 282.) SEC. 12. Proof of the requisite publication of any ordinance, resolution, or other proceeding, required to be published in any newspaper, by the affidavit of a printer or publisher thereof, taken before any officer authorized to administer oaths and take affidavits, and duly filed with the Clerk of the city, or any other competent proof, shall, in all courts and places, be conclusive evidence of the legal publication of such ordinance, resolution, or other proceeding.

(§ 283.) SEC. 13. All ordinances and by-laws of the Common Council, printed and published by their authority, shall, in all courts, places, and proceedings, be received without further proof as *prima facie* evidence thereof, and of their legal enactment and publication.

---

[f] See Section 92.

[g] See Comp. Laws, Sections 3196, 4311.

Perjury.

(§ 284.) SEC. 14. Any person required to take any oath or affirmation, or to make any affidavit or statement, under oath or affirmation, under any provision of this act, who shall, under such oath or affirmation, in any such statement or affidavit, or otherwise, willfully swear falsely as to any material matter, shall be guilty of perjury, and may be prosecuted therefor, and, on conviction, punished, as in the case of perjury under the general laws of this State.[h]

Public act.

(§ 285.) SEC. 15. This act shall be deemed a public act, and shall be construed benignly and favorably for any beneficial purpose therein intended.

This act may be amended.

(§ 286.) SEC. 16. This act may at any time be altered or amended by the Legislature of this State.

---

[h] See Section 45, *ante*. Also, Comp. Laws, sections 49, 128, 5820.

CHAPTER XII.

ACTS CONTINUED AND REPEALED.

SECTION
287. Acts continued in force.

SECTION
288. Acts repealed.

(§ 287.) SECTION 1. The following acts and part of acts, being now in force, shall be continued, subject to this act, viz.:

The act entitled[a] "An Act to incorporate the Fire Department of the City of Detroit," approved February 14th, 1840.

The act entitled[b] "An Act to amend the laws relative to supplying the City of Detroit with pure and wholesome water, and to provide for the completion and management of the Detroit Water Works," approved February 14th, 1853.[c]

The act entitled "An Act to authorize the Water Commissioners of the City of Detroit to loan money for the purpose of extending and improving the Water Works of said city," approved February 6th, 1855;[d]

All acts and parts of acts relating to schools in the City of Detroit;[e]

---

[a] See Section 442.

[b] See Section 448, *et post.*

[c] See Part II, Chapter II.

[d] See section 336. Section 337 embraces an act for a similar purpose.

[e] See Part II, Chapter IX.

The act entitled "An act amending an act relative to the registry of certain deeds, approved March 9th, 1844," approved May 7th, 1846;[f]

The act entitled "An Act relative to conveyances in the City of Detroit," approved April 1st, 1850;[g]

The act entitled "An Act to incorporate the City of Detroit Gas Company," approved March 14th, 1849, and all acts amendatory thereof.[h]

Sections eight, nine, ten, eleven, and twelve, of chapter one hundred and three of the Revised Statutes of 1846, relating to the selection and return of jurors from said city, to serve in the Circuit Court for the County of Wayne;[i]

Section forty-nine, of chapter thirty-five, of the Revised Statutes of 1845, relating to Boards of Health in cities and villages;[j]

The act entitled "An Act to establish a Police Court in the City of Detroit," approved April 2d, 1850, and all acts and parts of acts amendatory thereof;[k]

The act entitled "An Act to provide for draining certain low lands in the vicinity of Detroit," approved March 29th, 1849;[l]

(§ 288.) SEC. 2. The following acts and parts of acts are hereby repealed, viz.:

---

[f] See section 572.

[g] See section 573.

[h] See section 575, *et post.*

[i] See section 560, *et post.*

[j] See section 567.

[k] See Part II, Chapter IV.

[l] See Part II, Chapter X.

The act of the Legislative Council of the Territory of Michigan, granting a charter of incorporation to "The Mayor, Recorder, Aldermen, and Freemen of the City of Detroit," and entitled "An Act relative to the City of Detroit," approved April 4th, 1827, and all acts and parts of acts amending or altering said act or charter, and not hereby continued; and all other acts and parts of acts relating to the City of Detroit, and not hereby continued, the subjects whereof are revised and re-enacted, in this act, or which are repugnant to or inconsistent with the provisions of this act.

CHAPTER XIII.[a]

POLICE DEPARTMENT.[b]

SECTION
289. Police Commissioners; how appointed; term of office; powers, clerk of; compensation.
290. Power to subpœna witnesses on investigation.
291. Who may suspend policemen; trial of; notice; penalty.
292. Chief of Police; how appointed; powers and duties.
293. Police Station.
294. Board power to appoint watchmen.
295. Additional policemen; how appointed.
296. Board to make rules and regulations.
297. Power to arrest without warrant.
298. Council may confer on Police Justice jurisdiction of offenses against ordinances.
299. Duty of Police Justice to attend station-houses.
300. Council may designate Justice of the Peace to act in case of sickness or absence of Police Justice.
301. Council may offer rewards.

Board of police commissioners. (§ 289.) SECTION 1. The Mayor and two other persons, who shall be appointed by the Common Council, shall constitute a Board of Police Commissioners for the Powers of. City of Detroit; such Board, or a majority of them, shall have full power to try and determine all complaints against the Chief of Police, or any policeman or watchman of the city, and to remove them, or any of them, summarily, on conviction for insubordination, neglect of duty, or violation of any of the ordinances, or the rules and regulations made, or hereafter to be made, for the government of the Police Department of the Clerk of. city of Detroit. The City Clerk shall be the clerk of

[a] This chapter was added to the Charter as Chapter XIII, by Laws of 1861, p. 199.

[b] The first nine sections of this act, and the amendatory sections of Laws of 1864, p. 20, are repealed by Section 38 of the Act to establish a Police Government of the City of Detroit. Laws of 1867, Vol. II, p. 99. See 375, *post*.

said board, and shall keep its records. Said Commissioners shall receive no compensation. The persons first appointed by the Common Council shall hold their office, one until the second Tuesday of January, A. D. eighteen hundred and sixty-five, and the other until the second Tuesday of January, eighteen hundred and sixty-seven. All persons subsequently appointed, save for the purpose of filling unexpired terms, shall hold office for the term of four years, and until their successors are appointed and qualified. Such Commissioners may be removed for the same causes, and upon the same proceedings, as a member of the Common Council. In case any vacancy occurs, the Common Council shall appoint some person to fill the unexpired portion of the term. [*As amended by Laws of* 1864, *p.* 20.]

Terms of office.

Removal.

Vacancies.

(§ 290.) SEC. 2. Such Board, when convened for the purposes mentioned in the preceding section, shall be vested with full power to subpœna witnesses, issue warrants to compel the attendance of witnesses, administer oaths, take and record testimony, and to do such other acts as may lawfully be done by any court, for the purpose mentioned in section one of this chapter.

Power to subpœna witnesses on investigation.

(§ 291.) SEC. 3. The Mayor or Chief of Police may suspend any Policeman from his office, on charge of misconduct, until the trial and decision of the Board of Police Commissioners shall be had. Notice in writing, that charges or accusations are made, or are to be presented before the Board of Police Commissioners, shall be given to such member or members of the Police Department as are accused of official misconduct, neglect of duty, or other offenses to be tried by said Board, at least twenty-four hours before such trial shall be had.

Who may suspend policemen.

Trial of.

Notice.

Penalty. The Board may continue the suspension, remove the accused from office, or restore him to duty.

Chief of police and watchmen. (§ 292.) SEC. 4. The Chief of Police, and all policemen and watchmen, provided for in this act, save those mentioned in section six,[c] shall be appointed by the Common Council, on the nomination of the Board of Police Commissioners, and shall hold their office until removed or suspended, as provided for in this act. Powers of chief of police. The Chief of Police shall, under said Board, be the chief Executive Officer of the Police Department; he shall have the same power conferred upon policemen by this act, and shall posess all the powers of the Police Justice of the city of Detroit, to entertain complaints for criminal offences, and to issue warrants for the arrest of persons charged with such offences, but such warrants shall be made returnable before the Police Justice of said city, at his office. He shall also have power to commit persons charged with criminal offences, until examination had before the Police Justice; Duties of. he shall obey and cause the Police Department to obey the rules and regulations prescribed by the ordinances of the Common Council, and the rules and regulations prescribed by the Board of Police Commissioners, and shall perform such other duties as shall, from time to time, be prescribed by the Common Council. Policemen, oath of. All policemen appointed under this act shall, before entering upon the duties of the office, make and file with the City Clerk the official oath provided for by section fifteen, of chapter two, of said charter. Powers of. After filing said official oath, the policemen so appointed shall have power to serve any summons, subpœna, warrant,

---

[c] See Section 294.

order, notice, paper, or process whatever, issued or directed by any justice of the peace, judge, court, or officer whatever, in the execution of the laws of the State, for the prevention of crimes and the punishment of offenders, or of the police laws and regulations of the State or city, in any proceeding collateral to, or connected with, the execution of such general laws, or police laws and regulations. They shall have power to serve process for any violations of the city ordinances, and, generally, shall have and exercise the powers as conservators of the peace which township constables, under the general laws of the State, possess, but such policemen shall have no power to serve any paper or process in any civil action, or any paper connected therewith. It shall be the duty of such policemen, or such of them as may be designated, upon the requirement of the Board or Chief of Police, to at once report themselves at any designated place in the city, and to enter upon and continue the performance of the active duties of their office, until the Common Council, said Board, or said Chief, notify them that they are no longer required to perform such active service; for the time engaged in such active service, each member so engaged shall be paid such sum as shall be recommended by the Board and approved by the Common Council: *Provided, however,* That if the Council does not approve the sum agreed upon by the Board, it may fix the amount of compensation at any sum not exceeding that agreed upon by the Board. Policemen shall receive no pay, save for the time when they are so engaged in active service, nor shall they be required to render any service save when called on as hereinbefore provided. [*As amended by Laws of* 1864, *p.* 21.]

Duties of policemen.

Compensation of.

Police station. (§ 293.) SEC. 5. The Common Council shall provide suitable accommodation for the Police, to be designated "The Police Station."

Board may call into active service all policemen. (§ 294.) SEC. 6. The said Board of Police Commissioners shall have power, whenever, in their judgment, the safety or the interest of the city require it, to organize and call into active service, directly or through the Chief of Police, all or such number of the policemen so appointed as they deem necessary, and to dismiss them, or any portion of them, from such active service as to them shall seem proper: Proviso. *Provided, however*, That whenever it is deemed expedient, the Common Council may require said board to increase or diminish the number of such men in such active service, and it shall be the duty of the Board to comply with such requisition of the Council. Watchmen, powers of. Said Board shall also have power to appoint watchmen, without compensation, who shall possess the same powers, as conservators of the peace, which township constables possess under the general laws of the State. [*As amended by Laws of* 1864, *p.* 21.]

Additional policemen; how appointed. (§ 295.) SEC. 7. The Common Council, on the nomination of the Board of Police Commissioners, when, in their opinion, it is necessary for the preservation of the peace and good order of the city, may appoint additional temporary Policemen, but such appointment shall not continue beyond forty-eight hours, unless otherwise ordered by the Common Council.

Board power to make rules and regulations. (§ 296.) SEC. 8. The Board of Police Commissioners shall have power, and it shall be their duty, from time to time, to prescribe the duties, and make such rules and regulations for the management and government of the Police Department, as they shall think proper, not inconsistent with the provisions of this chapter, and the ordinances of the Common Council.

(§ 297.) SEC. 9. Whenever any person or persons shall violate any of the ordinances of the city, relative to breaches of the peace, any member of the police department may, under general regulations, to be prescribed by the Board of Police Commissioners, and without process, arrest such person or persons, and take them before the Chief of Police, and make complaint, who is empowered to hold to bail or commit such person or persons, to appear before the Police Court, or the Recorder's Court.

Power to arrest without warrant.

(§ 298.) SEC. 10. The Police Justice of the City of Detroit[d] shall have jurisdiction to hear and determine such offenses for any violations of the city ordinances, as the Common Council shall, by ordinance, prescribe.[e] All fines so imposed and collected by said Police Justice, shall be paid into the city treasury immediately after their collection.

Councilmay give Police Justice jurisdiction of offenses againstordinances.

(§ 299.) SEC. 11. It shall be the duty of the Police Justice to attend the police station house at such times as shall be prescribed by the Common Council; he shall summarily examine into the case of every person confined in said station house, and if he adjudge any person guilty of vagrancy, disorderly conduct, or any violation of the city ordinances, relative to breaches of the peace, he may convict such person or persons thereof, and commit him or her to the Wayne County

Duty of Police Justice.

To attend station houses.

[d] See "Act to establish a Police Court in the City of Detroit," approved April 2, 1850. Section 381, *et post.*

[e] As to further jurisdiction, see sections 382, 383, 384.

12

jail, or house of correction, for not more than six months, and impose a fine not exceeding fifty dollars, and in default of the immediate payment thereof, to commit such person or persons to the Wayne County jail, or to the house of correction, for a term not exceeding six months, or until such fine be paid. All fines imposed, shall be paid into the city treasury. He shall detain, for examination, all persons charged with offenses against the laws of the State, and not punishable under the ordinances of the city, as aforesaid, for examination before the Police Court: *Provided*, The Common Council, at any regular meeting thereof, may designate any Justice of the Peace of the City of Detroit, who shall have the power to perform the duties prescribed by this section; but in case of the death, absence from the city, sickness, or other disability, the Police Justice shall perform said duties; said Police Justice, or Justice of the Peace, shall receive such compensation for performing the duties required by this and the foregoing section, as the Common Council shall prescribe, and the Police Justice, and the Justice of the Peace, so designated, shall have exclusive jurisdiction in all cases properly cognizable by the Police Justice.

Fines; to whom paid.

Proviso.

Council to designate Justice of the Peace to act in case of sickness, etc., of Police Justice.

(§ 300.) SEC. 12. The Common Council shall designate, on the second Tuesday of January in each year, or at some regular meeting thereof, one of the Justices of the Peace elected in said city, to act as Police Justice, in case of the death, sickness, absence, or other disability of the Police Justice; and the Justice so designated, shall, during such disability, or the continuance of any vacancy in the office of Police Justice, have exclusive jurisdiction of all cases properly cognizable in the

Power of Justice of the Peace.

Police Court of said city, and shall have, and may exercise the same powers as may be exercised by the Police Justice of said city; and the Justice so exercising the duties of Police Justice, shall be paid such compensation as the Common Council shall direct — such compensation to be drawn from the fund applicable to the payment of the Police Justice. Such designation may be revoked by the Common Council, upon the recommendation of the Mayor, and another Justice designated. The Justice first designated, under the above provision, shall hold his office until the second Tuesday of January, eighteen hundred and sixty-two. The Police Justice of said city may be removed in the same manner and for the same causes as Justices of the Peace.

Compensation.

How app'ntment is revoked.

How Police Justice removed.

(§ 301.) SEC. 13. The Common Council shall have power, by a vote of two-thirds of all the Aldermen elected, to authorize the Board of Police Commissioners to offer a reward for the detection and apprehension of any offender against the city ordinances, or of the perpetrator of any high crime or misdemeanor, committed within the city, to be paid on the conviction of such offender or criminal.

Council may offer rewards.

PART SECOND.

ACTS OF THE LEGISLATURE

RELATING TO THE

CITY OF DETROIT.

CHAPTER I.

CORPORATE LIMITS OF THE CITY OF DETROIT.

SECTION
302. Boundaries.
303. Wards.
304. Election of Aldermen and other Ward Officers.

SECTION
305. Place of holding elections in Ninth and Tenth Wards; mode of conducting elections.
306. Appointment of persons to fill ward offices in Ninth and Tenth wards.
307. Act to take immediate effect.

An Act to Enlarge the Corporate Limits of the City of Detroit.

[*Approved February 12th*, 1857. *Laws of* 1857, *p.* 209.]

(§ 302.) SECTION 1. *The People of the State of Michigan enact*, That from and after the passage of this act the following district of country shall constitute the City of Detroit, to wit: Beginning at the national boundary line in Detroit River on the continuation of the dividing line between private claims numbered (21) twenty-one and (78) seventy-eight, as confirmed by the Board of Land Commissioners of the United States; thence northerly along said dividing line to the southerly line of the Detroit, Monroe and Toledo Railroad; thence north-easterly along said line to the present western boundary of the City of Detroit; thence northerly along said boundary to the north-western corner of said Boundaries.

city; thence eastwardly along the present northerly boundary line of said city to the north-east corner of private claim number (14) fourteen, known as the St. Aubin farm; thence southerly along the line between said claim number (14) fourteen and private claim number (91) ninety-one, to a point where the northerly line of Leland street, when extended in a right line eastwardly from the said city, would intersect the line between said claims; thence eastwardly at right angles with the side lines of said claims to the easterly line of private claims number (9) nine and (454) four hundred and fifty-four; thence southerly along the line between private claims number (9) nine and (454) four hundred and fifty-four and private claims number (11) eleven and (453) four hundred and fifty-three, being between the farms known as the McDougal and Chapoton farms, to the northerly line of the Fort Gratiot turnpike; thence north-easterly along said northerly line of said turnpike to the easterly line of private claim number (15) fifteen; thence southerly along the easterly line of said claim number (15) fifteen to said national boundary line; thence westwardly along said national boundary to the place of beginning.

Wards. (§ 303.) SEC. 2. So much of the above described district as lies below, or westward, of the present corporate limits of said city, shall constitute one ward, to be known and designated as the ninth ward of said city; and so much of said district as lies above, or eastward, of the present corporate limits of said city, shall constitute one ward, to be known and designated as the tenth ward of said city. And from and after the time above fixed for the taking effect of this act, the said district hereby annexed to said city shall be subject to all laws, ordinances and regulations which shall at any time be in force over the remainder of said city, and shall cease to be subject to the regulations or government of any other township: *Provided*, That the Common Council of the City of Detroit may at any time alter or divide the said wards in the manner provided by the Charter of said city for the regulation or alteration of the present wards thereof.[a] Proviso.

(§ 304.) SEC. 3. There shall be elected, at the next ensuing charter election to be held in said city, two persons in each of said wards to serve as Aldermen, one in each ward to serve one year, and one in each ward to serve for two years, and the time of service for which each Alderman is elected shall be designated on the ballots cast for such officers respectively; and such other ward officers shall be elected at such election, as are provided for the other wards of said city, and the terms of office of all such Aldermen and officers shall correspond with those of similar Aldermen and officers in such other wards. Election of Aldermen. Other ward officers.

(§ 305.) SEC. 4. The Common Council of the City of Detroit may at any time before said charter election appoint the places for holding the same in the said ninth and tenth wards, and said election shall be conducted in like manner with those in the other wards of said city, except that, at eight o'clock in the forenoon of the day for holding said charter election, the electors of said wards present at the place of holding the polls shall elect, *viva voce*, three of their own number to act Place of hold'g charter election in ninth and tenth wards may be appointed by Council. Modeofconduct'g election therein.

---

[a] See Section 2, p. 10. Also, Section 506.

as inspectors of said election, who shall be sworn rightfully to discharge the duties of such inspectors, (which oath either of them may administer to the others,) and who shall be the legal inspectors of said election, and said inspectors in each ward may appoint one or more electors of each of said wards to act as constables at and about the polls of such wards during said election day.

Persons may be appoint'd to fill ward offices.

(§ 306.) SEC. 5. The Common Council may appoint any persons to fill any office in either of said wards, which is provided for in the other wards of said city, (except that of Alderman,) and the officers so appointed shall continue to act, until their successors are elected at said charter election, and are duly qualified, and no longer.

To take immediate effect.

SEC. 6. This act shall take effect and be in force from and after its passage.

CHAPTER II.

BOARD OF WATER COMMISSIONERS.

SECTION
307. Board of Commissioners created; Powers and seal of.
308. Term of office; Vacancies; how filled.
309. President and Secretary.
310. Power to borrow money; registry of bonds.
311. Duty to supply water.
312. May employ Superintendent; Commissioners to receive no compensation.
313. May purchase land, etc.
314. May construct reservoirs and fountains.
315. Assessment of water rates; Lien on property; By-laws.
316. Sale of property to pay water rates.
317. Record of proceedings.
318. Report to Common Council.
319. Surplus funds to be invested; payment of bonds; new bonds; purchase of bonds, and canceling old bonds.
320. Oath of Commissioners.
321. Materials exempt from execution.
322. Commissioners may be removed; Vacancy; how filled.

SECTION
323. Power to enter on lands and water, to make surveys.
324. In case of disagreement, appraisers to be appointed.
325. Confirmation by Judge; Payment; Fee of property.
326. Where money to be deposited; City Treasurer to pay on draft.
327. Injuries to property; Pollution of water.
328. Penalty for boring pipe or connecting logs without permission.
329. Power to extend pipes and build reservoir beyond city limits.
330. Report of Commissioners to Council as to interest; Council to raise same by tax.
331. Commissioners not to be interested in contracts.
332. Present works conveyed to Commissioners.
332. Board may make by-laws, to be entered in a book.
334. Acts repealed.
335. Act may be amended or repealed.
336. Board authorized to borrow money.
337. Same.

An Act to amend the Laws relative to supplying the City of Detroit with pure and wholesome water.

[*Approved February* 14, 1853. *Laws of* 1853, *p.* 180.]

(§ 307.) SECTION 1. *The People of the State of Michigan enact*, That Shubael Conant, Henry Ledyard, Edmund A. Brush, William R. Noyes and James A. Van Dyke, be, and they are hereby named and constituted as a "Board of Water Commissioners of the City of Detroit;" who, and their successors in office, shall

Name and style.

be known by the name and style of the "Board of Water Commissioners of the City of Detroit,"[a] and by that name shall have power to contract, sue and be sued, to purchase, hold and convey personal and real estate, to have a common seal, to alter and change the same at pleasure, to make by-laws and ordinances, and do all legal acts which may be necessary and proper to carry out the effect, intent and object of this Act.

Powers.

Seal.

Term of office.

(§ 308.) SEC. 2. The said Commissioners shall hold their offices respectively for the term of three, four, five, six and seven years, from the first Tuesday in May, of the year one thousand eight hundred and fifty-three. Said Commissioners shall, within sixty days after the passage of this act, decide by lot their respective terms, which decision shall be notified by a written statement, to the Common Council of said city, which shall be entered of record on the books of the said Common Council; and at their first regular meeting in the month of April, in the year one thousand eight hundred and fifty-six, and annually thereafter, the said Common Council shall elect and appoint a citizen of said city, being a qualified voter and a freeholder, as a Commissioner, who shall hold his office for five years from the first Tuesday in the May next following:[b] *Provided*, That this section shall not be so construed as to disqualify any member of the said Board for re-appointment. And in case of the death or resignation, or removal from the city, of any of said Commissioners, the Common Council shall, as soon thereafter as possible, appoint to fill

Vacancy; how filled.

[a] See Section 5, *ante*.

[b] See Section 16, *ante*.

such vacancy, for the remainder of the term, some citizen of said city, being a qualified voter and a freeholder.

(§ 309.) SEC. 3. The said Commissioners shall choose one of their own number as President, who shall hold his office until the first Tuesday of May next ensuing the date of his election; they shall also appoint some suitable person as Secretary, who shall hold his office at the pleasure of the Board. And in case of the death, resignation, or removal from the city of the President, the said Commissioners shall have power to fill the vacancy so happening as in the first instance.

President and Secretary.

(§ 310.) SEC. 4. The said Commissioners shall have power to loan, from time to time, upon the best terms they can make, after giving public notice by advertising in the city papers for sixty days, and in one paper in Boston and two in New York, for such time as they shall deem expedient, a sum of money not exceeding two hundred and fifty thousand dollars,[c] upon the credit of said city of Detroit, and shall have authority to issue bonds pledging the faith and credit of said city for the payment of the principal and interest of said bonds, which bonds shall issue under the seal of said Board of Commissioners, and shall be signed by them, or a majority of them, and bearing interest not exceeding eight per cent. per annum. And it shall be the duty of said Commissioners to cause to be kept an accurate register of all bonds issued by them, showing the number, date and amount of each bond, and to whom the same was issued; and it shall also be their duty to cause to be

Power to loan money on bonds.

Registry of bonds.

[c] Power to make additional loans is conferred by Sections 337, 338, *post*.

Copy furnished Auditor.

furnished to the auditor of said city a copy of such register, as soon as the same is made, which shall be preserved by said Auditor, and copied into the records of said city.[d]

Supply of water.

(§ 311.) SEC. 5. It shall be the duty of said Commissioners to examine and consider all matters relative to supplying the city of Detroit with a sufficient quantity of pure and wholesome water, to be taken from the Detroit River, or such other source as may be deemed expedient, for the use of its inhabitants.

Power to employ Superintendents, etc.

(§ 312.) SEC. 6. Said Commissioners shall have power to employ superintendents, clerks, collectors, assessors, engineers, surveyors and such other persons as, in their opinion, may be necessary to enable them to perform their duties under this act, and to specify the duties of such persons so employed, and to fix their compensation: *Provided*, That in no case shall said Commissioners receive, directly or indirectly, any compensation for their own services.

Commissi'ners not to rec've compensation.

Power to purchase land, etc.

(§ 313.) SEC. 7. Said Commissioners shall have power, and it is hereby made their duty, as soon as may be, after the necessary funds shall have been procured, as herein provided, to purchase such land and materials, and to construct such reservoirs, buildings, machinery and fixtures, as shall be deemed necessary or desirable to furnish a full supply of water for public and private use in said city.

Reservoirs, hydrants, jets, etc.

(§ 314.) SEC. 8. Said Commissioners shall have power to construct reservoirs, jets, and fire hydrants, at such localities in said city as they may deem expedient and

---

[d] See Sections 337, 338, *post*.

necessary, and to lay pipes in and through all the alleys and streets of said city; and also to construct in such localities as they may deem expedient, not exceeding one to each block, hydrants, for public use, and to keep the same in repair; and also, with the consent of the Common Council of said city, to construct fountains in the public squares, or such other public grounds of said city as they shall deem expedient. Fount'ins in pub. squares

(§ 315.) SEC. 9. Said Commissioners shall, from time to time, cause to be assessed the water rate to be paid by the owner or occupant of each house or other building having or using water, upon such basis as they shall deem equitable; and such water rate shall become a continuing lien, until paid, upon such house or other building, and upon the lot or lots upon which such house or other building is situated. Assessm't of water rates. Lien on premises.

(§ 316.) SEC. 10. Said Commissioners shall have full power to make and enforce all necessary by-laws, rules and regulations for the collection of said water rates, either by the appointment of collectors to demand the same, requiring payment at the office, shutting off the water, or by a suit at law before any court of competent jurisdiction, or by sale of the lot or premises upon which such rates shall have become a lien: *Provided*, That such sales shall be conducted in the same manner, and shall have the same force, virtue and effect of sales of lots delinquent for city taxes:[e] *And provided, further*, That the attempt to collect said rates by any process above mentioned shall not in any way invalidate the lien upon said lot or premises. Power to make by-laws. Sale of property for non-payment of water rates.

---

[e] See Section 345, *ante*.

Record of proceedi'gs.

(§ 317.) SEC. 11. The said Commissioners shall cause to be kept an accurate record of all proceedings, together with a list of all assessments for water rates, which shall be subject to inspection at all times.

Report to Com. Council.

(§ 318.) SEC. 12. It shall be the duty of said Commissioners to make a report to the Common Council of said city annually, which report shall embrace a statement of the condition and operation of the works, a statement of the funds and securities of said Board, and all debts due and owing to and from said Board, together with an accurate account of their expenses; which statement shall be certified by said Commissioners, and shall be entered of record by the Clerk of said city, and published in such manner as said Common Council may direct.

Surplus funds to be invested.

(§ 319.) SEC. 13. Whenever the receipts of said Board, from water rates, or other sources, shall accumulate so that there shall be a surplus, amounting to a sum of not less than five hundred dollars, not needed for the payment of the current expenses, or the extension of said works, it shall be the duty of the Commissioners, together with the Auditor of said city, who shall be associated with them for that purpose, to invest the same in some safe stocks, or upon other real or personal securities. Such investment shall be made in the name of said Board, and in such manner as to make the same available for the payment of interest and principal of the bonds issued as aforesaid, as soon as may be. It shall be the duty of said Commissioners to pay the interest on such bonds, and as fast as such surplus fund will permit, also the principal, as the bonds become due, as funds for such purpose shall, from time to time,

Payment of bonds and interest.

accumulate. The said Commissioners may, when they have funds for that purpose, purchase the bonds so issued as aforesaid, whether the same have become due or not; and in case the said Commissioners shall at any time not have funds on hand sufficient to meet any of the said bonds at the time when they shall become due, they shall have the right to issue new bonds, for such amount, and on such time as they shall deem expedient, in the place of bonds so becoming due as aforesaid; the said old bonds to be canceled in the registry thereof, and the said new bonds to be recorded in the manner hereinbefore provided.

Purchase of bonds.

New bonds may be issued.

Old bonds canceled and new bonds registered.

(§ 320.) SEC. 14. Before entering upon the duties of their office, said Commissioners shall each take and file with the City Clerk an oath or affirmation,[f] similar to that provided in the case of other officers of said city.

Oath of Commissioners.

(§ 321.) SEC. 15. All materials procured, or partially procured, under a contract with the Commissioners, shall be exempt from execution; but it shall be the duty of the Commissioners to pay the money due for such materials, to the judgment creditor of the contractor, under whose execution such material might otherwise have been sold, upon his producing to them due proof that his execution would have so attached, and such payment shall be held a valid payment on the contract.

Materials exempt fr'm execution.

(§ 322.) SEC. 16. Any member of said Board of Commissioners may at any time be removed, by a vote of two-thirds of the members elect of the Common Council of said city, for sufficient cause, and the proceedings

Commissi'ners may be removed.

[f] For form of oath see Section 17, *ante*.

13

Copy of charges to be served.

in that behalf shall be entered on their journal: *Provided*, That the said Common Council shall previously cause a copy of the charges preferred against the Commissioners sought to be removed, and notice of the time and place of hearing the same, to be served on him ten days, at least, previous to the time so assigned;

Vacancy to be filled.

and in case of such removal, the Common Council shall, at their first regular meeting, or as soon thereafter as may be, appoint some person, being a citizen and a freeholder, to fill such vacancy, and the person so appointed to fill such vacancy may continue in office for the period his predecessor had to serve.[g]

Power to enter upon land or water.

(§ 323.) SEC. 17. The said Commissioners, and, under their direction, their agents, servants, and workmen, are hereby authorized to enter upon any land or water, for the purpose of making surveys, and to agree with the owner of any property, which may be required for the purposes of this act, as to the amount of compensation to be paid to said owner.

In case of disagreem't judge of c'rt to appoint appraisers.

(§ 324.) SEC. 18. In cases of disagreement between the Commissioners and the owner of any property which may be required for the said purposes, or affected by any operation connected therewith, as to the amount of compensation to be paid to such owner, or in case any such owner shall be an infant, a married woman, or insane, or absent from this State, the Judge of the Circuit Court of Wayne County may, upon the application of either party, nominate and appoint three disinterested persons to examine such property, and to estimate the

---

[g] See Section 26, *ante*.

value thereof, or damage sustained thereby, and to report thereon to the said court, without delay.

(§ 325.) SEC. 19. Whenever such report shall have been confirmed by the Circuit Judge of Wayne County, the said Commissioners shall pay to the said owner, or to such person or persons as the court may direct, the sum mentioned in said report, in full compensation for the property so required, or for the damage sustained, as the case may be, and thereupon the said Commissioners shall become seized in fee of such property so required, and shall be discharged from all claim by reason of any such damage.

Confirmat'n by judge.

Payment.

Fee of property.

(§ 326.) SEC. 20. And in case of the refusal, by any owner or owners, person or persons, to receive such sums awarded to them, for property required, or damages sustained, then the said Commissioners shall deposit with the City Treasurer the sums so awarded, subject to the draft of said owner or owners, person or persons; and thereupon the said Commissioners shall become seized in fee of such property, so required, and shall be discharged from all claim by reason of any such damage; and said City Treasurer shall keep strict account of all sums so deposited, and shall pay out the same on the drafts of the owner or owners, person or persons, to the credit of whom such moneys may have been deposited.[h]

Payment, when refused mon'y to be deposited.

City Treasurer to pay on draft.

(§ 327.) SEC. 21. If any person shall willfully do, or cause to be done, any act whereby any work, materials, or property whatsoever, erected or used within the City of Detroit, or elsewhere, by the said Commissioners, or by any person acting under their authority,

Injury to property or pollution of water.

---

[h] See Section 185, *ante*, for similar provision relative to damages in opening streets.

for the purpose of procuring or keeping a supply of water, shall, in any manner, be injured, or shall willfully pollute the water,[1] shall be deemed guilty of misdemeanor, and, upon conviction, shall be punished therefor, as other misdemeanors are punished.

Penalty for boring pipe or connecting logs without permission.

(§ 328.) SEC. 22. If any person shall, without the authority of said Commissioners, as delegated through any of their agents, perforate, or bore, or cause to be perforated or bored, any distributing pipe, or main log, belonging to the water works of said city, or make, or cause to be made, any connection or communication whatever with the said pipes or logs, every person so offending shall, for each offense, forfeit a sum not exceeding fifty dollars and costs of prosecution, to be recovered in the Mayor's Court of said city, or other court of competent jurisdiction.

Power to extend pipes construct reservoirs beyond limits of city.

(§ 329.) SEC. 23. The said Commissioners, in their discretion, shall have power to extend the distributing pipes and mains, and to construct reservoirs, hydrants, and jets, without the limits of said city; and to regulate, protect, and control such portions of said water works, without the bounds of said city, in and after the same manner that they regulate, protect, and control said works within said bounds.

Commisioners to report to Common Coun. what sum may be required to pay interest, etc.

(§ 330.) SEC. 24. It shall be the duty of said Commissioners, at least thirty days before the time fixed by the ordinance of said city for assessing city taxes, to make a special report to the Common Council of said city, what, if any sum, will be needed by said Commissioners, over and above the revenue of said board, to

[1] See 5th subdivision of Section 103, p. 53.

meet the payment of interest or principal of the bonds issued as aforesaid; and it shall be the duty of the Common Council to raise said amount by a special tax, in the same manner as general taxes, to be designated a water tax; and the said amount shall be paid over to said Board by the Treasurer of said city.

Com. Council to raise sum by tax.

(§ 331.) SEC. 25. No one or more of the said Commissioners shall be interested, either directly or indirectly, in any contract entered into by them, with any other person; nor shall they be interested, either directly or indirectly, in the purchase of any material to be used or applied in and about the uses and purposes contemplated by this act.

Com'issioners not to be interested in contracts or purchases of materials.

(§ 332.) SEC. 26. All lands, lots, docks, buildings, machinery, pipes, logs, hydrants, and all fixtures whatsoever, purchased, designated, or used for the present water works of the said City of Detroit, are hereby conveyed to and vested in said Board of Commissioners, who shall have full power to regulate, protect, and control the same; and all the authority, rights, and power heretofore exercised and had by said city, over said works, are hereby continued to and vested in said Board of Commissioners.

Lands, etc., of present works conveyed to the Board of Com'issioners.

(§ 333.) SEC. 27. The said Commissioners are hereby invested with full power to make and enforce such by-laws, regulations, and ordinances as may be necessary to carry into effect the object and intent of this act, and to supply any power or mode not already specified therein, and shall cause all such by-laws, regulations, and ordinances to be entered into a book to be kept for that purpose, and signed by the President and Secretary, which, when so entered and signed, shall be evidence in any court of justice.

Power to make by-laws, etc.

By-laws, etc. to be enter'd in a book.

Acts repealed. (§ 334.) SEC. 28. All acts, or parts of acts, contravening the provisions of this act, are hereby repealed.

Act amended. (§ 335.) SEC. 29. This act may at any time be altered, repealed, or amended.

An Act to authorize the Water Commissioners of the City of Detroit to loan money for the purpose of extending and improving the Water Works of said City.

[*Approved February* 6, 1855. *Laws of* 1855, *p.* 31.]

(§ 336.) SECTION 1. *The People of the State of Michigan enact*, That the Board of Water Commissioners of the City of Detroit shall have power to loan, upon the best terms they can make, and for such time as they shall deem expedient, a sum of money not exceeding two hundred and fifty thousand dollars, upon the credit of said City of Detroit, and shall have authority to issue bonds pledging the faith and credit of said city for the payment of the principal and interest of said bonds; which bonds shall issue under the seal of said Board of Commissioners, and shall be signed by them, or a majority of them, and bearing interest not exceeding eight per cent. per annum. And it shall be the duty of said Commissioners to cause to be kept an accurate register of all bonds issued by them, showing the number, date, and amount of each bond, and to whom the same was issued; and it shall also be their duty to cause to be furnished to the Auditor of said city a copy of such register, as soon as the same is made, which shall be preserved by said Auditor, and copied into the record of said city. And the said sum of money shall be expended by said Commissioners solely for the purpose of extending and improving the Water Works of the City of Detroit.

This act shall take effect immediately.

An act to authorize the Water Commissioners of the City of Detroit to borrow money for the purpose of extending and improving the Water Works of said City.

[*Approved February* 10, 1857. *Laws of* 1857, *p.* 200.]

(§ 337.) SECTION 1. *The People of the State of Michigan enact*, That the Board of Water Commissioners of the City of Detroit shall have power to borrow, upon the best terms they can make, and for such time as they shall deem expedient, a sum of money not exceeding two hundred and fifty thousand dollars, upon the credit of said City of Detroit, and shall have authority to issue bonds, pledging the faith and credit of said city for the payment of the principal and interest of said bonds; which bonds shall issue under the seal of said Board of Commissioners, and shall be signed by them, or a majority of them, and bearing interest not exceeding eight per cent. per annum; and it shall be the duty of said Commissioners to cause to be kept an accurate register of all bonds issued by them, showing the number, date, and amount of each bond, and to whom the same was issued; and it shall also be their

Board of Water Commissioners may borrow money.

duty to cause to be furnished to the Controller of said city a copy of such register, as soon as the same is made, which shall be preserved by said Auditor,[j] and copied into the records of said city; and the said sum of money shall be expended by said Commissioners solely for the purpose of extending and improving the Water Works of the City of Detroit: *Provided*, That the said Board of Commissioners shall not contract said loan until they are authorized and empowered so to do by the Common Council of the City of Detroit.

Money, how expended.

Proviso.

This act shall take effect and be in force from and after its passage.

---

[j] Under Law of 1855, p. 31, the copy of the register was to be furnished to, and preserved by, the Auditor. See Section 336.

CHAPTER III.

POLICE DEPARTMENT.

SECTION
338. Police powers vested in the Board.
339. Commissioners named.
340. Term of office; vacancies.
341. Oath of office; certificate of appointment.
342. Powers of the Board.
343. Officers of the Board.
344. Board to have control of Police force.
345. Board to preserve the peace, etc.; to appoint sealer of weights and measures; his powers. When auditors to allow accounts for pursuit of criminals; arrest of criminals.
346. Qualification of Police force; removals, salaries of officers and Policemen; presents, fees, etc.
347. Complaints against Officers and Policemen; costs; how taxed and collected.
348. Police insurance fund.
349. Expense during disability; how paid.
350. Powers of Police force; expense of serving warrant; service of process.
351. Gambling houses; persons found therein.
352. Police precincts; Stations.
353. Special Policemen; pay and powers of.
354. Patrolmen for private service; powers and duties of.
355. Resignations; persons removed not to be re-appointed.
356. Stolen property; record and inventory of; Proceedings, when claimed; when unclaimed; complaint book; registry of lost property; Record of police force; of Board.

SECTION
357. Station houses; Proceedings of arrest; accommodations for witnesses; special bail.
358. Expenses of Department; how paid.
359. Estimate of expenses; Police Fund.
360. How money paid from fund.
361. Restriction of expenses of Board. Books of Board to be open to Mayor.
362. Board to enforce city ordinances; may issue subpœna; administer oaths; attachment of witnesses.
363. Bond and oath of office.
364. Report of Superintendent.
365. Officers not liable to jury duty.
366. Certain acts made misdemeanors.
367. Removal of Commissioners.
368. When vacancies may be declared.
369. Tax for expenses.
370. Deputy Superintendent.
371. Policemen not to enter saloons, etc.
372. Service of criminal process.
373. Office of City Marshal abolished.
374. Bail in cases of commitment to House of Correction; when forfeited; failure of sureties to appear.
375. Repeal of certain acts; notice of organization.
376. When act to go into force.
377. Persons without trade or occupation; how dealt with; burglars tools; tools to be destroyed.
378. Offences not cognizable by Police Court.
379. Who to take bail.
380. Act to go into immediate effect.

An Act to establish a Police Government for the City of Detroit.

[*Approved February* 24, 1865. *Laws of* 1865, *p.* 99.]

(§ 338.) SECTION 1. *The People of the State of Michigan enact,* That all powers and duties connected Police powers, in whom vested.

with and incident to the Police Government and discipline of the city of Detroit shall be, as hereinafter more especially provided, vested in and exercised by a Board of Metropolitan Police, composed of four Commissioners of Metropolitan Police, and by a Superintendent of Metropolitan police, one or more Captains of Metropolitan Police, Sergeants of Metropolitan Police, and Patrolmen of Metropolitan Police. A majority of said board shall constitute a quorum for the transaction of business.

Com'issioners. (§ 339.) SEC. 2. There are hereby appointed, as such Commissioners of Metropolitan Police, Jacob S. Farrand, to hold office until the first day of February, one thousand eight hundred and seventy-three; Lorenzo M. Mason, to hold office until the first day of February, one thousand eight hundred and seventy-one; John J. Bagley, to hold office until the first day of February, one thousand eight hundred and sixty-nine; Alexander Lewis, to hold office until the first day of February, one thousand eight hundred and sixty-seven, and until their successors are chosen and qualified.

Term of office of commissioners. (§ 340.) SEC. 3. The term of office of each Commissioner of Metropolitan Police, after the respective determinations of the terms aforesaid, shall be eight years, and the Governor shall nominate, and by and with the advice and consent of the Senate, shall appoint from the citizens of Detroit, who shall be freeholders, a successor to the person whose term shall be about to expire as such commissioner. Vacancies. Any vacancy occurring during the term of any Commissioner shall be filled by appointment of the Governor, and the Commissioner so appointed shall continue in office until his successor shall be appointed in manner aforesaid.

(§ 341.) SEC. 4. The persons severally appointed Commissioners of Metropolitan Police by virtue of this act shall, before exercising the duties thereof, duly take, and file in the office of the Secretary of State, the oath of office prescribed for State officers.[a] Immediately upon receiving said oath of office, the Secretary of State shall give to each Commissioner a certificate of his appointment, whereupon he shall possess the power, and exercise the duties, of Commissioner of Metropolitan Police prescribed by this act.

Oath of office.

Certificate of appointment.

(§ 342.) SEC. 5. The said Board of Metropolitan Police shall have power to appoint a superintendent of the police force, a captain of police, one or more officers to be called and act as detectives, one captain in addition for each fifty patrolmen called into service, more than the first fifty, four sergeants of police, an attorney, surgeon, one or more roundsmen, doormen, janitors, and fifty or more patrolmen, who shall receive compensation, (provided the total number of patrolmen so appointed shall not exceed one hundred,) and as many patrolmen with or without compensation, in time of special emergency, or apprehended danger from riot, or other cause of alarm, as they shall deem expedient. Said Board shall also have power, for cause assigned on a public hearing, and on due notice, according to rules to be promulgated by them, to remove, or suspend from office, or for a definite time deprive of pay any member of such police force, (except that detectives, the attorney and surgeon, may be dismissed at any time by said

Powers of board.

[a] For form of oath see Constitution, Art. XVIII, Sec. 1. See also, Compiled Laws, Section 281.

board,) to make rules and regulations for the discipline and government of said force, and shall cause the same to be published, and to make and promulgate general and special orders to said force, through the Superintendent of Police, who shall be the executive head of the force. [*As amended by Laws of* 1867, *Vol. II*, *p.* 265.]

Officers of. (§ 343.) SEC. 6. The said Board shall appoint one of their own number to act as President, and some person not a member of the Board to act as Secretary and Property Clerk,[b] who shall give bonds to said Board in an amount and with sureties to be approved by said Board, conditioned for the safe keeping by him, and his rendition upon the order of the Board, of all money and other property which shall come into his hands by virtue of his office; and he shall receive such compensation annually as may be determined by said Board, and hold his office at the pleasure of said Board. [*As amended by Laws of* 1867, *Vol. II*, *p.* 266.]

To have control of police force, etc. (§ 344.) SEC. 7. Said Board shall assume and exercise the entire control of the police force of said city, and shall possess full power and authority over the police organization, government, appointments and discipline within said city. It shall have the custody and control of all public property, books, records and equipments belonging to the Police Department, and shall have power to erect and maintain all such lines of telegraph in such places within the said city as for purposes of police the Board shall deem necessary, whenever the Common Council shall authorize the establishment of such telegraph line or lines, and provide for the cost thereof.

---

[b] For duties of Property Clerk, see Section 356, *post*.

(§ 345.) SEC. 8. It shall be the duty of the Board of Police, and of the force hereby constituted, at all times of the day and night, within the boundaries of said city of Detroit, to preserve the public peace, to prevent crime, and arrest offenders, to protect rights of person and property, to guard the public health, to preserve order, to enforce all laws of the State, and all ordinances of the said city, relative to inspecting and sealing weights and measures; to designate, at any time of the year, and as often as they shall deem necessary, a member of the force to perform the duties of sealer of weights and measures in said city; and the person so designated shall have the exclusive power to perform said duties in said city, and shall, during the time he is directed by said Board to perform said duties, try, prove and seal all scales, beams, weights and measures, used in said city for the purpose of buying and selling, without giving any notice, as is now required by law:[c] *Provided*, The person so designated shall neither receive nor charge compensation or fee for performing said duties; to collect all license moneys under the laws of the State, the charter and ordinances of said city, and to account for and pay the same to the person authorized by law to receive them; to designate, from time to time, a member of the force to collect said license money; and the person so designated shall have exclusive power to collect said moneys in said city; to audit and allow all bills for traveling expenses incurred in the pursuit of criminals by members of the force, and to present the

To preserve the public peace, etc.

Sealer of weights and measures.

Powers of.

Proviso.

---

[c] See Section 4, p. 12. Also, 51st, 53d and 54th subdivisions of section 103, pp. 67, 68.

same to the Board of County Auditors of Wayne County for payment, in all cases where the criminals are charged with offenses committed in said city; and the said Board of Auditors shall in no case allow, or cause to be paid by said county, any bill or account for the pursuit or apprehension of criminals charged with or suspected of the commission of crime in said city, unless the said bill or account is presented by said Board of Police, and endorsed as allowed by the president and secretary thereof; to remove nuisances existing in public streets, roads, places and highways;[d] to report all leaks and defects in water-pipes and sewers to the proper authorities; to provide a proper force at every public fire, in order that thereby the firemen may be protected in the performance of their duties, and property preserved for the owners thereof; to protect strangers and travelers at steamboat and ship landings, and railway stations, and generally to carry out and enforce all ordinances of the city and laws of the State. Whenever any crime shall be committed in said said city, and the person or persons accused, or suspected of being guilty, shall flee from justice, the said Board of Police may, at their discretion, authorize any person or persons to pursue and arrest such accused or suspected person or persons, and return them to the proper court, having jurisdiction of the offense for trial. [*As amended by Laws of* 1867, *Vol. II, p.* 267.]

When Board of Auditors to allow accounts for pursuit of criminals.

Arrest of criminals.

Qualificat'ns of police force.

(§ 346.) SEC. 9. The qualification, enumeration and distribution of duties, mode of trial and removal from office of each officer and member of said police force,

---

[d] See 28th subdivision of section 103, p. 60.

shall be particularly defined and prescribed by rules and regulations of the board of police; and no person shall be appointed to or hold office in the police force who is not a citizen of the State of Michigan, shall not have resided in said State two years next preceding his appointment, who cannot read and write the English language, and who has ever been convicted of any crime: *And provided*, That no person (except the surgeon, attorney, detectives and secretary and property clerk) shall be removed from said force, except upon written charges preferred against him to the Board of Police, and after opportunity of being heard in his defense; but the Board of Police may suspend any member of the force pending the hearing of charges against him: *And provided*, Whenever any vacancy shall occur in the office of captain of police, the same shall be filled from among the persons then in office as sergeants of police, and a like vacancy in the office of sergeant of police, shall be filled from among the persons then in office as police patrolmen. The Police Commissioners shall receive no compensation whatever for their services during their term of office. The Superintendent of Police shall receive a salary not exceeding two thousand dollars per annum. Each captain shall receive a salary not exceeding twelve hundred dollars per annum; and each sergeant a salary not exceeding one thousand dollars per annum; and each patrolman a salary not to exceed nine hundred dollars per annum. All salaries shall be prescribed by the Board of Police, and shall be paid monthly to the person entitled thereto. The compensation to be paid to all other officers, appointees and employees of the force shall be determined by the said

Proviso.
Removals.
Proviso.
Salaries.
Com'issioners.
Superintendent.
Captain.
Sergeant.
Patrolmen.

Presents, fees, etc.

Board. No member of the Board of Police or of the police force shall receive or share in, under any pretenses whatever, any present, fee, gift or emolument for police service, other than the regular salary and pay provided by this section, except by the unanimous consent of said Board; and it shall be the duty of every member of said Board, or of the police force, to return to the property clerk (to be disposed of as hereinafter prescribed), every present, fee, gift or emolument received by him, with the consent of the Board, except said Board permits him to retain the same for his own use; and all moneys and proceeds of all property received from this source shall be disposed of by said Board as if the same had been paid or given for extra or ordinary services, as prescribed in the eleventh section of this act. Nor shall any member of said force receive or share in any fee, gift or reward from any person who may become bail for the appearance of any arrested, accused or convicted person, or who may become surety for any such person on appeal from the judgment or decision of any court or magistrate; or any fee, gift or reward, in any case, from any attorney at law who may prosecute or defend any person arrested or prosecuted for any offense within the county of Wayne; nor shall any member, either directly or indirectly, interest himself or interfere in any manner whatever in the employment or retainer of any attorney, to aid in the defense of persons arrested or accused; and for any violation of either of the foregoing provisions, the member so offending shall be immediately removed from office. [*As amended by Laws of* 1867, *Vol. II, p.* 268.]

Not to interfere in employment of attorney.

Complaints against officers and policemen.

(§ 347.) SEC. 10. Any citizen of Detroit, with a view to the trial and suspension, or removal from office, of any officer or patrolman of the police force may, on oath, in writing, prefer or make before the Board charges or complaint touching the character and competency, or affecting the acts, conduct or omission of such officer or policeman, or for violation of, or misconduct, as defined or prescribed by the rules and regulations of the Board; and said Board, after reasonable notice, in the discretion of the Board, to the person charged, shall proceed to the trial of said officer or policeman, on such charges or complaint, and shall have power to, and shall issue subpœnas,[c] tested in the name of the President of the Board, to compel the attendance of witnesses, to administer oaths and affirmations, and generally shall, for the purposes of such trial, have and exercise the powers and duties of justices of the peace in civil cases, so far as the same are applicable, and may make an order of removal or suspension for some certain period. If, on such trial, said charges or complaint shall be sustained, such officer or policeman shall pay the costs of such proceedings, and the same may be deducted and withheld from his pay, and in case of his suspension, his pay shall also cease from the date of the charge, and during the period of suspension. In trials under this section the same costs shall be charged and taxed as in trials before justices, and be collected on execution, as the case may be, from the court, or on execution to be issued by any Justice of the Peace, on certificate of the same by the Board, and order for execution, said costs, when collected, to be paid to the Treasurer of the Board, for the benefit of those concerned; but the said Board

Trial.

Costs.

How taxed and collected.

---

[c] See Section 362, *post*.

shall not tax or receive any fees for themselves, or for any member thereof.

Police life and health insurance fund.

(§ 348.) SEC. 11. All rewards, fees, proceeds of gifts and emoluments, that may be allowed by the Board of Police to be paid and given for or on account of extraordinary services of any member of the police force, and all moneys arising from the sale of unclaimed goods, shall be paid into the city treasury, and shall constitute a fund to be called the "Police Life and Health Insurance Fund;" and the persons who shall, from time to time, fill the office of President of the Board of Police, and that of the Comptroller of the City of Detroit, are hereby declared the trustees of said fund, and may invest the same as they shall see fit, either in whole or in part, and shall have power to draw the same from the treasury for that purpose.

Expense during disability may be paid from.

(§ 349.) SEC. 12. Whenever any member of the police force, in actual performance of his duty, and in consequence of the performance of such duty, shall become bodily disabled, his necessary expenses, during the time his disabilities as aforesaid continue, and consequent thereon, may become a charge upon the fund provided for in the preceding section, at the discretion of the said Board of Police. The Board shall inquire into the circumstances, and if satisfied the charge upon said fund is correct, may order the same to be paid by the draft of the said trustees upon the said fund, each writing his signature thereto; but the provisions of this section shall not apply to special patrolmen appointed as hereinafter provided, at the request and expense of private parties.[r]

[r] Section 354.

(§ 350.) SEC. 13. The members of the police force of the city of Detroit shall possess all the common law and statutory powers of constables, except for the service of civil process; and any warrant for search or arrest, issued by any magistrate of the State of Michigan, may be executed in any part of said State, by any member of said police force,[g] without backing or endorsement from any other magistrate or officer of said State; and for all offenses committed in the county of Wayne, the expenses incurred in serving said warrant shall be certified by the board of police, and audited and paid by said county, and in all other cases such expenses shall be determined by, and paid under the direction of the proper auditing board of the county in which the offense charged in said warrant shall have been committed. The superintendent, deputy superintendent, or any captain of police, having just cause to suspect that any felony is being, or is about to be committed within any building, public or private, or on any wharf or enclosure, or on board of any ship, boat or vessel, within the said city of Detroit, may enter the same at all hours of the day or night, to take all necessary measures for the effectual prevention or detection of all felonies, and may take, then and there, into custody, all persons suspected of being concerned in such felonies, and also may take charge of all property which he or they shall have then and there just cause to suspect has been stolen. The members of said police force shall also serve and execute all process and subpœnas issued by the Recorder's Court[h]

Powers of police force.

Expenses of serving warrant.

Criminal process, service of.

---

[g] See Section 125, *ante*.

[h] See Sections 110, 125, *ante*.

and the Police Court of said city, and all process and subpœnas in criminal cases, issued by Justices of the Peace in said city.[i] [*As amended by Laws of* 1867, *Vol. II. p.* 269.]

Gambling houses, etc., proceedings against.

(§ 351.) SEC. 14. If any member of the force, or if any two or more house-holders shall report in writing, under his or their signatures, to the Superintendent of the force, that there are good grounds, (which shall be stated in said report,) for believing any houses, room, or premises within the said city, to be kept or used as a common gaming house, common gaming room, or common gaming premises, for therein playing for wagers of money at any game of chance, or to be kept or used for lewd and obscene purposes and amusements, or the deposit or sale of lottery tickets or lottery policies, or as a cock-pit, or for harboring criminals, or for concealing stolen property, or for carrying on any trade, occupation, calling, practice, or act, prohibited by law, it shall be lawful for the said Superintendent to authorize in writing, any member or members of the force, to enter the same, who may forthwith arrest all persons there found offending against the law, or aiding or abetting in such offense, but none others, and seize all implements of gaming or lottery tickets, or lottery policies, and convey any person so arrested, before a magistrate, and bring the articles so seized, to the property clerk.[j] It shall be the duty of such Superintendent to cause such arrested person to be prosecuted vigorously, and such articles seized to be destroyed, as the orders, rules

The persons found therein.

[i] See Section 372.

[j] See 40th and 41st subdivision of section 103, p. 65.

and regulations of the Board of Police shall direct. [*As amended by Laws of* 1867, *Vol. II, p.* 270.]

(§ 352.) SEC. 15. It is hereby made the duty of the Board of Police, for more effectually distributing and enforcing its police government and discipline, to divide the said city of Detroit into precincts, without regard to ward boundaries, and to assign captains of police, and sergeants of police, to each of the said precincts, as they shall deem for the best interests of said city. The Board may, from time to time, establish a station or substation in each precinct or division, for the accommodation of the police force on duty therein. It shall promulgate all regulations and orders through the Superintendent of Police; and it shall be the duty of the Police force to respect and obey the said Superintendent, as the head and chief of the same, subject to the rules and regulations and general orders of the board.

Police precincts.

Stations.

Promulgation of orders thro' superintendent.

(§ 353.) SEC. 16. The Board of Police is hereby authorized to appoint persons of suitable character, who may be in the employment of the city in other branches or departments, special policemen or patrolmen: *Provided*, Such special policemen shall not be paid for their services as policemen, either from the police fund or the city or county treasury. Such policemen shall possess the same power as the regular police patrolmen, and shall obey the rules and regulations of the board, and conform to its general discipline.

Special police.

Compensation and powers of.

(§ 354.) SEC. 17. The Board of Police, whenever it shall seem to them discreet, may on the application of any person or persons, showing the necessities thereof, appoint and swear in any number of additional patrolmen to do duty at any place within said city, at the

Patrolmen for private service.

charge and expense of the person or persons by whom the application shall be made; and the patrolmen so appointed, shall perform duty only at the places designated by said Board; shall continue in office at the pleasure of said Board for a term not exceeding one year; shall be subject to and obey the orders, rules and regulations of said board, and conform to the general discipline of the force, and to such special regulations as may be made by such board for their government. They shall wear such dress and emblem as said Board may prescribe, and shall possess, as conservators of the peace, all the powers and privileges, and perform all the duties of the force herein prescribed: *Provided*, That no patrolman shall be appointed under this section until he shall have paid into the trust fund, hereinbefore provided, the sum of five dollars. The persons so appointed may be removed at any time by the Board of Police without cause assigned for the removal. The Board of Police may also, upon any emergency, or mob, pestilence, invasion, or during any day of public election or celebration, appoint as many special patrolmen from among citizens of Detroit as it may deem advisable and for a specified time; and during the term of service of such special patrolmen, they shall possess all the powers and privileges and perform all the duties of patrolmen of the force herein created, and shall receive such compensation, not exceeding three dollars per day, as said Board may prescribe: *Provided always*, That nothing herein contained shall give said Board power to do anything in conflict with the powers of inspectors of election in said city: *Provided further*, That policemen stationed at the polls on election days, shall perform all the duties

Duties and powers of.

Proviso.

Special patrolmen.

Proviso.

of, and be subject to all provisions of law relating to the attendance of constables at polls on election days; and no constable in said city shall receive any compensation for attendance upon the polls. [*As amended by Laws of* 1867, *Vol. II, p.* 270.]

Resignation of members.

(§ 355.) SEC. 18. No member of the police force, under penalty of forfeiting the pay which may be due to him, shall withdraw or resign from the police force, unless he shall have given one week's notice thereof, in writing, to the Superintendent of Police; and no person, who shall ever have been removed from the police force established by this act, for cause, shall be re-appointed by the Board of Police to any office in the said police force.

Persons removed not to be re-appointed.

Stolen property, how disposed of.

(§ 356.) SEC. 19. All stolen, or other property seized officially by the members of the police force, shall be deposited with the property clerk, and kept in a place to be designated by the said Board; and in case of neglect or refusal of any officer to so deposit the property taken, or found in the possession of any person or persons arrested, he shall be deemed guilty of a misdemeanor, and be subject to indictment, on information, and upon conviction, be fined a sum not less than the value of the property, nor exceeding three thousand dollars, and be imprisoned not to exceed one year; and the sentence of the court shall vacate the office of the person so convicted. All property or money, taken on suspicion of having been feloniously obtained, or of being the proceeds of crime, and for which there is no other claimant than the person from whom it is taken, and all lost property coming into the possession of any member of said police force, and all money and property taken

Record of.

from pawn brokers, as the proceeds of crime, or by any such member from any insane or intoxicated person, or person otherwise incapable of taking care of himself, shall be registered by the property clerk, in a book kept for that purpose, together with the name of the owner, if ascertained, and the name of the place where found, and of the person from whom taken, with the general circumstances and the date of its receipt, and the name of the officer recording the same, and shall be advertised, if the owner's name is not ascertained, in such manner as the rules and regulations of the Board shall prescribe. An inventory of the money or other property shall be given to the person from whom the same is taken; and in case the same shall not, within ten days after such arrest and seizure, be claimed by any other person or persons, it shall be delivered to the person from whom it was taken, and to no other person, except by order of the Board. In case said money or other property shall, within said ten days, be claimed by any other person than the one from whom it shall be seized, it shall be retained by the property clerk, until after the discharge or conviction of the person from whom the same was taken; and if the claimant or claimants shall establish to the satisfaction of the court, before which the person from whom such goods and money are taken, that he or they are the rightful owners of the same, the same shall be restored to him or them upon the order of said court; but if the court makes no order, said property shall be returned to the accused personally. All property and money that shall remain in the custody of the property clerk, for the period of six months, without any lawful claimant thereto, shall be put into

Inventory.

Proceedings when property is claimed.

Disposal of unclaimed property.

the Police Life and Health Insurance Fund; and the property shall be sold, after being advertised three times in some public newspaper in said city, and the proceeds paid to said fund. The Board of Police shall cause to be kept general complaint books, in which shall be entered every complaint preferred upon personal knowledge of the circumstances thereof, with the name and residence of the complainant. It shall also cause to be kept, books for the registry of lost, missing or stolen property, for the general convenience of the public and of the police force of the city. It shall also cause to be kept books of record, wherein shall be entered the name of every member of the police force, his time and place of nativity, the time and place where he became a citizen, (if he was born out of the United States,) his age, his former occupation, number of his family and the residence thereof, the date of his appointment and dismissal from office, with the cause of the latter; and in every such record, sufficient space shall be left against all such entries wherein to make record of the number of arrests made by such members of the police force, or of any special service deemed meritorious by the captains of police. It shall also cause to be kept, in proper books, the accounts of the Board, and a record of their proceedings; and they shall preserve and file copies of all bills audited and allowed, and keep an accurate account of all expenses of the police department. The Board of Police shall also cause to be kept and bound, all police returns and reports. [*As amended by Laws of* 1867, *Vol. II*, *p.* 271.]

Complaint book.

Registry of property lost.

Record of police force.

Record of Board.

(§ 357.) SEC. 20. It shall be the duty of the Board of Police to provide, at the expense of said city, all

Station houses.

necessary accommodations within such precincts as shall be contained within the boundaries of said city, for the station houses required by the Board of Police, for the accommodation of the police force of such precincts, for the lodging of vagrant and disorderly persons, and for the temporary detention of persons arrested for offenses. It shall also be the duty of said Board of Police to furnish the same suitably, and to warm and light the same by day and night, and to provide food for any person or persons detained in any of said station houses, when such food is deemed necessary for such person or persons by the officer in charge; and in every case of arrest, the same shall be made known to the captain or sergeant upon duty in the precinct wherein such arrest was made, by the person making the same; and it shall be the duty of the said captain or sergeant, as soon as practicable after such notice, to make written return thereof, according to the rules and regulations of the Board of Police, together with the name of the party arrested, the offense, the place of arrest, and the place of detention. All persons arrested by the officers or members of the police force shall be detained, while in their custody, only in the places provided for that purpose; and no trial or examination of any person arrested shall be held in the office of the Superintendent of Police, or of the Board. Necessary and usual articles of clothing or personal apparel upon the person, or in the possession of persons arrested and detained, shall not be taken or seized by the police, unless there be reason to suspect that the clothing has been stolen or obtained unlawfully. The Board of Police shall provide suitable accommodations within said city for the detention of

Proce'dings of arrest.

Accommodations for witnesses.

witnesses who are unable to furnish security for their appearance in criminal proceedings,[k] and such accommodations shall be in places other than those employed for the confinement of persons charged with crime, fraud or disorderly conduct; and it shall be the duty of all magistrates, in committing witnesses, to have regard to the rules and regulations of the Board of Police in respect to their detention. Every person arrested by the police, charged with the violation of any city ordinance, shall be entitled to give special bail for his appearance to answer to such charge; but no member of the police force shall become or furnish bail for any person arrested. [*As amended by Laws of* 1867, *Vol. II*, *p.* 273.]

Special bail.

(§ 358.) SEC. 21. The necessary expenses incurred in the execution of criminal process, for offenses charged to have been committed in the city of Detroit, and the maintenance of the Police Department hereby created within the said city of Detroit, shall be a city charge.

Expenses of police department to be paid by city.

(§ 359.) SEC. 22. It shall be the duty of the Board of Police to prepare and submit to the Controller, on or before the first day of May, in every year, an estimate of the whole cost and expense, not to exceed one hundred and twenty-five thousand dollars in any one year, of providing for and maintaining the Police Department of said city, within the current fiscal year, which estimate shall be in detail, and shall be laid by the Controller before the Common Council, with his annual estimate; and the same shall be by the Common Council of said city provided for in the general tax assessment, by levy to be laid on said city, and the same shall not

Estimate of expenses.

[k] See Comp. Laws, sections 5968, 5995, 5998, 6097.

require or be conditioned upon the vote of the freemen of the city; said money shall be paid by the officer collecting the same into the hands of the treasurer of the Board of Metropolitan Police, once a week or oftener. Police fund. The moneys so collected shall constitute and be styled "The Metropolitan Police Fund." The said Board of Police shall appoint a treasurer, who shall be the custodian of the money of said fund, and deposit the same in such place and in no other as he shall be directed by said Board. He shall give security to said Board that he will keep said money in said place and no other; that he will pay the same upon the order of said Board, and in all respects account for the disposition of the same, and that he will perform faithfully the duties of treasurer. Said treasurer shall be appointed to serve during the discretion of the Board. [*As amended by Laws of* 1867, *Vol. II, p.* 274.]

How money paid from. (§ 360.) SEC. 23. All moneys hereafter to be paid to any person or persons out of the police fund shall be certified by the president or acting president of the Board of Police to the secretary, who shall draw his warrant on the treasurer therefor, stating therein the fund to which it is chargeable, and the person to whom payable, and such warrant shall be countersigned by the president, or in his absence, by the acting president of the Board of Police.

Expenses of board; restriction of. (§ 361.) SEC. 24. No expenses other than salaries and pay herein provided, shall be incurred by the Board of Police, except for rent, record books, stationery, printing, telegraphing, badges, clubs, furniture of necessary rooms and stations, the preservation, repair and cleansing of the buildings and rooms used by the Board, advertising, fuel, lights, board of prisoners, witnesses, and for the arrest, conveyance and custody of prisoners and witnesses, and the preservation of the discipline and good order of the force, unless the same shall be expressly authorized, and provision made therefor as a city charge, by the Common Council of the city of Detroit: *Provided,* That nothing herein contained shall prevent said Board from incurring all expenses which are actually necessary to perform all the duties and exercise all the powers by this act enjoined upon them and granted to them. The books and accounts kept by said Board shall at all times be subject to the inspection of the Mayor and Controller, or either of them; and the Common Council may at any time require information respecting the same, the disclosure of which will not impair the usefulness and efficiency of the force. [*As amended by Laws of* 1867, *Vol. II, p.* 275.]

Proviso.

Books of board to be open to Mayor.

(§ 362.) SEC. 25. The Board of Police shall at all times cause the ordinances of the city to be properly enforced, and it shall be the duty of said Board, at all times, whenever consistent with the rules and regulations of the Board, and with the requirements of this act, to furnish all information desired, and comply with all the requests made by the Common Council of said city, or by the Mayor thereof, to quell riots, suppress insurrections, protect the property and preserve the public tranquility. The Board of Police shall have the power to issue subpœnas,[1] tested in the name of its president, to compel before it the attendance of witnesses before any proceeding authorized by its rules and regulations. Each

Board to enforce city ordinances, etc.

May issue subpœnas.

[1] See Section 347, *ante*.

Admininister oaths. Commissioner of Police, the Superintendent of Police, and the secretary of the Board of Police, are hereby given power to administer, take, receive and subscribe all affirmations and oaths to any witnesses summoned and appearing in any matter or proceeding authorized as aforesaid, or to any depositions necessary by the rules and regulations of the Board. Perj'ry, punishment of. Any willful and corrupt false swearing by any witness or person making deposition before any of the officers last mentioned, to any material fact, in any necessary proceedings under said rules and regulations, shall be deemed perjury, and punished in the manner now prescribed by law for such offence. Attachment of witnesses The provisions of law now existing in respect to attachment of witnesses before justices of the peace,[m] and to the compulsory attendance of the said witnesses, to appear and testify before them, are hereby applied to the case of witnesses subpœnaed before the Board of Police.

Bond and oath of office. (§ 363.) SEC. 26. The Board of Police shall require and make suitable provisions concerning security to be entered into by the Superintendent, the captains of police, the property clerk and treasurer; and said Board may, in their discretion, require security from any member of the force, conditional for the performance of any duty involving the care and disposition of property. Said Board shall require each member of the force to take an oath of office,[n] and the registry of the certificate thereof in a book to be kept for the purpose, which oath may be taken before any one of the Commissioners, who is hereby empowered to administer the same. [*As amended by Laws of* 1867, *Vol. II, p.* 276.]

---

[m] See Compiled Laws, Sections 3743 to 3752, both inclusive.

[n] See Section 17, p. 19.

(§ 364.) SEC. 27. The Superintendent of Police shall make to the Board quarterly reports, in writing, of the state of the police force, with such statistics and suggestions as he may deem advisable for the enforcement of the police government and discipline. The Board of Police shall, on or before the first Monday in April in each year, report in writing the condition of the police within the said city to the Common Council.

Report of superintendent of police.

(§ 365.) SEC. 28. No person holding office under this act shall be liable to jury duty, or to arrest on civil process, while actually on duty.

Officers not liable to jury duty,

(§ 366.) SEC. 29. It shall be a misdemeanor, punishable by imprisonment in the county jail, not more than two years, for any person, without justifiable or excusable cause, to use personal violence upon any elector in said city of Detroit,[°] while attending the polls upon any election day, or upon any member of the police force thereof, when in the discharge of his duty; or for any person, not a member of the police force, to falsely represent himself as being such member with a fraudulent design. [*As amended by Laws of* 1867, *Vol. II*, *p.* 276.]

Certain acts declared misdemeanors.

(§ 367.) SEC. 30. Either of said Commissioners of Police may at any time be removed by the Governor, under the provisions of statutes relating to the removal from office of sheriffs, which provisions are hereby extended so as to relate to each one of the said Commissioners, and in all cases where charges are made out against a Commissioner, he shall have an opportunity to present evidence in his behalf.

Removal of commissioners.

° See Section 54, p. 32, and note.

When positions declared vacant.

(§ 368.) SEC. 31. Any one of the said Commissioners, or any member of the police force, who shall, during his term of office, accept or hold any office elective by the people, or who shall, during his term of office, be publicly nominated for any office elective by the people, and shall not, within ten days succeeding the same, publicly decline the said nomination, shall be, in either case, deemed thereby to have resigned his commission, and to have vacated his office.

Tax for expenses.

(§ 369.) SEC. 32. The Common Council of Detroit are hereby empowered and directed annually to order and cause to be collected and raised by tax upon the estates, real and personal, subject to taxation according to law, within the said city of Detroit, the sums of money as aforesaid annually estimated for the said total expense of the Metropolitan Police, authorized by this act.

Deputy Superintend't.

(§ 370.) SEC. 33. In case at any time, or for any cause, the services of a deputy superintendent shall be required, the senior captain of police is hereby authorized to act in that behalf, so long as necessary, and the place of said captain shall be filled, for the time being, by any appointee of the board from the sergeants of police.

Policemen not to enter saloons, etc.

(§ 371.) SEC. 34. No policeman or officer of police shall, while on duty, be at liberty to enter any drinking or gaming saloon, or other place where liquors are sold to be drunk on the premises, or house of prostitution, except for the purpose of discharging some of the duties of his office.

Service of criminal process.

(§ 372.) SEC. 35. The members of the metropolitan police force shall have the exclusive power, and it shall be their duty, to serve all process within the city of Detroit, issuing from the Recorder's court, police court, and from justices of the peace in criminal cases, within said city, whether directed to constables, the sheriff or otherwise,[p] and shall be detailed by the proper officers, to attend, instead of deputy sheriffs[q] or constables, all courts of criminal jurisdiction of said city; all the duties now performed by deputy sheriffs in serving writs, executing orders of said court, attending said court, conveying prisoners to and from the county jail for arraignment or trial before said court, and in conveying prisoners to the Detroit House of Correction, the reform school, county jail, State prison or other place of punishment and imprisonment, under the judgment, sentence, order or process of said court,[r] shall be performed by the members of said police force; and in no case shall deputy sheriffs, or any constable of said city, receive or be paid by the county or State, any fee or compensation for services directed in this section, or in any part of this act, to be performed by the members of said force. The actual expenses of travel and of performing duties under this section, shall be paid by the County of Wayne, upon bills allowed by said Board of Police, and endorsed by the President and Secretary thereof. [*As amended by Laws of* 1867, *Vol. II, p.* 276.]

City Marsh'l office of abolished.

(§ 373.) SEC. 36. The offices of city marshal and assistant marshal of the city of Detroit is hereby abolished, and the duties of said office[s] shall hereafter be performed by the Superintendent of Police, or by the

---

[p] See Section 350, *ante*. See also, Section 125.

[q] By Section 110 the sheriff and his deputies were to attend upon the sittings of the Recorder's Court.

[r] See Section 110.

[s] See Sections 66, 67, 125, 159, 162, 164.

captains and sergeants of police, under his directions, in accordance with the provisions of this act, but this section shall not be operative until the Superintendent of Police, or captain of police, authorized by this act to be appointed, shall be sworn into office.

Bail of persons committed to house of correction.

(§ 374.) SEC. 37. No person committed to the house of correction for want of bail, shall be discharged therefrom on bail, until the order of discharge, by the magistrate or court who committed said person, or by the judge of some circuit court, or the Recorder of said city, (all of whom are authorized to approve of and take such bail,) together with the original recognizance approved by such magistrate, court, judge or Recorder, shall have first been delivered to the Superintendent of the House of Correction; and said Superintendent is hereby directed in every case to transmit said recognizance to the Superintendent of Police, who shall, whenever the said recognizance is forfeited by the principal therein named, deliver the same to the attorney of the Board of Police for prosecution; and said attorney shall forthwith proceed to collect the same by applying to the Recorder's court of said city for an order upon the sureties in said bond, to show cause why said recognizance shall not be forfeited and judgment entered for the amount of penalty therein mentioned against them, on a day in said order set forth. Said order shall be served personally upon said sureties, if they can be found in said city, and if they cannot be found, by leaving a copy at their last place of abode, at least four days before the day therein set forth, and shall be granted only upon the filing with said court of an affidavit or affidavits, showing to the satisfaction of said court, that the principal

When forfeited.

named in said recognizance has, during the time for which such recognizance is conditioned for his or her good behavior, been found guilty by a competent court, of being a disorderly person, of any crime or misdemeanor, or that he or she has been and is a disorderly person, at any time within the life of said recognizance, and since his or her discharge from said House of Correction. And the said sureties, or either of them, upon the service on them, or either of them, of said order and affidavit, or affidavits, shall come into court upon the day in said order named, and show cause by affidavit, or otherwise, as the court may direct, why judgment shall not be entered against them, or either of them, on said recognizance; and if they, or either of them, after service of said order, fail to appear, or do not show sufficient cause, said court shall enter judgment against both, all or either of them, upon their said recognizance, and shall issue execution thereon, and collect the same in the same manner as in cases of judgments on forfeited recognizances in said court. All moneys collected on such executions shall be paid by the officer collecting the same, or by the person or persons against whom the judgment was rendered, to the clerk of said said court, who shall, within three days after receiving the same, pay it to the officer empowered by law to receive it. [*As amended by Laws of* 1867, *Vol. II, page* 277.]

When sureties fail to appear.

(§ 375.) SEC. 38. Sections one, two, three, four, five, six, seven, eight and nine, of chapter thirteen, of an act entitled "an act to revise the charter of the city of Detroit," approved February fifth, one thousand eight hundred and fifty-seven, which chapter was added by

Acts repealed.

"an act to amend an act entitled an act to revise the charter of the city of Detroit, approved February fifth, one thousand eight hundred and fifty-seven," approved March twelfth, one thousand eight hundred and sixty-one; also sections one, two and three, of an act entitled "an act to amend an act entitled an act to revise the charter of the city of Detroit, approved February fifth, one thousand eight hundred and fifty-seven," and approved February fourth, one thousand eight hundred and sixty-four, and all acts and parts of acts inconsistent with the provisions of this act, are hereby repealed, such repeal, however, to take effect and become operative only when the Board of Police appointed by this act shall be duly organized, and a police force shall be appointed by said Board and sworn into office. The President of the Board of Metropolitan Police shall notify the City Marshal and Assistant Marshal in writing, and publish a notice in two daily papers published in Detroit, stating the fact and time, the organization of the said police force, for the purpose of fixing the time when sections thirty-five and thirty-six, and this section shall become operative.

When operative.

Notice of organization.

(§ 376.) SEC. 39. This act shall take immediate effect.

Persons without trade or occupation.

(§ 377.) SEC. 40. Any person who has no trade or occupation at which he actually labors, and has no visible means of support, and frequents houses of ill-fame, or places for the retailing of spirituous liquors, or places where gaming for money is carried on, and any person who has been sentenced to and served a term in State prison, by a court of competent jurisdiction in this State, who has no trade or occupation at which he actually labors, and frequents places for the retail of ardent spirits, houses of ill-fame, or places where gaming for money is carried on, and any person in whose possession burglars' tools shall be found, for the possession of which he or she cannot account satisfactorily, shall be deemed a disorderly person and shall be complained against, examined and dealt with as is provided by the statutes of this State for disorderly persons.[t] And it shall be the duty of the member of the police force to seize all burglars' tools, wherever found, and if the owner thereof can be discovered, to complain of him under this section, and if he is found guilty under such complaint, the Superintendent or some captain of police shall destroy or mutilate such tools, so that they cannot be used for burglarious purposes again, and if the said owner is not convicted, said tools shall be returned to him. If the owner of said tools shall not be found within ten days after they are seized, the Superintendent or some other member of said force shall take the same to the Police Justice, and make oath before him, of the time when and place where said tools were found; and if the said Police Justice shall find that said tools are burglars' tools, he shall order the same to be destroyed by the Superintendent or some captain of the police; and if the said Police Justice, upon the examination of any person upon complaint under this section, shall decide that any of the tools are not burglarious, such tools shall be returned to the owner, or if upon tools being brought before him, the owner of which cannot be discovered, he sball decide that all or part of them are not burglarious, then such as he decides are not burglarious shall be left and disposed of in the same manner

How dealt with.

Possessors of burglar's tools.

Tools destroyed.

[t] See Comp. Laws, 1550, *et post.*

as is provided for property found by the police. [*As added by Laws of* 1867, *Vol. II, p..* 278.]

Offense not cognizable by police justice.

(§ 378.) SEC. 41. Whenever the Police Justice of said city shall find, upon examination before him, that an offense not cognizable by him has been committed, and that there is probable cause to believe the person charged is guilty thereof, if the offense is bailable, said justice shall bind the said person with sufficient sureties to appear before the Recorder's court; and in default of the said person entering into a recognizance for his appearance at said court, as ordered by said justice, said justice shall commit him or her to the county jail for trial; and the person so committed may, during the time he or she is confined in said jail awaiting trial, appear before said justice and give bail for his or her appearance at the Recorder's court, and no other court, magistrate or officer shall, under any circumstances, admit said person to bail, except judges of the supreme and circuit courts, or the Recorder of said city. If said person is brought by writ of *habeas corpus* before a circuit court commissioner, said commissioner, upon return being made to him on said writ, that said person is imprisoned by virtue of being committed for trial by said police justice, shall not admit said person to bail nor proceed to further hear the case under the writ, except to receive evidence sustaining or denying the truth of the return. In no case shall said police justice, or any judge, court, magistrate or officer authorized to take bail for the appearance of any person charged with crime in said city, receive as surety for said person any person who is a party to a recognizance for the appearance of a person charged with crime, and which recognizance has been

Habeas corpus.

Parties not taken as sureties.

forfeited and is unpaid, or upon which recognizance judgment has been rendered but is unpaid and unsatisfied. Every judge, court, magistrate and officer, and the said police justice, shall, before receiving and accepting any person as surety under this section, require said person to swear that he is not a party to any forfeited and unpaid recognizance, nor a party to any unsatisfied judgment rendered upon any recognizance for the appearance of any person charged with or convicted of crime or misdemeanor. [*As amended by Laws of* 1867, *Vol. II*, *p.* 279.]

Oath of surety.

(§ 379.) SEC. 42. In all cases of trial or examination of any defendant before the police court of the city of Detroit, if any adjournment of any such trial or examination shall be had, and in all cases of the postponement of the examination of any party under arrest before said court, it shall not be competent for any other officer than the police justice or the person acting as such to take bail for the appearance of the accused at the said adjourned day. [*As amended by Laws of* 1867, *p.* 280.]

Person to take bail on adjournm't.

(§ 380.) SEC. 43. This act shall take immediate effect.

CHAPTER IV.

COURTS OF THE CITY OF DETROIT.

SECTION
381. Election of Police Justice; oath of office.
382. Powers and duties of Police Justice.
383. Same.
384. Same; vacancy.
385. Justices of the Peace not bound to act in criminal cases.
386. Warrants.
387. Security for costs, when demandable.
388. Clerk of; his salary and duties.
389. Appeals.
390. Salary of Police Justice.
391. When act to go into effect.
392. *Capias* for witnesses may issue from Recorder's Court.
393. Sentence in Recorder's Court in excess of Law not invalid.
394. Jurors in a Court of Record; when disqualified.
395. Jurors in Police and Justices' court; when disqualified.

An Act to establish a Police Court in the City of Detroit.

[*Approved April* 2, 1850. *Laws of* 1850, *p.* 364.]

Police justice.

(§ 381.) SECTION 1. *Be it enacted by the Senate and House of Representatives of the State of Michigan*, That there shall be a Police Justice in the City of Detroit. The first election for said Justice shall be held on the first Monday of May next, in the City of Detroit, to be conducted in the same manner as justices of the peace are elected at the charter election of said city; and the first incumbent of said office shall hold his office from the time he is elected till the fourth day of July, in the year 1854; and at the charter election of said city and the interval of every four years, the said Justice shall be elected in the manner provided for the election of Justices of the Peace in said city, to hold his office for four years, the term of which shall commence on the fourth day of July of the year in which

Election.

he is elected; and in case of a vacancy occurring in the said office of police justice, the Common Council shall order a special election, giving twenty days' notice thereof. And the said Police Justice shall, before entering upon the duties of his office, take and subscribe the oath prescribed by the constitution of this State,[a] before some officer authorized by law to administer oaths, and deposit the same with the Clerk of the County of Wayne, who shall file and preserve the same in his office. Oath.

(§ 382.) SEC. 2. He shall, except in case of his absence, or inability to act, have sole and exclusive jurisdiction to hear all complaints, to conduct all examinations in criminal cases, and to try all offenses which by the laws of this State are now brought and established within the jurisdiction of justices of the peace,[b] and which may hereafter arise within the corporate limits of the said city of Detroit. Powers and duties.

(§ 383.) SEC. 3. Warrants may be issued in criminal cases for the apprehending of offenders by any justice of the peace in said City of Detroit; but they shall be made returnable before the said Police Justice, except in case of his absence or inability, or a vacancy in said office. Ibid.

(§ 384.) SEC. 4. He shall reside and keep an office in the city of Detroit, and attend to all complaints of a criminal nature which may be brought before him at Ibid.

---

[a] Constitution, Article XVIII, Section 1.

[b] See Compiled Laws, Section 3924, *et post.* Also, Section 1666. In the matter of Samuel V. Berry, 7 Mich., 467, it was held that the jurisdiction of the Police Justice did not extend to cases where the punishment might exceed a fine of one hundred dollars, or three months imprisonment, or both.

all reasonable hours, and in case of his removal from said city, his death, or resignation, his office shall be vacated, and another person then acting in said city as a justice of the peace, shall be appointed by the Common Council of said city, who shall serve as such Police Justice until after the next ensuing charter election, when a Police Justice shall be elected to fill the vacancy.

Vacancy.

Justices of the Peace.

(§ 385.) SEC. 5. No justice of the peace residing in said city of Detroit, shall be entitled to receive any fees for, or bound to render any services in criminal cases, except during the sickness, absence or inability of the said Police Justice as aforesaid; in which case it shall be the duty of the several justices of the peace in said city, to render the same services, and they shall receive the same fees, as though this act had not passed.

Warrants.

(§ 386.) SEC. 6. When any warrant returnable before said Police Justice shall be returned during his absence, sickness, or inability to act, or during a vacancy (if such occurs) in said office, any further proceedings on such warrant may be had before any justice of the peace residing in said City of Detroit; and all warrants issued by the said Police Justice for the apprehending of criminals, shall have the same effect and be subject to the same restrictions as warrants issued by justices of the peace in similar cases.

Security for costs.

(§ 387.) SEC. 7. The said Police Justice shall have authority in all cases, at his discretion, either before or after the issuing of process, to require of the complainant security for costs to the satisfaction of said justice, and the person becoming such security shall sign a memorandum, in writing, to that effect, which said justice shall keep as a part of the record of the case; and in all cases, non-resident complainants shall give security before process shall issue. If the defendant or prisoner be discharged on examination, by said Police Justice, or acquitted on trial, the said Police Justice shall enter a judgment for costs against the surety and the complainant, either or both of them, which shall be of like force and effect, and shall be collected on execution, as any other judgment rendered by a Justice of the Peace:[c] *Provided*, That said justice shall certify, on the record of the court, that such payment of costs by the prosecutor, or his surety, in his opinion, is just and equitable. [*As amended by Laws of* 1863, *p.* 331.]

Proviso.

(§ 388.) SEC. 8. There shall be a Clerk of said court, who shall be appointed by the Common Council of the City of Detroit, who shall receive such salary as such Common Council may prescribe, which shall be allowed and paid in the same manner as provided for the payment of the Police Justice; he shall give a bond to the people of the State, in the penal sum of two thousand dollars, to be approved by said Common Council, for the faithful discharge of the duties of his office. It shall be his duty to keep a true record of the proceedings of said court, in proper books to be provided therefor, and file and safely keep all books and papers belonging or pertaining to said court; he shall have power generally to administer oaths and take affidavits; it shall also be the duty of said Clerk to receive all costs, fines and dues, of every description, from either party to complaints or prosecutions before said Police

Clerk of court.

Salary of.

Bond.

Duties of.

[c] See Comp. Laws, sections 3940, 3942.

Court, and which by law are taxable as justices' costs, and shall pay the same weekly to the County Treasurer of the County of Wayne, and shall take his receipt for the same; and all fines or other moneys, coming into his hands, shall be paid out and disposed of as is now provided by law with reference to justices of the peace. [*As added by Laws of* 1863, *p.* 331.)

Appeals. (§ 389.) SEC. 9. In all cases in said Police Court, where the sentence of imprisonment shall amount to thirty days or more, or where the fine imposed shall amount to twenty-five dollars or over, the Recorder of said city, or the Circuit Judge presiding in Wayne county, may allow an appeal to the Recorder's Court, upon satisfactory affidavit, presented to him within five days after the trial, showing the nature of the case, the circumstances of the trial, and the substance of the evidence taken thereon, if, in the opinion of such Recorder or judge, justice shall require an appeal, and on filing such affidavit and allowance with the Police Justice, such appeal may be taken in the same manner, and with the same effect and restrictions, as prescribed for appeals to the circuit courts in cases of sentences by justices of the peace in criminal cases.[d] [*As added by Laws of* 1863, *p.* 332.]

Salary. (§ 390.) SEC. 10. The said Police Justice shall not be entitled to receive to his own use any fees for services performed under this act, but in lieu thereof he shall receive an annual salary of twelve hundred dollars per year for the time he shall exercise the duties of

[d] Prior to this amendment, the Supreme Court was equally divided upon the question whether an appeal could be taken from the Police Court. People vs. the Police Justice, 7 Mich., 456.

such office, to be fixed from year to year by the Board of County Auditors for said County of Wayne, which shall be allowed, raised, and paid by said board as other county charges are allowed and paid; and during the time he remains such Police Justice he shall not perform the duties of a civil magistrate.

(§ 391.) SEC. 11. This act shall take effect and be in force from and after its passage; but nothing in this act contained shall be so construed as in anywise to affect the jurisdiction of justices of the peace in criminal proceedings, until said Police Justice shall be elected and qualified according to the provisions of this act.

An Act in relation to issuing Capiases for Witnesses in Criminal Proceedings.

[*Approved March* 15, 1861. *Laws of* 1861, *p.* 423.]

Recorder's court may issue capias for witnesses.

(§ 392.) SECTION 1. *The People of the State of Michigan enact,* That the Circuit and District Court of any county, and the Recorder's Court of the City of Detroit, shall have power to issue capiases in the first instance, for any witness or witnesses in criminal cases, when it shall satisfactorily appear that such witness or witnesses are material, and that there will be danger of the loss of their testimony unless such writ be issued.

An Act relative to Judgments in Criminal Cases.

[*Approved March* 27, 1867. *Laws of* 1867, *Vol. I, p.* 223.]

Judgment in Recorder's court not annulled by excess of punishment.

(§ 393.) SECTION 1. *The People of the State of Michigan enact*, That whenever, in any criminal case tried in any Circuit Court, or in the Recorder's Court of the City of Detroit, the defendant shall be adjudged guilty, and a punishment by fine or imprisonment shall be imposed in excess of that allowed by law, the judgment shall not for that reason alone be judged altogether void, nor be wholly reversed or annulled by any court of review, but the same shall be valid and effectual to the extent of the lawful penalty, and shall only be revised or annulled on writ of error, or otherwise, in respect to the unlawful excess.

An Act disqualifying Persons in Wayne County to sit as Jurors in certain cases.

[*Approved March* 27, 1867. *Laws of* 1867, *Vol. I, p.* 172.]

Circuit cor't

(§ 394.) SECTION 1. *The People of the State of Michigan enact*, That no person shall be qualified to be or become one of a panel of jurors, in any circuit court or court of record, in Wayne county, who within one year prior thereto, has been or acted as a member of a panel of jurors, whether summoned on the original panel, or added thereto as talesman, in the same court; and it shall be the duty of the circuit or presiding judge, to discharge

If acted as juror within one year.

Discharged.

any such person if summoned as a juror, who within one year has been a member of a panel of jurors in said court, and it shall be a just cause of challenge to any juror in any cause, over and above all other challenges allowed by law, that he has been within a year a member of a panel of jurors, in said court. Juror challenged.

(§ 395.) SEC. 2. No person shall be qualified to sit as a juror in any Justice or Police Court of Wayne county, or on an inquest before any Coroner, who has already sat as a juror in said Justice or Police Court, or on an inquest before said Coroner, more than three times during the calendar year, next preceding the time when he is summoned or offered as a juror on said court, or on said inquest. And it shall be the duty of Justices of the Peace, and Police Justices and Coroners, to enforce and carry out the provisions of this law, and to discharge any such juror. It shall be a good cause of challenge, over and above all challenges otherwise allowed by law, that any person summoned or offered as a juror, shall have acted as a juror in the same tribunal or court, more than three times during the prior calendar year. Police court or inquest. Over three times within the year. Discharged. Juror challenged.

CHAPTER V.

HOUSE OF CORRECTION.

SECTION
396. Name. How to be used.
397. How controlled; Board of Inspectors; how appointed. Term of office.
398. Board to adopt rules; Officers, how appointed; salaries; expenditures.
399. Meetings of Board; when at House of Correction; Board to examine its management; Records of Board.
400. Books of House of Correction, how kept; statements, when made; accounts, how audited; annual report.
401. Employees, and how removed.
402. Duties and powers of Superintendent and Deputy.
403. Contracts with Counties for keeping criminals; notice of contract.
404. Duties of Courts in counties making contracts.
405. Duties of Sheriffs in counties making contracts; fees of officers.
406. State Prison Inspectors may contract; compensation; notice of contract.
407. Duty of Sheriffs; fees of.
408. Certain males and females under age to be sent to House of Correction.

SECTION
409. Expenses, how defrayed.
410. Inspectors to make certain certificates.
411. Certificates to be published. What offenders from Wayne County to be confined in. Duty of officers conveying prisoners to; fees of officers.
412. Vagrants may be sentenced to.
413. Breaking from, with intent to escape; penalty.
414. Females in State Prison may be transferred to.
415. Record of infraction of rules to be kept; reward for good behavior.
416. Females liable to State Prison may be sent to.
417. Commutation of sentence.
418. Confinement in for not giving bail in State Courts.
419. Sentence to House of Correction by United States Court.
420. Laws applicable to State Prison convicts applied to those in House of Correction.
421. Acts repealed.
422. Governor may terminate operation of Sections 416 and 417.

An Act to establish the Detroit House of Correction and authorize the confinement of convicted persons therein.

[*Approved March* 15, 1861. *Laws of* 1861, *p.* 262.]

Name of.

(§ 396.) SECTION 1. *The People of the State of Michigan enact,* That the building erected for that purpose by the City of Detroit,[a] shall be known and recognized

[a] See 60th subdivision of Section 103, p. 69.

as the "Detroit House of Correction," and shall be used for the confinement, punishment and reformation of criminals, or persons sentenced thereto, under the provisions of this act, or any law of this State authorizing the confinement of convicted persons in said House of Correction.

How to be used.

(§ 397.) SEC. 2. The management and direction of the said House of Correction, subject to periodical inspection by the State authorities in their discretion, shall be under the control and authority of a Board of Inspectors to be appointed for that purpose by the Common Council of the City of Detroit, but the chairman of the Board of Inspectors of the State Prison and the Mayor of said city, shall, by virtue of their office, be members of said Board of Inspectors, who, together with three persons to be appointed on the nomination of the Mayor by the Common Council of said city, shall form said board. The term of office for the appointed members of said board, shall be three years; but the members first appointed, shall hold their office respectively as shall be determined by lot at the first meeting of said board, for one, two and three years, and thereafter one member shall be appointed each year for the full term of three years.

How controlled.

Board of Inspectors, how appointed.

Term of office.

(§ 398.) SEC. 3. The said Board of Inspectors is hereby authorized and empowered to establish and adopt rules for the regulation and discipline of said House of Correction, and upon the nomination of the Superintendent thereof, to appoint the subordinate officers, guards and employees thereof, to fix their compensation and prescribe their duties generally, to make all such bylaws and ordinances in relation to the management and

To adopt rules and regulations.

Officers, how appointed.

Salary of officers, Com. Council to sanction.

government thereof as they shall deem expedient. But no order, ordinance, resolution or act of said Board, fixing the salary or compensation of any officer or employee of said institution, shall be binding and valid until it shall have received the sanction of the Common Council of said city, by a vote of a majority of all the aldermen elect in said city, at some regular meeting subsequent to the meeting on which such proposed salary or compensation shall have been presented to said Common Council,[b] and no appropriation of money shall be made by the said Board of Inspectors for any purpose other than the ordinary and necessary expenses and repairs of said institution, except with the sanction of said Common Council as provided in the case of salaries and compensation of officers and employees.[c]

Expendit'rs, how made.

Meetings of Board, when

(§ 399.) SEC. 4. Said inspectors shall serve without fee or compensation. There shall be a meeting of the entire Board at the House of Correction once in each year, at such time as shall be fixed by said Board. One or more of said appointed inspectors shall visit the said House of Correction once, at least in each month. There shall be a meeting of said appointed inspectors at said House of Correction once in every three months, when they shall fully examine into its management in every department, hear and determine all complaints or questions not within the province of the Superintendent, to determine and make such further rules and regulations for the good govenment of said House of Correction, as to them shall seem proper and necessary. All

Meetings at House of Correction when; to examine into managem't; to hear complaints.

[b] See Sections 98, 218.

[c] See 1st subdivision of Section 103, p. 52.

rules, regulations or other orders of said Board, shall be recorded in a book to be kept for that purpose, which shall be deemed a public record, and with the other books and records of said House of Correction, shall be at all times subject to the examination of any member or committee of the Common Council, the Controller, Treasurer, or Attorney of said city, or any officer or person duly authorized by any court of record in this State, to make such examination. Records of. Open to inspection.

(§ 400.) SEC. 5. The books of said House of Correction shall be so kept as to clearly exhibit the state of the prisoners, the number received and discharged, the number employed as servants, or in cultivating and improving the premises, the number employed in each branch of industry carried on, and the receipts from, and expenditures for and on account of each department of business, or for improvement of the premises. A quarterly statement shall be made out, which shall specify minutely all receipts and expenditures, from whom received, and to whom paid, and for what purpose, proper vouchers for each, to be audited and certified by the inspectors and submitted to the Controller of said city, and by him to the Common Council for examination and approval. The accounts of said House of Correction shall be annually closed and balanced on the first day of January of each year, and a full report of the operations of the preceding year, shall be made out and submitted to the Common Council of said city, a copy of which shall be transmitted to each department of the State Government, and to each county in the State having contracts with said city for the confinement and Books of, how kept. Statements, when to be made, and what to show. Accounts, how audited. Annual report.

How published. maintenance of convicted persons,[d] and such report shall be published in some newspaper published in the city, or in such other form as shall be directed by the Common Council.

Employees, how removed. (§ 401.) SEC. 6. The Common Council of said city may require such further reports and exhibits of the condition and management of such institution as to them shall seem necessary and proper, and may, with the approval of the Mayor and Inspectors, for misconduct or willful neglect of duty, and upon sufficient evidence thereof, remove any officer or employee, or Inspector of said institution, except the Superintendent thereof, who shall be removable for the causes, and as provided in the charter of said city.[e] But any subordinate officer or employee may be removed by the Superintendent at his discretion, or by the Board of Inspectors with the approval of the Superintendent.

Superintendent, his powers and duties. (§ 402.) SEC. 7. The Superintendent of the said House of Correction shall have entire control and management of all its concerns, subject to the authority established by law and the rules and regulations adopted for its government; it shall be his duty to obey and carry out all written orders and instructions of the Inspectors not inconsistent with the laws, rules and regulations relating to the government of said institution. He shall be responsible for the manner in which said House of Correction is managed and conducted. Residence of. He shall reside at said House of Correction, devote his time and attention to the business thereof, and visit and examine into

---

[d] See Section 403, *post*.

[e] See Sections 13, 21, 22, 100, *ante*.

the condition and management of every department thereof and of each prisoner therein confined, daily, or as often as good order or necessity may require. He shall exercise a general supervision and direction in regard to the discipline, police and business of said House of Correction. The Deputy Superintendent of said House of Correction shall have and exercise the powers of the Superintendent, in his absence, so far as relates to the discipline thereof and the safe keeping of prisoners.

Deputy Superintendent, his powers and duties.

(§ 403.) SEC. 8. The Board of Supervisors of any organized county of the State shall have full power and authority to enter into an agreement with the Common Council of the City of Detroit, or with any authorized agent or officer in behalf of said city, to receive and keep in the Detroit House of Correction, any person or persons who may be sentenced to confinement by any court or magistrate in any of said counties, for any term not less than sixty days. Whenever such agreement shall have been made, it shall be the duty of the Board of Supervisors for any county in behalf of which such agreement shall have been made, to give public notice thereof in some newspaper published within said county, and in case no paper is published in said county, then such notice shall be published in some newspaper within the judicial district to which said county is attached, for a period not less than four weeks, and such notice shall state the period of time for which such agreement will remain in force.

Counties may contract for keeping of criminals.

Notice of contract how given.

(§ 404.) SEC. 9. In every county having such agreement with the said City of Detroit, it shall be the duty of every court, Police Justice, Justice of the Peace, or other magistrate, by whom any person, for any crime or

Duty of courts and justices in counties in counties making contract.

misdemeanor not punishable by imprisonment in the State Prison, may be sentenced for any term not less than sixty days, to sentence such person to the Detroit House of Correction, there to be received, kept and employed, in the manner prescribed by law, and the rules and discipline of the said House of Correction; and it shall be the duty of any such court, Police Justice, Justice of the Peace, or other magistrate, by a warrant of commitment duly issued by the court, justice or magistrate declaring such sentence, to cause such person so sentenced, to be forthwith conveyed by some proper officer to said House of Correction.

Duty of Sheriffs and Constables in counties making contract.

(§ 405.) SEC. 10. It shall be the duty of the Sheriff, Constable, or other officer in and for any county having such agreement with said city of Detroit, to whom any warrant or commitment for that purpose may be directed by any court or magistrate in such county, to convey such person so sentenced, to the said Detroit House of Correction, and there deliver such person to the keeper or other proper officer of said House of Correction, whose duty it shall be to receive such person so sentenced, and to safely keep and employ such person for the term mentioned in the warrant or commitment, according to the laws of said House of Correction, and the officer thus conveying and so delivering the person or persons so sentenced, shall be allowed such fees or compensation therefor as shall be prescribed or allowed by the Board of Supervisors for the county in which such person shall have been convicted.

Fees of officers.

State Prison Inspectors may contr'ct for confinem't of criminals.

(§ 406.) SEC. 11. The Inspectors of the State Prison may contract with the said City of Detroit, or any duly authorized agent or officer in behalf of said city, for the confinement and maintenance, in the Detroit House of Correction, of persons convicted of any offense punishable by imprisonment in the State Prison:[f] *Provided*, That the compensation to be paid for such confinement and maintenance, shall not exceed the sum of one dollar per week; and upon the completion and execution of any such contract, the Inspectors of the State Prison and of the said House of Correction shall give public notice thereof, in some weekly newspaper, in each county in which a weekly newspaper is published, after which any male person, under the age of twenty-one years and above the age of sixteen years, who shall be convicted of any offense, murder and treason excepted, punishable by imprisonment in the State Prison, may, in the discretion of the court before whom such conviction shall be had, be sentenced to imprisonment in the Detroit House of Correction; and every male between the ages of sixteen and twenty-two years, who shall, for the first time, be so convicted, shall be sentenced to said Detroit House of Correction. And every female, who shall be so convicted, shall be sentenced to said House of Correction.[g] And every person so sentenced shall be received into the said House of Correction, and shall be kept and employed in the manner prescribed by law, and shall be subject to the rules and discipline of said House of Correction.

Compensation.

Notice of contract, how given.

(§ 407.) SEC. 12. It shall be the duty of the Sheriff of any county within which any person shall be convicted and sentenced, as in the eleventh section of this

Duty of the Sheriffs.

---

[f] See Section 416, *post*.

[g] See case of Elliott vs. The People, 13 Mich., 365.

act provided, to convey such person to the said House of Correction, and deliver him or her to the Superintendent thereof, for which such Sheriff shall be paid the same fees and compensation allowed for conveying persons to the State Prison.

Fees of.

(§ 408.) SEC. 13. All provisions of law authorizing the commitment and confinement of males under sixteen, and females under fourteen years of age, in the jails, work-houses or houses of correction in the City of Detroit, are hereby made applicable to all persons who may or shall be, under the provisions of this act, sentenced to the said Detroit House of Correction.

Expenses of House of Correction, how to be defrayed.

(§ 409.) SEC. 14. The expenses of maintaining the said House of Correction, over and above all receipts for the labor of persons confined therein, and for the support of those whose support shall not be chargeable to the County of Wayne, or be otherwise provided for, shall be audited and paid, from time to time, by the Common Council of the City of Detroit, and shall be raised, levied and collected as part of the ordinary expenses of said city.

Inspect'rs to make certificates; where filed and upon whom served.

(§ 410.) SEC. 15. Whenever the said House of Correction shall, in the opinion of the Board of Inspectors, by this act created and established, or a majority of them, be so far completed as to insure the safe confinement and employment therein, of persons intended to be therein confined, they shall make duplicate certificates thereof under their hands and seals, one of which they shall file in the office of the Clerk of Wayne County, and the other shall be served upon the Sheriff of said county, and the said Sheriff shall thereupon transfer all such persons to the said House of Correction, and the

Superintendent thereof shall receive such persons and safely keep them for the term for which they are sentenced, and employ them according to the discipline and rules established for the government of said House of Correction.

Certificate to be published.

(§ 411.) SEC. 16. Immediately after filing the certificate of completion as aforesaid, the said Inspector shall cause a copy thereof to be published in at least three newspapers published in said county, and thereafter it shall be the duty of every court or magistrate in the said County of Wayne, authorized by law to sentence or commit any person to the county jail[h] of said county as vagrants, common drunkards, disorderly persons, common prostitutes, or for assault and battery, petit larceny, or other offenses punishable by imprisonment in the county jail, or by virtue of any final sentence of conviction except for contempt, to sentence such person to be confined in the said House of Correction, there to be received, kept and employed according to law under the rules and regulations of said House of Correction. And it shall be the duty of all officers having the execution of the final process of any court or magistrate sentencing convicted persons to said House of Correction, to cause such convicts to be conveyed forthwith to said House of Correction, and such officer or officers shall be paid therefor, the fees allowed by law for conveying persons to the county jail. But this section shall

Wh't offenders from Wayne Co. to be confined in.

Duty of officers to convey prisoners to.

Fees of officers.

Exception.

[h] Under this section it was held in Elliot vs. The People, 13 Mich., 365, that there is no power in any court to sentence persons to the House of Correction, except those who may be punishable by imprisonment in the county jail. Also, that such persons can be sentenced to the House of Correction for no longer period than would have been lawful in the county jail.

not apply to those juvenile offenders, who, by law, may be sent to the reform school at Lansing.[1]

Power to sentence vagrants to House of Correction.

(§ 412.) SEC. 17. It shall be lawful for any justice of the peace, police justice, or other magistrate having jurisdiction thereof, in the County of Wayne, or in any other county, having an agreement with the City of Detroit, for the confinement and maintenance of convicted persons in said House of Correction in all cases of complaint for vagrancy to commit any person except such juvenile offenders as are mentioned in the last preceding section, convicted on such complaint before such justice or magistrate to said House of Correction for a term not exceeding six months.

Escape or breaking House of Correction with intent, etc.

(§ 413.) SEC. 18. Every person lawfully committed to said House of Correction, who shall escape from or break said House of Correction with intent to escape therefrom, or who shall attempt by any force or violence, or in any other manner to escape from said House of Correction, whether such escape be effected or not, shall, upon conviction thereof, be punished by confinement in said House of Correction for a term not exceeding double the term for which he or she was so sentenced, to commence from and after the expiration of his or her former sentence.

Penalty.

Transfer of females fr'm the State Prison.

(§ 414.) SEC. 19. Upon the completion and execution of a contract for the confinement and maintenance of persons liable to imprisonment in the State Prison in the said House of Correction, as provided in section eleven of this act, it shall be competent and lawful for the Inspectors of the State Prison to transfer to said House

[1] See Compiled Laws, Section 6243.

of Correction all females confined in the State Prison, and such persons so transferred shall be received into said House of Correction, and there confined and employed for the unexpired term of their sentences respectively.

(§ 415.) SEC. 20. The Superintendent of said House of Correction shall cause to be kept a record of each and all infractions of the rules and discipline of said House of Correction, with the names of the convict or convicts offending, and the date and character of each offense; and every convict sentenced for one or more years, whose name does not appear upon such record, shall be entitled to a deduction of three days per month from his or her sentence, for each month they shall continue to obey all the rules of said House of Correction.

Superintendent to keep record of offences against discipline.

An Act supplementary to an act entitled "An Act to establish the Detroit House of Correction, and authorize the confinement of convicted persons therein.

[*Approved March* 27, 1867. *Laws of* 1867, *Vol. I, p.* 175.]

(§ 416.) SECTION 1. *The People of the State of Michigan enact*, That hereafter, whenever any female shall, in any court of the State of Michigan, be convicted of any crime or offense, except murder, which would under the existing laws of this State subject her to confinement in the State Prison, that the court by or before whom she shall be so convicted, shall sentence her to confinement in the Detroit House of Correction, instead

Females liable to State Prison to be sent to House of Correction.

of the State Prison, for such term as the said court shall deem just; and it shall be the duty of the Superintendent of said House of Correction to receive and securely keep all females so convicted, sentenced and committed to said House of Correction, until the term of her or their sentence has expired, or until she or they are otherwise duly discharged by law or competent authority.[j]

Duty of Superintendent.

Commutation of sentence.

(§ 417.) SEC. 2. Whenever the sentence of any female now confined in the State Prison shall be by the Governor or other competent authority, commuted to confinement for any period in the Detroit House of Correction, it shall be the duty of the agent of said State Prison to at once transmit such person in proper and safe custody, to the Superintendent of said House of Correction, whose duty it shall be to receive and safely keep her in said House of Correction until the expiration of her sentence as commuted, or until she is otherwise discharged by due process of law.[k]

Confinem'nt in House of Correction for non-giving bail to State court.

(§ 418.) SEC. 3. Hereafter, when any person found guilty of disorderly conduct or breach of the peace by any court of said State, in any county, having, with the City of Detroit or its duly authorized agent, an agreement such as is specified and provided for in section eight of said act, to which this is amendatory, shall be sentenced to give bail for good behavior, or upon other condition, it shall be competent for the court by or before which such person is convicted, to sentence her or

[j] See Section 406, *ante*.

[k] The operation of this and the foregoing section, may be terminated by the Governor. See Section 422.

him to confinement in said House of Correction for the non-giving of or until such bail is given, and the Superintendent of said House of Correction shall receive and safely keep the person so committed until the term of commitment has expired, or until he is served with a certificate signed by a circuit judge of the circuit in which is included the county where such person was convicted, stating that by giving of bail, or otherwise, the terms of the sentence or commitment of such person have been complied with.

(§ 419.) SEC. 4. Whenever any court of the United States, in or sitting within the State of Michigan, or any officer thereof, shall order or sentence any person, upon conviction, to be confined in the Detroit House of Correction for any period of time, or for want of bail, or for any other cause, it shall be the duty of the Superintendent to receive such person, and him or her safely and securely keep until the terms of such order or sentence are fully complied with.

Sentence to House of Correction by U. S. Courts.

(§ 420.) SEC. 5. All laws now in force, applicable to persons confined in the State Prison, shall be and are hereby made applicable to all persons who are, or hereafter shall be confined in said House of Correction, who have been transferred to said house from the State Prison, or who shall be sentenced to confinement in said house, on conviction of any offense punishable by confinement in the State Prison.

Laws applicable to persons in House of Correction same as in State Pris'n.

(§ 421.) SEC. 6. All acts and parts of acts inconsistent with the provisions of this act are hereby repealed.

Acts repealed.

(§ 422.) SEC. 7. At any time after two years from the passage of this act, the Governor of the State of Michigan may, in his discretion, by a certificate under

Governor to terminate operations of sections one and two.

CHAPTER V. HOUSE OF CORRECTION.

his hand and seal of the State, filed in the Secretary of State's office, terminate the operation of sections one and two of this act, at a time therein to be stated, a copy of which certificate shall be published in three papers in this State for three weeks prior to the time so stated, and a copy of such certificate shall be sent by the Secretary of State to each judge of a circuit court and to each prosecuting attorney in the State, at least sixty days before the time so stated.

CHAPTER VI.

FIRE DEPARTMENT.

SECTION
423. Board of Fire Commissioners created.
424. Commissioners named; terms of office.
425. Removals.
426. Oath of office.
427. Powers and duties of Board.
428. By what name to be known.
429. Powers and duties of the Commission; exclusive power.
430. Fire apparatus; houses, hydrants, etc.
431. Possession of property, implements, etc.
432. When office is deemed vacant.
433. Estimate of expenses to be submitted to citizens' vote; Fire Commission fund; Treasurer of Board.
434. Money drawn on warrant.
435. Offices to be provided; Fire Marshall; Salaries of firemen.
436. Right of way; penalty for refusing.
437. Property transferred to Commissioners.
438. Firemen exempt from military and jury duty.
439. Seal of Commission; right to sue; fines and penalties.

SECTION
440. Hydrants and fire cisterns; when engines may be sent out of city.
441. Former Fire Marshall's office abolished.
442. Acts repealed.
443. Board may establish rules.
444. Annual report of Commissioners.
445. Expenses of Department to be paid by tax.
446. Books, etc., to be subject to inspection of Mayor and Controller.
447. Act to take immediate effect.
448. Fire Department incorporated; may have a seal and hold real estate.
449. May make by-laws; disposition of funds.
450. Officers of Department; Board of Trustees.
451. Annual meeting of Department.
452. First officers appointed.
453. Interest of funds; how appropriated.
454. Certificates, how obtained; their effect.
455. Yearly list of members to be made for City Clerk.
456. The act made a public act.
457. Act may be modified or repealed.
458. Repeal of inconsistent acts.

An Act to create a Fire Commission in the City of Detroit.[a]

[*Approved March* 26, 1867. *Laws of* 1867, *Vol. II, p.* 931.]

(§ 423.) SECTION 1. *The People of the State of Michigan enact*, That all the powers and duties connected with and incident to the government and discipline of the Fire Department of the City of Detroit, shall be, as hereinafter more especially provided, vested in and

Board of commissioners.

[a] This act supercedes Chapter X, Part I.

exercised by a board, composed of four commissioners, a majority of whom shall constitute a quorum for the transaction of business.

Names of. (§ 424.) SEC. 2. There are hereby appointed as such

Term of office. commissioners, William Duncan, who shall hold his office for the term of five years; Theodore H. Hinchman, who snall hold his office for the term of four years; James W. Sutton, who shall hold his office for the term of three years; and Lucretius H. Cobb, who shall hold his office for the term of two years; and every commissioner appointed at the end of said terms shall hold his office for four years, or until his successor is appointed, except in cases of death, resignation or removal, and all successors shall be appointed by the Common Council on the nomination of the Mayor.

Removals. (§ 425.) SEC. 3. Any member of said Board of Commissioners, may at any time be removed by a vote of two-thirds of the members elect of the Common Council of said city for sufficient cause, and the proceedings in

Proviso. that behalf shall be entered on their journal: *Provided*, that the said Common Council shall previously cause a copy of the charges preferred against such member sought to be removed, and notice of the time and place of hearing the same, to be served on him ten days at least previous to the time so assigned, and opportunity be given him to make his defense personally and by counsel.

Oath of office. (§ 426.) SEC. 4. Immediately after their appointment, such Commissioners shall meet in the office of the City Comptroller of the City of Detroit, and file with the Comptroller the oath of office prescribed for the city officers,[b] and the Comptroller shall give to each a

[b] See Section 17, *ante*.

certificate of appointment for the respective terms of office aforesaid.

(§ 427.) SEC. 5. Said Commissioners, on being qualified, shall meet and organize by electing one of said Commissioners to be president, and appointing a person to be secretary; whereupon they shall possess and have all the power and authority conferred upon or possessed by any and all persons in the City of Detroit, for the prevention and extinguishment of fires, and to the exclusion of all such persons, together with such other powers and duties in said city, as are hereinafter conferred. Meeting to organize. Power and authority.

(§ 428.) SEC. 6. Such Commissioners shall take and have, as provided by this act, control and management of all officers, men, property, measures and action for the prevention and extinguishment of fires within the said city, to be organized as herein provided, and to be known as the "Fire Commission of the City of Detroit." How known.

(§ 429.) SEC. 7. The said Fire Commission is hereby empowered and directed to possess and exercise fully and exclusively all the powers and perform all the duties for the government, management, maintenance and direction of the Fire Department of the City of Detroit and the premises and property thereof, which at the time of the organization of the said commission, were possessed by or under the control of the Common Council of said city, and the officers of the Fire Department of said city or the officers or employees of said city, said powers and duties to be performed and exercised, and said property used in the said city or otherwise, as hereinafter provided. And the said commission shall hereafter have sole and exclusive power and authority to Powers and duties. Exclusive power.

Acts repealed. extinguish fires in said City of Detroit; and all acts conferring upon any other officer and officers any powers in relation to the extinguishment of fires in said city are hereby repealed.

Fire apparatus. (§ 430.) SEC. 8. It shall be the duty of the Board of Commissioners, subject to the provisions of this act, to provide in and for said city, all needed supplies, horses, tools, implements, engines, and apparatus of all kinds, for the extinguishment of fires; to provide fire

Houses and hydrants. telegraphs; to select suitable locations for engine houses, reservoirs and fire-hydrants, and to buy and to sell the same, in their discretion; and also, to construct, repair and maintain engine houses, reservoirs, and fire-hydrants, as they shall judge best, where [and] so long as the construction, repair and maintenance thereof are not otherwise by law committed to another board, and to take all such action in the premises, as may be necessary and proper for carrying into effect the duties herein required.

Possession of premises, implements, etc. (§ 431.) SEC. 9. The Commission hereby created is hereby empowered and directed to possess and exercise full and exclusive power and discretion for the government, management, and direction of the several buildings, premises and property, and appurtenances thereto, and all apparatus, hose, implements, and tools of any and all kinds, which, at the time of the appointment of the Commissioners aforesaid, shall be under the charge and control of any and all city officers, or officers of the Fire Department in said city, for the use and benefit of the Fire Department of the City of Detroit; and it shall be the duty of any and all persons in possession of any property, real or personal, belonging to or set apart for, or in use by or for the Fire Department of said city, to deliver the same to the possession and control of the said Commission.

(§ 432.) SEC. 10. Any one of said Commissioners shall be considered as vacating his term of office in the event of his accepting or holding any political office, and any Commissioner who shall, during the term of his office, be publicly nominated for any office elective by the people, and shall not decline the said nomination within ten days succeeding notice of the same, shall in either case be deemed to have vacated his office.

When office is deemed vacated.

(§ 433.) SEC. 11. It shall be the duty of the Commissioners to prepare and submit to the Common Council, on or before the first day of May in each year, an estimate of the whole cost and expense of providing for, and maintaining the Fire Department of said City, within the current fiscal year, not exceeding eighty thousand dollars for any one year, which estimate shall be in detail, specifying the objects of expenditure, the sums desired for each, and the reasons for the same; such estimates, or so much thereof as the Common Council shall approve, shall be submitted to the approval of the citizens of said city, at the meeting required by law for the approval of certain annual taxes, voted by said Common Council, and so much of said estimates as shall be approved by said citizens' meeting, shall be placed upon the general or other proper assessment rolls, and shall be assessed, levied and collected the same as other city taxes. Said money, when collected, shall be paid into the city treasury, and shall be styled the "Detroit Fire Commission Fund," and shall be drawn out therefrom for the purpose of said commission. Under the fiscal regulations established by this act, the city treasurer for the

Commissioner's estimate of expenses.

Estimate submitted to vote of citizens.

Detroit fire commission fund.

Treasurer of the Board.

time being is hereby appointed treasurer of the Fire Commission Board, who shall on check or voucher, duly disburse said fund by order of such Commissioners, for the purpose of this act, and paid over to the treasurer appointed by said Commissioners for disbursement under their direction.

Moneys drawn upon warrant.

(§ 434.) SEC. 12. All moneys hereafter to be paid to any person or persons out of the fire commission fund, shall be certified by the president or acting president of said commission to the secretary, who shall draw his warrant on the treasurer therefor, stating therein the fund to which it is chargeable, and the person to whom payable; and such warrant shall be countersigned by the president, or in his absence by the acting president of the Fire Commission, [and] the city treasurer shall pay said warrant.

Offices provided.

(§ 435.) SEC. 13. Said Commissioners shall provide such offices and business accommodation for the transaction of their business, and that of their subordinates, in

Fire Marshal.

said City of Detroit, as shall be necessary; they shall have power to select a chief and one or more assistant engineers — one of whom, to be designated by the Commissioners, shall discharge the duty of fire marshal —[c] who may be allowed proper compensation, together with engineers, foremen, drivers, pipemen, firemen and other officers that may be necessary for the efficient working

Proviso.

of said department: *Provided*, That the number of men to each fire engine, or hook and ladder company shall not exceed twelve, who shall discharge such duties as

[c] See Section 441, *post*.

may be designated, and be at all times under the control of and subject to removal by said Commissioners: *Provided further*, That the salary of the chief engineer and assistant engineers shall not exceed two thousand [dollars] per annum; the salaries of engineers of steam engines shall not exceed one thousand one hundred [dollars] per annum; the salaries of supply-men and foremen shall not exceed nine hundred dollars; the salary of the secretary of said board shall not exceed one thousand dollars per annum, and the salary of no other member of said force shall exceed eight hundred [dollars] per annum.

Proviso.

Salaries of firemen.

(§ 436.) SEC. 14. The aforesaid officers and men, with their apparatus of all kinds, when on duty, shall have the right of way going to and at any fire, or in any highway, street or avenue, over any and all vehicles of any kind, except those carrying the United States mail; and any person in or upon, or owning any vehicle, who shall refuse the right of way, or in any way obstruct any fire apparatus, or any of said officers while in the performance of duty, shall be guilty of a misdemeanor, and be liable to punishment for the same.

Right of way.

Penalty for refusing.

(§ 437.) SEC. 15. On and after the organization of the commission, all real estate, fire apparatus, hose, implements, tools, bells and bell towers, fire telegraph, and all property of whatever nature then or theretofore in use by the firemen or Fire Department of the City of Detroit, belonging to said city, shall be transferred by all persons having charge of the same to the keeping and custody of the Fire Commissioners hereby created, and for the use thereafter of said Commissioners; but the said property shall remain the property of the Mayor,

Transfer of all property to Commissioners.

Aldermen and Common Council of the City of Detroit, subject to the public uses of the said Commissioners as aforesaid, and for the purposes provided by this act.

Compensation of Commissioners. Firemen exempt fr'm military and jury duty. (§ 438.) SEC. 16. Said Commissioners shall receive no compensation whatever for their service, but all persons employed by them as firemen shall be exempt from military and jury duty while so employed.

Common seal and powers of Commission. (§ 439.) SEC. 17. The Commission hereby created may adopt a common seal and direct its use, and in the name of its president may institute and maintain suits and proceedings at law and in equity, and may pay any costs, expenses or judgments therein, for the enforcement of its rights and contracts, and for the protection, possession and maintenance of the property under its control, and may also, in like manner, sue for and shall have exclusive right to recover the fines and penalties mentioned in or imposed by the city ordinances, for the more effective prevention of fires and the better protection of life and property in the City of Detroit, and all sums recovered shall be for the benefit of the funds of said Commission.

Fines and penalties.

Hydrants. (§ 440.) SEC. 18. All cisterns and fire hydrants belonging to or now in use by the Fire Department of the City of Detroit, are hereby transferred to the control of said Commission, and it shall be competent for said Commissioners at any time, in their best judgment, to send any steam, fire or other engine with hose and apparatus, to the relief of any community in the vicinity of said city.

Engines s'nt out of the city.

Office abolished. (§ 441.) SEC. 19. The office of Fire Marshal, as now existing in said City of Detroit, is hereby declared to be abolished from and after the organization of said

Commission, and the duties thereof transferred to the person who shall be designated therefor, as provided in section fourteen of this act.[d]

(§ 442.) SEC. 20. All acts and parts of acts contravening the provisions of this act are hereby repealed, but such repeal shall not take effect until the actual organization of the Commission hereby created, and provided that nothing herein contained shall affect the rights of the corporation known as the Fire Department of the City of Detroit, organized January twentieth, eighteen hundred and forty,[e] under its acts of incorporation, and acts amendatory thereof. Acts repealed.

(§ 443.) SEC. 21. Said Board shall have power to adopt such rules and regulations for the government of the force created by this act, as they shall deem fit and proper, not inconsistent with the laws of this State, and the violation of such rules and regulations shall be sufficient and good cause for dismissal from the force. Rules established by the Board.

(§ 444.) SEC. 22. The Board of Commissioners shall, on or before the first Monday in April in each year, report in writing, the condition of the Fire Department within the said city, to the Common Council, together with a list of fires, alarms, losses and insurances on all property destroyed during the year. Commissioner's annual report.

(§ 445.) SEC. 23. The Common Council of Detroit are hereby empowered and directed, annually to order and cause to be collected and raised by tax upon the estates, real and personal, subject to taxation according to law, within the said city of Detroit, the sums of Expense of department to be paid by tax.

[d] This evidently refers to Section 13 of this act. See Section 435, *ante*.

[e] See Section 448, *et post*.

money, as aforesaid, annually estimated, for the said total expense of the said Fire Department, authorized by this act.

Inspection of books and acc'nts.

(§ 446.) SEC. 24. The books and accounts kept by said Board shall, at all times, be subject to the inspection of the Mayor and Controller; and the Common Council may, at any time, require any information respecting the same, the disclosure of which will not impair the usefulness and efficiency of the Fire Department.

(§ 447.) SEC. 25. This act shall take immediate effect.

An Act to incorporate the Fire Department of the City of Detroit.

[*Approved February* 14, 1840. *Laws of* 1840, *p.* 13.]

Preamble.

Whereas, The members of an association, known as the "Fire Department of the City of Detroit," have petitioned the Legislature to grant them an act of incorporation, to enable them the more effectually to accomplish the objects of their organization, and to provide means for the relief of disabled firemen and their families: Therefore,

Fire Department of Detroit a body corporate.

(§ 448.) SECTION 1. *Be it enacted by the Senate and House of Representatives of the State of Michigan*, That all persons who now are, or may hereafter become members of the Fire Department of the City of Detroit, and their successors, shall be, and hereby are ordained, constituted, and delared to be, and continue a body politic and corporate, in fact and in name, under the name and style of "The Fire Department of the City of Detroit," for the purposes recited in the above preamble, and by that name they and their successors may and shall have perpetual succession, and shall be known in law, capable of suing and being sued, of pleading and being impleaded, of answering and being answered unto, of defending and being defended, in all suits, complaints, matters, causes, courts, and places whatsoever, and both in law and equity; and capable of having a common seal; of acquiring, by purchase, gift, devise, or otherwise; and of holding and conveying any real, personal, or mixed estate, necessary, proper, or expedient, for the objects of this incorporation: *Provided*, That the amount of said estate shall at no time exceed the sum of sixty thousand dollars. [*As amended by Laws of* 1859, *p.* 8.]

May have a seal and hold real estate.

Proviso.

(§ 449.) SEC. 2. The members of the Fire Department of the City of Detroit, hereby incorporated, shall have, and are hereby declared to have, full power and authority to make and prescribe such by-laws, rules, ordinances, and regulations, and the same to alter, amend, and change at pleasure, as to them, from time to time, shall seem needful or proper, touching the management and disposition of their funds for the objects aforesaid; touching the regular and special meetings of the department; the regulation, duty and conduct of their members, delegates, and Board of Trustees; the election and displacing of officers and delegates; the admission and expulsion of members; the filling of vacancies in offices; and touching every other matter and thing necessary or

May make by-laws, etc.

Relative to disposal of funds.

Meetings.

Conduct of members and officers.

Election of same.

Admission and expulsion of members.

Filling vacancies, etc.

expedient for the good government and promotion of this incorporation, or which appertains to the business and objects for which the said incorporation is, by this act, instituted: *Provided*, That such by-laws, rules, ordinances, and regulations be not repugnant to the constitutional laws of the United States, or of this State.

Proviso.

Officers of department.

(§ 450.) SEC. 3. The officers of said department, by this act incorporated, shall be a President, Vice President, Secretary, Treasurer, and Collector, who, together with the Chief Engineer of the Fire Department, and the delegates from the several fire companies, and other bodies, pursuant to the provisions of the constitution and by-laws of the department, shall constitute a board of trustees, a majority of whom shall be a quorum for the transaction of business; and said officers and delegates, separately, and as a board of trustees, shall do and perform such duties and things as may be incumbent upon, or required of them, by the constitution or by-laws of the department.

Board of Trustees.

Annual meeting of Fire Department.

(§ 451.) SEC. 4. There shall be an annual meeting of the members of said corporation on the third Monday of January in each year, at which the officers shall be elected by ballot, by a majority of the members present, from their own body. And the officers elected shall hold their offices for one year, or until others be chosen in their places; but in case it at any time happens that an election of officers shall not be made or had on that day, the said corporation shall not be dissolved, but it shall and may be lawful to hold such election thereafter, pursuant to public notice given in one or more of the newspapers printed in said city.

(§ 452.) SEC. 5. Of the Fire Department of the City of Detroit, Robert E. Roberts shall be President; Frederick Buhl, Vice President; Edmund R. Kearsley, Secretary; Darius Lamson, Treasurer; and Elijah Goodell, Collector; who, together with the Chief Engineer of the Fire Department, duly appointed by the Common Council of the City of Detroit, and the delegates chosen as aforesaid, shall constitute the first Board of Trustees, and shall hold their offices until the third Monday of January next, or until others shall be chosen in their stead. Names of officers for first year.

(§ 453.) SEC. 6. The interest arising from the funds of the said corporation, except sufficient to defray incidental expenses, shall be appropriated to the relief of such indigent and disabled firemen and their families as may be interested in the fund, and who may, in the opinion of a majority of the trustees, be worthy of assistance. Interest of funds appropriated to relief of indigent and disabled firemen and their families.

(§ 454.) SEC. 7. All certificates now required to be obtained by firemen, from the Clerk of said city, pursuant to the provisions of any law of this State, shall hereafter be obtained from the department, by this act incorporated; which certificate, signed by the President and Treasurer of this department, and countersigned by the City Clerk of said city, and under the seal of this incorporation, shall have the like effect of those heretofore obtained from the said City Clerk, and shall be satisfactory evidence of the facts therein contained. And each person applying for such certificate, shall pay therefor such sum as the by-laws of the department shall prescribe, for the benefit of the corporation, and the objects thereof. Certificates, how obtained. Their effect.

(§ 455.) SEC. 8. It shall be the duty of the Board of Trustees to make out and deliver to the City Clerk, List of members to be made out yearly and giv'n to City Clerk.

once in each year, or whenever he may request it, an accurate list of all the members of this corporation, who are exempt from jury or military duty, that they are, or may become, entitled to the benefits thereof.

This is a public act.

(§ 456.) SEC. 9. This act is hereby declared to be a public act, and the same shall, in all courts and places, be regarded benignly and favorably for every beneficial purpose hereby intended.

May be repealed or modified.

(§ 457.) SEC. 10. The Legislature may alter, modify, amend, or repeal this act, by a vote of two-thirds of each House.

Acts inconsistent herewith, repealed.

(§ 458.) SEC. 11. All acts and parts of acts which contravene the provisions of this act, are hereby repealed; and this act shall take effect from and after its passage.

CHAPTER VII.

TAXES.[a]

SECTION
459. Duty of Assessor; warrant.
460. Duty of County Treasurer; account of.
461. Powers of Collector; Clerk to give notice of filing bonds; Treasurer to give notice of amount of bonds; Collectors to file bonds.
462. When tax rolls to be delivered to collectors.
463. Duty of Treasurer on return of rolls.
464. Act not applicable to certain taxes.
465. Citizens to vote on tax to raise bounty bonds.
466. Interest on bonds; tax to pay the principal.
467. Limitation to the bounty fund of 1862.
468. Act to take immediate effect.

An Act to provide for the collection of State and County taxes in the City of Detroit.

[*Approved March* 20, 1863. *Laws of* 1863, *p.* 423.]

(§ 459.) SECTION 1. *The People of the State of Michigan enact*, That hereafter, when the assessment rolls of the different wards in the City of Detroit, for city taxes, are annually, fully and finally confirmed, as prescribed by the provisions of the city charter,[b] it shall be the duty of the assessor of said city to make a copy of the assessment roll of each of said wards, to be known as the State and county tax rolls, upon which he shall, upon receipt of the certificate of the Clerk of the Board of Supervisors of said county, stating the amount of taxes apportioned to each ward, ratably assess the county and State taxes, as provided by the general laws of the State, to each of which tax rolls he shall annex a

Duty of assessor.

Warrant.

---

[a] For laws relating to school taxes, see Chapter IX, Part II.

[b] See Section 242, p. 139.

warrant signed by him, directed to the proper ward collector, and made returnable on the first day of February then next, commanding said collector to collect from the persons severally named in said roll the several sums mentioned in the last column thereof, opposite their respective names, with four per cent. as fees for collection, and to account for and pay over to the County Treasurer of Wayne county all the moneys so collected, on or before the said first day of February then next ensuing, except said four per cent. collection fees, and said warrant shall authorize every such collector, in case any person named in any such tax roll shall neglect or refuse to pay his tax, to levy the same by distress and sale of the goods and chattels of such persons, wheresoever the same may be found within the limits of said city, and shall also require the due and prompt return of all unpaid taxes to be made, which State and county tax rolls and warrants the assessors shall deliver over to the treasurer of said county on or before the fifteenth day of November in each year.

Duty of co'nty treasurer. (§ 460.) SEC. 2. The County Treasurer, upon the receipt of said rolls, is required to cause a notice to be published in two daily papers published in said city for three weeks, stating that said rolls and warrant have been made and deposited in his office by the assessors, where they will remain for thirty days from the date of such notice, during which time said taxes may be paid to the County Treasurer without being subject to payment of any per centage for collection, and such treasurer will grant his receipt for every tax so paid, and mark the same as paid on the roll; and said treasurer shall keep a correct account of all the extra

Account of treasurer.

expenses incident to the collection of said taxes under this act, and deliver a true statement of the amount thereof to the Board of Supervisors at their annual session in each year, who shall apportion the same among the several wards of said city, according to their respective valuations, which shall be collected and paid into the county treasury, the same as other county taxes, and credited to the contingent fund of said county. [*As amended by Laws of* 1865, *p.* 147.]

(§ 461.) SEC. 3. The collectors of said wards respectively, shall have the same power, and perform the same duties, in the collection of said taxes, as are now required by the general tax law to be performed by a township treasurer, so far as the same may not be inconsistent with this act.[c] Whenever any person elected or appointed collector of any ward in said city shall have qualified and filed his bond, as required by the charter of said city, it shall be the duty of the City Clerk to give written notice thereof to the County Treasurer; it shall be the duty of the County Treasurer, on or before the tenth day of December, in each year, to notify in writing each of said collectors of the amount of bond required to be given by him, which amount shall be fixed by said treasurer, and shall be at least double the amount to be collected by the collector. The collectors shall respectively, and within five days after receiving such notice, file their official bonds to said treasurer, and his successors, with the County Treasurer, and they shall be conditioned as township treasurer bonds now are required to be; they and the sureties thereto

Powers of collectors.

Cl'rk to give notice of filing of bonds and oath.

Tre'surer to give notice of amount of bonds required.

Collect'rs to file bonds within five days.

[c] See Section 73, p. 42. See also, Compiled Laws, p. 298, *et post.*

shall be approved by said treasurer, and the said collectors and their respective sureties shall be subject to be proceeded against for the non-performance of their duties, as said township treasurers may be;[d] in case any collector shall fail or neglect to file his official bond within the time prescribed, his office shall be deemed vacant, and the Common Council may appoint some person, who shall in his stead collect the State and county taxes of the ward, and who shall qualify, and file a bond, as the collector should have done, and who will be subject to all the liabilities and duties, and entitled to all the emoluments of a collector of said ward, in respect to State and county taxes. [*As amended by laws of* 1865, *p.* 508.]

Failure to vacate office.

Common Council may fill vacancy.

When tax rolls to be delivered to collectors.

(§ 462.) SEC. 4. On the expiration of the time limited for the payment of taxes into the County Treasurer's office, as aforesaid, and as soon as said collector's [bonds] shall have been approved of, it shall be the duty of said County Treasurer to deliver to said several collectors their appropriate tax rolls and warrants for collection, taking their respective receipts therefor.

Duty of Co. Tre'surer on return of tax rolls.

(§ 463.) SEC. 5. When the said State and county tax rolls are returned to said treasurer by said collectors, and the proper returns made, as required by the general tax law, and the requisite affidavit annexed of the unpaid taxes, it shall be the duty of said County Treasurer carefully to preserve all such tax rolls, warrants, returns and affidavits in his office; and it shall be the duty of said County Treasurer, in due time, to make returns to the Auditor General of such unpaid taxes, according to law.

[d] See Compiled Laws, Section 844, *et post.*

(§ 464.) SEC. 6. This act shall not apply to the assessment and collection of taxes in the City of Detroit for the year one thousand eight hundred and sixty-three. Not to apply to taxes of 1863.

An Act to provide for paying or funding the Bounty Fund raised by the citizens of Detroit.

[*Approved March* 6, 1863. *Laws of* 1863, *p.* 66.]

(§ 465.) SECTION 1. *The People of the State of Michigan enact*, That at the public meeting of the citizens of Detroit, to be held during the present year, to take into consideration the taxes proposed to be raised for the fiscal year eighteen hundred and sixty-three, the said citizens shall also vote whether or not they will consent to the imposition of a tax, or the issuing of bonds, to repay, with interest, the sum advanced by sundry persons or associations, under authority of resolutions passed by the Common Council of the City of Detroit, July twenty-fourth and August twenty-sixth, eighteen hundred and sixty-two, as a bounty fund to such inhabitants of said city as might volunteer into the military service of the United States; and in case a majority of said citizens, at such meeting, shall refuse their assent to the levying such tax, or the issuing of such bonds, then no such tax shall be levied, or bonds issued, under this act; but in case the majority of the Imposition of a tax; citizens to vote thereon. In case of refusal.

In case of assent, tax to be levied. citizens at such meeting, so to be held as aforesaid, shall consent to the levy of such tax, or the issue of such bonds, then the Common Council of said city are hereby authorized to levy a tax sufficient to pay said money so advanced, with interest not exceeding seven per cent., Bonds. or to issue bonds for the amount of said advance, to be known as "Volunteer Bounty Bonds," bearing an annual interest not exceeding seven per cent., and redeemable within four years from the time of their issue; the said tax to be levied, or the said bonds to be issued, according as a majority at said meeting shall specifically determine.

Interest on bonds. (§ 466.) SEC. 2. If the majority of said citizens, at their aforesaid meeting, shall determine that bonds shall be issued for such advance, the said Common Council are hereby empowered, and directed to levy an annual tax to pay the interest on said bonds, and an annual Principal; tax for payment of. tax of ten thousand dollars to provide for the retirement of said bonds at their maturity.

Limitation of authority. (§ 467.) SEC. 3. The authority under this act shall be confined solely and entirely to the bounty fund raised during the summer of eighteen hundred and sixty-two, usually called the "Forty thousand dollars Bounty Fund," and shall not apply to any other or future bounties, or issue of city bonds.

(§ 468.) SEC. 4. This act shall take immediate effect.

CHAPTER VIII.

REGISTRATION AND ELECTIONS.

SECTION

469. Registration ordered; Board of; Books; What to contain.
470. City bound to publish notice of meeting; Time and place of meeting; What notice to contain; Vacancies in Board; Expenses, how paid.
471. Duty of Board; Sessions of to be public; Registration, how made; Board may question applicants on oath; Penalty for false statement.
472. Who may not register; Penalty for fraudulent registration.
473. Registration in cities after 1859.
474. Notice to be given; What to contain; Duty of Inspectors.
475. List to be filed with City Clerk.
476. When registers to be delivered to Inspectors; Name may be registered on election day.
477. Registration in townships.
478. Registration in townships in 1859.
479. Registration in townships after 1859; Penalty for fraudulent registration.
480. Sessions of Township Boards, when held; Powers and duties; Penalty for false statement.
481. Who not entitled to register; Penalty for fraudulent registration.
482. When registers to be delivered to Inspectors; Names may be registered on election day; Oath may be administered; Penalty for false statement.
483. Vote may be challenged.
484. Penalty for illegal voting.
485. Only actual residents to be registered.
486. Death and removal of electors; Board to review lists; Provision for subsequent registration; Oath; Penalty for false entry.
487. Copy of township register to be furnished Township Clerk.
488. Penalty for destroying or falsifying register.

SECTION

489. Township Clerk to file copies of register with County Clerk and Town Treasurer.
490. Village elections; Duty of President and Trustees.
491. Voting under assumed name; Penalty.
492. What courts have jurisdiction.
493. Violation of duty a misdemeanor; Duty of Courts and Prosecuting Attorneys.
494. Report to Secretary of State; Duty of Secretary of State.
495. Compensation of Board.
496. Members of Board to take oath of office.
497. Form of registry.
498. Re-registration in Detroit; Notice of meetings of Board; Sessions of; Powers and duties of Board; Former registrations invalid.
499. Review of registration; How names to be entered; Note of persons ceasing to be electors; What applicants are to state.
500. City Board of Registration; Meeting and duties of; Persons registered in more than one ward; Oath of applicant; When Board may direct registration; Interpreter; Penalty for false statement.
501. Proceedings when persons not registered apply to vote; Oath.
502. Review prior to special elections; Notice; Vacancies in Board.
503. Violation of act a misdemeanor.
504. Sessions of Board of Registration.
505. Repeal of certain sections.
506. Division of wards.
507. Continuance in office after division; Election in new wards; Inspectors; Session of Board of Registration; Duties and powers of Board; Rules in registration; Conduct of elections.
508. Acts repealed.

An Act further to preserve the purity of Elections, and guard against the abuses of the Elective Franchise, by a Registration of Electors.

[*Approved February* 14, 1859. *Laws of* 1859, *p.* 483.]

Registraton ordered.

(§ 469.) SECTION 1.[a] *The People of the State of Michigan enact*, That there shall be, in the year one thousand eight hundred and fifty-nine, a registration of the qualified electors of the State. The Aldermen of every incorporated city, and the Supervisor, Treasurer, and Clerk of every township, shall constitute a Board of Registration for such city or township, and their duties shall be as follows: They shall, respectively, provide suitable bound books, or registers, one for each township, and one for each ward, so made and arranged as to contain an alphabetical list of the respective books, names, christian or baptismal, and surnames, in full, of all persons declared by the Constitution of the State to be electors and entitled to vote, residing in their townships or wards, and the date of the registration;[b] and, if the elector resides in a city, or incorporated village, also his residence by the number of the dwelling and the name of the street, if any, and if none, a description of the locality of the same.

Board of Registrat'n.

Board to provide books; how arranged and what to contain.

REGISTRATION IN CITIES.

City boards to publish notice of meetings of board.

(§ 470.) SEC. 2. Each city board shall, at least two weeks previous to the time of their meeting, in each ward, cause to be published in one or more newspapers

[a] See Section 505.

[b] See Section 497.

printed and published in such city, a notice that the Board of Registration will meet on the first Monday of October, in the year one thousand eight hundred and fifty-nine, at nine o'clock in the forenoon, to make a perfect list, as near as may be, of all persons residing in such ward, qualified as electors, under the constitution; and designating the place in each ward where said board will meet for that purpose. And they shall also cause handbills to be posted in at least twenty conspicuous places in each ward, containing a similar notice of the time and place of such meeting of the board for that ward, which notice shall also contain a true copy of section one of article seven of the Constitution, relative to the qualifications of electors. And the board may so divide and classify themselves, that two or more of them may be assigned to different wards, the more speedily to complete the registration; and in case of the sickness or absence of any Alderman, or his inability or refusal to serve at the session, in any ward, the Board shall, in writing, under the hand of their chairman, immediately appoint the Assessor of the ward,[c] or any Justice of the Peace, to act in his stead, who shall be, for the purposes of registration in that ward, deemed a member of the Board of Registration. They shall continue in session not less than three, nor more than five days, in each ward. All necessary blanks and instructions to aid the Board in the discharge of their duties, and all other expenses in performing the same, including the employment of printers, for printing such notices, and the registry lists, shall be provided by the Board, and be paid for by the city.

Time and place of meeting designated.

Handbills to be posted.

What notice to contain.

Vacancies in board.

Length of session.

Expenses, how paid.

[c] Office of Ward Assessor in Detroit abolished. Section 55.

Duty of board.

(§ 471.) SEC. 3. At the time and place mentioned in such notice, the Board, or those members thereof so classified and assigned for that ward, shall meet and proceed to the registration in such book, which book shall be called the "Register of Electors," for such ward, of the names of persons at the time residing in such ward, and so qualified as follows, to wit: Their sessions shall be public, and during the first two days thereof, they shall not write in the register the name of any person, without a request made by him personally, and in their presence; but shall allow him, if able and willing so to do, to write his own name therein, in the proper place. In case of such request, the name of the elector shall be plainly written, by a member of the Board, who shall also note his residence, as required by section one of this act. After the first two days of the session, it shall be the duty of such Board to proceed to complete the list, by writing in such register the names of all the remaining residents of the ward, known by them to be such, and to be qualified as aforesaid, with the proper description above mentioned; but they shall, during their whole session, permit any such qualified person, residing in the ward, whose name has not already been entered in the register, to write it there himself. Opposite to every name, on such register, shall be noted by the Board the day and year of its entry, and during such session, and all future sessions of the Board, in any city or township, they may, for their better information in making the registration, have before them the poll list of the next preceding general election, charter election, or township meeting, to be returned to the proper keeper, at the close of the session, and all such entries

Sessions to be public.

Registration, how made.

shall be made with ink. The Board, at every session, shall have power, and it shall be their duty to question every person presenting himself for registration, touching his residence and other qualifications, as an elector of the ward, and it shall be the duty of the applicant to make truthful answers to all such questions, and the Board may, for the more perfect examination of the applicant, swear, and employ an interpreter, truly and impartially to interpret all such questions and answers, and if the applicant shall, in his answers, make any material statement which is false, he shall, upon conviction thereof, pay a fine of not more than one hundred nor less than five dollars, and be imprisoned in the county jail not more than thirty nor less than five days.

Board may question and require applicants to make oath.

Penalty for making false statement.

(§ 472.) SEC. 4. The name of no person but an actual resident of the ward at the time of the registration, and entitled under the constitution, if remaining such resident, to vote at the next general or charter election, shall be entered in the register. Neither the Board, nor any member thereof, shall write or enter in the register the name of any person, nor suffer him to write or enter his name therein, whom they know, or have good reason to believe, not to be such resident and so qualified; nor shall any person, knowing or having good reason to believe himself not to be such resident, and so qualified, write his name therein, or cause it to be done; and every person so offending shall, upon conviction, be punished for each offense by a fine of not more than five hundred nor less than twenty-five dollars, and be imprisoned in the county jail not more than ninety nor less than ten days.

What persons not entitled to register.

Penalty for fraudulent registration

REGISTRATION IN CITIES AFTER 1859.

Time for registration in cities after 1859.

(§ 473.) SEC. 5.[d] On the Thursday, Friday, and Saturday next preceding the general election,[e] and on the Thursday and Friday next preceding the day of the regular charter election of the city, and during the two days (Sundays excepted) which next precede any special election, after the year one thousand eight hundred and fifty-nine, the Board of Registration of the city, to be constituted as aforesaid, shall be in session at such places in the several wards as they shall designate in their notices, to be published and posted up as hereinafter provided, from nine o'clock in the forenoon until five o'clock in the afternoon, for the purpose of completing the lists of qualified voters, during which session it shall be the right of each and every person then actually residing in the ward, and who at the then next approaching election may be a qualified elector, and whose name is not already registered, to have his name entered in the register, which shall be done in the manner above described; and such board, and each member thereof, and each applicant for registration, is hereby vested and charged with the same rights, powers, duties, and penal liabilities, touching the examination of applicants, as hereinbefore provided.

Notice to be given.

(§ 474.) SEC. 6. At least two weeks previous to the commencement of any such session, the board, at the expense of the city, shall cause a notice thereof to be

---

[d] See Section 504, 505.

[e] See Section 498.

printed and published in one or more newspapers published in such city, designating the place of holding the same; and shall also cause the same notice to be printed in handbill form, and posted up in at least ten conspicuous places in each ward; which handbill shall also contain a true copy of the list of names then appearing in the register for the ward. And immediately after the close of the polls of such election, the Clerk of the Board of Inspectors of that election, and before the counting of the votes, shall, under the direction and by the assistance of the Inspectors, insert and write upon, or attach to such printed handbill, all the names of electors appearing on the register, and not on such handbill, so that such handbill, so corrected, shall be a true copy of the list then appearing in such register, and shall, with the Inspectors, or a majority of them, certify and sign such copy, and file the same in the office of the County Clerk, who shall carefully keep and preserve the same; and the same shall be evidence, *prima facie*, of the original; and in case of the loss or destruction of the original, the same or a certified copy thereof shall be used in its stead.

What notice shall contain.

Duty of inspectors.

(§ 475.) SEC. 7. At the close of their sessions, the board, or the members who made the registration in the particular ward, shall sign the list, adding the date of their signature, and shall immediately deposit the same for safe keeping with the City Clerk, who shall carefully preserve the same in his office until delivered, as hereinafter provided.

List to be filed with City Clerk.

(§ 476.) SEC. 8. At any such general, special, or charter election, in the city, and as soon, at least, as the poll in each ward is opened, the City Clerk shall

Registers to be delivered to inspectors, when.

cause the proper register to be placed in the hands of the Inspectors of Election, to be used by them during the same, and returned to the City Clerk immediately thereafter. And they shall not receive the vote of any person whose name is not written therein; but if any person shall offer and claim to vote at such election,

Name may be registered on day of election.

whose name is not so registered, his name may be registered by the Clerk of the Election, under the direction of the Inspectors, upon the same terms and conditions hereinafter prescribed for the like cases, arising at elections in townships, substituting *ward* for *township;* and both the applicant and the qualified elector shall be subject to the same penalties prescribed in cases so arising.

REGISTRATION IN TOWNSHIPS.

Registrat'n in townships who to constitute board.

(§ 477.) SEC. 9. It shall be the duty of the Board of Registration in each township, to wit: The Supervisor, Treasurer, and Clerk thereof, and in case of the absence of any of them, or his inability to serve, the Justice of the Peace, not holding the office of Supervisor or Town Clerk, whose term of office will first expire, to provide, at the expense of the township, the like book for their township, for the purpose of the like registration of the qualified electors thereof, to be arranged in

Books, how arranged.

the same manner, save that in cases where the elector does not reside within the limits of an incorporated village, a description of his residence may be omitted; but in case he resides within such limits, and in the township, a description of his residence, by the street, and the number of the dwelling, or other brief but intelligible method; and the names of such resident electors of the village shall be written in said register, in a list separate and distinct from those of other electors of the townships, so as to exhibit a correct registration for the village, which list shall be called the *Village Election Register.*

REGISTRATION IN TOWNSHIPS IN 1859.

Proce'dings at township election in 1859.

(§ 478.) SEC. 10. At the annual meeting of each township, on the first Monday of April, in the year one thousand eight hundred and fifty-nine, the Township Treasurer shall, at a place as near as practicable to that of the meeting, and of convenient access to the electors, have said book or register in readiness for the entry of their names, and each qualified elector, residing in the township, may then write his name, at length, in the proper place in said register, if able and willing to do so, or the Treasurer shall, upon request made in his presence, by the elector personally, write the name of such elector in its proper place. And in all cases, under this act, the board, or the members thereof, receiving or making the entry of a name, shall note or cause to be noted, the day and year thereof. During such township meeting, and during all future sessions of the board, the township poll list of the next preceding general election or township meeting, shall be before him or them for their better information in making the registration, to be returned to the Clerk at the close of the meeting or the session. The Supervisor, or other person

Board to have access to township poll list.

Supervisor to register names while making assessments.

or persons charged by law with the assessment of property in the township, for the purpose of State taxation, shall, while making such assessment, and in connection with the performance of that duty, in the year one thousand eight hundred and fifty-nine, have with him the said register, and shall allow each qualified elector, residing in the township, whose name has not been entered therein, to write the same, or shall himself, at the like personal request of the elector, write the same therein, at the proper place, and shall, after completing his valuation of property, and on or before the first day fixed by law for reviewing his assessment, deposit said register with the Township Clerk, who shall carefully keep and preserve the same in his office.

Registration after 1859, how made.

(§ 479.) SEC. 11. After the year one thousand eight hundred and fifty-nine, it shall be the right of any such qualified elector, residing in the township, and entitled to vote at the next election therein, and whose name has not been registered, on any day except Sunday, the days of the session of the Board of Registration, and the days intervening between them and the next approaching election, to apply to the Township Clerk, in person, for the registration of his name, and if, upon such examination as is required by the next following section of this act, the Clerk shall be satisfied that such applicant is a resident of the township, and otherwise qualified and entitled to vote in such township, at the then next election, to be held therein, the name of such applicant shall be written, either by himself or the Clerk, upon a separate paper, to be kept by the Clerk, his residence described, and the date of the entry noted, as required in the two last preceding sections; which paper shall be laid before the Board of Registration of each township, at its next meeting for examination and review. And the names of such persons, appearing thereon, as the Board shall be of opinion are qualified electors at the then next election, and entitled to vote thereat, may, by some member of the board, and under their direction, be entered in the proper register, in the manner above set forth. And every applicant to the Clerk, so causing his name to be entered upon such separate paper, knowing or having good reason to believe himself not to be such resident, and qualified to vote in such township at the then next election, shall, upon conviction thereof, be punished by fine and imprisonment, as provided in the thirteenth section of this act. Penalty for fraudulent registration

REGISTRATION IN TOWNSHIPS AFTER 1859.

(§ 480.) SEC. 12. On the Saturday next preceding the general election, the annual township meeting, and preceding any special election, after the year one thousand eight hundred and fifty-nine, the Board of Registration of each township shall be in session at the office of the Township Clerk, from nine o'clock in the forenoon, until five o'clock in the afternoon, for the purpose of completing the list of qualified electors; during which session it shall be the right of each and every person who, at the next approaching election, or township meeting, may be a qualified elector and entitled to vote thereat, and whose name is not already registered, to have his name duly entered on said register, which shall be done in the manner above set forth. The board shall Sessions of township boards, wh'n held. Powers and duties.

have the power, and it shall be their duty, and the duty of the Clerk, and of the Supervisors individually, when acting under this statute, to question every person presenting himself for registration, touching his residence, and his other qualifications as an elector of the township; and it shall be the duty of the applicant to make truthful answers to all such questions. And the Board, Supervisor, Clerk, or Treasurer, as the case may be, may, for the more perfect examination of the applicant, swear, and employ an interpreter truly and impartially to interpret such questions and answers. And if any such applicant shall, in his answers, make any material statement which is false, he shall, upon conviction thereof, pay a fine of not more than one hundred dollars, nor less than five dollars, and be imprisoned in the county jail not more than thirty nor less than five days.

Penalty for false statement.

Who not entitled to register.

(§ 481.) SEC. 13. The name of no person but an actual resident of the township, at the date of the registration, and entitled under the constitution, if remaining such resident, to vote at the then next election or township meeting, shall be entered in the register. Neither the board, nor any member thereof, shall write, or enter therein, the name of any person, nor suffer him to write or enter his name therein, whom they know, or have good reason to believe not to be such resident and so qualified; nor shall any person, knowing or having good reason to believe himself not to be such resident, and so qualified, write his name therein; and every person so offending shall, upon conviction, pay for each offense a fine of not more than five hundred nor less than twenty-five dollars, and be imprisoned in the county jail not more than three months, nor less than ten days.

Penalty for fraudulent registrati'n.

(§ 482.) SEC. 14. At such election, or township meeting, and as soon, at least, as the poll is opened, the Township Clerk shall cause the register to be placed in the hands of the Inspectors of Election, to be used by them during the election, and to be returned to the Clerk, immediately thereafter; and they shall not receive the vote of any person whose name is not written therein. But in case any person shall offer and claim the right to vote, whose name is not so registered, his name may then be registered by the Clerk, under the direction of the Inspectors, upon the terms and conditions following: One of the Inspectors shall administer to him an oath, in the following form, viz: You do solemnly swear that you will true answers make to such questions as shall be asked you, touching your qualifications as an elector at this poll, so help you God;[f] or an affirmation to the same effect, which oath or affirmation, if he be unable to understand the English language, may be interpreted to him by an inspector, or interpreter, sworn by an inspector, which interpreter shall also interpret his answers to the Inspectors. If, in his answers, on oath, he shall state positively that he has resided in the township ten days next preceding said election, designating particularly the place of his residence, and that he possesses the other qualifications of an elector, under the constitution, stating such qualifications; and shall, furthermore, swear that, owing to the sickness or bodily infirmity of himself, or of some near relative, residing in the same household, (giving the name of said relative,) or owing to his absence from the township, on public or official business,

Clerk to deliver register to inspectors on day of registration.

Names may be registered on election day.

Oath.

[f] See Section 44, p. 29.

or his own business, and without intent to avoid or delay his registration, during the then last session of the board, he has been prevented from causing his name to be previously registered; and if, furthermore, some qualified elector of the township, and not a candidate for any office, at that election, shall take an oath before said Inspectors, which oath any one of them may administer, that he is well acquainted with such applicant, that he has, in fact, resided in the township ten days previous to such election, and that he, the freeholder, [qualified elector,] has good reason to believe, and does believe, that all the statements of such applicant are true, the Inspectors may, in their discretion, direct the Clerk to register his name in the proper place, with the proper date; and if such applicant or such qualified elector shall, in said matter, willfully make any false statement, he shall be deemed guilty of perjury, and, on conviction, be subject to the pains and penalties thereof.

Penalty.

Vote may be challenged.

(§ 483.) SEC. 15. Any person offering to vote at any such election, in a city, township, or village, whose name is not written in the proper register, may be objected to, and his vote challenged, for that cause, by any elector present, and entitled to vote at that poll; and on such challenge being made, the Inspectors shall, if on inspection they find his name not so written in the proper register, refuse the vote. But nothing in this act contained shall be held or construed in any way to affect or impair the right of any Inspector or elector to challenge any person offering to vote, nor the effect of such challenge, as now established by law, or as such right and such effect may hereafter be established: *Provided, however*, That the vote of no person shall be received whose name is not so registered.

Proviso.

(§ 484.) SEC. 16. Any person, knowing that his name is not so registered, who shall vote, or offer to vote at any such election, either in a city or township, and every Inspector, knowing such name not to be so registered, willfully and corruptly consenting to receive such vote, shall, if the vote be received by reason of such consent, be, for every such offense, punished as above provided in section thirteen of this act; and on the trial of the person so voting or offering to vote, the presumption shall be that he knew that his name was not so registered. Penalty for illegal voting.

(§ 485.) SEC. 17. The name of no person shall be registered in any township or ward where he does not actually reside[g] at the time of the registration; and every person who shall willfully register, or cause or procure, by enticements, or other means, the name of any person to be registered contrary to the provisions of this act, shall, upon conviction of any such offense, be also punished as above provided in section thirteen of this act. Actual residence a conditi'n of registration. Penalty.

DEATH AND REMOVAL OF ELECTORS.

(§ 486.) SEC. 18. At every session of the Board of Registration of any township or ward, after the year one thousand eight hundred and fifty-nine, it shall be their duty to review the list of names in their register, and if it shall have come to their knowledge that any person whose name has been registered has died or has removed therefrom and ceased to reside therein, they Board to review and correct lists.

[g] For what constitutes a residence see section 38, p, 27.

shall place the letter D against the name of the deceased person, and the letter R against the name of the person who has so removed, with the date of the entry and the initials of the name of the member making it, so as to show by whom and when made, and thereafter such name shall be considered and treated as no longer in the list, and shall be omitted in the copies above provided for. But if it shall happen that such entry was erroneously made, and such person shall thereafter appear at any election and claim the right to vote thereat, his name may, on his application, be again registered, but upon the following terms: he shall, upon his oath or affirmation, which any member of the Board of Inspectors or the Board of Registration may administer, declare that he has not removed from, but is still a resident of the township or ward, and is otherwise a qualified elector, and entitled to vote. And on making such oath or affirmation, his name may be registered in the manner above described, either by the Board of Registration or the Board of Inspectors. And if such applicant shall swear or affirm falsely, he shall be liable to the pains and penalties of perjury. But in case such entry shall be made falsely, maliciously, and without credible information, the member of the Board making it shall be deemed guilty of a misdemeanor and be punished as such, and the party aggrieved shall be entitled to recover of him in an action on the case trible damages for the injury, and trible costs of suit in any court having jurisdiction of the cause, and the record of the defendant's conviction of the criminal offense, duly authenticated, shall be *prima facie* evidence of his liability.

Provisions for subsequent registration.

Conditions.

Penalty.

Penalty for false entry.

(§ 487.) SEC. 19. It shall be the duty of any city or township clerk, except during the session of the Board or on days of election, on the demand of any qualified elector of the ward in such city, or of such township, on payment or tender of his legal fees, to make out, certify, and at his office deliver to such elector a true copy of the contents of the register of election of such ward or township; for which he shall be entitled to receive at the rate of fifty cents for every one hundred names.

Copy of township register to be furnished by T'wnship Clerk.

(§ 488.) SEC. 20. Whoever shall willfully cut, burn, mutilate, or destroy any such register of electors, or copy thereof filed for preservation, or shall unlawfully take and carry away the same, or unlawfully conceal or refuse, or neglect to surrender the same, with intent to prevent its being used as authorized by law, shall be deemed guilty of larceny; and whoever shall falsify any such register or copy, by unlawfully erasing or obliterating any name or entry lawfully made therein, or by unlawfully inserting therein any name, note or memorandum, with intent thereby to influence or affect the result of any election, or to defraud any person of an election to office, shall be deemed guilty of forgery; and the person so offending shall, for every such offense, be punished by imprisonment in the State Prison not more than five years, or by a fine not exceeding five hundred dollars, and imprisonment in the county jail not more than one year, nor less than ninety days.

Penalty for destroying register.

Penalty for falsifying register.

(§ 489.) SEC. 21. To the end that the contents of such registers may not be lost, it shall be the duty of every township clerk, within twenty days after each general election, to make, certify and transmit to the county

Township Clerk to file copies with Co'nty Cl'rk and Township Treasurer.

clerk of the proper county, and also to the township treasurer, a true copy of such contents, to be by such county clerk and township treasurer filed and preserved in his office; for which, when received, he shall give such township clerk a receipt; and such township clerk shall be entitled to receive therefor from the township at the rate of fifty cents for every one hundred names; and such copy, or a copy thereof, certified by the county clerk or township treasurer, shall be *prima facie* evidence of the contents of the original, and in case of the loss or destruction of the original, shall be used in its stead.

Fees.

Copy evidence.

VILLAGE ELECTION.

Village elections. Duty of President and Tr'stees

(§ 490.) SEC. 22. It shall be the duty of the President and Trustees of every incorporated village, or the persons who are by law authorized to make by-laws and charged with the general powers to regulate and control the municipal affairs of the village, to procure from the Clerk of the township or of the townships, respectively, within which said village may wholly or in part lie, and it is hereby made his duty to furnish to them, at the expense of the village, from the register of electors of the township or townships within which such village is situated, a true copy of the village election register, to be certified by such Township Clerk, and to be delivered to the Inspectors of Election in such village, and used for the purpose of the village election, in the same manner and to the same effect as is above provided for the general election and township meetings in townships, as near as may be; and there are hereby given to the Inspectors of any such village election the same power and authority, and to applicants for registration the same rights and privileges which are given to township inspectors and to applicants at township elections, respectively, at such elections; and such inspectors and applicants and other persons mentioned in the foregoing provisions regulating elections in townships, are charged with the same duties and subjected to the same penalties and liabilities as are provided in like cases at such elections in townships; and the vote of no person shall be received whose name is not written in such register, or in the copy thereof used by the Inspectors of the Election. Such copy of the village register shall be furnished at least ten days before the first village election in the year one thousand eight hundred and sixty, and as often as once in two years thereafter, and oftener if the proper municipal authority shall require it, and the township clerk shall be entitled to receive therefor at the rate of fifty cents for every one hundred names.

Voting under assumed name.

(§ 491.) SEC. 23. If any person falsely personating any qualified elector whose name is registered, shall at any election vote, or offer to vote, in the name of such elector, or if any person shall knowingly encourage or persuade any such person to vote or offer to vote, or if any person assuming a false or fictitious name, shall vote or offer to vote by that name, or shall enter or cause to be entered upon the register as his own a false name, the person so offending shall, for every such offense, be punished as above provided in section twelve of this act.

Penalty.

What courts to have jurisdiction.

(§ 492.) SEC. 24. The Recorder's Court in the City of Detroit shall have cognizance and jurisdiction of all offenses under this act committed within the limits of said city, and the offender may in all cases be there proceeded against by information, as provided by the charter of said city, or any other statute applicable thereto. In all other cases the Circuit or District Court for the proper county shall have cognizance of such offenses committed within the county; and in cases where the punishment is by such fine or such imprisonment, one or both, as a justice's court may impose, the proper justice's court shall have cognizance and jurisdiction thereof.

Violation of duty a misdemeanor.

(§ 493.) SEC. 25. Any willful violation of duty by any person charged with the execution of this act or any provisions thereof, not herein particularly provided for, shall be deemed a misdemeanor, and the person guilty thereof shall be punished accordingly. And it is hereby made the duty of every circuit and district court in its charge to the grand jury, to call their special attention to the necessity of making diligent and careful inquiry touching offenses arising under this act; and also, the duty of every prosecuting attorney whenever he shall receive credible information that any such offense has been committed, to cause the same to be prosecuted.

Duty of c'rts and Prosecut'g Attorneys.

Report to Secretary of State.

(§ 494.) SEC. 26. It shall be the duty of every City Clerk and Township Clerk, annually, in the month of November, to forward, by mail, to the Secretary of State, at the seat of government, the aggregate number of names, not marked with the letter D or R, appearing in the register for such city or township, omitting the names; and the Secretary of State is hereby required to keep a record thereof in such manner as to show the

Duty of Secretary of State.

number of votes in such city and township, arranged in alphabetical order, in a book to be kept for that purpose. And he shall, within twenty days from the approval of this act by the Governor, cause a printed copy of the same to be forwarded by mail, to every such City and Township Clerk in the State.

(§ 495.) SEC. 27. Each member of a City Board of Registration, while acting under this act, shall be entitled to receive two dollars a day, for every day he shall actually serve in performing his duties, to be paid by the city; and each member of a township Board shall receive the same compensation as now provided for Inspectors of Election. Compensation.

(§ 496.) SEC. 28. Each member of a Board of Registration shall, before he enters upon the discharge of his duties under this act, make and subscribe the oath of office contained in the first section of article eight of the constitution.

(§ 497.) SEC. 29. Every register shall be of good paper, well bound and arranged alphabetically in the following form as near as practicable: Registers, in what form arranged.

DATE.	NAME.	RESIDENCE.	REMARKS.

This act shall take effect immediately.

(§ 498.) SEC. 30. The City Board of Registration of the city of Detroit shall cause a session of the Board of Registration of each ward, or election district of said city, to be held on the first Monday in October, in the year eighteen hundred and sixty-four, and on the first Monday in October in every fourth year thereafter, for Re-registration in the City of Detroit.

the purpose of making a re-registration of the qualified electors of each ward or election district in said city; and for such purpose the Aldermen of each ward, or substitutes to be appointed, as provided by section two of the act to which this act is amendatory, shall constitute the Board of Registration for such ward, but said city Board may appoint other persons than ward officers as such substitutes; and in case said wards, or any of them, shall be divided in the formation of election districts, said City Board may appoint the necessary number of five persons to act as a Board of Registration for any district which may otherwise be without such Board. Said Board shall cause a like notice of such meeting and registration, and of the time and place of holding the same, to be published and printed in like manner, and for the same period, as is required by said section two of the act aforesaid.[h] The said several ward or district Boards shall be in session on the first Monday in October aforesaid, and for not less than three nor more than six days thereafter, from nine o'clock in the morning to one o'clock in the afternoon, and from three o'clock to five o'clock in the afternoon, and shall be provided with the proper blank books for registering the names of voters, of the form heretofore used, and shall have the same powers, and perform the same duties, as are conferred upon or required of Boards of Registration under the act aforesaid; and the same rules and requirements shall be observed in such re-registration, in all respects, as were required in the original registration under said act to which this is amendatory. When such

Board of Registration

Notice of meetings of the Board.

Time of sessions.

Powers and duties of Board.

Former registrations invalid.

[h] Section 470.

registration shall be completed, the former registry of electors in such wards or district shall henceforth be deemed invalid, and shall not be used at the ensuing elections; and no person shall vote at any public election in said wards or districts after such re-registration whose name shall not be registered anew, under the provisions of this section, or be afterwards properly entered on such new register, according to the provisions of the act aforesaid, or of this act. [*As added by Laws of* 1863, *p.* 69.]

(§ 499.) SEC. 31. At the session of the Board of Registration in the several wards or election districts of said city of Detroit, except in a year in which a new registration has been made, they shall review and complete the list of qualified voters, as provided by law; and in order to prevent, so far as possible, the blotting, mutilation, or disfigurement of said registration of electors, it is enacted that no name shall be entered in such registers excepting in the handwriting of one of the Board of Registration, and then only by direction of the proper Board during its session; and no member of said Board shall write or make any entry in said register excepting the same be permitted by law, and no other person shall make any entry or mark whatever therein excepting inspectors of election, as provided by this act: *Provided*, That any elector desiring to enter his name in his own handwriting may do so, if the Board shall have decided that such elector is entitled to be registered; but when any person shall have ceased to be an elector of any ward or election district, the Board of Registration for such ward or district, at its session, may note the fact in red ink across the name of such elector, in addition

Review of registration.

Names to be entered by one of the Board.

Proviso.

When persons cease to be electors, note thereof to be made.

to the marks provided to be set opposite his name by this act.[h] No name shall be entered in said registers excepting upon the personal application of an elector desiring his name to be registered, and upon due examination made, as required by this act,[i] unless the person whose name is registered is personally known to the Board of Registration, or at least one member of said Board, to be a qualified elector of the ward or district in the register of which such name is registered. The Board of Registration in each ward and district shall require each applicant for registration to state whether he has previously been registered in or resided in any other ward or district. Each Board shall make a separate list of the new registrations made at their then session, particularly specifying in such lists those who have previously resided or been registered in any other ward or district, noting the previous place of residence of such person, and shall deliver such separate list to the City Board of Registration, at its session hereafter provided to be held. [*As added by Laws of* 1864, *p.* 70.]

How names may be registered.

Applicants to state whether or not they have been previously registered, etc.

List of new registrat'ns.

(§ 500.) SEC. 32. The city Board of Registration, which shall be composed of the members of the Board of Registration assigned to the several wards and election districts of said city of Detroit,[j] shall assemble at the Common Council chamber in the said City of Detroit, on the Monday preceding any election to be held in said city, excepting special elections held for election of ward officers, at nine o'clock in the forenoon. On

City Board of Registration.

Meetings of.

---

[h] See Section 486.

[i] See Sections 471, 480.

[j] See Sections 469, 473.

the organization of said city board by the appointment of a chairman and clerk, said city board shall proceed to examine the register of electors of the several wards and districts of said city; said board may correct any errors appearing therein, but no new name shall be added thereto, or marked so as to indicate that any person has ceased to be an elector in any ward or district, excepting as provided in this section. Whenever said board shall find that any person is registered in two or more wards or districts of said city, the board shall ascertain the ward or district in which such person is entitled to be registered, and shall indicate in the register of any other ward or district the fact that such person is not entitled to vote in such other ward or district, retaining the name of such person in the ward or district in which such person is entitled to vote. Said board may register any person applying to be registered in the register of the district or ward in which said applicant resides: *Provided*, Said board shall require such applicant to state positively, on oath or affirmation, which oath or affirmation any member of said board may administer, to answer to such question as shall be asked him touching his right to be registered by said board, that he has resided in such ward or district at least ten days preceding the session of said city board, designating particularly the place of his residence, and that he possesses the other qualifications of an elector under the constitution, stating such qualifications, and that owing to the sickness or bodily infirmity of himself, or some near relative residing in the same household, (giving the name of such relative,) or owing to his absence from said city of Detroit on public or official business, or on

Duties of.

Proceeding, when pers'n is registered in more than one ward.

Board may register upon application.

Proviso.

Oath of applicant.

his own business, and without intent to avoid or delay his registration during the then last session of the board of registration in the ward or district in which he resides, he has been prevented from causing his name to be previously registered, or that he was not registered in the ward or district of his then residence, during the then last session of the board therein, because of his not having resided in such ward or district ten days prior to the conclusion of the said session of said board, and that he moved into the said ward or district, (stating the time he so moved,) and has continued since to reside therein with intent to become a resident thereof;

Oath of applicant.

and if, furthermore, some qualified elector of said city, and not a candidate for office at the then approaching election, shall take an oath before said board, which oath any member of said board may administer, that he has in fact resided in such ward or district at least ten days prior to the then session of said city board, and that he has good reason to believe, and does believe, that

Board may question applicant.

all the statements of such applicant are true. Said board may question such applicant and qualified elector as they may think proper, in order that they may be satisfied

May direct his registration.

of the truth of such statements. If they shall deem such applicant a qualified elector of such ward or district, and entitled to be registered, they shall direct the chairman of the board to register the name of the applicant, with the date of registration, and his place of residence, in the register of the ward or district in which

Interpreter.

he is entitled to vote. Said board may employ an interpreter, in case either said applicant or qualified elector shall be unable to speak the English language, who shall be sworn by one of said board to truly interpret the oath to said applicant and elector, and to interpret to them said questions, and the answers made thereto, to said board. If such applicant, or such qualified elector, shall in such manner willfully make any false statement, or if such interpreter shall willfully and falsely misstate said oath, questions or answers, he shall be deemed guilty of perjury, and on conviction, be subject to the pains and penalties thereof. No name shall be added to any of said registers by said city board of registration, or entries made therein by said board, unless at least one member of the board assigned to the ward or district in the register of which said name is added or entry made shall be present. [*As added by Laws of* 1864, *p.* 71.]

Penalty for false statement.

(§ 501.) SEC. 33. When any person shall apply to the inspectors of any election, excepting special elections for ward officers, in said City of Detroit, who has not been registered, to be registered by said inspectors, alleging that he was absent during the then last session of the board of registration of the ward or district, said inspectors shall require such applicant to state, on oath, in addition to the statements required by section fourteen of this act, that he was absent from the City of Detroit during said session, and during the session of the City Board of Registration, on the Monday preceding such election. [*As added by Laws of* 1864, *p.* 74.]

Proceedings when persons not registered apply to vote.

Oath.

(§ 502.) SEC. 34. Whenever the Common Council shall order a special election to be held in any of the wards of said city for election of ward officers, said Council, by resolution, shall direct the board of registration that last held its session in such ward to review and complete the list of qualified electors of such ward,

Review prior to special elections.

on a day and at a place to be named in such resolution. Notice of the time and place of the session of said board shall be published in at least one of the daily newspapers published in said city, for at least four successive days prior to such session. It shall not be necessary to insert in such notice the names of registered electors, or post handbills containing the same, as in case of general or charter elections. The provisions of this act, or so much thereof as may be applicable, shall govern and regulate the action of said board, each member thereof, and all other persons, in reviewing and completing the register of electors at such session, and all persons are hereby made liable to the penalties prescribed therein for any violation of the same at such session as if the same were here again enacted. In case there may be any vacancy in the then board for such ward or district, said Council may fill the same. [*As added by Laws of* 1864, *p.* 74.]

N'tice thereof.

Provisions of this act to govern the Board.

Vacancies.

Violation of this act a misdemeanor.

(§ 503.) SEC. 35. Any willful violation of duty by any person charged with the execution of this act, or of any provision thereof not herein particularly provided for, shall be deemed a misdemeanor, and the person guilty thereof shall be punished accordingly.

An Act to amend an Act, entitled "An Act further to preserve the Purity of Elections and guard against the abuses of the elective franchise by a registration of electors."

[*Approved March* 16, 1861. *Laws of* 1861, *p.* 549.]

(§ 504.) SECTION 1. *The People of the State of Michigan enact*, That on the second Thursday, Friday and Saturday next preceding the general election, and on the second Thursday and Friday next preceding the day of the regular charter election of the City of Detroit and not afterward, the Board of Registration shall be in session at such places in the several wards and districts as they shall designate in their notices as prescribed by law, from nine o'clock in the forenoon until five o'clock in the afternoon, for the purpose of completing the list of qualified voters in pursuance of said act, approved February 14th, 1859, and any member of said board may administer an oath or affirmation to the applicant, that he shall true answers make to all questions put to him touching his qualification as an elector. Sessions of Board of Registr'ti'n.

(§ 505.) SEC. 2. So much of sections one and five[k] of the act aforesaid, approved February 14th, 1859, as may be inconsistent with this act, and all other acts and parts of acts contravening the provisions of this act, are hereby repealed: *Provided*, That this act shall apply and have force only in the City of Detroit, in the County of Wayne.[1] Repeal. Proviso.

---

[k] Sections 469, 473, *ante.*

[1] NOTE BY THE CITY COUNSELLOR.—As amended by the Acts of 1861 and 1864, the law is:

1. The several ward boards shall meet on the first Monday in October, 1864, and on the first Monday in October every fourth year thereafter. They

An Act to authorize the Common Council of the City of Detroit to divide any ward of said c ty into two wards or election districts, and to provide for the registration of qualified electors therein.

[*Approved March* 27, 1867. *Laws of* 1867, *Vol. II*, *p.* 1033.]

Division of wards authorized.

(§ 506.) SECTION 1. *The People of the State of Michigan enact*, That the Common Council of the City of Detroit shall have power by ordinance, whenever they deem it expedient, to divide any existing ward in said city into two wards, or into two election districts; the ordinance shall specifically describe the boundaries of each of such wards or districts.

---

shall be in session not less than three, nor more than six days, and from 9 A. M. to 1 P. M., and from 3 to 5 P. M., each day. Their duty is to make a re-registration of electors, and after its completion, every former registry shall be invalid. The act of 1864 gives the city power to fill vacancies in the ward boards, by persons other than ward officers. [*See Section* 498.]

2. During the first two days, the boards shall only register the names of those who make personal request to be registered. After said two days, it is the duty of the board to add the names of all others known to them to be residents of the ward, and qualified electors. [*See Section* 471.]

3. This may be done as provided in section 471, but if the application is made on the ground of absence, the applicant, in addition to the proof and oath required by section 482, must swear that he was absent from the city, (not ward,) during the last preceding sessions of the ward and city boards. [*See Section* 501.]

REVIEWING, ETC.

4. In the years when there is no new registration, the several boards shall meet in such places as the city board shall designate, upon the second Thursday, Friday and Saturday next preceding a general election, and upon the second Thursday and Friday next preceding the regular charter election. [*See Section* 504.]

The duties of the boards, their mode of proceeding, etc., are regulated by sections 473, 474, 475 and 476, as amended by section 499, viz:

No name shall be entered save by a member of the board, or the elector himself.

If an elector has ceased to be a resident, it shall be noted in red ink.

(§ 507.) SEC. 2. Whenever a ward is divided into two wards, pursuant to the provisions of this act, all officers theretofore elected or appointed for the original ward so divided, shall continue to hold their respective offices, unless sooner removed pursuant to the revised charter, until new officers are elected by or appointed for the new wards, or until their successors are elected by or appointed for such new wards. The first election in said new wards shall not be held until the Common Council, by resolution, order or direct the same; such resolution may direct such first election to be held at the next general election ensuing its adoption, or may order a special election for that purpose.

C'ntinuance in office after division.

Election in new wards.

(§ 508.) SEC. 3. Whenever new wards are created by the division of an existing ward, or whenever any ward is divided into election districts, the Common Council shall, at least twenty days prior to the first general or special election to be held in said wards or districts after such division, appoint for each of such wards and

Inspector of election.

No person to be registered save on personal application, etc., unless known to at least one member of the board, to be a resident, etc.

Each applicant to state if he has previously resided or been registered in any other ward.

A separate list shall be made of the new registrations, noting the previous residence of the persons so registered, which shall be delivered to the city board at its next session.

SPECIAL ELECTIONS.

5. [*See Section* 502.]

MEETING OF THE CITY BOARD.

6. This board, to be composed of those assigned to the several wards, must meet at the City Hall upon the Monday preceding each election, (save special elections.) to correct the registers, register new applicants, etc. The section requiring this meeting, provides fully the duties, powers, etc., of the board. [*Section* 500.]

Board of registration, session of. election districts, an inspector of election, who, with one of the aldermen of the original wards so divided, shall act as a Board of Registration in the ward or election district, and who, with one inspector of election, to be elected by *viva voce* vote of the electors present at the opening of the polls at said election, shall form a board of inspectors for such election, but vacancies in any board of inspectors may be filled by the electors present, as in other cases of such vacancies. Time and continuance of session. It shall be the duty of the board of registration hereby provided for, to hold a session in the registration wards or districts for which they act, for the purpose of making a registration of the qualified electors of such ward or district; such session shall commence at least fifteen days before the said first general or special election to be held in such wards or election districts; Duties and powers. such boards shall continue in session not less than three nor more than five days, and shall perform all the duties, and have all the powers required from or conferred upon boards of registration by and under an act entitled "an act further to preserve the purity of elections, and guard against the abuses of the elective franchise by a registration of electors," approved February fourteenth, eighteen hundred and fifty-nine, and the acts amendatory thereof, and all the same rules and Rules in registrat. requirements shall be observed in the registration hereby provided for, as now required in the original registration under said acts; and all the provisions of said acts are hereby, so far as the same can apply, made applicable to all proceedings under this act. When such registration is completed, When completed. it shall stand as and be, in all respects, regarded and acted upon as the original registration of electors of the ward or district for which it was made. All elections in new wards after the said election, shall be conducted and governed as to registration, inspectors and otherwise, in conformity with the provisions of law now in force in reference to other wards. In cases where a ward is divided into two election districts, for the purposes of all elections subsequent to said first election, the Common Council shall, at least twenty days prior to any election, appoint two inspectors, one of whom, with one of the aldermen of the said ward so divided shall act as a board of registration in each of said districts, and with one inspector, to be elected by a *viva voce* vote of the electors of the district present at the polls at any election, shall form a board of inspectors for said election; vacancies in such board may, at any election, be filled by the electors present as in other cases.

Conduct of elections.

Proceedings when divided into two election districts.

(§ 509.) SEC. 4. All acts and parts of acts inconsistent with the provisions of this act, are hereby repealed

CHAPTER IX.

PUBLIC SCHOOLS.

SECTION
510. City to be one District; Schools made free.
511. School Inspectors to be elected; Term of office.
512. Vacancy in office of Inspector; how filled.
513. Persons elected refusing to serve; Board of Inspectors may establish rules.
514. Who constitute Board of Education; Its powers; Property, how disposed of.
515. Quorum.
516. City Clerk to be clerk of the Board.
517. Recorder may meet with Board.
518. General Powers of Board; may make by-Laws.
519. Mayor's Court to have jurisdiction in certain cases.
520. Board to publish annual statement.
521. To establish Library.
522. Taxes for support of schools.
523. Treasurer of the Board.
524. Duty of Collectors relative to school moneys.
525. Collectors and Treasurer to give bonds.
526. Repeals prior acts.

SECTION
527. School taxes to be placed separate on assessment rolls.
528. Who to collect school taxes; collectors to give bonds.
529. Board to elect President.
530. Quorum of Board.
531. Taxes for building school houses.
532. Freemen to vote on taxes.
533. Meeting to be called for that purpose.
534. Meeting may be called by two members of the Council.
535. How school house tax to be collected.
536. Board of Education may borrow money; bonds may be issued.
537. Bonds a lien on property of Board.
538. Board to pay interest on bonds.
539. Amends other sections.
540. Amends other sections.
541. Removal of School Inspectors from the ward.
542. Council may authorize levy of taxes for building school houses.
543. Act to take immediate effect.
544. Estimates to be made.
545. To be communicated to Council.
546. Repeals acts.
547. Act to take immediate effect.

An Act in relation to Free Schools in the City of Detroit.[a]

[*Approved Feb.* 17, 1842. *Laws of* 1842, *p.* 112.]

Detroit to be one School District.

(§ 510.) SECTION 1. *Be it enacted by the Senate and House of Representatives of the State of Michigan*, That the City of Detroit shall be considered as one School District, and hereafter all schools organized therein, in

[a] For the laws relating to the "colored children" of the city, see Session Laws of 1841, page 48.

pursuance of this act, shall, under the direction and regulations of the Board of Education, be public and free to all children residing within the limits thereof, between the ages of five and seventeen years, inclusive. Schools free to scholars of certain ages.

(§ 511.) SEC. 2. In lieu of the School Inspectors now required to be elected in said city, there shall be twelve[b] School Inspectors to be elected in the manner following: At the next annual charter election, there shall be elected in each ward of said city, two School Inspectors, one of whom shall hold his office for two years, and the other for one year; and at every annual charter election thereafter, there shall be elected in each ward, one School Inspector, who shall hold his office for two years. No School Inspector shall be entitled to receive any compensation for his services. School Inspectors to be elected. Their term of office. Not to receive compensation.

(§ 512.) SEC. 3. In case of a vacancy in the office of School Inspector, the Common Council of the City of Detroit may fill the same, until the next annual election, when, if such vacancy happen in the first year of the term of said office, the electors of the proper ward may choose a suitable person to fill the remainder of such term: *Provided*, The City Clerk shall give notice of such vacancy prior to such election, as may be required in other cases. Vacancy in office of School Inspector, how filled. Proviso.

(§ 513.) SEC. 4. Every person elected to the office of School Inspector, who, without sufficient cause, shall neglect or refuse to serve, shall forfeit to the Board of Education for the use of the library, the sum of ten dollars, to be recovered in an action of debt in some Persons elected scho'l Inspectors refusing to serve, may be fined.

[b] By the increase in the number of wards of the city, the number of School Inspectors has been increased to twenty.

Proviso.

Board may establish rules and regulations and fine its members.

competent court: *Provided*, No person shall be compelled to serve two terms successively; and the said Board shall make all necessary rules and regulations relative to its proceedings, and punish by fine, not exceeding five dollars for each offense by any member of the Board, who may, without sufficient cause, absent himself from any meeting thereof, to be collected as they may direct.

Who to constitute Bo'rd of Education.

Bo'rd a body corporate.

Its powers and privileges.

How proceeds of property received by Board to be disposed of.

Proviso.

(§ 514.) SEC. 5. The School Inspectors, together with the Mayor and Recorder of said city, (who are declared to be *ex officio* School Inspectors,) shall be a body corporate, by the name and style of "The Board of Education of the City of Detroit," and in that name may be capable of suing and being sued, and of holding or selling, and conveying real and personal property, as the interest of said Common Schools may require; and shall also succeed to, and be entitled to demand all moneys and other rights belonging to or in possession of the Board of School Inspectors, or any member thereof, or any real and personal property or other rights, of any such district in said city; and the clear proceeds of all such property which may come into the possession of said Board, as last aforesaid, shall be expended and disbursed by and under the authority of said Board of Education, for the support of said schools, after paying all just and legal demands existing against the several school districts heretofore existing in said city: *Provided*, That said Board shall not be liable to pay an aggregate amount of indebtedness against any one district, greater than the amount received from the same by said Board. [*As amended by the Laws of* 1843, *p.* 23.]

What a quorum of Board.

(§ 515.) SEC. 6. The Board of Education (eight members whereof may form a quorum,) may meet from time to time,[c] at such place in said city as they may designate.[d]

(§ 516.) SEC. 7. The Clerk of said city shall be *ex officio* Clerk of said Board, and shall perform such duties as the Board of Education may reasonably require. In case of the absence of said Clerk, or for any other cause, the Board may choose some suitable person to perform his duties, either as principal or deputy Clerk. **Who to be Clerk of Board.**

(§ 517.) SEC. 8. The Recorder of said city shall be entitled to a seat at the meeting of said Board, for the purpose of deliberation, and of acting on committees, but shall have no vote therein. **Recorder of Detroit may meet with the Board.**

(§ 518.) Sec. 9. The Board of Education shall have full power and authority, and it shall be their duty, to purchase school houses, and apply for and receive from the County Treasurer or other officer, all moneys appropriated for primary schools and district library of said city, and designate a place where the library may be kept therein. The said Board shall also have full power and authority to make by-laws and ordinances relative to taking the census of all children in said city between the ages of five and seventeen years[e]; relative to making all necessary reports and transmitting the same to the proper officers, as designated by law, so that said city may be entitled to its proportion of the primary **General powers and authority of the Board.** **May make by-laws and ordinances relative to certain matters.**

---

c See Section 530. By the Laws of 1846, p. 102, six members were made a quorum.

d The remainder of this section, relative to the Mayor or Recorder being the presiding officer of the Board, was repealed by Section 2 of the Act of 1846, Laws of 1846, p. 101. See Section 529.

e By the Laws of 1850, p. 50, and 1855, p. 3, (see Section 522 *post*,) the assessment for School Taxes is to be based on the number of children between "four" and "eighteen." See also Compiled Laws, Section 2261.

school fund; relative to the visitation of schools; relative to the length of time schools shall be kept, which shall not be less than three months in each year; relative to the employment of and examination of teachers, their powers and duties; relative to regulation of schools and the books to be used therein; relative to the appointment of necessary officers, and prescribe their powers and duties; relative to anything whatever that may advance the interests of education, the good government and prosperity of common schools in said city, and the welfare of the public concerning the same.

Mayor's Court to have jurisdiction under by-laws of the Bo'rd.

(§ 519.) SEC. 10. The Mayor's Court[f] shall have jurisdiction of all suits wherein the said Board may be a party, and of all prosecutions for violation of said by-laws and ordinances.

Board to publish an an'ual statement.

(§ 520.) SEC. 11. The said Board shall annually, in the month of February, publish in some newspaper of the city, a statement of the number of schools in said city, the number of pupils instructed therein the year preceding, the several branches of education pursued by them, and the expenditures for all things authorized by this act, during the preceding year.

To establish a library.

The People ex rel., vs. the Treasurer of Wayne County, 8 Mich., 392.

Tax for, how levied.

(§ 521.) SEC. 12. The Board of Education shall establish a district library, and for the increase of the same, the Common Council are authorized annually to lay a tax on the real and personal property within said city of a sum not exceeding two hundred dollars, which tax shall be levied and collected in the same manner as the moneys raised to defray the general expense of said city.[g]

---

[f] Now Recorder's Court. See Section 274, p. 157.

[g] As to fines for library, see Compiled Laws, Section 2358.

(§ 522.) SEC. 13.[h] The Common Council of said city are hereby authorized, once in each year, to assess and levy a tax on all the real and personal property in said city according to the city assessment rolls of that year, which shall not exceed two dollars for every child in said city, between the ages of four and eighteen years, the number of children to be ascertained by the last report on the subject, on file in the office of the Clerk of the County of Wayne, or in the office of the Secretary of said Board of Education, and certified by the President thereof; and the said tax shall be collected in the same manner as the moneys raised to defray the general expenses of said city. All said money shall be disbursed by the authority of said Board for the maintenance and support of said schools, and for no other purpose. The said Board of Education shall have authority to establish a high school in said city, and also to appoint a Superintendent of the public schools, under the charge of said Board, with such salary and with such powers and duties as shall be prescribed by said Board of Education. [*As amended by Laws of* 1855, *p.* 3.]

Common Council may levy taxes for support of schools.

How taxes collected and disbursed.

Board may establish high school, and appoint a Superintendent of public schools.

(§ 523.) SEC. 14. The Treasurer of said city shall be the Treasurer of said Board, unless otherwise directed by said Board; he shall keep all moneys belonging to said schools separate from the moneys belonging to the corporation of said city, and he shall not pay out or expend the school moneys without the authority of the said Board.

Who to be Treasurer of Board, his duties.

(§ 524.) SEC. 15. The Collector of said city, when he shall have paid any school money to said Treasurer

Duty of collectors relative to scho'l moneys.

[h] See Section 527, *post*.

or other person, shall take a receipt therefor, and file the same with the Clerk of said board; and it shall be the further duty of the Collector, when he shall have made his final return concerning the collection of said tax, to make a report to said Board, stating the whole amount of school tax, the amount collected, and the amount returned by him to the Common Council as unpaid or uncollected. If any Collector shall neglect or refuse to pay to said Treasurer the sums of money required by his warrant, or to account for the same as unpaid, at the time and in the manner required by law the Recorder of the city of Detroit, or the President of the Board of Education of said city, shall forthwith issue a warrant under his hand, directed to the Sheriff of said county, commanding him to levy such sums as shall remain unpaid and unaccounted for, together with his fees for collecting the same, of the goods and chattels, lands and tenements of such Collector and his sureties, and to pay the same to the Treasurer of said Board of Education, and return such warrant within twenty days after the date thereof.—[*As amended by Laws of* 1855, *p.* 3.]

Collectors refusing to pay moneys collected, how proceeded against.

Collectors and Treasurer to give bonds.

(§ 525.) SEC. 16. The Collector and Treasurer shall, before they enter on their duties under this act, enter into such bonds to said Board, and with such sureties as may be deemed necessary, conditioned for the faithful discharge of their duties respectively under this act.[1]

Prior acts repealed.

(§ 526.) SEC. 17. All parts of acts, so far as they relate to the City of Detroit, inconsistent with this act, are hereby repealed. And it shall not be necessary to elect any school district officers in said city, as heretofore required by law.

[1] See Section 528, *post.*

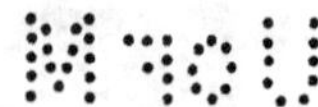

An Act to amend "An Act relative to Free Schools in the City of Detroit."

[*Approved Feb.* 13, 1843, *Laws of* 1843, *p.* 22.]

(§ 527.) SECTION 1. *Be it enacted by the Senate and House of Representatives.* That all taxes which have been or may hereafter be assessed and levied by the Common Council of the City of Detroit, under and by virtue of the authority conferred on said Council by the thirteenth section of an act entitled "An act relative to Free Schools in the City of Detroit," shall be set forth in the assessment roll of said city, in a separate column, apart and distinguished from all other city taxes;[j] and that the Collector of said city shall collect and is hereby authorized and required to collect, said taxes in money, and said Collector shall not be required or permitted to receive in payment of said taxes any liabilities or evidences of debt against said city.[k]

School taxes to be placed in sep'rate column on assessment roll.

What Collector shall receive for school taxes.

An Act to amend an act entitled "An Act relative to Free Schools in the City of Detroit." Approved Feb. 17, 1842.

[*Approved April* 28, 1846. *Laws of* 1846, *p.* 101.]

(§ 528.) SECTION 1. *Be it enacted by the Senate and House of Representatives:* That the Collectors of the City of Detroit, elected in the different wards of said city,

Who to collect school taxes.

---

[j] See Section 243, p. 139.

[k] Section 2 of this act, is incorporated into Section 514, *ante.*

shall act as Collectors of the school tax assessed and levied in said city, in their respective wards, under and by virtue of the provisions of the act to which this act is amendatory; and that each of said Collectors, previous to his entering upon his duties, shall, in addition to the bond now required by law,[l] make and execute to the Board of Education of said City of Detroit a bond, with two good and sufficient sureties, to be by them approved, in the penal sum directed by said Board, conditioned for the faithful performance of his duties as such Collector; and that in case of neglect or refusal of any one of said Collectors to execute and obtain such bond according to the provisions of this section, he be subject to a penalty of one hundred dollars, to be collected in an action of debt, which may be brought in any court in this State, at the suit and in the name of the said Board of Education of the City of Detroit.

Collect'rs to give bonds.

Conditions of bonds.

(§ 529.) SEC. 2. The Board of Education of the City of Detroit may elect one of their own number President of the Board, who shall perform all the duties, and be vested with all the powers conferred by the act to which this act is amendatory, upon the Mayor and Recorder of said City of Detroit, or either of them; and all the provisions of the act to which this act is amendatory, providing that the Mayor or Recorder of said city shall be the President of said Board, are hereby repealed. The term of office, and time and mode of said election of said President, to be prescribed by said Board.

(§ 530.) SEC. 3. Eleven members of the board shall constitute a quorum for the transaction of business.[m] [*As amended by Laws of* 1867, *Vol. II, p.* 115.]

[l] See Section 525, also Sections 18, p. 20, and § 30, p. 23.

[m] See Section 515.

An Act to amend an act entitled "An Act relative to Free Schools in the City of Detroit." Approved Feb. 17, 1842.

[*Approved March* 12, 1847. *Laws of* 1847, *p.* 50.]

(531.) SECTION 1.[n] *Be it enacted by the Senate and House of Representatives:* That in addition to the taxes mentioned in the act to which this act is amendatory, the Common Council of the City of Detroit is hereby authorized and empowered to levy and collect a tax, not exceeding fifteen hundred dollars in any one year, to be expended in the purchase of lots in said city, for the use of the public schools thereof, and the erection and building a school house or school houses, with the necessary out buildings and fixtures, on any lot or lots which may be so purchased, or any other lots now owned by the Board of Education of said city, or which the said Board may hereafter acquire: *Provided,* That said tax, when so levied and collected, shall be paid to the Treasurer of said Board of Education, and be vested in said Board to and for the purpose hereinbefore stated, and no other, and also that the title to such lots purchased shall also be in said Board for the purpose aforesaid.

Taxes for building school houses and purchasing lots ther'for may be levied.

Proviso.

Title to sch'l lots in wh'm vested.

(§ 532.) SEC. 2. Said tax shall not be levied or collected, unless at a meeting of the freemen of said city, called for such purpose, as hereinafter provided; a majority of the freemen present shall assent to the same.[o]

Freemen to vote on taxes for school houses.

---

[n] See Section 542 amending this Section.

[o] See Section 545.

Mayor or Recorder to call meeting of freemen to vote on taxes.

(§ 533.) SEC. 3. It shall be the duty of the Mayor, or Recorder, in case of the absence of the Mayor, or a vacancy in his office, to call such a meeting of the freemen of said city, for the purpose of giving their assent or dissent to such tax, when it shall be requested by petition, signed by twenty-four freemen of said city; which call shall particularly express the object of such meeting, and shall be published in two of the daily newspapers published in the said City of Detroit, one week previous to such meeting: *Provided*, That the Mayor may call such meeting upon the notice herein mentioned, without such petition, at his own option.

Proviso.

Meeting of freem'n may be called by two members of Co'ncil in certain cases.

(§ 534.) SEC. 4. If the said Mayor or Recorder shall refuse to call such meeting, upon the presentation to either of them of such petition, or shall neglect to do so for three days after the presentation of such petition, any two members of the Common Council of said city may on the like petition, call such meeting, upon a like notice and publication thereof, in the manner and for the time hereinbefore specified in the case of a call by the Mayor or Recorder. Such meeting may be adjourned, from time to time, by vote of a majority of those present.

How taxes for school houses and lots to be collected.

(§ 535.) SEC. 5. The said tax shall be levied and collected in the same manner as the tax provided for in the thirteenth section[p] of the act to which this act is amendatory, and shall be consolidated therewith on the tax rolls; but it shall be the duty of the said Board of Education, in each and every year, when such tax is levied and collected, to separate the amount thereof from the gross amount of money received by said Board

[p] Section 522, *ante*.

for such year, and set it apart as a fund to be reserved for the purposes specified in the first section of this act.

(§ 536.) SEC. 6. The Board of Education of the City of Detroit is hereby authorized, from time to time, on such term or terms of payment as they may deem proper, to borrow a sum of money not exceeding in all the sum of five thousand dollars, for the purposes specified in the first section[q] of this act, at a rate of interest not exceeding seven per cent. per annum, payable semi-annually and to issue the bonds of said Board in such form, and executed in such manner as said Board may direct: *Provided,* That said Board shall issue no bond for a less sum than fifty dollars. [*As amended by Laws of* 1850, *p.* 50.]

Board of Education may b'rrow money and issue bonds for payment.

Proviso.

(§ 537.) SEC. 7. The bonds issued under this act shall be a charge upon all the property of said Board, which shall constitute a security for the payment thereof: *Provided,* That no legal proceedings shall be instituted to enforce such lien, or to sell any property of said Board for the payment of the principal money of any of said bonds, until one year after such principal shall become due, according to the tenor and effect thereof.

Bonds to be a lien on property of Board.

Proviso.

(§ 538.) SEC. 8. It shall be the duty of the Board of Education, whenever they shall borrow any money, under the provisions of this act, annually to appropriate a sufficient sum out of any money which may come into their hands, to pay the interest upon the same; and also in addition thereto, an annual sum equal to five per cent. upon the amount so borrowed, to be invested, under the direction of said Board, in bonds of the City of Detroit,

Board to keep interest on bonds paid and provide sinki'g fund to pay principal.

---

[q] Section 531, *ante.*

bearing interest at such prices as the same can be purchased, to accumulate as a sinking fund for the payment of the principal of the sum so borrowed; both of which appropriations shall take precedence of all others.

An Act to amend an Act entitled "An Act relative to Free Schools in the City of Detroit."

[*Approved March* 5, 1850. *Laws of* 1850, *p.* 50.]

(§ 539.) SECTION 1.[r]

(§ 540.) SECTION 2.[s]

Removal of School Inspector fr'm ward for which he is elected not to vacate his office.

(§ 541.) SEC. 3. The removal of any member of the Board of Education of the City of Detroit, from the ward for which he is elected School Inspector, after such election, shall not operate to vacate his office;[t] but notwithstanding such removal, any inspector, so removing, shall continue to hold his said office, and to be a member of said Board, and all provisions of any act or acts, which make such removal a vacation of said office, are hereby repealed: *Provided*, The removal of such member shall not be from the city.

Proviso.

---

[r] Amends Section 13 of the Act of 1842, by simply changing the ages on on which the school assessment is based, from "five to seventeen," to "four" and "eighteen." Section 13 was again amended by Laws of 1855, p. 3. See Section 522, *ante*.

[s] Amends Section 6 of Act of 1847. See Section 536.

[t] See Section 7, p. 15.

An Act to amend an Act, entitled "An Act in relation to Free Schools in the City of Detroit." Approved Feb. 7th, 1857.

[*Approved March* 7, 1861. *Laws of* 1861, *p.* 127.]

(§ 542.) SECTION 1. *The People of the State of Michigan enact*, That in lieu of the fifteen hundred ($1,500) dollars mentioned in the first (1) section of an act approved March twelfth, (12,) eighteen hundred and forty-seven, (1847,)[u] and in addition to all other taxes, authorized by law to be assessed and levied for school purposes in the City of Detroit, the Common Council of said city is hereby authorized and empowered to levy and collect a tax not exceeding twenty thousand ($20,000) dollars in any one year, to be expended in the purchase of lots, and in paying for lots already purchased in said city for the use of the public schools thereof, and in the erection and building of school houses with the necessary outbuildings and fixtures, on any lots now owned by the Board of Education, in said city, or which said Board may hereafter require. Said tax, when so levied and collected, shall be paid to the Treasurer of said Board, and shall vest in said Board for the sole purposes hereinbefore stated, unless the said Board shall, by resolution, direct the same to be applied in whole or in part for the maintenance and support of the schools of said Board, in which case said tax may be so applied; said tax shall be collected in the same manner, and with

Common Council authorized to levy taxes for building school houses.

Tax to be paid to treasurer of Board of Education.

[u] See Section 531, *ante*.

the same right, duties, powers and obligations, as the general school taxes in said city.[w]

(§ 543.) SEC. 2. This act is ordered to take immediate effect.

An Act to provide for the levying and collecting of taxes for the maintenance of Free Schools in the City of Detroit.

[*Approved March* 16, 1865. *Laws of* 1865, *p.* 350.]

Estimates of expenses to be made.

(§ 544.) SECTION 1. *The People of the State of Michigan enact*, That it shall be the duty of "the Board of Education of the City of Detroit," to annually make an estimate of the amount of taxes deemed necessary for the ensuing or then current year, for all purposes of expenditure within the powers of said Board, which estimate shall specify the amounts required for the different objects of expense, as particularly as may be, including the teachers' salaries, purchase of lots, buildings, repairs, fuel and general current expenses.

Estimates to be communicated to Common Council.

(§ 545.) SEC. 2. When said estimate shall have been so made, it shall be the duty of the President of said Board, to communicate the same to the Common Council of said city; and it shall be the duty of said Common Council to assess and levy the amount of said estimate, and cause the same to be collected and paid over to said Board of Education for the purposes of the free

Levy and collecti'n of.

[w] The only change made in the original section of the Laws of 1857, p. 163, is introducing the word "require" in the place of "acquire;" also, the words "unless said board shall," etc., between the words "hereinbefore stated" and the words "said tax shall be collected."

schools of said city under their jurisdiction: *Provided*, That if the amount of such estimate shall exceed in any one year, a sum equal to three dollars for each child in said city, according to the last report of the school census of said city, on file in the office of the Clerk of the County of Wayne, or in the office of the Secretary of said Board of Education, and certified by the President thereof,[x] then and in that case, as to so much of said aggregate estimate as exceeds the amount of three dollars for each child as aforesaid, if the said Common Council approve, the whole or any part thereof, they shall cause the said excess, or so much thereof as they approve, which shall not however, exceed said three dollars per child by more than the sum of twenty-five thousand dollars, to be submitted to the approval of the citizens of said city at the meeting required by law, to be held for the approval of such annual taxes voted by said Council,[y] as require such approval of a citizens' meeting; and if such excess be submitted over and above said sum, equal to three dollars per child, and not being more than twenty-five thousand dollars beyond said sum, shall be approved by said citizens' meeting, then the total amount of such tax for school purposes for such year, shall be a sum equal to three dollars per child as aforesaid, together with the additional amount so approved by said Common Council and by said citizens' meeting, otherwise it shall be so much of said estimate as shall not exceed three dollars per child aforesaid, and no more.

When estimate exceeds $3 per child, surplus to be submitt'd to approval of citizens.

[x] See Section 522, *ante*.

[y] See Section 200, p. 117. Also, Section 532, *et post*.

Acts repealed.

(§ 546.) SEC. 3. All acts and parts of acts inconsistent with the provisions of this act, are hereby repealed.

(§ 547.) SEC. 4. This act shall take immediate effect.

CHAPTER X.

DRAINAGE.

SECTION
548. Council to certify nuisance.
549. Proceedings thereupon; Jury to view.
550. Proceedings on view of premises.
551. Same.
552. Statement of damages to be signed by Jury.

SECTION
553. Entry on premises authorized.
554. Right to maintain ditches.
555. Trespass on the same.
556. Failure to attend as Juror, fineable.
557. Act to have immediate force.

An Act to provide for draining certain low lands in the vicinity of Detroit.[a]

[*Approved March* 29, 1849. *Laws of* 1849, *p.* 185.]

Whereas, It is represented and believed by the Mayor, Aldermen and Freemen of the City of Detroit, that great and serious injury to the health of the citizens of said city results from the overflow of water on the low lands, in the rear of and adjacent to said city, thereby overflowing a large portion of the lots of ground on which buildings are now being erected; and as the drains constructed, although of large dimentions, are by no means capable of carrying off at once the floods of water resulting from sudden rains or dissolving of snows, it follows that many cellars are filled with water, and the *debris* thus carried into them, from which the injury to health must be apparent; therefore,

(§ 548.) SECTION 1. *Be it enacted by the Senate and House of Representatives of the State of Michigan*, That the Common Council of the City of Detroit, shall inquire

Common Council to certify nuisance, etc.

[a] See Section 287, p. 262.

into, and certify, whether any, and what marsh, swamp, or other low lands are a source of disease to the public health of said city, and whether said public health will be promoted by draining the same; and if they shall so certify, shall file said certificate with the Clerk of the Mayor's Court of said City.

Proceeding thereupon.

(§ 549.) SEC. 2. The Common Council shall thereupon issue a summons directed to the Marshall of said city, Sheriff, or any constable of the County of Wayne, requiring him to summons nine reputable freeholders of such county, who are not interested in the lands through which any ditch contemplated to be cut shall pass, nor in anywise of kin to the parties interested in the land, to be and appear on the premises at a certain time to be specified in such summons, not less than fifteen nor more than twenty days from the date thereof, which summons shall also direct the officer to serve the same, and give six days notice to the owner of such lands, of the time at which the jury is to appear; and which summons shall be executed and return made thereof, in the same manner and with like authority, as upon services issued in cases pending before justices of the peace, and certify that the notice required has been given.[b]

Jury of view

Proce'dings on view of premises.

(§ 550.) SEC. 3. The Mayor, or any alderman or justice of the peace thereto designated and required by the Common Council, shall attend at the time and place specified in the summons, and if it appear that the notice above prescribed has been given, and if six or more of the nine freeholders as above specified shall then and there appear, he shall administer to each of them an

[b] See Section 556, *post*.

oath or affirmation well and truly to examine and certify in regard to the benefits or damages which will result from the opening of said ditch or ditches.

(§ 551.) SEC. 4. The Common Council shall deliver to the jury a map of the land through which said ditch or ditches are proposed to be opened, on which map the plan, length, width and depth thereof shall be particularly designated, with a space sufficient on each side to receive the deposit of the excavation; and thereupon the jury shall personally examine the premises and hear any reason that may be offered in regard to the questions submitted to them; and if the jury shall be satisfied that the opening of said ditch or ditches is necessary or proper, they shall so certify in writing; and further certify, whether the benefits which will accrue to the owner of the lands for the opening of said ditch or ditches, will or not, be equal to any damages that he will sustain thereby; and if such benefits are certified not equal to the damages, the jury shall assess and certify the damages which in their judgment will be sustained by the owner. Ibid.

(§ 552.) SEC. 5. Such inquisition shall be signed by all the jurors, and delivered to the Mayor, Alderman, or justice in attendance; and for all services rendered, the same fees shall be paid as are allowed for similar services in cases tried before [a] justice of the peace. Inquisition.

(§ 553.) SEC. 6. Upon the delivery of the certificate of the jury to the Mayor, Alderman, or Justice in attendance, which certificate, together with the inquisition and map shall be filed with the Clerk of the Common Council, and upon payment of cost of proceedings, and payment or tender of the damages assessed by the jury, Entry on premises authorized, etc.

if any, it shall be lawful for the Common Council to enter by their agent, teams and necessary implements, upon said lands, and cut and open such ditch or ditches, designated on said map, as adopted and sanctioned by such jury, not deterioating materially from the dimensions there laid down.

Right to maintain ditches.

(§ 551.) SEC. 7. After said ditch or ditches shall have been opened, it shall be lawful for said Common Council, their successors or agent, forever thereafter, from time to time, as it shall be necessary, to enter the lands through which the same are opened, and clear and scour such ditch or ditches, so as to preserve the original dimensions thereof.

Trespasses on same.

(§ 555.) SEC. 8. Any person who shall in any way obstruct or injure any ditch or ditches so opened, shall be liable to pay the Common Council aforesaid double the damages that shall be assessed by the jury for such injury, and in case of a second or other subsequent offense by the same person, treble such damages.

Failure to attend as juror, fineable.

(§ 556.) SEC. 9. If any person summoned to attend as a juror, in accordance with the provisions contained in section two of this act, shall fail or neglect to attend at the time and place specified, unless satisfactory excuse be given for such non-attendance or neglect, he shall be liable to a fine of five dollars, which may be imposed by the officer who shall officiate at the swearing of the jury, which officer may order such delinquent juror to be imprisoned until such fine is fully paid.

(§ 557.) SEC. 10. This act shall take effect and be in force from and after its passage.

CHAPTER XI.

MISCELLANEOUS PROVISIONS.

SECTIONS.

558. First Senatorial District.
559. Second Senatorial District.
560. Assessor to make a list to serve as jurors.
561. What persons to be selected as jurors.
562. Number which the list shall contain.
563. Who not to be selected
564. Duplicate lists to be made.
565. Census statistics; twenty-five copies of, to be deposited with the Mayor.
566. Council to appoint persons to take census.
567. Mayor and Aldermen to be Board of Health.
568. Recorder to have the powers of a Circuit Court Commissioner.
569. To have same fees.
570. Duties of Register of Deeds relative to conveyances of lands in the city.

SECTION.

571. When record of such deed may be read in evidence.
572. When deed may be read in evidence.
573. Same.
574. City may not issue due bills, etc., to circulate as currency.
575. Detroit Gas Light Company incorporated; duration of Company.
576. Powers of Corporation.
577. Capital stock; officers.
578. Powers of Board of Directors; liabilities of stockholders.
579. Time of commencing operations.
580. Corporate liability.
581. Act to be public act.
582. Report to Common Council.
583. Price of gas.
584. Acceptance by the Company.
585. Act to have immediate effect.

SENATORIAL DISTRICTS.

(§ 558.) SECTION 1. The *First* District shall consist of the second, third, fourth, seventh and tenth wards of the City of Detroit, and the townships of Greenfield, Hamtramck and Grosse Point, in the County of Wayne, and the election returns shall be made to the Clerk's office in the County of Wayne.

(§ 559.) SEC. 2. The *Second* District shall consist of the first, fifth, sixth, eighth and ninth wards of the City of Detroit, and the election returns shall be made to the Clerk's office in the County of Wayne. [*Laws of* 1861 *page* 252.]

JURORS FOR THE WAYNE CIRCUIT COURT.

Lists of pers'ns to serve as jurors.

(§ 560.) SEC. 3. The assessors and township clerk of each Township, and the assessor and aldermen of each ward in the City of Detroit,[a] shall, at the time appointed by law for said assessors to review their assessment roll in each year, make a list of persons to serve as petit jurors, and a list of persons to serve as grand jurors for the ensuing year. [*Comp. Laws, Section* 4350.]

Selection how made.

(§ 561.) SEC. 4. The said officers shall proceed to select from those assessed on the assessment roll of the township or ward for the same year, suitable persons, having the qualifications of electors, to serve as jurors; and in making such selection, they shall take the names of such only as are not exempt from serving on juries; who are in possession of their natural faculties, and not infirm or decrepit; of fair character, of approved integrity, of sound judgment, and well informed, and free from all legal exceptions. [*Comp. Laws, Section* 4351.]

Number to be selected.

(§ 562.) SEC. 5. Such lists shall contain not less than one for every one hundred inhabitants of such township or ward, computing according to the last preceding census, and having regard to the population of the county, so that the whole number of jurors selected in the county shall amount at least to one hundred, and not exceeding four hundred, one half of whom shall be designated as petit jurors, and one half as grand jurors. [*Comp. Laws, Section* 4352.]

---

[a] The office of ward assessor being abolished, (Section 55, p. 33.) and a single assessor for the city being created, (Section 232, p. 133.) the duties prescribed by this and the four following sections devolve upon the latter officer. See also section 140, p. 88, as to selection of persons to serve as jurors in the Recorder's Court.

(§ 563.) SEC. 6. In making such selection, the said officers shall avoid, as far as practicable, selecting any of the same persons who were actually drawn, and who served as jurors, during the preceding year. [*Compiled Laws, Section* 4353.] Who not to be selected.

(§ 564.) SEC. 7. Duplicate lists of the persons so selected, shall be made out and signed by the officers making such selection, or the major part of them, and within ten days thereafter one of each of said lists shall be transmitted to the County Clerk, and the other shall be filed with the Clerk of the Township, or Assessor of the ward, as the case may be. [*Comp. Laws, Section* 4354.] Duplicate lists to be made.

CENSUS, AND APPOINTMENT OF PERSONS TO TAKE CENSUS.

(§ 565.) SEC. 8. The Secretary of State shall condense, in a tabular form, the census and statistical returns made to him, and as soon as may be, cause three thousand copies to be published in pamphlet form, and transmit four copies to each organized township in the State, one for the use of the Supervisor, one for the use of the Township Clerk, and two to be deposited in the township library; and twenty-five copies to the Mayor of the City of Detroit, and ten copies to the Mayor of any other city in the State, for the use of the several city libraries, and one copy to each of the members of the present Legislature and its officers: *Provided*, That in counties having less than five thousand inhabitants, the supervisor in each town shall be entitled to three dollars for taking the Census and Statistics in his town extra. [*Comp. Laws, Section* 637.] Distribution of cens's and statistical returns.

Council to appoint persons to take census.

(§ 566.) SEC. 9. In the City of Detroit, the Common Council shall appoint a person in each ward to discharge the duties required by this act, (to take census,) to be performed by the Supervisor of each township or ward: *Provided*, There is no Assessor elected in said wards. [*Comp. Laws, Section* 638.]

BOARD OF HEALTH.

Who to constitut' Board of Health.

(§ 567.) SEC. 10. The Mayor and Aldermen of each incorporated city, and the President and Council, or Trustees, of each incorporated village in this State, shall have and exercise all the powers, and perform all the duties of a Board of Health as provided in this chapter, within the limits of the cities or villages respectively of which they are such officers.[b] [*Comp. Laws, Section* 1385.]

POWERS OF THE RECORDER.

To have the powers of a Circ't Court Commissioner.

(§ 568.) SEC. 11. The Recorder of the City of Detroit shall have and exercise the same powers as are now exercised by the Circuit Court Commissioner of the County of Wayne.[c] [*Comp. Laws, Section* 4000.]

Fees.

(§ 569.) SEC. 12. The Recorder is authorized to demand and receive the same fees for the services so rendered as are now by law permitted to be demanded and received by the Circuit Court Commissioner.[d] [*Compiled Laws, Section* 4001.]

---

[b] See 27th subdivision of Section 103, p. 60.

[c] See Sections 121, 122, p. 83.

[d] By the Session Laws of 1867, Vol. I, p. 88, jurisdiction in cases of forcible entry and detainer is conferred upon the Recorder.

An Act relative to the Registry of certain Deeds.

[*Approved March* 9, 1844. *Laws of* 1844, *p.* 60.]

(§ 570.) SEC. 13. The Register of deeds of the County of Wayne shall record at length in the registry of deeds in his office, any conveyance or deed of land, duly executed and delivered by the Governor and Judges of the late Territory of Michigan, by virtue and in pursuance of an Act of Congress, entitled "An act to provide for the adjustment of titles of land in the town of Detroit and Territory of Michigan, and for other purposes," approved April 21, 1806; and the record of such conveyance or deed, or a transcript thereof duly certified by said Register, may be read as *prima facie* evidence in any Court of Record within this State, if produced in court, could be read in evidence of the title of the land therein described, under said Act of Congress.

Deeds by Governor and Judges.

(§ 571.) SEC. 14. In any case where any such conveyance, duly executed by virtue and in pursuance of said act of Congress, as aforesaid, has been heretofore recorded in the registry of conveyances in the office of the Registry of Deeds, in the City of Detroit, or the Register of Probate, or the Register of Deeds of the County of Wayne; the record of such conveyance or deed, or a transcript thereof, duly certified by the Register of Deeds of said County, may be read as *prima facie* evidence in any Court within this State, in case the original of such record, if produced in Court could be read in evidence of the title of the land therein described, under said Act of Congress: *Provided,* That this act shall not be construed so as to effect any proceeding now pending in

Record of such deeds.

When it may be read in evidence.

any Court of law or equity of this State: *And Provided,* That it shall not be so construed as to effect the rights now vested in any person or persons.

An Act, amending an Act, relative to the Registry of certain Deeds. Approved March 9, 1844.

[*Approved May* 7, 1846. *Laws of* 1846, *p.* 156.]

(§ 572.) SEC. 15. It shall not be necessary to acknowledge or prove the execution of any deed of land which may have been or shall be granted by the Mayor, Recorder, and Aldermen of the City of Detroit, under the provisions of an Act of Congress, entitled "An Act supplementary to an Act to provide for the adjustment of titles to land in the town of Detroit, and territory of Michigan, and for other purposes," approved August twenty-ninth, one thousand eight hundred and and forty-two, to entitle the same to be recorded; but every such deed which may have been, or shall be executed by said Mayor, Recorder, and Aldermen, under their respective hands and seals, shall be entitled to be duly recorded, and every such deed so recorded, or the record or transcript of such deed, duly certified, may be read in evidence in any Court within this State, without further proof thereof: *Provided,* That this act shall not be construed so as to affect any proceedings now pending in any Court of law or equity in this State, or to affect the rights now vested in any person or persons.

An Act relative to Conveyances in the City of Detroit.

[*Approved April* 1, 1850. *Laws of* 1850, *p.* 232.]

Whereas, Many or most of the conveyances of lots in the City of Detroit, made and executed by the late Governor and Judges of the Territory of Michigan, were made without any acknowledgment by the said Governor and Judges as required by the law of the time, requiring conveyances in general to be acknowledged to entitle them to be recorded:

And Whereas, Many or most of these conveyances have been recorded in the proper registry of the County of Wayne, or of the City of Detroit as heretofore existing, and now remain of record in the said County Registry:

And Whereas, Many of said original conveyances have, by time, accident, or otherwise, been lost, or are out of the possession or control of those owning and claiming the said lots; therefore,

(§ 573.) SEC. 16. *Be it enacted by the Senate and House of Representatives of the State of Michigan,* That all deeds and conveyances of lots or lands in the City of Detroit by the late Governor and Judges of the late Territory of Michigan, that have heretofore been recorded in the registry of deeds of the County of Wayne or the City of Detroit, the record of said deeds, or a certified copy thereof by the Register of Deeds of the County of Wayne, may be used and read in evidence in all Courts and places with the same force and effect as if the original deeds or conveyances from the said Governor and Judges were produced and proved: *Provided,* It shall first be made to appear that such original deed or deeds have been lost or destroyed.

CITY NOT TO ISSUE DUE BILLS.

Corporation not to issue due bills.

(§ 574.) SEC. 17. Section three of an act to amend an act, entitled "An Act relative to the City of Detroit," authorizing the issue, by the corporation, of due bills in payment of the debts of said corporation, be and the same is hereby repealed; and said corporation is expressly prohibited from issuing any new due bills, checks, drafts or tickets, designed to circulate as paper currency, or to pass from individual to individual as a circulating medium, or re-issuing any such due bills, checks, drafts or tickets; and any person who shall as Mayor, Recorder, or Alderman, or otherwise sign any such due bills, checks, drafts or tickets, for such corporation, or shall put such due bills, checks, drafts or tickets, in circulation for such corporation, shall be deemed guilty of a misdemeanor, and, on conviction thereof, shall be fined a sum of not less then five hundred dollars, nor more then one thousand dollars, and be imprisoned in the county jail until said fine is paid. [*Laws of* 1842, *p.* 28.]

Not to re-issue.

Punishm'nt.

An Act to incorporate "The City of Detroit Gas Company."[f]

[*Approved March* 14, 1849. *Laws of* 1849, *p.* 82.]

Whereas, Certain persons have associated themselves under the style of "The City of Detroit Gas Company," for the purpose of carrying on and establishing in said City of Detroit a gas manufactory, of the kind now generally used, or any improved gas or inflammable substance, and of supplying the citizens with gas, who desire the same, at rates to be agreed upon, the following being the names of the persons who have signed the articles of association and taken shares of stock, viz: L. C. Rose, Jason Braman, J. M. Slater, Jeffrey Coles, James Cooper, John N. Williams, James Beck, Mathew Anderson, T. R. Davenport, Henry H. Leroy, Samuel Howlet, F. F. Parker, and of whom at present said —— —— is President, said Beck, Secretary, said Parker, Treasurer, and said Leroy, Rose, Braman and Slater are Directors. Preamble.

And whereas, The Common Council of said city have given the necessary permit to said corporation to locate said establishment in said city, and to run their pipes through the streets of the same, and have given them the exclusive privilege so to do for the period of ten years, on condition and under certain restrictions, as appears by an agreement, in writing, signed by a committee of said Council, and to which reference is hereby had; *And whereas*, said persons have applied to this Legislature to be incorporated, the more effectually to enable them to accomplish the said objects of their organization. The same.

---

[f] See Section 574, changing name of the company.

(§ 575.) SECTION 18. That said persons above named, who have signed said articles of association, and all such other persons as have or shall become stockholders and associated with them for said purpose, and their successors or assigns, shall be and are hereby constituted and declared to be a body politic and corporate, under the name and style of the "Detroit Gas Light Company," for the object and purpose contemplated and stated in the above preamble, for the period of forty-eight years from and after the passage of this act;[g] *Provided always*, That within the period of three years[h] they commence operations, and continue the same with all reasonable dispatch. [*As amended by Laws of* 1851, *p.* 19.]

Name of corporation changed.

Duration of corp'ration.

Powers of the corporation.

(§ 576.) SEC. 19. The Corporation hereby created by the name aforesaid, and the successors thereof, shall have continual succession for the period aforesaid, and shall be persons in law, capable of suing and being sued, pleading and being impleaded, answering and being answered unto, defended and defending in all courts, suits, proceedings, places and matters whatsoever, and capable of having a common seal; of acquiring, holding and conveying estate, real, personal and mixed, necessary or expedient for the Corporation for the purposes and objects thereof.

Capital stock.

(§ 577.) SEC. 20. The capital stock of said Company shall not exceed one million of dollars;[i] such stock may be subscribed for and issued from time to time as the business of the Company shall make necessary under the

[g] By the original act the life of the corporation was limited to fifty years.

[h] By act of 1849, one year.

[i] By Act of 1849, the stock was limited to one hundred thousand dollars, and by the Laws of 1855, p. 420, to five hundred thousand dollars.

direction of the Board of Directors; the property affairs and concerns of said Corporation shall be managed and conducted by a Board of seven Directors, who shall consist of a President, Secretary, Treasurer, and four other Directors, all of whom shall be stockholders, except the Secretary. [*As amended by Laws of* 1867, *Vol. II, p.* 923.] Officers.

(§ 578.) SEC. 21. The majority of the Board of Directors and stockholders, on account of said corporation hereby created, shall have, and hereby are declared to have, full power and authority to make, prescribe, and carry into effect all such rules, by-laws and regulations, and the same to alter, amend and renew, as the majority of the Board of Officers and stock, at a meeting of the holders thereof, regularly called, shall think proper to make, which are necessary and proper for the purpose of carrying out the true intent and meaning of this act; and among other things to provide for calling new elections when any election fails to be made when duly called, and may form, if they think proper, a constitution or articles of agreement, to be signed or to govern them within the provisions of this act, containing the elements of their organization, the rights, privileges and duties of officers and members; the modes and times of calling elections and holding the same, the accounts of stock, and liabilities and privileges of holders, and the exercise of the powers above contained, and concerning all other matters and things in and about the regulation, control, conduct of the corporation, its objects, and all matters pertaining thereto, and for the changing and amendment thereof from time to time, as may be necessary. And for the purpose of commencing to organize and making necessary rules, the Powers of Board of Directors.

said present Board of Officers and persons, who have signed said articles of association, or a majority thereof, as soon as this act becomes a law, may get together and exercise, all and singular, the powers aforesaid necessary or expedient. It being expressly provided that this corporation shall never exercise banking powers or brokerage business, or anything in the nature thereof; that it shall make no regulations or rules contrary to law; that it shall at all times be subject to the inspection of the Legislature, or a committee thereof, and shall make a full report of all its affairs and doings whenever required by said Legislature. All the shareholders shall be jointly and severally liable for all debts and contracts of the company until forty per cent. of the capital stock shall have been paid in, and also for all debts of the company of every description after the capital stock of the company shall have been exhausted.

Liability of share holders.

Time of commenci'g operations.

(§ 579.) SEC. 22. Unless the said corporation shall have established their manufactory, and so far progressed as to begin to supply gas to some portion of the city, within four years,[j] from the passage of this act, this act shall cease and become null and void. [*As amended by Laws of* 1851, *p.* 20.]

Corporate liability.

(§ 580.) SEC. 23. That the property of every individual vested in said corporation shall be liable to be taken on execution for the payment of his or her just debts, in such manner, as is or may be prescribed by law.

Public act.

(§ 581.) SEC. 24. That this act be and the same is hereby declared to be a public act, and that the same

[j] By the original act the time was limited to twenty-four months.

be construed in all courts and places favorably for every beneficial purpose therein mentioned.

(§ 582.) SEC. 25. The said company shall annually, on the first week of January, make an accurate report, in writing, to the Common Council of Detroit, showing the amount of capital stock actually paid, the amount issued, all real or personal estate had or owned by said company, and the cost of the same; a statement of the extent of pipe laid down; the number of street lamps erected;—which report and statement shall be verified by the oath of the Secretary and one of the directors of said company. [*As added by Laws of* 1855, *p.* 21.] Report to the Comm'n Council.

(§ 583.) SEC. 26. The said company shall not increase the present price charged for gas without the consent of the Common Council of said city. [*As added by Laws of* 1855, *p.* 21.] Price of gas.

(§ 584.) SEC. 27. Said company shall be entitled to all the benefits and subject to the provisions of this act, on filing in the office of the Secretary of State a written acceptance of this act, signed by its President and Secretary, and sealed by its corporate seal.[k] [*As added by Laws of* 1855, p. 21.] Acceptance.

(§ 585.) SEC. 28. This act shall take effect immediately.

---

[k] The acceptance of the company was filed June 27, 1855.

INDEX.

	SECTION.	PAGE.
ACCOUNTS.		
To be audited by Council,	80	45
When to be accompanied by affidavit,	80	45
Same,	215	126
When Controller to audit and allow,	62	36
Doubtful, to be returned by Controller to Council,	62	37
Doubtful, proceedings on if allowed by Council,	62	37
Audited and allowed, Controller to make annual report of,	62	37
Controller to open with Treasurer,	63	38
Against the City, when barred from action,	80	45
Prosecuting Attorney to render,	120	83
Of Board of Police Commissioners subject to inspection,	361	213
Of Board of Fire Commissioners subject to inspection,	446	256
Of House of Correction, how audited,	400	235
ACKNOWLEDGMENT,		
Of deeds may be taken by Controller,	76	43
Of deeds, when may be taken by City Clerk,	251	146
Deeds, of Mayor, Recorder, etc., may be recorded without,	572	326
ACQUITTALS,		
Clerk of Recorder's Court to report number of,	155	94
ACTIONS,		
On accounts against City, when barred,	80	45
When to be conducted by City Attorney,	60	36
Pending when charter revised, to be continued,	273	157
ACTS CONTINUED,		
Incorporating Fire Department of City Detroit,	287	161
Amending laws relative to supply of water,	287	161
To authorize Water Commissioners to borrow money,	287	161
Relating to Schools in City of Detroit,	287	161
Relating to registry of certain deeds,	287	162
Relating to certain conveyances in City of Detroit,	287	162
Certain sections relative to jurors,	287	162
Certain sections relative to Boards of Health,	287	162
To establish Police Court,	287	162
To provide for drainage of certain low lands,	287	162
ADJOURNMENT.		
Of sessions of Council,	85	47
Of special sessions of Council,	86	48
Of drawing of Jurors,	144	90
Of drawing of Jurors, notice of, to Recorder and Sheriff,	144	90

	SECTION.	PAGE.
Affidavits.		
When to accompany claims and accounts,	80	45
Same,	215	126
May be submitted to Board of Review of Taxes,	237	137
False, to be deemed perjury,	284	160
What officers may take,	76	43
When Chairmen of Committees may take,	78	44
Same,	102	52
Clerk of Recorder's Court may take,	109	79
Clerk of Police Court may take,	388	227
Complaints to be in form of,	126	84
Of printer, of what to be evidence,	282	159
Agricultural Lands.		
To be assessed at actual cash value,	233	134
Aldermen.		
When elected,	3	12
Terms of office of,	15	19
Shall constitute the Common Council,	82	46
Ineligible to office of Recorder,	11	16
Ineligible to certain offices,	11	16
Ineligible to certain offices for one year after his term,	11	16
Shall vacate office if interested in contracts,	13	17
Shall vacate office for receiving bribe,	14	18
Penalty for offering bribe to,	14	18
Vacancy in office of, how filled,	27	22
To have powers of Policemen,	36	25
To be Inspectors of Election,	39	28
To be members of Board of Registration,	38	27
Same,	469	268
Same,	498	288
With Assessor, to have powers of Supervisors,	234	134
With Assessor, to represent corporation in Board of Supervisors,	234	134
To vote on all questions in Council, except when interested,	99	51
Certain contracts with, to be void,	217	126
Powers of, at fires,	263	152
Power of Council to expel,	21	20
May administer oaths and take affidavits,	76	43
Majority of, constitute quorum of Council,	82	46
Absent, how brought before Council,	82	46
Absent, power of Council to compel attendance of,	96	50
Proceedings by, to call special session of Council,	86	47
Compensation of,	96	50
Majority vote of, necessary for appointments and removals,	100	51
May direct Street Commissioner to notify owners to repair sidewalks,	105	75
May inspect records of Recorder's Court,	132	86
Alleys. See *Highways*, *Streets*.		
When Street Commissioners may direct the working, etc., of,	71	41
When Overseers of Highways to work and improve,	72	41
May be cleaned by contract,	72	42
Power of Council to work and improve,	103	54
Power of Council to open, extend, vacate, etc.,	103	54
Power of Council to open, extend, vacate, etc.,	157	95
Power of Council to pave, grade and repair,	103	54
Power of Council to levy tax to pave, grade, etc.,	203	119
How cost of grading, paving, repairing, etc., to be paid,	103	55
Power of Council to dispose of dirt in,	103	55
Power of Council to clean,	103	55
Power of Council to prevent encumbrances on,	103	55

	SECTION.	PAGE.
Power of Council to prescribe the use of, ...	103	56
Power of Council to survey and ascertain boundaries of, . .	103	59
Damages by opening, vacating, etc., how apportioned, . . .	168	102
Damages by opening, vacating, etc., to be paid from Contingent Fund, ...	168	102
Benefits from opening, vacating, etc., how assessed, . . .	168	102
Assessments of benefits by opening, to be paid Treasurer, . .	184	108
Sale of lands in default of payment of assessment for opening,	184	108
Platting and recording of plats to be dedication of, . . .	191	11
Power to lay water pipes through, ...	314	1 2
Police authorized to remove nuisances in, ...	345	198
Alms House.		
Power of Council to establish, ...	103	69
Power to imprison in, ...	103	72
Power to employ inmates of, on public works, ...	67	72
Superintendent of, how appointed, ...	4	12
Amendments.		
Of Complaints and Pleadings in Recorder's Court, ...	126	84
Amusements.		
Unsafe, power to prohibit, in streets, etc., ...	103	56
Animals,		
Power to impound, ...	103	58
Power to compel fastening of, in streets, etc., ...	103	58
Appeals,		
From Recorder's Court, power to take, ...	130	85
From proceedings to open streets, highways, etc., ...	177	105
Bond for, in such cases, ...	177	105
Return of Clerk of Recorder's Court in such cases, ...	178	106
Proceedings on, in such cases, ...	179	106
From Board of Review to Council, ...	240	138
From Board of Review to be summarily determined, ...	241	138
From Board of Review, how long hearing may be continued, .	242	139
From Police Court, ...	389	228
Appointments,		
Of officers by Council, ...	4	12
Appropriations,		
Controller to report when exhausted, ...	02	07
Power of Council to make, ...	103	71
Arrests,		
When electors not subject to, on civil process, ...	54	32
To be made known to proper public officer, ...	357	210
Of persons without warrant, ...	297	169
Of persons at fires, refusing to obey orders of Engineer, etc.,	264	153
Of disorderly persons at fires, ...	264	153
Of persons wilfully setting fires, ...	269	154
Arson,		
Information or complaint for, to be endorsed by Recorder, . .	114	81
Ash Houses,		
Power to regulate construction of, ...	103	64
Asses,		
Power to prevent the running at large of, ...	103	58
Assessments,		
Special, to be collected by City Collector, ...	69	41
Special, property bid in by Corporation on sales for, how held,	252	147
For paving, grading, etc., streets, highways, etc., power to levy,	103	54
For numbering buildings, power to levy, ...	103	59
For abatement of nuisances, power to levy, ...	103	60

	SECTION.	PAGE.
For filling up sinks, cellars, etc., power to levy, ...	103	61
For building lateral sewers, power to levy, ...	103	62
To be made by Assessor, ...	70	41
When to be paid by the city, ...	103	55
On cellars drained into public sewers, power to levy, . . .	103	59
Power to make regulations for, ...	103	71
Illegal when paid, power to refund, ...	105	76
Illegal, power to vacate, ...	105	76
On Insurance Companies, ...	105	76
New, when may be made to pay certain deficiencies, ...	106	77
New, Council may limit time for making, ...	106	77
For public works to be levied, before work commenced, . .	206	122
Ordinances, etc., for, when to be passed, ...	218	127
On agricultural lands, how made, ...	233	134
On lots lying in two or more wards, ...	235	135
Description of lands subject to, ...	235	135
Not vitiated by wrong name of owner, ...	235	135
May be equalized, corrected, etc., by Board of Review, . .	237	136
Not to be increased or made by Board without notice, . .	237	137
Complaint of, may be made to Board of Review, ...	237	137
Erroneous, when may be changed by Board of Review, . .	237	137
Appeal from decision of Board relative to, ...	240	138
Not to be increased by Council without notice, ...	241	138
Local, when warrants to issue for collecting, ...	254	148
For water rates, power to make, ...	315	183
For water rates, list of to be kept, ...	317	184
For water rates, to be a lien, ...	315	183
For paving, grading, etc., to be a lien, ...	103	55
Assessment Rolls,		
Special, to be made out by Surveyor, ...	68	41
Special, to be placed in hands of Receiver, ...	254	148
When to be made out for the Wards, ...	233	134
To be reviewed and approved by Board of Review, ...	237	136
Powers of Board relative to, same as that of Supervisors, . .	238	137
To be returned by Board of Revew to Council, ...	237	137
To be considered by Council, ...	240	138
May be corrected by Council, ...	241	138
How long may be considered by Council, ...	242	139
To be the basis of all taxes, ...	242	139
Taxes to be extended on, in separate columns, ...	243	139
When to be delivered by Assessor to Controller, ...	243	139
To be delivered by Controller to Receiver, ...	243	139
Receiver to give notice of reception of, ...	243	140
When warrants may issue for taxes unpaid thereon, ...	241	141
Assessment of Benefits. See *Benefits.*		
Assessor,		
How appointed and term of office of, ...	232	133
May appoint Assistants, ...	232	133
Compensation of, ...	232	133
When to assess proprerty, ...	233	133
To discriminate between certain classes of property, . . .	233	134
How to assess agricultural lands, ...	233	134
When to make out Assessment rolls, ...	233	134
Action subject to revision of Board of Review and Council, .	234	134
With Aldermen, to have powers of Supervisors, ...	234	135
With Aldermen, to represent Corporation in Board of Supervisors,	234	135
May demand list of property from owner or agent, . . .	236	135
How such demand to be made by, ...	236	135
How to proceed when list not furnished, ...	236	136

	SECTION.	PAGE.
To extend tax on rolls in separate columns, ...	243	139
When to deliver tax rolls to Controller, ...	243	139
Duty of, relative to State and County taxes, ...	243	142
To make out State and County tax rolls, ...	459	261
To annex warrant to State and County tax rolls, ...	459	261
To prepare list of persons to serve as jurors, ...	70	41
Same, ...	140	88
How to make selection of persons to serve as jurors, . . .	561	322
Same, ...	563	323
To make duplicate lists of persons to serve as jurors, . . .	564	323
Ward, office of abolished, ...	55	33
Assignation Houses.		
Power to suppress, ...	103	64
Assistant Marshalls,		
How appointed, ...	4	12
Powers and duties of, ...	67	40
Assumpsit,		
When tax may be recovered in an action of, ...	248	145
Attorney, City.		
When elected, ...	3	11
Term of office of, ...	15	19
Qualifications of, ...	8	16
To file official bond, ...	29	23
To conduct suits and proceedings in Recorder's Court, . . .	60	36
To collect fines and penalties, ...	131	86
To draw up resolutions for opening, vacating streets, etc., . .	158	96
To conduct proceedings for opening, vacating streets, etc., .	160	98
To advise jury in proceedings for opening, vacating streets, etc.,	165	101
To give notice of report of jury for opening, vacating streets, etc.,	172	103
When vacancy in office of, may be filled by the Court, . .	127	85
Compensation of person appointed to act in place of, . .	127	85
Auctions.		
Mock, power to prohibit and suppress, ...	103	65
Power to regulate, ...	103	66
Auctioneers.		
Power to license and regulate, ...	103	66
Auditor, City.		
Associated with Water Commissioners for certain purposes, . .	319	184
Auditors of Wayne County.		
To pay certain accounts for apprehension of criminals, . . .	345	198
May inspect records of Recorder's Court, ...	132	86
Awnings.		
Power to regulate, ...	103	56
Bail.		
Power to hold to, for good behavior, ...	103	72
Clerk of Recorder's Court to report nnmber of persons held to,	155	94
Special, allowed on charge of violating ordinances, ...	357	211
No member of police to become or furnish, ...	357	211
Persons committed in default of, how discharged, ...	374	218
Who authorized to take, ...	374	218
When Police Justice may take, for appearance at Recorder's Court,	378	222
For appearance at Recorder's Court, who may take, . . .	378	222
Confinement in House of Correction, for want of, in State Courts,	418	244
Ballast.		
Power to regulate throwing of, into Detroit River, ...	103	53
Ballots.		
For persons to fill vacancies, to designate the vacancy, . . .	50	31

	SECTION.	PAGE.
BALLOT BOXES.		
One for each ward or district to be kept by the Clerk,	41	28
When to be delivered to Inspectors of election,	41	29
BANKS.		
Power to make contracts with, for keeping public moneys,	221	128
BARNS.		
Power to cleanse or abate,	103	61
Power to regulate the construction of,	103	61
Power to regulate use of lamps in,	103	63
BATHING.		
Power to prevent and regulate,	103	64
BATH HOUSES.		
Power to license and regulate,	103	67
BEEF.		
Power to inspect,	53	68
BEGGARS.		
Power to punish and restrain,	103	64
BENEFITS, ASSESSMENT OF.		
In opening ditches to drain low grounds, how made,	103	59
Same,	551	319
In cases of opening, altering, vacating, etc., alleys,	168	102
Amount collected from, to be paid Treasurer,	168	102
Same,	184	108
When land may be sold to pay,	184	108
When to be offset against damages in the opening of streets, etc.,	194	112
BELLS.		
Power to regulate the ringing of,	103	69
BILLIARDS.		
Power to suppress gambling with,	103	65
BILLIARD TABLES,		
Power to license and regulate keepers of,	103	67
BILLS OF MORTALITY,		
Power to compel the keeping and returning of,	103	69
BIRTHS,		
Power to regulate the registration of,	103	69
BLACKSMITH SHOPS.		
Subject to regulations as to their construction and management,	103	63
BLOCKS AND STREETS, See *Plats*,		
Plats of, to be approved by Commissioners on plan of city,	189	111
Plats of, to be acknowledged and recorded,	189	111
Approved by Commissioners, copies of to be deposited with Clerk,	190	111
Not approved, acknowledged and recorded, of no validity,	191	111
Platting and recording plats of, evidence of dedication,	191	111
Record of former plats of, evidence of dedication,	191	111
BOARDS,		
Members of, may administer oaths and take affidavits,	102	52
May issue subpœnas, and compel production of papers,	102	52
BOARD OF AUDITORS OF WAYNE COUNTY. See *Auditors of, etc.*,		
BOARD OF CITY CANVASSERS,		
How composed,	48	31
BOARD OF COMMISSIONERS ON PLAN OF THE CITY,		
How appointed,	189	110
Lands not to be laid out into blocks and streets, without approval of a majority of,	189	111
Limitation of powers of,	189	111

	SECTION.	PAGE.
City Clerk to be clerk of,	190	111
Plats not approved by and recorded, of no validity,	191	111
Vacancy in, how filled,	192	112
To receive no compensation,	193	112
BOARD OF EDUCATION,		
How constituted,	514	302
Same,	5	13
Made a body corporate,	514	302
Schools to be under the direction of,	510	300
General powers and duties of,	514	302
Same,	518	303
Quorum of, how constituted,	515	301
Same,	530	308
City Clerk to be clerk of,	516	303
Recorder may sit with,	517	303
Same,	514	302
Power to take census of children,	518	303
Jurisdiction of Recorder's Court in matters relating to,	519	304
To make annual report,	520	304
May establish High School and appoint Superintendent,	522	305
City Treasurer to be treasurer of,	523	305
Power to elect President of,	529	308
Title of real estate to vest in,	531	309
May make loans and issue bonds,	536	311
Bonds of, to be a lien on property of Board,	537	311
To make annual appropriations for payment of bonds of,	538	311
Removal of members of, when not to vacate office,	541	312
To make annual estimate of expenses,	544	314
Estimates of, to be submitted to Council,	545	314
BOARD OF COMMISSIONERS OF SINKING FUND. See *Sinking Fund,*		
BOARD OF HEALTH,		
Power to establish,	103	60
How constituted under general State law,	567	324
Certain section of Revised Statutes of 1846, relative to, continued,	287	162
BOARD OF INSPECTORS OF ELECTION. See *Inspectors of Election.*		
BOARD OF INSPECTORS OF HOUSE OF CORRECTION. See *House of Correction.*		
BOARD OF REGISTRATION. See *Registration, Board of.*		
BOARD OF REVIEW,		
May revise and correct action of Assessor,	233	134
How appointed, and of whom to consist,	237	136
Term of office of,	237	136
Sessions of, when and where held,	237	136
Power to equalize, correct, amend, etc., assessments,	237	136
Not to increase any assessment without notice,	237	137
Power to review assessments complained of,	237	137
Majority of, may correct erroneous asessments,	237	137
To return assessment roll to Council,	237	137
Compensation of,	237	137
Have powers of Supervisors, to correct assessment rolls,	238	137
Notice of meetings of, to be given by City Clerk,	239	138
Appeals from the Common Council,	240	138
Members of, may sit with Council to consider appeals,	240	138
BOARD OF SEWER COMMISSIONERS,		
How appointed,	5	13
To have control of all public and private sewers,	5	13
To furnish Council with list of sewers recommended,	5	13
Terms of office of, and compensation,	5	14
May appoint Engineer,	5	14

	SECTION.	PAGE.
Board of Water Commissioners. See *Water Commissioners.*		
Boilers,		
Power to regulate the putting up of,	103	64
Bonds,		
May be issued to provide money for public buildings,	204	120
For public buildings not negotiable for less than par value,	204	121
Public meeting to consent to issue of, for Building Fund,	205	121
Not to be issued unless authorized by law,	208	123
New, may be issued to refund outstanding bonds,	208	123
New, when issued, to show class of indebtedness,	210	124
New, to be dated, sealed; for what sum to be issued,	210	124
New, Controller to keep list of,	210	124
Old, when refunded to be cancelled and destroyed,	211	124
Old, list of cancelled and destroyed to be kept,	211	124
Issued, contrary to provisions of Charter, void,	212	124
Committee to negotiate, how constituted,	222	128
Refunded, to become property of Commissioners of Sinking Fund,	226	130
Public faith and property pledged to secure,	229	131
Volunteer Bounty, Council authorized to issue,	465	265
Volunteer Bounty, tax authorized for payment of,	466	266
Water Commissioners anthorized to issue,	310	181
Same,	336	190
Same,	337	191
Issued by Water Commissioners, to be registered,	310	181
Water Commissioners, to make investment for payment of,	319	184
New, when Water Commissioners may issue,	319	185
New, when issued by Water Commissioners, to be registered,	319	185
Board of Education authorized to issue,	536	311
Made a lien on property of Board of Education,	537	311
Board of Education to make appropriations to pay,	538	311
On appeal in cases of street openings, etc.,	177	105
Of Corporation to be countersigned by Controller,	62	36
Treasurer to be charged with,	63	38
Treasurer to have custody of certain,	65	39
Bonds, Official.		
When to be filed,	18	20
What officers to give,	29	23
Council may direct what officers shall give,	29	23
Condition of,	30	23
Of Constable, special conditions of,	31	23
Council may order renewal of,	32	24
Neglect to file, vacates office,	33	24
When sureties on, required to justify,	34	25
Clerk to report officers failing to file,	35	25
Of Property Clerk of Metropolitan Police,	343	196
Of Treasurer of "Metropolitan Police Fund,"	359	212
Of Clerk of Police Court,	388	227
Of Collectors, for collection of State and County taxes,	461	263
Of Collector and Treasurer, for security of school moneys,	525	306
Of Collectors for collection of school taxes,	528	308
To be given before license shall issue,	103	71
On issue of license, Mayor to examine sureties of,	103	71
Books and Papers.		
Refusal to deliver over, punishable as a misdemeanor,	74	42
Books and Pictures, Indecent.		
Power to prevent exhibition and sale of,	103	58
Boundaries.		
Of City,	2	9
Same,	302	175

	SECTION.	PAGE.
Of Wards,	2	10
Of Wards, Ninth and Tenth,	303	176
Of Wards, how altered,	2	10
Same,	303	177
Of Highways, Streets, etc., power to survey, ascertain, etc.,	103	59
BOUNTY FUND. See *Bonds.*		
Tax authorized to pay,	465	265
Bonds may be issued, to be known as "Volunteer Bounty Bonds,"	465	266
Interest on Bonds to pay,	466	266
Limitation of power to impose tax to pay,	467	266
BREAD.		
Power to inspect and regulate weight of,	103	67
BREWERIES.		
Power to regulate construction and management of,	103	63
BRIBERY.		
Punishment for offering or receiving,	14	18
BRICK.		
Power to regulate the size of,	103	64
Same,	104	73
Same,	105	74
BRIDGES.		
Street Commissioners to superintend construction of,	71	41
Power of Council to establish, construct, maintain etc.,	103	58
BUILDINGS.		
Power to assess expenses of numbering,	103	59
Wooden, power to prevent erection of, within certain limits,	103	63
Power to prevent removal and repair of, in certain limits,	103	63
Stone and brick, power to regulate construction of,	104	73
Same,	105	74
Not to be erected on certain docks and wharves,	103	53
Public, power to provide for erection of,	103	69
Unsafe, power to remove, and assess expense of removal of,	79	44
Same,	103	56
Right to remove, erected on lands purchased at tax sales,	246	145
Same,	247	145
Same,	250	146
BUILDING MATERIALS.		
Power to regulate the inspection of,	103	67
BURGLAR'S TOOLS.		
To be seized by police,	377	221
When to be destroyed,	377	221
BURIALS.		
Of Strangers and Paupers, power to provide for,	103	68
Power to regulate generally,	103	68
BUTCHERS.		
Power to license and regulate,	103	66
BUTCHERS' SHOPS AND STALLS.		
Power to compel the cleaning or abating of,	103	61
Power to prohibit erection of, within certain limits,	103	62
BUTTER.		
Power to provide for the inspection of,	103	68
BY-LAWS.		
Power of Council to pass,	96	50
CABS. See *Vehicles.*		
In streets, power to prescribe stands for,	103	57
At depots, wharves, etc., power to prescribe stands for,	103	57

	SECTION.	PAGE.
Cabmen.		
Power to regulate, at depots, steamboat landings, etc.,	103	57
Power to license and regulate,	103	66
Camphene Factories.		
Power to cleanse or abate,	103	62
Canvassers. See *Board of City Canvassers.*		
Canvass.		
Of votes, how made,	47	30
Caravans.		
Power to license or prohibit,	103	66
Cards.		
Power to suppress gaming with,	103	65
Carpenter and Cooper Shops.		
Power to regulate the construction and management of,	103	63
Cars.		
Power to prescribe speed of, in city limits,	103	70
Carmen.		
Power to license and regulate,	103	66
Carriages, Carts, etc.		
Power to regulate at depots, docks, etc.,	103	57
Power to prescribe stands for, in streets,	103	57
Cattle.		
Power to restrain running at large,	103	57
Cellars.		
Power to compel cleansing or abatement of,	103	61
Power to regulate construction of,	103	61
Power to assess expenses of altering, cleaning, etc.,	103	61
Drained into public sewers, power to levy tax on,	103	59
Cemetery.		
Power to hold real estate for,	103	73
Census.		
Power to provide for taking,	103	69
Council to appoint person to take,	566	324
Mayor entitled to certain copies of returns of,	565	323
Of Children, Board of Education to take,	518	303
Of Children, School Taxes to be based on,	522	305
Certificate.		
By Clerk of presentation of ordinances to Mayor,	90	49
By Clerk of presentation of ordinances to Mayor, to be evidence,	280	158
Of such presentation to be recorded,	90	49
Of expenses of State prisoners in House of Correction,	133	87
Of Treasurer, when evidence of fee of property in the city,	186	109
Of Clerk of copies of ordinances, proceedings, etc., to be evidence,	281	159
Of sale of land for taxes, Council may direct execution of,	246	144
Of sale of land for taxes, when Controller to execute,	251	146
To Commissioner of Metropolitan Police,	341	195
Of service as fireman,	262	152
Same,	454	259
Challenge.		
Of vote at elections, proceedings on,	44	29
Of vote for want of registration,	483	280
Of Jurors in Recorder's Court,	138	88
Same,	394	231
Of Jurors in Police Court,	395	231
Of Jurors in proceedings for opening, etc., streets, etc.,	163	100

	SECTION.	PAGE.
CHARTER.		
Power to punish violations of,	103	72
Prosecutions for violations of,	126	84
Attorney to collect fines for violations of,	131	86
City to pay costs, etc., for prosecutions under,	133	86
Offenses against, may be tried without jury,	139	88
Clerk of Recorder's Court to report prosecutions under,	155	94
CHECKS.		
Corporation not to issue, to circulate as money,	574	328
CHIEF ENGINEER.		
Council may appoint and prescribe duties of,	257	150
To be deemed a fireman, and exempt from militia and jury duty,	262	152
May be appointed by Fire Commissioners,	435	252
Salary of,	435	253
CHIEF OF POLICE.		
Complaints against, may be tried by Board of Commissioners,	289	164
When, may suspend policemen,	291	165
CHIMNEYS.		
Power to regulate construction and compel cleaning of,	103	64
CHIMNEY SWEEPER.		
Ignorance of the English language not to disqualify,	10	16
CIRCUSES AND CARAVANS.		
Power to prohibit or license,	103	66
CITY ATTORNEY. See *Attorney.*		
CITY CLERK,		
When elected,	3	11
Term of office of,	15	19
Official bond of,	29	23
To give notice of election and appointment to officers,	33	24
Shall report neglect of officer to qualify,	35	25
To give notice of elections,	37	26
To keep ballot boxes,	41	28
To be clerk of Council,	61	36
Same,	83	47
To possess powers of township clerk,	61	36
May administer oaths and take affidavits,	76	43
May take fees for administering oaths,	76	43
To countersign licenses,	81	45
Licenses not valid unless countersigned by.	81	45
To preside over Council until President elected,	84	47
When to give notice of special session of Council,	86	48
To make certificate of presentation of ordinance to Mayor,	90	49
To keep and record ordinances,	91	49
To sign record of ordinances,	91	49
To certify resolutions to open, widen streets, etc.,	159	97
To deliver to attorney copy of resolution to open streets, etc,	160	98
To record certified copy of report of jury relative to opening streets, &c.,	183	108
To be clerk of Commissioners on plan of the city,	190	111
To give notice of meetings of Board of Review,	239	138
To take acknowledgment of and attest deeds from city,	251	146
Effect of certificate of, relative to presenting ordinances to Mayor,	280	158
Copy of ordinance certified by, to be evidence,	281	159
To be clerk of Police Commissioners under law of 1861,	279	164
To countersign Firemens' certificates,	454	259
To be clerk of Board of Education,	516	303
When to make Register of Electors,	487	283
To send to Secretary of State number of registered voters,	494	286
To notify County Treasurer when ward collectors have qualified,	461	263

23

	SECTION.	PAGE.
CITY OF DETROIT. See *Corporation*,		
Boundaries of,	2	9
Same,	302	175
To pay costs of certain prosecutions, etc.,	133	86
Faith and property, pledged for payment of debts,	229	131
To pay expenses of Metropolitan Police,	358	211
To be one school district,	510	300
Certain acts relating to, repealed,	288	262
CITY HALL,		
Power to erect,	103	69
CITY SURVEYOR. See *Surveyor*.		
CLERKS OF ELECTION,		
How appointed, and oath of,	40	28
When to register names on election day,	476	274
CLERKS OF MARKET,		
How appointed,	4	12
To file official bond,	29	23
CLERK OF POLICE COURT,		
To be appointed by the Council,	388	227
Salary, bond, duties of,	388	227
May administer oaths and take affidavits,	388	227
CLERK OF RECORDER'S COURT,		
To be appointed by the Council,	4	12
Powers and duties of,	64	38
May administer oaths and take affidavits,	76	43
Same,	109	79
To keep records of the court and to sign process,	109	79
Complaints to be sworn to before,	126	84
When to open and adjourn court,	128	85
When to give information relative to records, etc., of court,	132	86
Salary of, how paid,	134	87
List of jurors to be returned to,	140	89
List of jurors to be filed in office of.	141	89
To put names of jurors in "jury box,"	141	89
To destroy old ballots before new names put in,	142	89
To notify Recorder and Sheriff of drawing of jurors,	143	90
May adjourn drawing of jurors,	144	90
How to proceed in drawing jurors,	145	90
To destroy names of jurors drawn known to be dead, etc.,	145	91
To make and file minute of drawing of jurors,	146	91
To issue *venire facias* to Sheriff,	146	91
To destroy ballots of jurors excused,	149	92
How to preserve names of jurors serving,	150	92
To report to Council criminal business of the court,	155	94
To draw jury in proceedings to open streets, etc.,	165	100
Objections to report of jury in street opening cases, to be filed with,	177	105
To make return on appeal in street opening cases,	178	106
When to file with City Clerk certified copy of report of jury,	183	107
COAL AND COKE,		
Power to designate and regulate places for sale of,	103	57
Power to regulate the inspecting of,	103	67
COCK PITS,		
Power of Metropolitan Police relative to,	351	204
COLLECTORS, CITY,		
To be appointed by the Council,	4	12
To file official bond,	29	23
To file bond for security of school money,	525	306

	SECTION.	PAGE.
To collect special assessments, ...	69	41
When warrants for unpaid taxes to be issued to, ...	243	141
When to levy on and sell personal property for unpaid taxes,	244	142
To pay over moneys received to Receiver, ...	244	143
Duties of, relative to collection of school tax, ...	524	305
COLLECTORS, WARD,		
Election of, ...	3	12
To file official bond, ...	29	23
To file official bond with County Treasurer, ...	461	263
To collect State and County taxes, ...	73	42
Powers and duties of, as to State and County taxes, . . .	461	263
When qualified, City Clerk to notify County Treasurer, . .	461	263
Proceedings on neglect of, to file bond with County Treasurer,	461	264
When warrants to issue to, for unpaid taxes, ...	243	141
When to levy on and sell personal property for unpaid taxes, .	244	142
To pay over moneys collected to Receiver, ...	244	143
To collect certain city taxes, ...	73	42
To give bond for collection of school moneys, ...	528	308
Duties of, relative collection of school moneys, ...	528	307
COMBUSTIBLE ARTICLES,		
Power to regulate, etc., storage of, ...	103	63
COMMISSIONERS TO APPORTION RENT,		
To be appointed when lease is affected by opening streets, etc.,	187	110
To take oath, and make report, ...	187	110
Report of, when confirmed, to be conclusive, ...	187	110
COMMISSIONERS ON PLAN OF THE CITY. See *Board of, etc.*		
COMMITTEES.		
Chairman of, may administer oaths, etc., ...	78	44
Same, ...	102	52
May subpœna witness and compel production of papers, . .	102	52
To be appointed by President of Council, ...	101	51
Duties of, to be prescribed by ordinance, ...	101	51
For negotiating loans, how constituted, ...	222	128
COMMON COUNCIL,		
How constituted, and quorum of, ...	82	46
To judge as to qualification of members, ...	96	50
May expel its own members, ...	21	20
May compel attendance of absent members, ...	82	46
Same, ...	96	50
When to elect President of, ...	84	47
City Clerk to be clerk of, ...	61	36
Same, ...	83	47
Clerk to preside over until President is elected, ...	84	47
To hold regular sessions, ...	85	47
Special sessions of, how called, ...	86	47
May pass by-laws and rules, ...	96	50
Right of petition to, ...	95	50
Officers to be appointed by, ...	4	12
Same, ...	5	13
How to remove officers holding by election, ...	21	21
How to remove officers holding by appointment, ...	22	21
When may suspend officers, ...	23	22
How to fill vacancy in office held by appointment, ...	26	22
How to fill vacancy in office held by election, ...	28	22
Resignations in office to be made to, ...	25	22
When to order special election to fill vacant office, ...	27	22
When to declare result of special elections, ...	49	31
May direct what officers shall give bonds, ...	29	23

	SECTION.	PAGE.
May prescribe condition of official bonds,	30	23
May order renewal of official bonds,	32	24
May prescribe additional duties of officers,	75	43
May examine sureties of bonds and contracts,	34	24
What proceedings of, to be presented to Mayor,	87	48
Reconsideration by, in case of Mayor's veto,	89	49
Record of proceedings of, to be kept,	91	49
Proceedings of, to be published,	92	49
Meetings of, to be public,	94	50
Records of, open to inspection,	94	50
To have control of finances and corporation property,	97	50
May sell, lease, convey, etc., corporation property,	97	51
Ordinances, resolutions, etc., of, when may be passed,	98	51
Ordinances, resolutions, etc., of, when may be passed,	218	127
When ordinances, etc., may be passed at special session of,	98	51
Appointments to and removals from office, to be by majority vote of,	100	51
General powers of, relative to compensation of officers,	103	52
General powers of, relative to appointment and removal of officers,	103	52
General powers of, relative to fees and costs of officers,	103	52
General powers of, relative to fees of jurors and witnesses,	103	52
General powers of, relative to waters of Detroit River,	103	53
General powers of, relative to wharves and docks,	103	53
General powers of, relative to leasing of wharves and docks,	103	53
General powers of, relative to working of highways, streets, etc.,	103	54
General powers of, relative to improvement of parks, etc.,	103	54
General powers of, relative to opening of streets, etc.,	103	54
General powers of, relative to disposition of dirt, manure, etc.,	103	55
General powers of, relative to the cleaning of streets and sidewalks,	103	55
General powers of, relative to the prevention of riots, etc.,	103	56
General powers of, relative to maintainance of quiet at depots, etc.,	103	56
General powers of, relative to prescribing stands for drays, etc.,	103	57
General powers of, relative to fireworks,	103	57
General powers of, relative to paving of sidewalks,	103	57
General powers of, relative to indecent exposures,	103	57
General powers of, relative to running at large of animals,	103	58
General powers of, relative to running at large of dogs,	103	58
General powers of, relative to fastening of teams,	103	58
General powers of, relative to constructing bridges, culverts, etc.,	103	58
General powers of, relative to cellars drained into public sewers,	103	59
General powers of, relative to boundaries of streets, etc.	103	59
General powers of, relative to numbering of buildings,	103	59
General powers of, relative to draining of swamps, etc.,	103	59
General powers of, relative to markets,	103	60
General powers of, relative to public health,	103	60
General powers of, relative to abatement of nuisances,	103	60
General powers of, relative to nauseous shops, privies, etc.,	103	61
General powers of, relative to dead carcasses, unsound meat, etc.,	103	61
General powers of, relative to cellars, drains, sinks, etc.,	103	61
General powers of, relative to lateral sewers,	103	62
General powers of, relative to fire department,	103	62
General powers of, relative to storage of explosive substances,	103	62
General powers of, relative to soap, candle factories, etc.,	103	62
General powers of, relative to extra hazardous buildings,	103	63
General powers of, relative to powder and lights in stables, etc.,	103	63
General powers of, relative to wooden buildings,	103	63
General powers of, relative to partition fences, walls, etc.,	103	63
General powers of, relative to chimneys,	103	64

	SECTION.	PAGE.
General powers of, relative to bathing,	103	64
General powers of, relative to houses of ill fame,	103	64
General powers of, relative to beggars, vagrants, etc.,	103	64
General powers of, relative to unsound meats,	103	65
General powers of, relative to games and gaming,	103	65
General powers of, relative to lotteries,	103	65
General powers of, relative to intoxicating liquors,	103	65
General powers of, relative to porters, runners, etc.,	103	66
General powers of, relative to auctioneers, peddlers, etc.,	103	66
General powers of, relative to public exhibitions,	103	66
General powers of, relative to hotels, saloons, etc.,	103	66
General powers of, relative to butchers, provision dealers, etc.,	103	66
General powers of, relative to billiard tables and pin alleys,	103	67
General powers of, relative to police,	103	67
General powers of, relative to weighers and gaugers,	103	67
General powers of, relative to bread,	103	67
General powers of, relative to inspection of wood, provisions, etc.,	103	67
General powers of, relative to weights and measures,	103	68
General powers of, relative to paupers,	103	68
General powers of, relative to burials,	103	68
General powers of, relative to census and public meetings,	103	69
General powers of, relative to public buildings,	103	69
General powers of, relative to alms houses,	103	69
General powers of, relative to jails, work houses, etc.,	103	69
General powers of, relative to imprisonment of criminals,	103	69
General powers of, relative to speed of cars and engines,	103	70
General powers of, relative to granting of licenses,	103	71
General powers of, relative to taxes, their levy and collection,	103	71
General powers of, relative to appropriations,	103	71
General powers of, relative to violations of the charter, etc.,	103	72
General powers of, relative to employment of prisoners,	103	72
General powers of, relative to printing,	103	73
General powers of, relative to public peace,	103	73
General powers of, relative to subdivision of wards,	103	73
General powers of, relative to real estate for corporation purposes,	103	73
General powers of, relative to real estate for cemetery purposes,	103	73
General powers of, relative to construction of stone and brick buildings,	104	73
General powers of, relative to construction of stone and brick buildings,	105	74
General powers of, relative to appointment of policemen,	104	74
General powers of, relative to perpetuation of evidences of real estate titles.	105	75
General powers of, relative to repairs of sidewalks,	105	75
General powers of, relative to taxes illegally collected,	105	76
General powers of, relative to taxes on insurance companies,	105	76
General powers of, relative to illegal assessments,	105	77
May order removal of unsafe buildings, etc,	179	44
May inspect records of Recorder's Court,	132	86
May prescribe punishments for violations of charter. etc.,	137	88
Power to lay out, extend streets, alleys, etc.,	157	95
To declare by resolution necessity of public improvement,	158	96
How to give notice of intended improvements,	159	96
When may elect to pay damages claimed,	181	107
When to pay damages found by jury,	185	108
When to take possession of land for public improvement,	186	109
Evidence of right of, to take such possession,	186	109
To appoint commissioners on plan of the city,	187	110
Power of, to raise funds for special purposes,	196	116
May levy and collect taxes for certain funds,	197	116

	SECTION.	PAGE.
May levy and collect taxes for district road fund, ...	198	117
May levy and collect taxes for constructing sewers, ...	199	117
To direct Mayor to call meeting to consider taxes. . . .	200	118
When, may call second meeting to consider taxes, . . .	200	118
To levy sufficient taxes to pay interest, ...	201	119
To levy certain tax for purposes of the sinking fund, . -	201	119
May levy tax on lots drained into public sewer, ...	202	119
May levy tax for paving, grading, etc., streets, etc., . . .	203	119
May provide money for public building fund, ...	204	120
When may contract for purchase of real estate, ...	205	122
Must approve public works, before commenced, ...	206	122
Not to issue unauthorized bonds, ...	208	123
May issue new bonds to refund old bonds, ...	208	123
Not to borrow money unless authorized, ...	209	124
When may authorize Controller to borrow, ...	209	124
To create no debt contrary to charter, ...	212	125
To determine fiscal year and publish Controller's report, . .	219	127
May require statements and estimates of officers, . . -	220	128
May contract for keeping of public moneys, ...	221	128
To approve loans, ... - . . .	222	129
When, may direct to what fund, tax to be credited, . . .	223	129
May revise and correct action of assessor, ...	233	134
To appoint Board of Review, ...	237	136
When to consider assessment rolls, ...	240	138
May correct assessment rolls, ...	241	138
Not to increase assessment without notice, ...	241	139
How long may consider assessment rolls, ...	242	139
May extend or renew warrants for collection of taxes, . .	243	142
Notice by, to pay delinquent taxes, ...	245	143
When may order sale of land to pay taxes, ...	246	144
May charge interest on redemption of land, ...	249	146
When may direct land bid in, to be held in trust for contractor,	252	147
May procure and control fire apparatus, ...	255	149
May organize and prescribe duties of fire companies, . . .	256	149
To appoint and prescribe duties of engineers, ...	257	150
May appoint fire marshal, ...	267	154
May remove fire marshal, ...	270	155
May appoint Board of Police Commissioners, etc., ...	289	164
May fill vacancies in Board of Police Commissioners, . . .	289	165
May appoint policemen and watchmen, ...	292	166
To provide accommodations for police, ...	293	168
May appoint temporary policemen, ...	295	168
When may prescribe jurisdiction of police justice, ...	298	169
To appoint justice of the peace to act as police justice, . .	300	170
May fill vacancy in office of police justice, ...	384	226
When may offer reward for detection of criminals, . . .	301	171
Water Commissioners to make report to, ...	318	184
When to raise water tax, ...	330	188
To levy tax to pay expenses of Metropolitan Police, . . .	359	211
Same, ...	369	216
May require information as to accounts, etc., of Metropolitan Police, ...	361	213
May appoint Clerk of Police Court, ...	388	227
To sanction salaries, etc., of officers of House of Correction, .	398	234
To sanction expenditures of Inspectors of House of Correction,	398	234
When to levy tax for expenses of House of Correction, . .	409	240
To appoint Fire Commissioners, ...	424	248
How to remove Fire Commissioners, ...	425	248
To submit estimates of Fire Commissioners to public meeting, .	433	251
Power to levy tax to support Fire Department, ...	445	255

	SECTION.	PAGE.
May require information relative to Fire Department, ...	446	256
When, may appoint person to collect State and County taxes,	461	264
When to direct review of registration, ...	502	293
May direct election on division of ward, -	507	297
To appoint Inspector of election on division of ward, ...	508	298
To fill vacancy in office of School Inspector, ...	512	301
May levy tax for school library, ...	521	304
May levy tax for support of schools, ...	522	305
Same, ...	545	314
To appoint persons to take census, ...	566	324
Proceedings by, under the drainage act of 1849, ...	549	318

COMPENSATION. See *Salary*.

Of Sewer Commissioners, ...	5	14
Of Aldermen, ...	96	50
Of officers, power of Council relative to, ...	103	52
Of officers, when and how to be increased or diminished, .	103	52
Of hack drivers, etc., ...	103	66
Of policemen, ...	103	67
Of weighers and measurers, ...	103	67
Of person appointed to act as attorney, ...	127	85
Where private property is taken for public purposes, ...	157	96
Awarded by jury, in cases of opening streets, etc., ...	167	101
How awarded in such case, where there is mortgage, etc., . .	167	101
How apportioned in opening alleys, ...	168	102
In cases of opening streets, etc., jury to report, ...	170	102
In cases of opening streets, etc., to be assessed to property benefited, ...	171	103
In cases of opening streets, etc., to be awarded the city, .	171	103
In cases of opening streets, etc., may be inquired into, . .	173	104
Of the jurors in cases of opening streets, etc., ...	188	110
Of policemen, ...	292	167
Of Justice of the Peace, acting as Police Justice, ...	299	170
Of owners of land, to be paid by Water Commissioners, . .	323	186
Proceedings as to, where owners do not agree with Water Commissioners, ...	324	186
Limit of number of policemen who may receive, ...	342	195
Of Property Clerk of Metropolitan Police, ...	343	196
Of special policemen, ...	353	205
Same, ...	354	206
Of officers conveying prisoners to House of Correction, . .	405	238
For maintenance of State prisoners in House of Correction, .	406	239
For conveyance of State prisoners to House of Correction, .	407	240
Of Board of Registration, ...	495	287

COMPLAINTS.

Prosecutions may be by, ...	112	80
Rules relative to, ...	113	80
Proceedings on, against persons licensed, ...	77	43
Different degrees of offenses may be joined in, ...	113	80
Certain, to be endorsed by Recorder, ...	114	81
When defendant may be found guilty of less degree than laid in,	115	81
Joinder of persons in, ...	116	81
May be in form of affidavits, ...	126	84
What to set forth and trials on, ...	126	84

COMPLAINT BOOKS.

Of Metropolitan Police, and what to be entered therein, . .	356	209

CONCERTS.

Power to prevent or license, ...	103	66

	SECTION.	PAGE.
CONSTABLES.		
When elected,	3	12
To file official bond,	29	23
May be suspended or removed by Mayor,	21	21
To have same duties as township constables,	73	42
Special, condition of bond of,	31	23
Duties of, at fires,	265	153
CONTINGENT FUND.		
Illegal taxes, if paid, to be refunded out of,	105	76
Damages in opening alleys, to be paid out of,	108	102
For what purpose raised,	196	114
Power to raise tax for,	197	116
CONTRACTS.		
Sureties on, may be examined by Council, etc.,	34	25
Persons interested in, not eligible to certain offices,	12	17
Officers becoming interested in, to be removed from office,	13	17
Not to be let to Aldermen or other officers,	217	126
Unauthorized, not to be made,	206	122
Unauthorized, to be void,	212	124
Made after the proper fund is exhausted, void,	216	126
Streets, alleys, etc., may be paved, graded, etc., by,	72	42
When claims on, to be accompanied by affidavit,	80	45
When actions on, to be barred,	80	45
When certain, to be commenced,	203	120
To be let to the lowest bidder,	207	122
Not to be let to defaulters or persons in arrears,	207	123
No additional allowance to be made on,	213	125
Of old Corporation to be discharged by new Corporation,	271	156
Water Commissioners not to be interested in certain,	331	189
For imprisonment of criminals in House of Correction,	403	237
Of Inspectors of State Prison, relative to same,	406	238
CONTROLLER.		
How and when appointed,	4	12
Term of office of,	15	18
When office of, to commence,	16	19
To file official bond,	29	23
How and when may be removed,	22	21
General powers and duties of,	62	36
To open account with Treasurer,	63	38
To keep list of Corporation property,	63	38
May administer oaths and take affidavits.	76	43
May take acknowledgment of deeds,	76	43
To present to Council estimate of amount of taxes,	200	117
To countersign bonds for the Public Building Fund,	204	121
To keep record of bonds for the Public Building Fund,	204	121
To give information to Council relative to the finances,	200	118
When Council may authorize Controller to make loan,	209	124
To keep record of new bonds to refund old bonds,	210	124
To countersign new bonds to refund old bonds,	210	124
To keep record of bonds, etc., cancelled,	211	124
No money to be paid except on warrant signed by,	214	125
May require affidavit to accompany claim,	215	126
Annual report of, and what to contain,	219	127
To be member of committee to negotiate loans,	222	128
May divide funds for special purposes,	225	130
To be one of the Commissioners of Sinking Fund,	226	130
To draw warrants on Sinking Fund,	228	131
To deliver tax rolls to Receiver of Taxes,	243	139
When to sign warrant of collection of certain taxes,	243	141

	SECTION.	PAGE.
To execute deed of lands sold for taxes,	246	144
Same,	251	146
May execute certain conveyances to the Corporation,	252	147
When to bid in property for benefit of the Corporation,	252	146
To be a trustee of "Police, Life and Health Insurance Fund,"	348	202
To submit estimates of expenses of Metropolitan Police,	359	211
May inspect accounts, etc., of Metropolitan Police,	361	213
May inspect accounts, etc., of Fire Commissioners,	446	256
CONVEYANCES. See *Deeds*.		
Upon tax sales, Controller to execute,	246	144
Same,	251	146
To the Corporation, when to be executed by Controller,	252	147
When to be evidence of regularity of proceedings,	246	144
Same,	253	147
Of lands upon tax sales, may be recorded,	251	146
Certain, to the Corporation, may be recorded,	252	147
CONVICTIONS.		
Clerk of Recorder's Court to report number of,	155	94
CORPORATION OF "THE CITY OF DETROIT."		
Name, powers, seal of,	1	9
Clerk to keep seal of,	61	36
Controller to keep list of property of,	63	38
Council to have control of property of,	97	50
Council to provide for erection of buildings of,	103	69
Council to purchase, etc., real estate for use of,	103	73
Faith and property of, pledged for payment of debts of,	229	131
Embezzlement by officers of property of,	230	131
To pay the debts of the old Corporation,	271	156
Rights and property of old corporation to vest in,	272	156
Act incorporating, not to invalidate legal acts of old Corporation,	277	158
To retain right of property in fire apparatus, etc.,	437	253
Not to issue due bills to circulate as currency,	574	328
COSTS AND EXPENSES.		
Power to impose payment of, in certain cases,	103	72
Of officers, power to regulate,	103	52
Incurred in prosecutions, when city liable for,	133	86
On appeals in cases to open streets, etc.,	179	106
On trials of Metropolitan Policemen for misconduct,	347	201
On trials before the Police Justice,	387	226
COUNSELOR.		
How appointed, and term of office of,	4	12
Duties and compensation of,	4	12
COUNTY.		
Offices, Aldermen not eligible to,	11	16
CROSSWALKS. See *Walks*.		
Surveyor to make assessments for,	68	41
Street Commissioners to superintend construction of,	71	41
How expenses of, may be paid,	103	55
Power to clean,	103	55
CULVERTS.		
Power to construct,	103	58
Street Commissioners to superintend construction of,	71	41
DAMAGES.		
For opening ditches, how assessed,	103	59
Same,	551	319
For obstructing ditches,	555	320
From defective sidewalks, when owners liable for,	105	75
For private property taken for public use, how ascertained,	157	96

	SECTION.	PAGE.
In opening, altering, etc., streets, etc., when to be paid, . .	167	101
In opening, altering, etc., streets, etc., how paid, ...	167	101
To Mortgagees, lessees, etc., when to be awarded, . . .	167	101
In opening, etc., alleys, how awarded, ...	168	102
When to be paid from the Contingent Fund, ...	168	102
To mortgagees, lessees, etc., in opening alleys, jury to report, .	170	102
Apportioned on property benefitted in opening alleys, . .	171	103
Apportioned to the City of Detroit in opening alleys, . . .	171	103
Awarded, may be inquired into, ...	173	104
City may elect to pay, on annulment of report of jury, . .	181	107
Assessed on property, in what cases to be a lien, . . .	182	107
In case of opening streets, etc., when to be tendered, . . .	185	108
In case of opening streets, etc., when may be deposited, . .	185	109
On payment of, Council may take possession of land, . . .	186	109
Benefit to be offset against, in opening of streets, etc., . .	194	112
Awarded to estate of deceased persons in opening streets, etc.,	195	112
DEATHS.		
Of officers, to vacate office, ...	24	22
Power to provide for registration of, ...	103	69
Of electors, proceedings by Board of Registration relative to, .	486	281
DEBTS.		
Of the Corporation, Controller to keep list of, ...	63	38
Of the Corporation, power to make appropriations to pay, .	103	71
Unauthorized evidences of, not to be issued, ...	208	123
Same, ...	212	124
Unauthorized by law, not to be created or paid, ...	212	125
Same, ...	213	125
Evidences of, when refunded, to be cancelled, ...	211	124
Of the old corporation, to be paid, ...	271	156
DECEASED PERSONS.		
Damages awarded to estates of, in opening streets, etc., . .	195	112
DEDICATION.		
Of alleys, parks, streets, etc., by platting and recording plats, .	191	111
DEEDS AND CONVEYANCES.		
Controller may take acknowledgments of, ...	76	43
Of lands sold for taxes, when to be executed and effect of, .	246	144
Of lands sold for taxes, who to execute, ...	251	146
Of lands sold for taxes, what to be evidence of, ...	253	147
To the Corporation, when to be executed by Controller, . .	252	147
Of Governor and Judges, may be recorded by Register, . .	570	325
Of Governor and Judges, effect of, as evidence, ...	570	325
Same, ...	571	325
Same, ...	573	327
Of Mayor, Recorder, etc., recording and effect of as evidence,	572	326
DEFAULTERS.		
Who to be considered, ...	9	16
Ineligible to elective or appointive office, ...	9	16
Offices held by, to be declared vacant, ...	9	16
Contracts not to be let to, ...	207	123
DETROIT HOUSE OF CORRECTION. See *House of Correction.*		
DETROIT RIVER. See *Wharves.*		
Power to preserve purity of water of, ...	103	53
Power to remove obstructions in, ...	103	53
Power to regulate anchoring of vessels in, ...	103	53
Power to license bath rooms or vessels on, ...	103	67
DICE.		
Power to suppress gaming with, ...	103	65

	SECTION.	PAGE.
DIRECTOR OF THE POOR.		
When elected,	3	11
Term of office of,	15	19
To have same powers and duties as Township Directors,	73	42
DIRT.		
In streets and public places, power to dispose of,	103	55
DITCHES.		
For drainage of low lands, proceedings to open,	103	59
Same,	551	319
Power to maintain,	554	320
Power to punish for obstructing,	555	320
DISEASES.		
Power to prevent the introduction and spread of,	103	60
DISORDERLY ASSEMBLAGES.		
Power to restrain or suppress,	103	56
DISORDERLY HOUSES.		
Power to suppress, and punish keepers of,	103	64
DISORDERLY OR DRUNKEN PERSONS.		
Power to restrain and punish,	103	64
Who to be deemed, and proceedings against,	377	220
May be sent to House of Correction,	411	241
DISTILLERIES,		
Power to prevent erection of, in certain limits,	103	62
DISTRICT ROAD FUND. See *Taxes*,		
Power to raise, and for what purposes,	195	115
May be raised by tax,	198	117
Limitation of amount of,	198	117
Estimates of amount of, to be submitted,	200	117
Surplus not to be transferred to sinking fund,	224	129
Expenses of crosswalks to be paid from,	231	132
DOCKS. See *Wharves*.		
DOGS,		
Running at large of, power to restrain,	103	58
DRAINAGE. See *Ditches*,		
Of swamps, low lands, etc., power to provide for,	103	59
Of swamps, low lands, etc., Council to inquire relative to,	548	317
When jury to be summoned relative to,	549	318
Jury to assess benefits and damages arising from,	551	319
Power to maintain ditches for purposes of,	554	320
DRAINS,		
Power to build,	103	58
Private, power to compel building of,	103	58
Private, power to regulate construction of,	103	58
Same,	103	61
Private, power to assess expense of,	103	61
Private, running into public sewer, power to levy assessment for,	103	59
Same,	202	119
Lateral, power to maintain,	103	58
Lateral, power to assess expense of building,	103	62
Lateral, assessment rolls for, made by surveyor,	68	41
DRAYMEN,		
Power to regulate,	103	57
Power to license and fix compensation of,	103	66
DUE BILLS,		
Corporation not to issue, to circulate as currency,	574	328

	SECTION.	PAGE.
Elections. See *Register. Inspectors of Elections. Special Elections,*		
Of officers,	3	11
Special, for mayor or alderman may be called,	27	22
Annual, time, place, and notice of holding,	37	26
Clerks of, how appointed,	40	28
Polls of, when to open and how long to be kept open,	42	29
Proceedings on challenge of vote at,	44	29
Punishment for voting more than once at,	46	30
Mode of conducting,	47	30
Returns of, inspectors to certify,	48	31
For state and county officers, how conducted,	53	32
Powers of police at,	354	206
Of police justice,	381	224
May be ordered by Council on division of wards,	507	297
Election Districts,		
How constituted,	38	27
Wards may be divided into,	38	27
Same,	506	296
Council to appoint inspectors on establishment of,	508	297
Elector to vote in, where he resides,	38	27
What constitutes residence in,	38	27
Electors.		
Must vote in ward or district where they reside,	38	27
What constitutes residence of,	38	27
Qualifications of,	43	29
If challenged, oath may be administered to,	44	29
Punishment of, for taking false oath,	45	30
Not to vote more than once at any election,	46	30
Not subject to arrest on civil process, on election day,	54	32
Attending polls, violence on, made a misdemeanor,	366	215
Proceedings of Board of Registration on death or removal of,	485	281
Board of Registration to note names of persons ceasing to be,	499	289
City Clerk to forward to Secretary of State number of registered,	494	286
Embezzlement.		
Of public property by Corporation officers, how punished,	230	131
Encroachments.		
On streets, alleys, etc., power to prohibit and remove,	103	59
Engineers.		
Of Sewer Commissioners, how appointed and duties of,	5	13
To be appointed by Fire Commissioners,	435	252
Salaries of,	435	253
Appointment of, by Council,	257	150
Exempt from jury and militia duty,	262	152
Engine Houses.		
Council to provide,	255	149
Fire Commissioners to construct and maintain,	430	250
Fire Commissioners to have the control of,	431	250
Engines.		
On railroads in the city, power to regulate speed of,	103	70
Fire, Council to provide,	255	149
Fire, Company to take care of,	259	151
Fire, Company to work and examine,	260	151
Fire, Fire Commissioners to provide,	430	250
Fire, Fire Commissioners to have control of,	431	250
Fire, to have the right of way to fires,	436	253
English Language.		
Officers must be able to read and write,	10	16

	SECTION.	PAGE.
ERECTIONS. See *Buildings.*		
Unsafe, power of Council relative to,	79	44
EVIDENCE.		
Of title, power to provide for the perpetuation of,	104	73
Same,	105	75
Of regularity of proceedings, when conveyance to be,	246	144
Same,	253	147
Of right to enter and possess land, when Treasurer's certificate to be,	186	109
Certified copy of report of jury in opening streets to be received as	183	108
Of firemen's exemption from militia and jury duty,	262	152
Certificate of presentation of ordinances to Mayor to be	280	158
How records in Clerk's office and ordinances made,	182	159
Printer's affidavit of publication, when to be,	282	159
Certain printed copies of ordinances, etc., to be,	283	159
Conveyances of the Governor and Judges, effect of as,	570	325
Same,	571	325
Same,	573	327
Conveyances of Mayor, Recorder, etc., effect of as,	572	326
EXECUTIONS.		
When to issue on judgments on recognizances,	117	82
Materials procured by Water Commissioners exempt from,	321	185
EXEMPTION,		
Of firemen from militia and jury duty,	262	152
Same,	438	254
List of firemen claiming, to be kept,	455	259
Of policemen from jury duty,	365	215
From jury duty in Recorder's Court, who may claim,	148	92
In street opening case, who may claim,	162	99
From execution, of materials purchased by Water Commissioners,	321	185
EXHIBITIONS,		
Indecent, power to prevent,	103	58
Power to license and regulate,	103	66
EXPENSES. See *Costs and Expenses.*		
EXPLOSIVE SUBSTANCES,		
Power to prevent manufacture of, within certain limits,	103	62
Power to regulate storage of,	103	63
EXPRESS COMPANIES,		
Power to regulate runners, agents, etc., of,	103	56
EXPULSION,		
From office, proceedings to effect,	21	20
From office, vacates office,	25	22
FACTORIES,		
Power of Council over starch, soap, glue, etc.,	103	62
Same,	103	61
FAST DRIVING,		
In streets, power to prevent,	103	56
FEES. See *Compensation,*		
Of jurors and witnesses,	103	52
Of officers, power to regulate,	103	52
For administering oaths, etc., what officers may not take,	76	43
FEMALES,		
When to be sentenced to House of correction,	406	239
Same,	416	243
Under fourteen years of age, may be sent to House of Correction,	408	240
Sentence of, commuted from State Prison to House of Correction,	417	244

	SECTION.	PAGE.
FENCES,		
Unsafe, Council may order removal of,	79	44
Unsafe, order for removal of, how served,	79	44
Partition, power to regulate construction of,	103	63
Encroaching on streets, etc., power to remove,	103	59
FERRIES,		
Power to license and regulate,	103	53
FINANCES,		
Controller to keep books showing state of,	62	37
Controller to take general supervision of,	62	37
Controller to give information to Council respecting,	200	118
FINES AND PENALTIES,		
Power to impose,	103	72
Power to imprison for non-payment of,	103	72
Limitation of amount of,	103	72
Imposed on Street Commissioners for neglect to give notice of defective sidewalks,	105	75
Duty of attorney relative to,	131	86
Clerk of Recorder's Court to give information relative to,	132	86
Clerk of Recorder's Court to report number of imposed,	155	94
May be imposed on defaulting jurors,	148	62
Same,	162	99
May be imposed on firemen for breach of duty,	256	150
Imposed and collected by police justice to be paid to treasurer,	298	169
Same,	399	170
Persons may be committed in default of payment of,	299	170
Fire Commissioners may sue for and recover certain,	439	254
For refusing to serve as school inspector,	513	301
FIRES.		
Power to provide for prevention of,	103	62
Same,	103	64
Powers of officers at,	103	64
Powers of Mayor at,	263	152
Power to arrest for disobedience of lawful orders at,	264	153
Disorderly persons may be arrested at,	264	153
Certain officers to repair to, and their duties at,	265	153
Cause of, to be investigated by Fire Marshal,	267	154
Cause and origin of, to be reported to Council,	268	154
Fire Marshal to cause arrest of persons wilfully setting,	269	154
Duties of Metropolitan Police at,	345	198
Fire Commissioners to have exclusive power to extinguish,	429	249
Engines to have right of way to and at,	436	253
Fire Commission may sue for fines for the prevention of,	439	254
FIREMEN.		
Exemption of, from military and jury duty,	262	152
Certificates of exemption, by whom issued,	454	259
Council to prescribe duties of,	256	150
May impose fines and penalties on,	256	150
When on duty, to be protected by police,	345	198
Salaries of,	435	253
To have right of way to fires,	436	253
FIRE COMMISSION OF THE CITY OF DETROIT.		
Powers and duties of Fire Department vested in,	423	247
Same,	429	249
Majority of Board of, to constitute a quorum,	423	248
First members of Board named, and term of office of,	424	248
Future members of Board of, to be appointed by Council,	424	248
How members of, to be removed from office,	425	248
Official oath of members of,	426	248

	SECTION.	PAGE.
May elect President and appoint Secretary,	427	249
To have exclusive power to extinguish fires,	427	249
Same,	429	249
Name by which to be known,	428	249
To provide and maintain houses, engines, etc.,	430	250
To possess and control all fire apparatus and property,	431	250
Office of, vacated by acceptance of political office,	432	251
To submit to Council estimate of expenses,	433	251
Treasurer of,	433	251
To provide offices for transaction of business,	435	252
May appoint Chief and Assistant Engineers, etc.,	435	252
May appoint person to act as Fire Marshal,	435	252
Property used by former Department transferred to,	437	253
Same,	440	254
To receive no compensation,	438	254
May have seal and institute suits,	439	254
Right of, to sue for and recover certain fines,	439	254
May send engines, etc., out of the city,	440	254
Power to adopt rules, etc.,	443	255
To make annual report, what report of, to contain,	444	255
Books and accounts of, subject to inspection,	446	256
FIRE COMMISSIONERS' FUND,		
How constituted,	433	251
How treasurer to pay out,	433	252
To be paid only on warrants,	434	252
FIRE COMPANIES,		
Power to authorize,	103	62
Power to organize and prescribe duties of,	256	149
May appoint their own officers, etc.,	259	150
To take care of fire apparatus and proceed to fires,	259	151
To assemble whenever Council shall direct,	260	151
FIRE DEPARTMENT,		
Power to establish,	103	62
Incorporated,	448	256
Act of 1840, incorporating, continued,	287	161
May have and hold real estate,	448	257
May make rules and regulations,	449	257
Meetings and election of officers of,	449	257
Officers and Board of Trustees of,	450	259
Annual meeting of,	451	258
Trustees to make list of members,	455	259
Disposition of interest of funds of,	453	259
Powers and duties of, vested in Fire Commissioners,	423	247
Fire Commissioners not affect rights of the corporation of the,	442	255
Fire Commissioners to make annual report of condition of,	444	255
Council to levy tax for support of,	445	255
FIRE DEPARTMENT FUND,		
Tax on insurance companies to be credited to,	105	76
For what purpose raised,	196	115
Power to raise by tax,	197	116
Estimates for, to be submitted before raising,	200	117
FIRE MARSHAL,		
Power to appoint,	267	154
To investigate causes of fires,	267	154
To report to Council results of investigation as to fires,	268	154
To cause arrest of persons setting fires,	269	154
Term of office of, and how removed,	270	155
Office of, abolished,	441	254
Fire Commission to appoint person to act as,	435	252

	SECTION.	PAGE.
FIRE WARDENS.		
Ex-officio, who to be,	258	150
Council may appoint,	258	150
General powers and duties of,	261	151
Exempt from military and jury duty,	262	152
May order any person to assist in extinguishing fires,	263	152
Their duties at fires,	265	153
FIREWORKS, FIREARMS, ETC.		
Power to prevent exhibition and firing of,	103	57
FISCAL YEAR.		
Council to determine,	215	127
FISH.		
Unsound, power to prevent sale of,	103	65
Power to license and regulate sellers of,	103	67
Power to inspect,	103	68
FLOUR.		
Power to inspect,	103	68
FORESTALLING.		
Power to prohibit,	103	60
FORGERY.		
When falsifying Register of Electors deemed to be,	488	283
FOUNDRIES.		
Power to regulate construction and management of,	103	63
FREEMEN'S MEETINGS. See *Meetings*.		
FUNDS.		
Into what, revenues divided,	196	114
Power to raise additional, for special purposes,	196	116
Money raised for particular, to be credited to such funds,	223	129
When Council may credit moneys to other,	223	129
Raised for particular purpose, to be applied to such purpose,	224	129
Surplus of, to be transferred to sinking fund,	224	129
Not to be transferred from one fund to another,	225	130
May be divided by Controller into special funds,	225	130
Controller to report to Council when exhausted,	62	37
GAMES.		
Fraudulent, power to suppress,	103	65
GAMING.		
Power to suppress,	103	65
GAMING HOUSES.		
Power to suppress,	103	65
Power of Metropolitan Police relative to,	351	204
GAS LIGHT COMPANY.		
Incorporated,	575	330
Powers of,	576	330
Capital stock of,	577	330
Officers of,	577	331
Powers of Board of Directors of,	578	331
Property of members vested in, liable to execution,	580	332
GEESE.		
Power to prohibit running at large,	103	58
GENERAL FUND.		
For what purpose raised,	196	114
Power to raise by tax,	197	116
Estimates for, to be submitted before raising,	200	117
When moneys may be credited to,	223	129

	SECTION.	PAGE.
GENERAL ROAD FUND.		
For what purpose raised,	196	115
Power to raise by tax,	197	116
Estimates for, to be submitted before raising,	200	117
GLUE FACTORIES.		
Power to abate or cleanse,	103	61
Power to prohibit within certain limits,	103	62
GOATS.		
Power to prevent the running at large of,	103	58
GOODS.		
Power to prohibit crying of, in streets,	103	56
GRADING. See *Highways. Streets.*		
GROCERIES.		
Power to compel owner to clean or abate,	103	61
Power to license keepers of,	103	66
GAUGERS.		
Power to appoint and prescribe duties and fees of,	103	67
HABEAS CORPUS.		
Recorder may issue writ of,	121	83
When persons brought on writ of, not entitled to bail,	378	222
HACKMEN.		
Power to regulate,	103	57
Power to license,	103	66
HACKS AND HACKNEY COACHES. See *Vehicles.*		
HAWKERS.		
Power to license and regulate,	103	66
HAY.		
Power to designate and regulate places for sale of,	103	57
Power to inspect,	103	67
HEADING.		
Power to inspect,	103	67
HEALTH.		
Power to provide for preservation of,	103	60
Power to establish Board of,	103	60
Who constitute Board of,	567	324
Public, duty of Metropolitan Police to guard,	345	197
HEARTHS.		
Power to regulate construction of,	103	64
HIGH SCHOOL.		
Power to establish,	522	305
HIGHWAYS. See *Overseer of Highways, Street Commissioners.*		
Power to work and improve,	103	54
Power to clean,	103	55
Power to clean, pave, etc., by contract,	72	42
Power to open, widen, vacate, etc.	103	54
Same,	157	95
Power to dispose of dirt, cleanings, etc., of,	103	55
Street Commissioners to superintend working of,	71	41
To be worked and improved by Overseer of Highways,	72	41
Power to grade, pave, etc.,	103	54
How expenses of paving, grading, etc., of, to be paid,	103	54
Power to prevent the encumbering of,	103	55
Power to remove encroachments on,	103	59
Power to regulate the use of,	103	56
Power to survey and ascertain the boundaries of,	103	59
Notice of opening of how and on whom served,	159	96

	SECTION.	PAGE.
Return of service of notice of opening of,	159	97
Attorney to apply for jury to consider matter of opening,	160	98
Qualifications of jurors to consider matter of opening,	161	99
Summoning of jurors to open, extend, etc.,	162	99
Drawing of jurors to open, extend, etc.,	163	99
Challenge of jurors to open, extend, etc.	163	100
Summoning of talesmen to open, extend, etc.,	164	100
Clerk to draw jury to open, extend, etc.,	165	100
Jury to open, etc., to be sworn,	165	100
Jury to open, etc., to be advised by City Attorney,	165	101
Jury to open, etc., to view property to be taken to open, etc.,	166	101
Jury to determine necessity of taking property to open, etc.,	167	101
Jury to award just compensation for property taken to open, etc.,	167	101
Damages by opening, etc., how paid,	167	101
Damages by opening, to mortgagees, lessees, etc., how apportioned,	167	101
Jury to report damages by opening, etc.,	170	102
Damages to mortgagees, lessees, by opening, etc., how stated,	170	103
Of report of jury relative to opening, etc., how confirmed,	172	103
Objections to report of jury relative to opening,	172	104
Amount of damages given in opening, etc., may be inquired into,	173	104
Proceedings on objections to report of jury relative to opening etc.,	174	104
When new jury may be called relative to opening, etc.	175	104
Vacancy in jury to open, etc., how supplied,	176	105
Appeal from confirmation of report of jury to open, etc.,	177	105
Notice of appeal from such confirmation,	177	105
Return on appeal from confirmation of report of jury to open, etc.,	178	106
Proceedings in Supreme Court on review of report of jury to open, etc.,	179	106
Proceedings on reversal of confirmation of report of jury to open, etc.,	180	106
On reversal of confimation of report to open, etc., City may elect to pay damages,	181	107
When confirmation of report of jury to open, etc., conclusive,	182	107
Report of jury to open, etc., to be entered in "Street Records,"	183	108
Amount assessed for benefits by opening, etc., how collected,	184	108
When damages for opening, etc., to be paid,	185	108
Effect of payment of damages for opening, etc.,	186	109
Proceedings where lease affected by opening, etc.,	187	109
In opening, etc., benefits to offset against damages,	194	112
In opening, etc., where damages to be awarded estates of deceased persons,	195	112
Council may levy tax for paving, grading, etc.,	203	119
HIGHWAY TAXES. See *Taxes. Road Fund*,		
Power to assess and levy,	103	54
When persons not compelled to pay,	103	57
HOGS,		
Power to restrain running at large,	103	58
HORSES,		
Power to restrain running at large,	103	58
Power to compel fastening of, in streets,	103	58
HOTELS,		
Power to regulate runners of,	103	66
Power to license keepers of,	103	66
HOUSE OF CORRECTION,		
Power to build and regulate,	103	69
Power to appoint and remove officers of,	103	69

	SECTION.	PAGE.
Power to imprison in,	103	69
Power to employ inmates of, on public works,	103	72
Expenses of, how paid,	103	70
Same,	409	240
Board of certain prisoners in, how paid,	133	86
General laws as to safe keeping of prisoners, applicable to,	136	87
Police Justice may commit to,	299	170
Name and purposes of,	396	232
How controlled,	397	233
Officers of, how appointed,	398	233
Salaries and expenditures of, to be sanctioned by the Council,	398	134
Books of, how kept and what to show,	400	235
Quarterly statement of, to be made.	400	235
Accounts of, how audited,	400	235
Annual report of, to be made to the Council,	400	235
Officers and employees of, how removed,	401	236
Counties may contract for keeping convicts in,	403	237
Judges, in counties having contracts, to sentence certain criminals to,	404	237
Sheriff to convey certain convicts to,	405	233
Same,	407	239
Inspectors of State Prison may contract for confining certain convicts in,	406	238
When females may be sentenced to,	406	239
Same,	408	240
Same,	416	243
Same,	417	244
Certain persons liable to imprisonment in jails in Detroit to be sent to,	408	[illegible]
Vagrants, etc., convicted in Wayne county, to be sent to,	411	[illegible]
Magistrates may sentence to, for vagrancy,	412	[illegible]
Penalty for attempting to escape from,	413	243
In default of bail for good behavior, persons may be committed to,	418	244
Persons sentenced to, by United States Court,	419	245
Laws applicable to State Prison to apply to,	420	245
HOUSE OF CORRECTION, BOARD OF INSPECTORS OF THE.		
How appointed and terms of office of,	397	233
To adopt rules and appoint officers of,	398	233
Mayor to be member of,	397	233
Meetings of, and duties at such meetings,	399	234
To keep records, and who may inspect them,	399	235
Members of, how removed,	401	236
HOUSE OF CORRECTION, SUPERINTENDENT OF.		
To nominate officers,	398	233
How removed,	401	236
Power of, to remove officers and employees,	401	236
To have control of and reside at,	402	236
To carry out instructions of Inspectors,	402	236
Powers of Deputy,	402	237
To keep record of infractions of rules, etc.,	415	243
To receive certain prisoners sent from other counties,	405	238
To receive females sentenced to,	416	244
To receive females when sentence is commuted to imprisonment in,	417	244
To receive persons committed in default of bail,	418	245
To receive persons sentenced to, by U. S. Courts,	419	245
HOUSES OF ILL FAME.		
Power to suppress and punish keepers of,	103	64
Powers of Metropolitan Police relative to,	351	204

	SECTION.	PAGE.
HUCKSTERS.		
Power to license, regulate or suppress,	103	66
HYDRANTS.		
Water Commissioners may construct,	314	182
Fire Commission to provide,	430	250
Transferred to Fire Commission,	440	254
ICE AND SNOW.		
Power to compel cleaning sidewalks of,	103	56
IMPRISONMENT.		
For violations of Charter or ordinances,	103	72
INDECENT EXPOSURES.		
Of persons, paintings, etc., power to prevent,	103	57
At bathing places, power to prevent,	103	64
INDICTMENT.		
Power to prosecute by,	112	80
Complaints and informations to have preciseness of,	113	80
Found in Wayne Circuit Court to be certified to Recorder's Court,	118	82
Trials upon, to be by jury,	139	88
INFORMATIONS.		
Power to prosecute by,	112	80
Form of,	113	80
When not to be filed unless endorsed by Recorder,	114	81
Different degrees of offenses may be joined in,	113	80
When defendant may be found guilty of less offense than laid in,	115	81
Two or more persons may be joined in,	116	81
INSPECTION.		
Of bread,	103	67
Of wood, lumber, etc.,	103	67
Of coal, hay, vegetables and provisions,	103	67
Of oils, liquors, etc.,	103	68
Articles going out of the State not subject to,	103	68
Of weights and measures by City Sealer,	103	68
INSPECTORS.		
Power to appoint and prescribe duties and fees of,	103	67
INSPECTORS OF ELECTION, BOARD OF.		
How constituted,	5	13
Same,	38	27
One of, with Alderman, to form Board of Registration, in divided wards,	38	27
Oath of members of,	39	28
Vacancy in to be filled by electors,	38	27
Same,	39	28
Who to be members of, in wards not divided,	39	28
Who to be members of, in wards divided,	39	28
Same,	508	298
May appoint clerks,	40	28
Clerks of, to take oath,	40	28
Ballot boxes to be furnished to,	41	28
May administer oath to person challenged,	44	29
May administer oath to person asking registration,	486	282
To certify returns of election,	48	31
One of, to be chosen on Board of City Canvassers,	48	31
To add certain names to registration lists,	474	273
INTEREST,		
On public moneys, Council may contract for,	221	128
On public moneys to be credited to sinking fund,	221	128
When sinking fund to be invested on,	226	130

	SECTION.	PAGE.
On unpaid taxes,	243	140
On redemption of land sold for taxes,	249	140
On bonds issued by Water Commissioners,	310	181
On "Volunteer Bounty Bonds,"	466	266
On bonds of Board of Education,	536	311
INTEREST FUND,		
For what purpose raised,	196	115
Power to raise by tax,	201	119
INSURANCE COMPANIES,		
Power to levy tax on,	105	76
To make sworn statement of premiums received,	105	76
INTERPRETER,		
Board of Registration may employ,	471	271
Same,	500	292
JAILS,		
Power to build, control and appoint officers of,	103	69
Power to imprison in,	103	96
Power to employ inmates of, on public works,	103	72
Board of prisoners in, how paid,	133	86
General laws relative to prisoners, apply to prisoners in,	136	87
Clerk of Recorder's Court to report number sentenced to,	155	94
Police Justice may commit to,	299	169
Metropolitan Police to convey to and from,	372	217
JURORS,		
Assessor to make list of, for Wayne Circuit Court,	560	322
How Assessor to make selection of,	561	322
Number of, to be selected,	562	322
Who not to be selected to serve as,	563	323
List of, for Recorder's Court, prepared by Assessor,	140	88
Same,	70	41
Power of Council to fix fees of,	103	52
Same,	188	110
Challenges of,	138	88
Same,	395	231
Penalty on Assessor for not making list of,	140	89
Qualifications of,	140	89
Names of, to be deposited in "jury box,"	141	89
Old ballots destroyed, before new names of, put in "jury box,"	142	89
When and how many to be drawn by clerk,	143	90
Notice of drawing of, be given by clerk,	143	90
Recorder and Sheriff to be present at drawing of,	144	90
Drawing of, when to be adjourned,	144	90
Proceedings on drawing of,	145	90
Minute of drawing of, made by Recorder and Sheriff,	145	91
Minute of drawing of, filed in clerk's office,	146	91
Venire facias for summoning who to serve,	146	91
Venire facias for summoning, how served and returned,	147	91
Neglecting to attend, may be fined,	148	92
Ballots of, exempt by law to be destroyed,	149	92
Names of, serving to be deposited in separate box,	150	92
Proceedings where sufficient number of, fail to attend,	151	92
When to be summoned forthwith,	152	93
When talesmen to be summoned as,	153	93
Qualifications of, to open, widen streets, etc.,	161	99
Fines and exemptions in such cases,	162	99
Drawing of, to open, extend streets, etc.,	163	99
Challenge of, to open, extend streets, etc.,	163	100
Insufficient number of, to open, extend streets, etc.,	164	100
Drawing and swearing of, to open, extend streets, etc.,	165	100

	SECTION.	PAGE.
To view the property to be taken for public improvement,	166	101
To ascertain necessity of public improvement,	167	101
To award damages and compensation in such cases,	167	101
Disqualification of certain persons to act as,	394	230
Same,	395	231
JURY. See *Jurors, Highways.*		
Persons tried, to have benefits of, as in Circuit Courts,	138	88
Right of trial by,	139	88
Offenses against charter, etc., may be tried without,	139	88
How drawn and sworn,	139	88
Who may claim exemption from sitting on,	148	92
Same,	162	99
Firemen exempt from sitting on,	262	152
Same,	438	254
Policemen exempt from sitting on,	365	215
Damages in opening streets, etc., to be ascertained by,	157	96
Attorney to apply for, in opening streets, etc.,	160	98
To report to Recorder's Court, in opening streets, etc.,	169	102
What report of, to state,	170	102
Same,	171	103
Notice of confirmation of report of, to be given,	172	103
Objections to confirmation of report of, to be filed,	172	104
Report of, not to be annulled for matter of form,	173	104
Report of confirmed, if no objections filed,	174	104
Proceedings if objections to report of, filed,	174	104
New, to be called on annulment of report or failure to agree,	175	104
Vacancy in, how supplied,	176	105
Appeal from confirmation of report of,	177	105
Proceedings on appeal from confirmation of report of,	179	106
Proceedings on reversal of confirmation of report of,	180	106
When errors in judgment of confirmation of report of, may be corrected,	181	107
When confirmation of report of, to be conclusive,	182	107
Copy of report of, when to be entered on "Street Records,"	183	108
Confirmation of report of, how to affect leases,	187	109
When to award damages to estates of deceased persons,	195	112
To consider necessity of drainage of low grounds,	103	59
Proceedings of, under the drainage act,	549	318
Same,	551	319
Council may fix compensation of,	103	52
Compensation of, in street opening cases,	188	110
JURY BOX.		
How and what names to be put in,	141	89
Old ballots in, to be destroyed before new names put in,	142	89
When and how many jurors to be drawn from,	143	90
Names of defaulting jurors to be returned to,	149	92
Proceedings when insufficient number of names remain in,	150	92
JURY TRIALS.		
To be according to general laws,	154	93
JUSTICES OF THE PEACE.		
Election, terms of office and powers of,	6	14
Power to designate one, to act at Station House,	299	170
Power to designate one to act as Police Justice,	300	170
Same,	384	226
Compensation of, in such cases,	300	171
Power to revoke appointment of, in such cases,	300	171
Criminal process issued by, to be served by Metropolitan Police,	350	204
Same,	372	216
May issue warrants returnable before Police Justice,	383	225

	SECTION.	PAGE.
Shall not act in criminal matters, but in certain cases,	385	226
When may sentence to House of Correction,	412	242
Not incompetent to act in matters pertaining to the corporation,	279	158
KITES.		
Power to prevent flying of,	103	56
LAMPS.		
Power to provide for erection of, in streets,	103	56
Power to regulate use of, in barns, etc.,	103	63
LARD.		
Power to regulate rendering of,	103	62
Power to inspect,	103	68
LEASES.		
Of Corporation property, Controller to report,	62	37
Treasurer to have custody of,	65	39
Damages to, by opening streets, etc., how awarded,	167	101
How stated in report of jury opening streets, etc.,	170	103
When to cease on account of opening streets, etc.,	187	109
When Commissioners appointed to apportion rent under,	187	110
Of public wharves, etc., power to make,	103	53
LIBRARY.		
District, power to levy tax for,	521	304
Fines for refusing to act as Inspector of Schools go to use of,	513	301
Board of Education to receive all moneys for,	518	303
LICENSES.		
Power to authorize Mayor to issue,	103	70
General provisions relative to issuing of,	103	71
Proceedings by Mayor to suspend or annul,	77	43
To be countersigned by Clerk and entered in proper books,	81	45
For sale of liquors,	103	66
Of runners of hotels, of draymen, etc.,	103	66
Of auctioneers, peddlers, hawkers, etc.,	103	66
Of circuses, theatrical representations, etc.,	103	66
Of keepers of hotels, grocers, etc.,	103	66
Of butchers, hucksters and sellers of provisions,	103	66
Of keepers of billiard tables and pin alleys,	103	67
Of bath houses,	103	67
Not to be granted for longer than one year.	103	71
Metropolitan Police to collect all moneys due for,	345	197
LIEN.		
Of assessments for opening alleys, etc.,	182	107
Of assessments for paving, grading, etc.,	103	55
Of assessments for abating nuisances,	103	61
Of assessments for cleaning cellars, privies, etc.,	103	62
Of assessments for building lateral sewers, etc.,	102	62
Of assessments for building sidewalks,	105	75
Of general taxes,	103	71
Same,	245	143
Of assessments for water rates,	315	183
Of bonds issued by Board of Education,	537	311
LIMITS. See *Fire Limits, Boundaries.*		
LIQUORS. See *Wines and Liquors.*		
LISTS OF PROPERTY.		
Assessor may demand,	236	135
How demand of, made, and proceedings when not furnished,	236	136
LOANS,		
Unauthorized, not to be made,	208	123
May be made for public building fund,	204	120
Committee to negotiate, how constituted,	222	128

	SECTION.	PAGE.
To be approved by Council,	222	129
The faith and property of Corporation pledged to secure,	229	131
Power of Water Commissioners to make,	310	181
Same,	336	190
Same,	337	191
LOTTERIES,		
Power to suppress, and punish managers of,	103	65
Power Metropolitan Police relative to,	351	204
LUMBER,		
Power to inspect,	103	67
MANURE,		
Lying in streets, power to dispose of,	103	55
MAPS,		
Council may provide for preservation of,	104	73
Same,	105	75
MARKETS,		
Power to establish and regulate,	103	60
Power to lease stalls of,	103	60
Power to license keepers of stands of,	103	66
Clerks of, how appointed,	4	12
Term of office of clerks of,	15	19
MARSHAL,		
How appointed,	4	12
Assistants of, how appointed,	4	12
Term of office of,	15	19
To file official bond,	29	23
General powers and duties of,	66	40
May serve process issued by Recorder's Court,	125	84
To serve notices in proceedings to open streets, etc.,	159	97
To summon jury in proceedings to open streets, etc.,	162	99
Further duties of, in proceedings to open streets, etc.,	164	100
To be *ex officio* fire warden,	258	150
To have power of fire warden,	261	152
Duties of, at fires,	265	153
May be suspended or removed by Mayor,	21	21
Office of, abolished,	373	217
Superintendent of Metropolitan Police to act as,	373	217
MARSHES,		
Proceedings for drainage of,	103	59
Same,	549	318
MAYOR,		
When elected,	3	11
Term of office of	15	19
Salary of,	57	35
General powers and duties of,	56	34
Who to act in absence of,	57	35
To nominate Receiver of taxes, Superintendent of House of Correction, Counsellor,	4	12
To nominate Sewer Commissioners,	5	13
To nominate Commissioners on plan of the City,	189	111
To nominate Assessor,	232	133
To nominate members of Board of review,	237	136
To nominate Fire Marshal,	267	154
To nominate Inspectors of House of Correction,	397	233
To nominate Fire Commissioners,	424	248
Powers relative to appointment of policemen,	103	67
Same,	104	74
Powers relative to removal of policemen,	103	67

	SECTION.	PAGE.
Member of committee for negotiating loans,	222	128
Member of Board of Commissioners of Sinking Fund,	226	130
To preside at meetings of Commissioners of Sinking Fund,	227	131
Ex officio Fire Warden,	358	150
Ex officio Police Commissioner,	289	164
Ex officio School Inspector,	514	302
Ex officio Inspector of House of Correction,	397	233
May suspend or remove certain officers,	21	21
May suspend policemen,	291	165
May grant licenses and examine sureties for,	103	70
Proceedings by, to annul or suspend licenses,	77	43
Ordinances to be presented to, and approved by,	87	48
Neglecting to return ordinances, etc., effect of,	88	48
Veto by, proceedings on,	89	49
When may call special meetings of Council,	86	47
When to call meetings to vote taxes,	200	118
Same,	533	310
May execute deeds in absence of Controller,	251	146
To sign certain bonds,	204	121
Same,	210	124
May administer oaths and take affidavits,	76	43
May inspect books, etc., of Police Commissioners,	361	213
May inspect books, etc., of Fire Commissioners,	446	256
Entitled to copies of census returns,	565	323
Special election of, in case of vacancy,	27	22
MAYOR'S COURT,		
Continued until organization of Recorder's Court,	156	94
Same,	274	157
Records of, transferred to Recorder's Court,	275	157
Power to impose penalty for boring water logs,	328	188
Power in matters concerning Board of Education	519	304
MEAL,		
Power to inspect,	103	68
MEASURER,		
Of articles to be measured, power to appoint,	103	67
MEASURES,		
Power to regulate,	103	68
Power of Board of Metropolitan Police relative to,	345	197
MEAT,		
Unsound, power to prohibit sale of,	103	65
Unsound, power to prohibit depositing of in city,	103	61
Power to license and regulate sellers of,	103	67
Power to inspect,	103	68
MEETINGS.		
Of inhabitants, power to provide for calling,	103	69
Of Board of Canvassers,	48	31
Of Council,	86	47
Of citizens to consider taxes,	200	118
To consider certain school taxes,	532	309
Same.	556	315
To consider expenses of Fire Department,	433	251
Of Fire Department,	451	258
Of Board of Commissioners of Sinking Fund,	227	131
Of Board of Review,	237	136
Of Fire Companies,	250	151
Of inspectors of House of Correction,	399	234
Of Board of Education,	515	302
To consider issuing of bonds for public building fund,	205	121

	SECTION.	PAGE.
MENAGERIES,		
Power to prohibit or license,	103	66
MENDICANTS,		
Power to restrain and punish,	103	64
MILITIA DUTY. See *Exemptions.*		
MISDEMEANOR,		
Bribery of aldermen made,	14	18
Not delivering books, papers, etc., to successor, punished as,	74	42
Embezzlement of public property by officers, punished as,	230	132
Polluting water and injuring water works, made,	327	188
When violence on elector or policeman, punished as,	366	215
When refusing right of way to firemen, made,	436	253
When violation of Registry act punished as,	493	286
Same,	503	294
METROPOLITAN POLICE,		
Established and how composed,	338	193
Power to appoint officers and patrolmen of,	342	195
Power to remove or suspend members of,	342	195
Power to appoint Superintendent of,	342	195
Superintendent to be executive head of,	342	196
Board of Commissioners to have control of,	344	196
Duty of, to preserve peace, etc.,	345	197
To report leaks in water pipes and sewers,	345	198
To remove nuisances in alleys, streets, etc,	345	198
Duty of, at fires,	345	198
Qualifications of members of,	346	199
Board may suspend members of,	346	199
Vacancy in office of captain or sergeants, how filled,	346	199
Salaries of members of,	346	199
Not to receive any presents, gifts, etc.,	346	200
Not to interfere with employment of attorney	346	200
Trial of members of, for misconduct,	347	201
When members of, to receive pay from "Police Life and Health Fund,"	349	202
When superintendent of, may enter buildings, etc.,	350	203
To serve process from Recorder's and Police Courts,	350	203
To serve criminal process issued by justices of the peace,	350	204
Powers of, relative to gambling houses, houses of ill fame, etc.,	351	204
Board to furnish accommodations for,	357	209
City to pay certain expenses of,	358	211
Estimates of expenses of to be submitted by Board,	359	211
Restriction of expenses of,	361	212
Power to levy tax to pay expenses of,	369	216
When senior captain may be Superintendent of,	370	216
METROPOLITAN POLICE, BOARD OF,		
Police powers vested in,	338	193
Appointment of,	339	194
Terms of office of,	340	194
Vacancies in, how filled,	340	194
To take oath of office,	341	195
When to receive certificates of appointment,	341	195
General powers of, relative to appointments and removals,	342	195
May promulgate general orders to police,	342	196
Same,	352	205
May appoint President, Secretary and Property Clerk,	343	196
To have entire control of police and its books, papers, etc.,	344	196
May erect telegraph for police purposes,	344	196
To appoint person to collect all license moneys,	345	197
To appoint person to act as sealer of weights, etc.,	345	197

	SECTION.	PAGE.
To preserve public peace,	345	197
To audit and allow expenses for pursuit of criminals,	345	197
When to authorize pursuit of criminals,	345	198
To define duties and mode of trial of policemen,	346	198
May suspend policemen during trial,	346	199
To receive no compensation,	346	199
May try charges against policemen,	347	201
When may issue subpœnas and have powers of Justices of the Peace,	347	201
Same,	362	213
When may order payments from Life and Health Insurance Fund,	349	202
To divide City into precincts,	352	205
May establish Station-houses,	352	205
May appoint certain special policemen,	353	205
Same,	354	206
Same,	342	195
May appoint policemen for special service,	354	205
Not to re-appoint any person who has been removed,	355	207
To keep complaint book and record of lost property,	356	207
To keep record of its proceedings and of the police force,	356	209
To provide accommodations for the police force,	357	209
To provide accommodations for witnesses detained,	357	210
To submit to Controller estimate of expenses,	359	211
To appoint Treasurer of "Metropolitan police fund,"	359	212
Restriction of expenses of,	361	212
Books and accounts of subject to inspection,	361	213
To cause observance of city ordinances,	362	213
May require security of its appointees,	363	214
To require official oath of policemen,	363	214
Quarterly reports to be made to,	364	215
To make annual report to Council,	364	215
How members of removed,	367	215
Members of to accept no elective office,	368	216
METROPOLITAN POLICE, PROPERTY CLERK OF,		
Power of Board to appoint,	343	196
To give official bond, and compensation of,	343	196
Gifts, presents, etc., to policemen to be handed over to,	346	200
Property seized in gaming houses, etc., to be deposited with,	351	204
Other property seized to be deposited with,	356	207
General duties of, relative to property deposited with,	356	208
METROPOLITAN POLICE, SUPERINTENDENT OF,		
Power to appoint,	342	195
To be executive head of Police force,	342	196
Salary of,	346	199
When may enter buildings, vessels, etc., on suspicion,	350	203
Powers of, relative to gambling houses, lotteries, etc.,	351	204
To cause arrest of persons found in gambling houses,	351	204
Orders and regulations to be promulgated through,	352	205
Same,	342	196
Police force to obey,	352	205
Notice of resignations to be given to,	355	207
No trial or examination of persons arrested to be held in office of,	357	210
May administer oaths in certain cases,	362	214
To make quarterly reports to Board,	364	215
Deputy, when senior Captain may be,	370	216
To perform duties of former City Marshal,	373	217
Certain recognizances to be transmitted to,	374	218
When to destroy burglar's tools,	377	221

	SECTION.	PAGE.
METROPOLITAN POLICE FUND,		
How constituted, and power to appoint treasurer of,	359	212
Treasurer of, to give security for,	359	212
How moneys paid from,	360	212
METROPOLITAN POLICE LIFE AND HEALTH INSURANCE FUND.		
How constituted,	348	202
Who to be trustees of,	348	202
What expenses to be paid from, and how paid,	349	202
Unclaimed property and money seized by police to be paid into,	356	208
METROPOLITAN POLICEMEN,		
Board of Commissioners may appoint and remove,	342	195
Special, power to appoint,	342	195
Same,	353	205
Same,	354	206
Number of, who may receive compensation,	342	195
Compensation of,	346	199
Special, compensation of, in certain cases,	354	206
Trial of, on charge of misconduct,	347	201
To have powers of Constables,	350	203
Not to serve civil process,	350	203
When expense of serving warrant by, to be paid by Wayne county,	350	203
For private service, power to appoint,	354	205
Resignations of,	355	207
Removed, not to be re-appointed,	355	207
May not become bail,	357	211
To take official oath,	363	214
When exempt from jury duty and arrest on civil process,	365	215
Assault on, when a misdemeanor,	366	215
Personating a, a misdemeanor,	366	215
Accepting elective office, deemed a resignation,	368	216
Not to enter saloons while on duty,	371	216
To have exclusive power to serve certain process,	372	216
To attend criminal courts,	272	217
To seize burglars' tools,	377	221
MORTGAGES,		
Treasurer to be charged with amount of,	63	38
Treasurer to have custody of,	65	36
May be executed by Council for purchase money,	103	73
Affected by opening of streets, etc., how damages awarded,	167	101
How stated in report of jury, opening streets, etc.,	170	103
MULES.		
Power to prevent their running at large,	103	58
MURDER.		
Information for, to be endorsed by Recorder,	114	81
NOISES.		
Disorderly, power to prohibit,	103	56
NOTARY PUBLIC.		
Alderman may hold office of,	11	16
NOTES.		
Treasurer to be charged with amount of,	63	38
Treasurer to have custody of,	65	39
NOTICES.		
Of annual and special elections by Clerk,	37	26
Of suspension or annulment of license,	77	44
Of special sessions of Council, how served,	86	48
Of drawing jurors, to be given by Clerk,	144	90
Of adjournment of drawing jurors,	144	90
Of resolution to open streets, etc., to be published,	159	96

	SECTION.	PAGE.
Of such resolution to be served on owners,	159	97
Of confirmation of report of jury in opening streets, etc.,	172	103
Of appeal from confirmation of such report,	177	105
Of meeting of citizens to consider taxes,	200	118
Of letting of contracts to be published,	207	123
Of loan by Water Commissioners,	310	181
Of meetings of Board of registration,	470	269
Same,	473	272
Same,	474	272
Same,	498	288
Same,	502	294
Same,	504	295
Of increase of any assessment by Board of Review to be given,	237	137
Of meetings of Board of Review,	239	138
Of reception of tax rolls by Receiver,	243	140
Of such reception to be demand of taxes,	243	140
By Receiver of unpaid taxes,	243	141
Of delinquent taxes,	245	143
NUISANCES.		
Power of Council relative to,	103	60
In streets, etc., to be removed by Metropolitan Police,	345	198
OATHS. See *Affidavits.*		
Of office, form of,	17	19
Of office, officers to take,	17	19
Of office, officers elected at special elections to take,	18	20
Of office, officers appointed to fill vacancies to take,	18	20
Of office, Inspectors of Election to take,	39	28
Of office, Clerks of Election to take,	40	28
Of office, Police Justice to take,	381	225
Of office, Water Commissioners to take,	320	185
Of office, policemen to take,	292	166
Of office, Commissioners of Metropolitan Police to take,	341	195
Of office, Fire Commissioners to take,	426	248
Of office, members of Board of Registration to take,	496	287
Of office, Commissioners to apportion rent to take,	187	110
Of office, when to be filed with City Clerk,	17	19
Of office, when be taken before City Clerk,	18	20
Of office, Clerk to report persons neglecting to file,	35	25
Of office, when neglect to take and file, vacates office,	33	24
What officers may administer,	76	43
When chairmen of Committees may administer	78	44
Same,	102	52
Clerk of Recorder's Court may administer,	109	79
Clerk of Police Court may administer,	388	227
Inspectors of Election may administer, to person challenged,	44	29
Informations and complaints to be certified by,	113	80
Administered to persons stricken from Registry list,	486	282
Administered to applicants for registration,	500	291
Same,	501	293
To witnesses, when Commissioners of Metropolitan Police may administer,	362	214
When to be administered to sureties on recognizances,	378	223
When to be administered to parties on license bond,	103	71
As to amount of premiums received by insurance companies,	105	76
Of Street Commissioners rendering account to Controller,	71	41
False, by persons challenged at elections, deemed perjury,	45	30
False, before Police Commissioners, when deemed perjury,	362	214
False, before Board of Registration, when deemed perjury,	486	282
Same,	500	293
False, to be deemed perjury,	284	160

	SECTION.	PAGE.
Obstructions,		
In streets, etc., power to remove.	103	55
Offenses,		
When persons may be convicted of less, than charged in complaint,	115	81
Prosecutions for, how commenced,	126	84
Office. *See Officers.*		
Terms of,	15	18
When to commence,	16	19
Not specially named, may be discontinued,	19	20
Expulsion from, proceedings for,	21	20
Removal from, proceedings for,	22	21
Suspension from, proceedings for,	23	22
When may be declared vacant,	24	22
Appointive, Council may fill vacancy in,	26	22
Elective, Council may fill vacancy in,	28	22
Defaulters, not eligible to,	9	16
Clerk to give notice to persons elected or appointed to,	33	24
Neglect of officer to qualify, vacates,	33	24
Plurality to elect to,	51	31
Proceedings in case of tie for same,	52	31
Books and papers of, to be delivered to successor,	74	42
Appointments to and removals from to be by majority of Council,	100	51
Power of Council to fill vacancies in,	103	52
Officers. *See Office, Oaths, Bonds, (Official.)*		
What, elected and when,	3	11
Same,	6	14
What, appointed and when	4	12
Same,	5	13
Terms of office, of,	15	18
Same,	4	12
Same,	6	14
To be residents of Detroit,	7	15
To be able to read and write English language,	10	16
Removal of from city or ward, when to vacate office,	7	15
Not to be interested in contracts,	12	17
Election or appointment of, void if interested in contracts,	12	17
Becoming interested in contracts vacates office,	13	17
Becoming interested in contracts, guilty of malfeasance,	13	17
Contracts with, to be void,	217	126
When to enter on official duties,	18	20
When to file official bonds,	18	20
To hold office until successors have qualified,	15	19
Elected, how Council may remove,	21	20
Appointed, how Council may remove,	22	21
How Council may suspend,	23	22
Certain, may be removed or suspended by Mayor,	21	21
Power of Council as to appointments and removals of,	103	52
Power of Council as to salaries and fees of,	103	52
Power of Council to increase salary of,	103	52
Resignations of, to be made to Council,	25	22
What, to give official bonds,	29	23
Condition of official bonds of,	30	23
May be required to file new bonds,	32	24
Clerk to notify, of their election or appointment,	33	24
Failure to qualify, Clerk to report names of,	35	25
To be elected by a plurality vote,	51	31
Appointments and removals of, to be by majority of Council,	100	51
To deliver books, papers, etc., to their successors,	74	42
To be deemed officers within the general laws of the State,	74	43

	SECTION.	PAGE.
Council may prescribe other duties of,	75	43
Statements and estimates of, may be required,	220	128
Embezzlements of public property by, how punished,	230	131
Of jails, work-houses, etc., power to appoint,	103	69
Not to issue unauthorized bonds or evidences of debt,	208	123
When to continue, on division of wards,	507	297
OILS,		
Power to inspect,	103	68
Power to prevent manufacture of, in certain limits,	103	62
OMNIBUSSES.		
Power to regulate drivers of,	103	57
Power to license drivers of,	103	66
ORDINANCES.		
To be presented to Mayor for approval,	87	48
How approved or disapproved by Mayor,	87	48
Not returned by Mayor to Council, to go into effect,	88	48
Vetoed by Mayor, how may be passed,	89	49
Clerk to make certificate of presentation of, to Mayor,	90	49
To be deposited with and recorded by Clerk,	91	49
When to be published and when to take effect,	92	50
Style of,	93	50
To be passed on yeas and nays,	98	51
Same,	218	127
When not to be passed at session when introduced,	98	51
Same,	218	127
May be passed at session when introduced by unanimous consent,	98	51
Same,	218	127
May be passed at special session called therefor,	98	51
Same,	218	127
Punishments for violation of, to be prescribed in,	103	72
Former, to continue in force until repealed,	278	158
Record of, evidence of due passage and publication,	281	159
Affidavit by printer, etc., evidence of due publication,	282	159
Printed by authority of Council, evidence of legal enactment,	283	159
Power to punish for violations of,	103	72
Limits of fines and imprisonment for violations of,	103	72
Recorder's Court to have exclusive jurisdiction of offenses against	129	85
Council may prescribe punishment for violations of,	137	88
Offenses against, may be tried without jury,	139	88
Clerk to report prosecutions for violations of,	155	94
Certain, arrest of persons without warrant for violations of,	297	169
When Police Justice may have jurisdiction for violations of,	298	169
Metropolitan Police to enforce,	345	197
Police Commissioners to cause enforcement of,	362	213
Persons violating may be admitted to bail,	357	211
Certain, valid without presentation to Mayor,	87	48
ORDINARIES.		
Power to regulate and license,	103	66
OVERSEER OF HIGHWAYS.		
When elected,	3	12
May be removed or suspended by Mayor,	21	21
To work and improve highways, etc.,	72	41
May contract to clean and improve streets, etc.,	217	127
PARTITION FENCES AND WALLS. See *Walls.*		
Power to regulate construction of,	103	63
PAVEMENTS.		
Street Commissioners to superintend construction of,	71	41
Contracts for, not to be let to officers,	217	126
Contracts for, to be let to lowest bidder,	207	122

	SECTION.	PAGE.
Of streets, etc., may be done by contract,	72	42
Of streets, power to provide for,	103	54
Cost of, how assessed.	103	54
PAVING. See *Street Paving Fund, Highways.*		
PAVED STREETS.		
When road tax not to be levied on,	103	57
PAUPERS.		
Powers of Council relative to,	103	68
Power to provide for burial of,	103	68
PAWNBROKERS.		
Power to license and regulate,	103	66
PEDDLERS.		
Power to license and regulate,	103	66
PENALTIES. See *Fines*,		
Power to impose and limitation of,	103	72
For taking false oath at elections,	45	30
For voting more than once,	46	30
For not delivering books to successor in office,	74	43
Imposed, Attorney to collect and pay to treasurer,	131	86
Clerk to give information relative to,	132	86
For illegal registration,	481	278
For illegal voting,	484	281
For mutilating or falsifying register of Electors,	488	283
For making false entry in registry of electors,	486	282
For voting under assumed name,	491	285
For false statement to Board of Registration,	500	293
For attempting to escape from House of Correction,	413	242
For refusing right of way to firemen,	436	253
PERJURY,		
False oath at elections	45	30
False oath, where oath required by Charter,	284	160
False oath, before Police Commissioners,	362	214
False oath, before Board of Registration,	486	282
Same,	500	293
PETITION,		
Right of, guaranteed,	95	50
PHYSICIANS,		
How appointed,	4	12
PICTURES,		
Indecent, power to prevent sale or exhibition of,	103	58
PIN ALLEYS,		
Power to suppress gaming with,	103	65
Power to license and regulate	103	67
PLATS. See *Board of Commissioners on plan of the city. Blocks and Streets*,		
To be approved by Commissioners,	189	111
Making and recording of, when to be dedication,	191	111
Council may provide for preservation of,	104	73
Same,	105	75
Power to provide for preservations of copie of,	105	75
POLLS. See *Elections*,		
POLL LISTS,		
How kept,	47	30
POLICE. See *Metropolitan Police*,		
Power of Council to establish.	103	67
Chief of, how appointed,	292	166
Power and duties of Chief of,	292	166

	SECTION.	PAGE.
When Chief, may let to bail,	297	169
Mayor may remove officers of,	21	21
Council to provide accommodations for,	293	168
POLICE COMMISSIONERS, BOARD OF,		
How constituted and powers of,	289	164
Terms of office of, and vacancies in,	289	165
Power of, to try and remove policemen,	291	165
Power to nominate policemen,	104	74
Same,	292	166
May request Mayor to nominate policemen,	104	74
May appoint watchmen,	294	168
May make rules and regulations,	296	168
POLICEMEN.		
Power to appoint,	103	67
Same,	104	74
Same,	292	166
Power to remove,	103	67
Same,	289	164
Powers of,	103	67
Same,	104	74
Same,	292	166
May serve criminal, but not civil process,	104	74
Oath of,	292	166
Compensation of,	292	167
Mayor and Chief of Police may suspend,	291	165
Notice of charges against to be in writing,	291	165
When may arrest without process,	297	169
Temporary, how appointed,	294	168
Same,	295	168
Aldermen to have powers of,	36	25
POLICE COURT. See *Clerk of Police Court.*		
Established,	381	224
Process from, to be served by Metropolitan Police,	372	216
Metropolitan Police to attend sessions of,	372	217
Adjournment of cases in, who to take bail,	379	223
Appeals from, to Wayne Circuit Court,	389	228
Disqualification of certain persons to act as jurors in,	395	231
POLICE JUSTICE.		
When elected and oath of office of,	381	224
Powers and duties of,	382	225
Same,	299	169
When to have jurisdiction of offenses against city ordinances,	298	169
Powers of, relative to burglars' tools seized by police,	377	221
Power to bind for appearance at Recòrder's Court,	378	222
When may commit in default of bail,	378	222
When to have exclusive power to take bail,	379	223
When warrants issued by Justices of the Peace to be returnable before,	383	225
Where to reside and keep an office,	384	225
To attend all criminal complaints,	384	225
May sentence for vagrancy to House of Correction,	412	242
Vacancy in office of, how filled,	384	226
When Justices of the Peace may act as,	385	226
Same,	386	226
May demand security for costs,	387	226
Power to appoint Justice of the Peace to act as,	300	170
Power to revoke such appointment,	300	171
Power to appoint Justice of the Peace to act as, at station house,	299	170
How removed,	300	171
Salary of,	390	228

	SECTION.	PAGE.
POLICE STATION.		
Power to provide,	293	168
Police Justice to attend and examine persons confined in,	299	169
Power to appoint Justice of the Peace to act at,	299	170
Board of Metropolitan Police to provide,	352	205
POOR FUND.		
For what purpose raised,	196	115
Power to raise by tax,	197	116
Estimates for, to be submitted,	200	117
PORK.		
Power to inspect,	103	68
PORTERS.		
Power to regulate,	103	56
Power to license,	103	66
POSTS.		
Power to inspect,	103	67
POULTRY.		
Unsound, power to prevent sale of,	103	65
Power to license sale of,	103	67
Power to inspect,	103	68
POUNDS.		
Power to provide,	103	58
POWDER,		
Power to regulate storage of,	103	62
Power to regulate conveyance of,	103	63
PRESIDENT OF BOARD OF FIRE COMMISSIONERS,		
Power to elect,	427	249
Warrants on Fire Commission fund to be signed by,	434	252
PRESIDENT OF BOARD OF EDUCATION,		
Power to elect,	529	308
PRESIDENT OF BOARD OF POLICE COMMISSIONERS,		
Power to appoint,	343	196
To be Trustee of Police, Life and Health Insurance Fund,	358	202
To teste subpœnas issued by Board,	362	213
PRESIDENT OF BOARD OF WATER COMMISSIONERS,		
Power to choose,	309	181
PRESIDENT OF COUNCIL,		
When to be elected,	58	35
Same,	84	47
Term of office of,	84	47
When to be acting Mayor,	57	35
Pro tempore, when to be acting Mayor,	57	35
Pro tempore, when to be elected,	58	35
Pro tempore, when to preside, and powers of,	59	35
Power of, to send for absent aldermen,	82	46
Duties of,	84	47
To sign record of proceedings of Council	91	49
To appoint committees,	101	51
PRINTING.		
Power to provide for,	103	73
Proposals for contracts,	207	123
Of proceedings of Council,	92	49
Of Controller's report,	219	128
Of report of Water Commissioners,	318	184
Of report of Board of Education.	520	304
Of Report of House of Correction,	400	236
Of report of Clerk of Recorder's Court,	155	94

	SECTION.	PAGE.
PRISONERS.		
Who liable for board and expenses of,	133	86
General laws for safe keeping applicable to,	136	87
May be confined in county jail,	135	87
To be conveyed by police to place of confinement,	372	217
PRIVATE PROPERTY.		
May be taken for public use,	157	95
PRIVIES.		
Power to compel cleansing or abatement of,	103	61
Power to regulate the construction of,	103	61
Power to levy assessment for cleaning,	103	61
PROCESS.		
From Recorder's Court, served by Marshal,	66	40
When Mayor may issue,	77	43
What may, and may not be served by police,	104	74
Clerk of Recorder's Court to sign and seal,	109	79
From Recorder's Court, when directed to Marshal,	125	84
From Recorder's Court, how signed, sealed and tested,	125	84
When persons may be arrested without,	297	169
Certain, may be served by police in any part of the State,	350	203
From Recorder's and Police Courts, to be served by police,	350	203
Same,	372	216
Criminal, from Justices of the Peace, to be served by police,	350	204
Same,	372	217
Issued by Justices of the Peace, when returnable before Police Justice,	383	225
Issued by Police Justice, effect of,	386	226
When Police Justice unable to act on,	386	226
Before issuing, Police Justice may require security for costs,	387	226
When City to pay expense of service of,	358	211
Civil, when policemen exempt from arrest on,	365	215
Civil, when electors exempt from arrest on,	54	32
PROPOSALS,		
For contracts to be advertised for,	207	122
PROSECUTIONS,		
How commenced,	126	84
Clerk of Recorder's Court to report number of,	155	94
PROSECUTING ATTORNEY,		
When to act in Recorder's Court,	120	83
To render account of moneys collected,	120	83
When to sign informations and complaints,	113	80
Duty of, relative to violations of Registry act,	493	286
PROVISIONS,		
Unsound, power to prohibit sale of,	103	65
Power to license and regulate sellers of,	103	67
Power to inspect,	103	68
PROSTITUTES,		
Power to punish,	103	64
May be sent to House of Correction,	411	241
PUBLIC BUILDINGS,		
Power to erect,	103	69
PUBLIC BUILDING FUND,		
For what purpose raised,	196	116
Power to raise by loan and issue bonds for,	204	120
Surplus of, not to be transferred to sinking fund,	224	129
May be divided into special building funds,	196	116
Bonds for, not to be issued without consent of public meeting,	205	121
PUBLIC BUILDING STOCK OF THE CITY OF DETROIT,		
Certain bonds to be known as,	204	121

	SECTION.	PAGE.
PUBLIC EXHIBITIONS,		
Power to prevent or license,	103	66
PUBLIC HOUSES,		
Power to license runners of,	103	66
Power to regulate runners and agents of,	103	56
Power to license keepers of,	103	66
PUBLIC PARKS,		
Power to grade, improve and regulate,	103	54
Power to open, extend, vacate, etc.,	103	54
Power to survey and ascertain boundaries of,	103	59
Platting and recording of plat of, to be dedication,	191	111
Water Commissioners may construct fountains in,	314	183
PUBLIC PLACES. See *Highways*, *Public Parks.*		
Street Commissioners to superintend working, etc., of,	71	41
When Overseers of Highways to work, improve, etc.,	72	41
May be cleaned, etc., by contract,	72	42
Power to work and improve,	103	54
Power to grade and regulate,	103	54
Power to open, extend, etc.,	103	54
Same,	157	95
How expenses of improving, etc., may be paid,	103	55
Power to prescribe use of,	103	56
Dedication of, how made,	191	111
PUBLIC WORKS,		
Power to employ prisoners on,	103	72
Contracts for, to be let to lowest bidder,	207	123
Tax for, to be first levied,	206	122
To be paid for, only from such tax,	206	122
PUNISHMENTS, See *Fines and Penalties,*		
Of Officers interested in contracts,	13	18
For bribery of Aldermen,	14	18
For perjury at elections	45	30
For voting more than once,	46	30
Power to impose,	103	72
For embezzlement of public property by officers,	230	132
For polluting water and injuring water works,	327	188
For boring water pipes,	328	188
For making false statement to Board of Registration,	471	271
For fraudulent registration,	472	271
For falsifying or destroying "Registry of Electors,"	488	283
QUALIFICATIONS.		
Of officers,	7	15
Same,	10	16
Of Attorney,	8	16
Of Water Commissioners,	308	180
Of jurors,	140	89
Same,	161	99
Of electors,	43	29
Of Metropolitan policemen,	346	199
Of sureties on certain recognizances,	378	223
QUORUM,		
Of Council,	82	46
Of Board of Education,	515	302
Same,	530	308
Of Commissioners of Sinking Fund,	227	131
Of Trustees of Fire Department,	450	258
Of Fire Commissioners,	433	248
Of Metropolitan Police Commissioners,	338	194

	SECTION.	PAGE.
RAPE.		
Information for, to be endorsed by Recorder,	114	81
ROAD FUNDS. See *General Road Fund, District Road Fund,*		
RACING,		
In streets, power to prevent,	103	56
RAILROADS.		
Power to regulate speed of cars on,	103	70
Power to preserve quiet at depots of,	103	56
Powers of Metropolitan Police at depots of,	345	198
REAL ESTATE.		
Power of Council to purchase,	103	73
Power to perpetuate evidence of titles of,	104	73
Same,	105	75
Power of Water Commissioners to purchase,	313	182
Power of Board of Education to hold,	531	309
Same,	514	302
Power of Fire Department to hold,	448	257
Certain, transferred to Fire Commissioner,	437	253
RECEIPTS.		
Controller to take, on delivery of tax rolls to Receiver,	243	140
Receiver to give, on payment of taxes,	243	140
RECEIVER OF TAXES.		
How appointed,	4	12
Term of office of,	15	19
Bond of,	29	23
How removed,	22	21
Controller to deliver tax rolls to,	243	139
To give notice of reception of tax rolls,	243	140
To give receipts on payment of taxes,	243	140
To make roll of unpaid taxes,	243	141
To give notice of unpaid taxes,	243	141
Collectors to pay taxes collected to,	244	143
To pay taxes received, to Treasurer,	244	143
Assessment rolls for sewers, paving, etc., to be placed in hands of,	254	148
RECORDS. See *Street Records.*		
Of ordinances, proceedings of Council, etc.,	91	49
Of Council, open to inspection,	94	50
Council may provide for preservation of,	104	73
Same,	105	75
Of Recorder's Court open to inspection,	132	86
Of Metropolitan Police,	356	209
Of stolen property,	356	207
Of House of Correction open to inspection,	399	235
Of conveyances by Governor and Judges,	570	325
Same,	571	325
Same,	573	327
Of conveyances by Mayor, Aldermen, etc.,	572	326
RECORDER.		
When elected,	3	11
Term of office of,	15	19
Salary of,	134	87
Power to nominate Clerk of Recorder's Court,	4	12
Aldermen ineligible to office of,	11	16
Subject to impeachment,	20	20
Powers and duties of,	64	38
May administer oaths and take affidavits,	76	43
To be Judge of Recorder's Court,	108	78
When Judge of Circuit Court may sit in place of,	108	78
May grant writ of *habeas corpus*,	121	83

	SECTION.	PAGE.
Powers of at chambers,	122	83
Process from Recorder's Court to be tested in name of,	125	84
Proceedings when unable to attend court,	128	85
To be present when names of jurors put in jury box,	142	90
To be present at drawing of jurors,	144	90
To direct number of jurors to be drawn,	143	90
When authorized to take bail,	374	218
Same,	378	222
To be *ex-officio* member of the Board of Education,	514	302
Entitled to seat at meetings of Board of Education,	517	303
To have powers as Circuit Court Commissioner,	563	324
When entitled to same fees as Circuit Court Commissioner,	569	324
RECORDER'S COURT. *See Clerk of Recorder's Court.*		
A Court of Record,	107	78
Jurisdiction of,	111	79
Marshal to attend sessions of, and serve certain process from,	66	40
Sheriff to attend sessions of, and serve certain process from,	110	79
When process from, to be directed to Marshal,	125	84
When process from, to be directed to Sheriff,	125	84
Process from, how signed, sealed, tested, etc.,	125	84
Not to affect jurisdiction of Wayne Circuit Court,	111	80
When Circuit Judge may sit in,	108	78
Prosecutions in, to be by information, etc.,	112	80
May enforce recognizances,	117	81
May establish rules,	123	83
May have seal,	124	84
Terms of,	128	85
Certain indictments found by Grand Jury, to be tried in,	119	82
When Prosecuting Attorney to act in,	120	83
Proceedings in, when Recorder unable to attend,	128	85
To have exclusive jurisdiction of offenses against ordinances,	129	85
Writ of error from, to Supreme Court,	130	85
Records of, may be inspected,	132	86
May fine jurors neglecting to attend,	148	92
When talesmen to be summoned on jury in,	153	93
Jury trials in, to be governed by general laws,	154	93
To take place of Mayor's Court,	156	74
To instruct jury in opening streets, etc.,	165	100
Appeal from, in street opening cases,	177	105
Process from to be served by Metropolitan Police,	350	203
Same,	372	216
Metropolitan Police to attend on,	372	217
Proceedings in, on forfeiture of recognizances,	374	218
When Police Justice may take bail for appearance at,	378	222
May issue capiases for witnesses,	392	229
Judgment of, not invalidated by excess of sentence,	393	230
To have cognizance of violations of registry act,	492	286
Jurisdiction of, in matters pertaining to Board of Education,	519	304
Records, etc., of Mayor's Court, to be transferred to,	275	157
Actions cognizable in Mayor's Court to be transferred to,	275	157
Inhabitants of the city not incompetent to act in,	279	158
RECORDER'S COURT FUND.		
For what purpose raised,	196	116
Power to raise by tax,	197	117
Estimates for, to be submitted,	200	117
RECOGNIZANCES.		
Power of Recorder's Court to enforce,	117	81
Proceedings on, when forfeited,	117	82
Form of,	118	82
Proceedings on forfeiture under Metropolitan Police act,	374	218
When Court may render judgment against sureties on,	374	219
Qualification and oath of sureties on,	378	223

	SECTION.	PAGE.
REDEMPTION.		
Of lands sold for taxes,	246	144
How made,	247	145
Of lands sold for taxes, interest on,	249	146
REGISTER OF ELECTORS.		
What to contain,	471	270
When to be delivered to Inspectors,	476	273
When City Clerk to make copy of,	487	283
Punishment for mutilating or falsifying, etc.,	488	283
Form of,	497	287
Names to be entered in, by members of Board of Registration,	499	289
Names of persons ceasing to be electors, to be noted in,	499	289
REGISTRATION.		
Of births and deaths, power to provide for,	103	69
Under the Registry act, how made,	471	270
Persons applying for, may be questioned,	471	271
What persons not entitled to,	472	271
Fraudulent, penalty for,	472	271
Lists, when and what names Inspectors to add to,	474	273
Challenge of vote for want of,	483	280
Penalty for voting without,	484	281
Actual residence necessary to,	485	281
Proceedings where name is stricken from, by mistake,	486	282
Former, made invalid,	498	289
Review of,	499	289
Applicants for, what to state,	499	290
Proceedings for, of persons unable to register at proper time,	500	291
Proceedings when persons apply to vote without,	501	293
Review of, prior to special elections,	502	293
REGISTRATION, BOARD OF,		
How composed,	38	27
Same,	469	268
Same,	498	288
Same,	500	290
Books of, how arranged,	469	268
To give notice of meetings,	470	269
Same,	474	272
Same,	498	288
Vacancies in, how filled,	470	269
Same,	502	294
Length of sessions of,	470	269
Same,	498	288
May question applicants for registration,	471	271
Same,	499	290
When may employ interpreter,	471	271
Same,	500	292
When may administer oath,	500	292
Same,	500	291
Same,	501	293
Same,	486	282
When to meet,	473	272
Same,	498	288
Same,	504	295
To deposit registration lists with City Clerk,	475	273
To review and correct lists,	486	281
Same,	499	289
Former powers and duties of, continued,	498	288
Names of electors to be entered by,	499	289
To note names of persons ceasing to be electors,	499	289
When may appoint Boards of Registration in election districts,	498	288

	SECTION.	PAGE.
Meetings of, to compare and correct lists,	500	290
Proceedings by, where elector is registered in two or more wards,	500	291
May register on application,	500	291
Compensation of,	495	287
Members of, to take official oath,	496	287
How constituted, when ward is divided,	508	298
Sessions, powers and duties of, when ward is divided,	508	298
REGISTRY LAW.		
Recorder's Court to have jurisdiction of violations of,	492	286
Duty of Prosecuting Attorney relative to,	493	286
Violations of made a misdemeanor,	493	286
Same,	503	294
REGRATING.		
Power to prohibit,	103	60
REPORTS. *See Jurors, Jury.*		
Annual, of Clerk of Recorder's Court,	155	94
Of Commissioners to apportion rent,	187	110
Annual, of Controller,	219	127
Of Commissioners of sinking Fund,	226	130
Annual, of Water Commissioners,	318	184
Relative to value of land taken by Water Commissioners,	324	187
On confirmation of such, payment to be made,	325	187
Of Water Commissioners relative to interest on their bonds,	330	188
Quarterly, of Superintendent of Metropolitan Police,	364	215
Annual, of Board of Metropolitan Police,	364	215
Quarterly, of House of Correction,	400	235
Of House of Correction, Council may require,	401	236
Annual, of Fire Commission,	444	255
Annual, of Board of Education,	520	304
RESIDENCE.		
How determined,	38	27
Necessary to registration,	472	271
Same,	485	281
Same,	500	291
RESIGNATIONS.		
Of officers, to be made to the Council,	25	22
Offices may be declared vacant on,	24	22
Of members of Metropolitan police force,	355	207
Same,	368	216
RESOLUTIONS.		
To be presented to and approved by Mayor,	87	48
Certain, valid without Mayor's approval,	87	48
How approved by Mayor, and when to go into effect,	87	48
How vetoed by Mayor,	87	48
Effect of neglect to approve or return to Council,	88	48
When to go into effect,	88	49
Same,	92	50
Passage of, over Mayor's veto,	89	49
Certificate of presentation of, to be recorded,	90	49
To be deposited with City Clerk,	91	49
Certain not to be passed at session when introduced,	98	51
Same,	218	127
To be passed on yeas and nays,	98	51
Same,	218	127
To make public improvements, what to contain,	158	96
To be drawn by Attorney,	158	96
To make public improvement, to be published,	159	97
To make public improvement, how served,	159	97
Certified copy of, to be delivered to Attorney,	160	98
Former, to remain in force until repealed,	278	158

	SECTION.	PAGE.
Rewards,		
When Council may offer, for detection of criminals,	301	171
Right of Way,		
Firemen going to fires, to have,	436	253
Riots,		
Power of Council to prevent,	103	56
Power of Metropolitan Police to quell,	362	213
Road Funds. See *General Road Fund. District Road Fund.*		
Rules, Regulations, and By-Laws,		
Power of Council to make,	96	50
Power of Recorder's Court to make,	123	83
Power of Water Commissioners to make,	316	183
Power of Police Commissioners to make,	296	168
Certain, power of Board of Metropolitan Police to make,	346	199
Power of Inspectors of House of Correction to make,	398	233
Power of Board of Education to make,	513	302
Power of Fire Commissioners to make,	443	255
Power of Fire Department to make,	449	257
Runners,		
Power to regulate,	103	56
Power to license and regulate compensation of,	103	66
Salary. See *Compensation,*		
Of Mayor,	57	35
Of Officers, power of Council as to,	103	52
Of Recorder and Clerk of Recorder's Court,	132	87
Of Members of Metropolitan Police,	346	199
Of Clerk of Police Court,	388	227
Of Police Justice,	390	228
Of Officers of House of Correction, to be approved by Council,	398	234
Of Firemen,	435	253
Sale,		
For taxes, power to make.	103	71
Same,	246	144
For taxes, notice of,	245	143
For taxes, when deed to be given,	246	144
For taxes, what officers to execute deeds,	251	146
For taxes, when Controller to bid in,	252	146
For taxes, purchaser neglecting to pay bids,	252	147
For local assessments, how conducted,	254	148
For non-payment of water rates,	316	183
Salt,		
Power to inspect,	103	68
Saloons,		
Power to license and regulate,	103	66
Schools. See *Board of Education,*		
Acts relating to, continued,	287	161
To be free to all children,	510	301
To be under direction of Board of Education,	510	301
Funds to be expended for support of,	514	302
Power to appoint Superintendent of	522	305
High, power to establish,	522	305
Power to raise tax for support of,	522	305
Taxes for, to be set forth in separate column,	527	307
Taxes for, to be paid in money,	527	307
School District,		
City to be considered as one,	510	300

	SECTION.	PAGE.
SCHOOL HOUSES,		
Board of Education to provide,	518	303
Power to levy tax for building,	531	309
Same,	542	313
Meeting to consider tax for building,	532	309
Proceedings to call meeting to consider tax for building,	533	310
Same,	534	310
Tax for building, how collected,	535	310
Power to borrow money to erect,	536	311
SCHOOL INSPECTORS. See *Board of Education*,		
When elected,	3	12
Term of office of,	15	19
Same	511	301
Vacancy in office of, how filled.	512	301
Not to vacate office by removal from ward,	541	312
Same,	7	15
Persons elected to office of, fined for refusing to serve,	513	301
To have no compensation,	511	301
To constitute Board of Education,	514	302
SCHOOL TAXES. See *School Houses*,		
Authority to levy,	522	305
Same,	545	314
Duty of Collectors relative to,	524	305
Same,	528	308
Collector refusing to pay over, proceedings on,	524	306
Collector and Treasurer to give bonds for,	525	306
Same,	528	308
To be placed in separate column,	527	307
To be paid in money,	527	307
Board of Education to present estimate of,	544	314
When meeting to be called to consider,	545	315
SCUTTLES,		
Power to compel providing of, on roofs,	103	64
SEAL,		
Of the Corporation,	1	9
Of the Corporation, City Clerk to keep,	61	36
Of Recorder's Court,	124	84
Of Board of Water Commissioners,	307	180
Of Fire Commissioners,	439	254
Of Fire Department,	448	257
SEALER OF WEIGHTS AND MEASURES,		
How appointed,	4	12
Powers of,	103	68
Appointment of, by Board of Metropolitan Police,	345	197
SENTENCES,		
Clerk of Recorder's Court to report number of,	155	94
SENATORIAL DISTRICTS.		
Of what to consist,	558	321
Same,	559	321
SEWERS. *See Drains.*		
Power to build,	103	58
Commissioners of, to have control of,	5	13
Not to be built, unless recommended by Commissioners,	5	14
Private, power to compel and regulate construction of,	103	58
Private, levy of assessment on cellars drained by,	103	59
Power to cleanse or abate,	103	61
Lateral, Surveyor to make assessments for,	68	41
Lateral, power to construct, etc.,	103	58
Lateral, power to regulate construction of,	103	62

	SECTION.	PAGE.
Lateral, power to assess expenses of,	103	62
Power to levy tax for construction of,	199	117
Contracts for, to be let to lowest bidder,	207	122
Metropolitan Police to report defects in,	345	198
Fund for repairs of,	202	119
SEWER FUND.		
For what purpose raised,	196	115
May be raised by tax,	199	117
Estimates for to be submitted,	200	117
Taxes on lots, etc., drained by private sewers to be credited to,	202	119
SHEEP.		
Power to prevent running at large,	103	58
SHERIFF OF WAYNE COUNTY.		
To attend sessions of, and serve process from Recorder's Court,	110	79
Certain process to be directed to,	125	84
To be present at drawing of jurors,	144	90
To serve *venire facias* for jurors,	146	91
Service and return of *venire facias* by,	147	91
When to summon jurors forthwith,	152	93
When to summon talesmen,	153	93
SHINGLES.		
Power to inspect,	103	67
SHOWS.		
Power to license and regulate,	103	66
SIDEWALKS.		
Surveyor to make assessments for,	68	41
Street Commissioners to superintend construction of,	71	41
How expenses of, to be paid,	103	55
Power to clean and prevent encumbering of,	103	55
Power to permit paving or planking of,	103	57
Power to prevent driving on,	103	58
Defective, liability for injuries occasioned by,	105	75
SIGNS.		
Power to prevent encumbering streets with,	103	55
Power to prevent exhibition of, on vehicles,	103	56
Power to regulate suspension of,	103	56
SINKING FUND.		
For what purpose raised,	196	115
Surplus of certain funds to be transferred to,	224	129
Interest on funds to be credited to,	221	128
Power to levy tax for purposes of,	201	119
Board of Commissioners of, their duties,	226	130
Commissioners of, subject to ordinances relative to,	227	131
Meetings of Commissioners of,	227	131
Commissioners of, may appoint Secretary,	227	131
Treasurer to have custody of,	228	131
How moneys paid from,	228	131
SLAUGHTER HOUSES.		
Power to cleanse or abate,	103	61
Power to prohibit within certain limits,	103	62
SLIPS.		
Power to regulate construction of,	103	61
Power to assess expense of cleaning,	103	61
SNOW AND ICE.		
Power to compel removal of,	103	66
SOAP FACTORIES.		
Power to cleanse or abate,	103	61
Power to prohibit,	103	62

	SECTION.	PAGE.
SPECIAL ELECTIONS.		
Officers elected at, when to enter upon their duties,	18	20
Of Mayor and Aldermen, when may be held,	27	22
Notice of,	37	26
How conducted,	49	31
When and by whom result of, declared,	49	31
Review of Registration prior to,	502	293
SPECIAL BUILDING FUNDS. See *Public Building Fund.*		
SQUARES. See *Public Places.*		
STABLES.		
Power to cleanse or abate,	103	61
Power to regulate use of lights in,	103	63
STARCH FACTORIES.		
Power to cleanse or abate,	103	61
Power to forbid within certain limits,	103	62
STATE PRISON.		
Metropolitan Police to convey prisoners to,	372	217
Inspectors of, may contract for keeping prisoners in House of Correction,	406	238
Transfer of females from, to House of Correction,	414	242
Commutation of sentence from, to House of Correction,	417	244
STEAMBOATS.		
Power to regulate runners at landings of,	103	56
Duty of Metropolitan Police at landings of,	345	198
STONE.		
Power to inspect,	103	67
STOVES.		
Power to regulate putting up of,	103	64
STREETS. See *Highways, Public Places, Jurors, Jury.*		
Overseers of Highways may contract to clean,	217	127
Power to lay water pipes in,	314	183
Metropolitan Police to remove nuisances,	345	198
STREET COMMISSIONERS.		
How appointed,	4	12
May be removed by Mayor,	21	21
Bond of,	29	23
General duties of,	71	41
When to notify owners to repair sidewalks,	105	75
Punishment of, for neglect to give such notice,	105	75
STREET OPENING FUND.		
For what purpose raised,	196	115
Estimates for, to be submitted,	200	117
STREET PAVING FUND. See *Paving.*		
For what purpose raised,	196	116
Power to raise tax for purposes of,	203	119
STREET RECORDS.		
Report of jury as confirmed, to be entered in,	183	108
What to be evidence of,	183	108
SUBPŒNAS.		
When Council may issue,	21	21
On complaints for violation of license, Mayor may issue,	77	43
May be issued by Committees,	102	52
Issued by Fire Marshal,	267	154
When Police Commissioners may issue,	347	201
Same,	362	213
Certain, to be served by Metropolitan Police,	350	203

	SECTION.	PAGE.
SUPERINTENDENT. See *House of Correction*, *Metropolitan Police*.		
Of Alms House, how appointed,	4	12
Of House of Correction, how appointed,	4	12
Of Water Works, power to employ,	312	182
Of schools, power to appoint,	522	305
Of Metropolitan Police, power to appoint,	341	195
SUPERVISORS OF WAYNE COUNTY.		
Assessor and Aldermen to have powers of,	234	134
Corporation, how represented in Board of,	234	135
SUPREME COURT.		
Power to remove proceedings to, by writ of error,	130	85
Proceedings on appeal to, in street opening cases,	177	105
Return of Clerk of Recorder's Court on appeal to,	178	106
Proceedings in, on appeal to,	179	106
SURETIES.		
On official bonds, contracts, etc., required to justify in writing,	34	25
Sufficiency of, on license bonds, to be inquired into,	103	71
On recognizances, when judgment may be entered against,	117	82
On recognizances, proceedings against,	374	218
To be furnished on contracts,	207	123
SURVEYOR,		
When elected,	3	11
Term of office of,	15	19
General powers and duties of,	68	40
Water Commissoners may employ,	312	182
SWAMPS,		
Power to provide for drainage of,	103	59
Proceedings to drain, under act of 1849,	549	318
TALESMEN,		
Power to summon in Recorder's Court,	153	93
Power to summon in street opening cases,	164	100
TALLOW,		
Power to prevent rendering of, in certain limits,	103	62
TALLOW CHANDLER'S SHOPS,		
Power to cleanse or abate,	103	61
TANNERIES,		
Power to cleanse or abate	103	61
Power to prohibit within certain limits,	103	62
TAVERNS. See *Hotels*.		
TAXES. See *School Houses. School Taxes. Sale*,		
Treasurer to be charged with.	63	38
What, to be collected by ward collector,	73	42
Power to assess, levy and collect,	103	71
Made a lien,	103	71
Same,	245	143
Power to sell for unpaid,	103	71
Illegal, when paid, power to refund,	105	76
Illegal, power to vacate,	105	76
On Insurance Companies, power to levy.	105	76
On Insurance Companies, to what fund to be credited,	105	76
For paving, etc., when to be assessed anew,	106	77
For various funds, power to levy and collect,	197	116
For District Road Fund, power to levy,	198	117
For constructing sewers, power to levy,	199	117
For Interest Fund, power to levy,	201	119
On lots, etc., drained in public sewers, power to levy,	202	119
For paving, grading, etc., power to levy,	203	120
Estimates of amount of, to be submitted,	200	117

	SECTION.	PAGE.
For public works, to be levied before work commenced,	206	122
For Sinking Fund, power to levy,	201	119
Ordinances imposing, when and how to be passed,	218	127
Same,	98	51
Ordinances imposing, to be presented to Mayor,	87	48
To be credited to the fund for which raised,	223	129
When credited to the general fund,	223	129
To be applied to the purposes for which raised,	224	129
To be based on assessment rolls,	242	139
How to be extended on assessment rolls,	243	129
Due when tax rolls delivered to Receiver,	243	140
Notice by Receiver, a sufficient demand of,	243	140
On payment of, receipt to be given,	243	140
Unpaid, percentage added to,	243	140
Unpaid, notice by Receiver of,	243	141
Unpaid, when warrant may issue for collection of,	243	141
Unpaid, warrants for, when may be extended,	243	142
Unpaid, notice sale of real estate for,	245	143
Unpaid, power to sell real estate for,	246	144
Unpaid, redemption of land sold for,	246	144
Same,	247	145
Unpaid, Controller to execute deed of land sold for,	246	144
Same,	251	146
Power to charge interest on redemption of land sold for,	249	146
For expenses of Metropolitan Police,	259	211
Same,	369	216
For expenses of House of Correction, power to levy,	409	240
For support of Fire Department, power to levy,	433	251
Same,	445	255
To pay Volunteer Bounty Bonds,	465	265
For District Library,	521	304
Water, power to levy,	330	189
TAXES, STATE AND COUNTY. See *Tax Rolls*,		
How to be assessed by Assessor,	243	142
Same,	459	261
Ward collectors to collect,	73	42
Duties of ward collectors relative to,	461	263
Assessor to make out warrant for collection of,	459	261
When may be paid to County Treasurer,	460	262
Collectors to give bonds for collection of,	461	263
When Council may appoint person to collect,	461	264
TAX ROLLS,		
Controller to examine,	62	37
Ward, what to be known as,	243	139
Ward, to be delivered by Controller to Receiver,	243	139
Notice of reception of, by Receiver, a demand of taxes,	243	140
State and County, what to be known as,	459	261
State and County, Assessor to annex warrant to,	459	261
State and County, notice by County Treasurer of,	460	262
State and County, when to be delivered to collectors,	462	264
State and County, County Treasurer to preserve,	463	264
TELEGRAPH.		
Where Police Commissioners may erect,	344	196
THEATRICALS.		
Power to license and regulate,	103	66
TIMBER.		
Power to inspect,	103	67
TIE VOTE.		
At elections, proceedings in case of,	52	31
In Council, effect of,	99	51

	SECTION.	PAGE.
TREASON.		
Information, etc., for, to be endorsed by Recorder, ...	114	81
TREASURER.		
When elected, ...	3	11
Term of office of, ...	15	19
Bond of, ...	29	23
Controller to keep account with, ...	63	38
To be charged with taxes and moneys receivable, . . .	63	38
General duties of, ...	65	39
Fines and penalties collected, to be paid to, ...	131	86
Assessments for benefits, when collected to be paid to, . .	184	108
Damages by opening streets, etc., when deposited with, . .	185	109
Orders on, for expenses of city, ...	208	123
To destroy evidences of debt, when refunded, ...	211	124
To keep list of cancelled evidences of debt, ...	211	124
To credit surplus of funds to Sinking Fund, ...	224	129
Member of Board of Commissioners of Sinking Fund, . . .	226	130
To have custody of moneys, etc., belonging to Sinking Fund,	228	131
May be Treasurer of Fire Commission, ...	433	251
To be Treasurer of Board of Education, ...	523	305
School taxes, when collected, to be paid to, ...	524	305
To give bond for security of school moneys, ...	525	306
Damages awarded for land taken by Water Commissioners, when deposited with, ...	326	187
Water tax, when raised, to be paid to, ...	330	189
Receiver to pay taxes collected to, ...	244	143
TREASURER, COUNTY. *See Taxes (State and County), Tax Rolls.*		
TREES.		
In streets, power to provide for preservation of, ...	103	56
TURPENTINE.		
Power to prohibit manufacture of in certain limits, ...	103	62
UNSAFE ERECTIONS. *See Buildings, Fences.*		
VACANCIES. *See Officers.*		
Made by officers ceasing to be residents, ...	7	15
Made by officers becoming interested in contracts, ...	12	17
Made by Aldermen accepting bribes, ...	14	18
Made by officers becoming defaulters, ...	9	16
Officers appointed or elected to fill, when to enter on duty, .	18	20
When may be declared, ...	19	20
Same, ...	24	22
In appointive offices, ...	26	22
In elective offices, ...	28	22
Certain, in office of Mayor or Alderman, ...	27	22
In Board of Inspectors of Election, ...	38	27
Ballots to fill, to state the same, ...	50	31
Power of Council to provide for filling, ...	103	52
Same, ...	103	69
In office of Recorder, who to act, ...	108	78
In Board of Commissioners on plan of city, ...	192	112
In Board of Water Commissioners, ...	308	180
Same, ...	322	186
In office of City Attorney, ...	127	85
In Board of Metropolitan Police, ...	340	194
In office of Captain and Sergeants of Metropolitan Police, . .	346	199
In office of Police Justice, ...	384	226
In Board of Registration, ...	470	269
Same, ...	502	294
In office of School Inspector, ...	512	301
In Board of School Commissioners under act of 1864, . . .	289	165
In Metropolitan Police, created by accepting office, ...	368	216
In Board of Fire Commissioners, created by accepting office, .	432	251

	SECTION.	PAGE.
VAGRANTS.		
Power to restrain and punish,	103	64
How punished,	299	169
Proceedings against under Metropolitan Police Act,	377	220
May be sent to House of Correction,	411	241
May be sent from other counties to House of Correction,	412	242
VEGETABLES.		
Unsound, power to prohibit sale of,	103	65
Power to license and regulate sellers of,	103	67
Power to inspect,	103	67
VEHICLES.		
Power to regulate standing of, at depots, etc.,	103	57
Power to license drivers of,	103	66
Power to prescribe stands for, in streets,	103	57
Power to regulate compensation of drivers of,	103	66
Power to prevent exhibition of signs on,	103	56
VENIRE FACIAS.		
To be issued from Recorder's Court to Sheriff,	146	91
Form of,	146	91
When and how to be served and returned,	147	91
VESSELS.		
Power to regulate stationing and anchoring of,	103	53
VETO.		
Of ordidances, etc., by Mayor,	87	48
Proceedings of Council on,	89	49
VICTUALLING HOUSES.		
Power to license and regulate,	103	66
VOLUNTEER BOUNTY BONDS.		
Council authorized to issue,	465	266
VOTING.		
More than once, punishment for,	46	30
Illegal, penalty for,	484	281
Under assumed name, penalty for,	491	285
VOUCHERS.		
To be filed by Controller,	62	36
WALKS. See *Crosswalks*, *Sidewalks*.		
WALLS.		
Unsafe, power of Council to remove,	103	56
Power to regulate construction of,	103	63
Same,	104	73
Same,	105	74
WARRANTS.		
Drawn and signed by Controller,	65	39
Same,	214	125
Not to be drawn if fund exhausted,	213	125
Moneys to be paid out of treasury only on,	214	125
If drawn after fund exhausted, to be void,	216	126
To be charged to fund on which drawn,	63	38
To specify purpose for which drawn,	65	39
To indicate purpose for and fund on which drawn,	214	125
On Sinking Fund, to be drawn by Controller,	228	131
On "Metropolitan Police Fund," how drawn,	366	212
On Fire Commission Fund, how drawn,	434	252
WARRANTS, TAX. See *Taxes*.		
When issued and annexed to tax rolls,	243	141
When may be renewed or extended,	243	142
For collection of tax for local improvements,	254	148
To be annexed to State and County tax rolls,	459	261
Certain, County Treasurer to preserve,	463	264

	SECTION.	PAGE.
Wards.		
Established, and how altered,	2	10
May be divided,	38	27
Same,	506	296
May be divided into election districts,	38	27
Same,	506	296
Power to subdivide city into,	103	73
Ninth and Tenth established,	303	176
Officers of, when and how elected,	3	12
In what, electors to vote,	38	27
Made election districts,	38	27
Divided, who to be Inspectors of Election,	39	28
Office of Assessors of, abolished,	55	33
Divided, when officers of, to continue,	507	297
Divided, power to order election in,	507	297
Divided, proceedings as to elections in,	508	297
Watchmen. See *Police*, *Metropolitan Police*,		
Water of Detroit River.		
Council may preserve purity of,	103	53
Water Commissioners to consider relative to,	311	182
Water Commissioners, Board of,		
Appointment of,	5	13
Term of office of,	15	18
Same,	308	180
When term of office to commence,	16	19
Incorporation of,	307	179
May have seal,	307	180
Qualifications of,	308	180
Vacancies in, how filled,	308	180
Same,	322	186
May appoint President and Secretary,	309	181
Power to loan money on bonds,	310	181
Same,	336	190
Same,	337	191
May employ superintendents, clerks, etc.,	312	182
To have no compensation,	312	182
Power of, to purchase lands, construct reservoirs, etc.,	313	182
May construct fountains, hydrants, etc.,	314	182
May assess water rates,	315	183
To keep list of assessments for water rates,	317	184
Power to make rules, etc.,	316	183
To make annual report to Council,	318	184
Surplus funds of, to be invested,	319	184
When may issue new bonds,	319	185
To take oath of office,	320	185
Materials procured by, exempt from execution,	321	185
Members of, how removed,	322	185
Authorized to enter on lands, etc.,	323	186
Proceedings where property is taken by,	324	186
Not to be interested in certain contracts,	331	189
Water Rates.		
Commissioners may assess,	315	183
To be a lien,	315	183
Commissioners to make rules as to collection of,	316	183
Sale of property for non-payment of,	316	183
List of assessments for, to be kept,	317	184
Wayne County.		
Auditors of, to pay certain expenses for the apprehension of criminals,	345	198

	SECTION.	PAGE.
To pay expense of service of certain warrants,	350	203
Auditors of, to fix salary of Police Justice,	390	228
Auditors of, may inspect records of Recorder's Court,	132	86
Aldermen not eligible to offices of,	11	16
WAYNE CIRCUIT COURT,		
Appeal from Court to,	389	228
WAYS AND MEANS, COMMITTEE OF,		
Chairman of, member of committee to negotiate loans,	222	128
To be Commissioners of Sinking Fund,	226	130
WEIGHERS,		
Power to appoint,	103	67
WEIGHTS,		
Power to regulate and compel use of sealed,	104	68
Board of Metropolitan Police may appoint sealer of,	345	197
WHARFING PRIVILEGES,		
Council may lease,	103	53
WHARVES AND DOCKS,		
Public, power to erect and regulate,	103	53
Private, power to regulate construction of,	103	53
Public, power to lease,	103	53
Public, buildings not to be erected on,	103	53
Public, power to prevent encumbering of,	103	53
Power to preserve order on,	103	56
Sold for taxes, power to remove buildings on after expiration of term,	250	146
WHISKY,		
Power to inspect,	103	68
WINES AND LIQUORS,		
Power to prohibit sale of,	103	65
Power to license sale of,	103	66
Power to inspect,	103	68
WITNESSES,		
Power to fix fees of,	103	52
When Council may subpœna,	21	21
When Mayor may subpœna,	77	44
When committees may subpœna,	102	52
When Fire Marshal may subpœna,	267	154
When Metropolitan Police Commissioners may subpœna,	347	201
Same,	462	213
Swearing falsely before Metropolitan Police Commissioners, guilty of perjury,	362	214
Detained, Police Commissioners to find accommodations for,	357	210
Power to issue capiases for,	392	229
WOOD.		
Power to designate places for sale of,	103	57
Power to measure and inspect,	103	67
WORK HOUSE. *See House of Correction, Alms House.*		
Power to build and control,	103	69
Power to imprison in,	103	69
Power to employ inmates on public works,	103	72
Board of prisoners in, how paid,	133	87
General laws to be applicable to,	136	87
Power to appoint officers of,	103	69
Expenses of confinement of prisoners in, how paid,	103	70
YEAS AND NAYS.		
Ordinances, etc., to be passed on,	98	51
When to be entered on the record,	98	51
Same,	218	127
When to be called in meetings of Commissioners of Sinking Fund,	227	131

www.ingramcontent.com/pod-product-compliance
Lightning Source LLC
LaVergne TN
LVHW020118110826
845151LV00001B/203

* 9 7 8 1 4 2 5 5 4 2 0 5 4 *